THE POLITICAL SYSTEM OF
THE UNITED STATES

THE POLITICAL
SYSTEM OF
THE UNITED STATES

John D. Lees

FABER AND FABER
3 Queen Square
London

First published in 1969
by Faber and Faber Limited
3 Queen Square London WC1
First published as a Faber Paperback in 1970
New edition 1975
Printed in Great Britain by
Butler & Tanner Ltd., Frome and London
All rights reserved

ISBN 0 571 04878 1 (Faber Paperbacks)
ISBN 0 571 04883 8 (hard bound edition)

To JOHN M. HOLMES

—whose generosity began it all

The author and publishers wish to thank the following for permission to quote brief extracts from the works listed below:

Atherton Press Inc., from R. A. Bauer *et al.*, *American Business and Public Policy*, R. C. Martin, *The Cities and the Federal System*, and F. J. Sorauf, *Party and Representation*.

Bobbs-Merrill Co. Inc., from L. N. Reiselbach, *The Roots of Isolation*.

Clarendon Press, Oxford, from M. J. C. Vile, *Constitutionalism and the Separation of Powers*.

A. A. Knopf Inc., from G. McConnell, *Private Power and American Democracy*.

ACKNOWLEDGEMENTS

This book is an attempt to provide an introduction to American politics which is as useful to students of the United States as to students of politics. The debts acquired in writing it are extensive on both sides of the Atlantic. At the University of Michigan from 1960–62 I profited from an educational experience without which such a study could never have been written. I am especially indebted to the stimulating teaching of Samuel Eldersveld, Joseph Kallenbach, George Peek and John White, and the company and patience of fellow teaching assistants, in particular Gerry Faye, Mark Reader, Larry Scheinman and David Smeltzer. I have also benefited from the comments of fellow members of the Department of American Studies at the University of Keele, and from a research grant from the University of Keele which helped me to spend some time in Washington in the summer of 1966. Keith Ovenden generously made available to me research findings which helped to form the basis of the case-study of Model Cities legislation in 1966.

During the final stages of completing the manuscript I have been grateful for the opportunity of discussing many specific questions with my good friend James P. Young. However, my major debt must be to Richard Rose, whose initial encouragement led me to begin the book and whose trenchant comment and pointed criticism of successive drafts of the manuscript have saved me from numerous errors of omission and commission and made more likely whatever merits the final product may possess. Gratitude and goodwill to those mentioned above compels me to absolve them from any responsibility for what is written here. The same cannot be said for my wife Moira, for without her patience, good humour, and practical aid this book would never have been completed.

JOHN D. LEES,
Keele, Staffs.

One of the pitfalls of writing about contemporary events, especially in the United States, is that analysis and examples quickly become dated. I have no illusions that the revisions made here to the original study, designed to take account of political changes since 1969 and of new writing on many of these matters, may already have been upstaged by events before they are read. However, I have sought to revise the basic chapters on the political institutions and have entirely re-written the last chapter, which seeks to outline significant patterns of change since 1969, in particular since the 1972 national elections. I have been helped immeasurably in the task of deciding what to retain by the comments, critical and commendatory, of students and professional colleagues in both Britain and the United States. One consequence is that in some of the new material I have been less concerned to provide a detailed analysis, but rather to give a more personal evaluation of the significance of contemporary changes on the future course of American national politics.

JOHN D. LEES,
Keele, Staffs.,
November 1974

CONTENTS

INTRODUCTION

The political tensions and conflicts which face the government of the United States in the current decade make it important to obtain some understanding of the nature of the American political system, how it was created, and how it has developed in order to provide political stability for a changing society. This book is intended to serve as an introductory guide to the American political system, tracing the interdependence of political institutions and social forces and examining the distinctive features of American political development.

It is necessary immediately to emphasise the introductory nature of this study, and also to justify the rationale for such a study. There is a formidable mass of literature on all aspects of the American political process written by Americans for Americans. Much of this can be confusing to the non-American, either because too much basic knowledge is taken for granted or because it is written in a style and language often unfamiliar to many British students of politics. There are also some studies of American government written by British or American authors for non-Americans. These are usually traditional in approach, providing a simple description of major political institutions and do not utilise the large body of knowledge now available on the workings of the American system following recent developments in empirical and behavioural research in the United States. This study seeks to incorporate many of the significant findings of such research into questions such as the development of political attitudes, in order to provide a more comprehensive analysis of the political process in the United States at the national level.

No one should expect to learn in this book all about the Presidency, Congress, or the Supreme Court as institutions of government, or obtain a detailed account of city government in the United States. More specialised information can be obtained by using the footnotes and general bibliography as a guide to further study. The book should, however, provide an impression of the role played by particular political institutions in a larger political system.

The book emphasises the importance of certain central values and their influence on American society and politics. These values – a distrust of government, a faith in divided and decentralised authority, the importance of equality, etc. – have affected the institutions of government and the behaviour of politicians from the creation of the first system of government in the United States to the present day. Consideration of social values and relationships is therefore imperative in obtaining a full understanding of political institutions, for the political system consists of a set of formal and informal arrangements (values, political institutions, laws, electoral procedures, political parties and interest groups, etc.) by which a society, or those who act on its behalf, decide or fail to decide, what is to be done. The United States possesses a particular style and system of politics which seeks to promote unity while allowing for social and political diversity. Of crucial importance has been the preservation of unity in the face of recurring conflicts which have been the result of such factors as territorial and economic expansion, immigration, and affluence. The typical pattern of American politics has been one of stability, periodic conflict (usually, though not always, moderate), and gradual political change. This has been achieved by a political process established in the eighteenth century which has changed little in form and which continues to emphasise the division and diffusion of political authority.

Political change has not, however, always followed social conflict. It cannot, for instance, be assumed because the United States has become a more pluralistic society that such change automatically led to an increase in political pluralism, or that because equality has been a central value in American society that all groups have obtained full political, economic and social equality. As the United States celebrates its bicentennial, over a century after the first major breakdown of the political process which resulted in a bitter civil war, the basic institutions of government are in serious disarray, providing a stern test of the abilities of political leaders to restore responsible government and the faith of many citizens in the legitimacy of the political system.

Chapter One

THE ENVIRONMENT OF POLITICS
IN THE UNITED STATES

The first settlers from Europe who founded those colonies in North America which later became the United States, likened their new environment to the Garden of Eden. In the words of Russell Nye, 'Americans, like Adam but without his fatal rejection, held Eden in their hands'.[1] This initial optimism remained as the United States grew in size with the expansion of the nation westwards across a continent. The great Mississippi Valley was transformed into a new garden, the Garden of the World, and this vast and growing agricultural society in the interior of the continent became a dominant symbol in nineteenth-century America, a collective representation which contemporary observers such as Crèvecœur and Tocqueville felt to be an affirmation of the promise of American life.[2] Here, free from the influence of European ideas and institutions, a new race of men could build a society unimpaired by ancient forms and feudal traditions.

In the middle of the twentieth century the United States has become the largest and richest industrial nation in the world, yet the connection with Eden still remains. As Nye has remarked: 'the American economic system has produced and distributed more of the goods and comforts of living to more people over a greater territory and for a longer period of time than any other system in any other country since Adam walked out of the Garden of Eden'.[3] This development has been affected by many environmental factors which have also influenced the nature of the American political system.

[1] R. B. Nye, *This Almost Chosen People*, East Lansing, Michigan: Michigan State University Press, 1966, p. 13.
[2] See H. N. Smith, *Virgin Land*, New York: Vintage Books, 1959, Part 3.
[3] R. B. Nye, *op. cit.*, p. 109.

The Geographical Environment of the United States

The most significant environment factors have been geographical, in particular the distance of the United States from countries of Western Europe, and the rapid expansion of the land area and population of the country. In 1790 the United States comprised thirteen states, with a gross area of 888,811 square miles and a population of almost 4 million (of which nearly one-quarter were Negro slaves) living almost entirely in a rural environment. By 1968 the United States consisted of fifty states stretching across a 'continent plus', with a gross area of 3,615,211 square miles and a population of over 200 million, about 75% living in an urban or suburban environment. Today a population larger than that of the United Kingdom, France, and Germany combined occupies a territory whose gross area is considerably larger than Western Europe, with the British Isles being smaller in area than the state of Texas.

The fact that the original thirteen states were territorially homogeneous, but occupied only a part of a vast and as yet undeveloped continent, had an important influence on the creation and the development of the American political system. The fact also that London and Europe were over 3,000 miles away was especially significant in the pre-airplane and pre-steamboat age when distances even within the original states were formidable. Such isolation allowed a new political system to be created in a society with little historic tradition of feudalism. If most European political systems have been the by-product of history, the political system of the United States may be said to be primarily a by-product of geography.

This geographic isolation produced a curious but continuous ambivalence toward Europe. A scepticism about political involvement with Europe found expression in the Farewell Address of the first President of the United States, George Washington, in September 1796, and staying clear of European entanglements became a guiding tenet of American policy for the next 140 years. Yet inescapable social and family links with Europe made complete isolation difficult.

Geographic expansion also created formidable internal problems of maintaining political unity and communication. The inevitable geographic remoteness of Washington, the nation's capital, to many citizens produced problems for the national government in terms of maintaining citizen support for their actions. This explains, in part, why national legislators seem forced to act as delegates of their states or districts in Washington rather than as 'national' representatives. They provide the link between the people and a national government that often seems geographically and physically remote from their everyday lives. This factor is only slightly alleviated by the rapid improvement in mass communications, for the United States does not have a newspaper with a truly national circulation.

Political differences based on regional differences have also had a constant effect on the political system. These were obscured at first by the common desire on the part of the original colonies to rid themselves of English political control, but they quickly became evident and illuminated the weaknesses of the Articles of Confederation, the first governmental system created by the new states. Such differences influenced the gathering at Philadelphia in 1787 that produced the American Constitution, which in turn failed to provide a complete constitutional remedy. Modern patterns of migration and communication have to some extent obscured traditional regional boundaries, but many factors have conspired to preserve distinctive ways of life and political traditions. The best contemporary example is the group of states in the Deep South such as Alabama, Georgia, Louisiana, Mississippi, and South Carolina, who formed the heart of the Confederacy which, in the middle of the nineteenth century, sought without success to secede from the United States. In such states a combination of social patterns such as slavery and racial segregation and events like the Civil War and Reconstruction produced a distinctive political 'style' which continues to affect national as well as state politics.[4]

Economic interests which have coincided with regional boundaries have also influenced political attitudes. They have produced political controversies and brought to the Presidency or to national prominence men representing specific regional attitudes and interests. The expansion of the United States west-

[4] See V. O. Key, Jr., *Southern Politics in State and Nation*, New York: A. A. Knopf, 1949; also A. Leiserson (ed.), *The American South in the Sixties*, New York: Praeger, 1964.

wards, beginning with the purchase of the extensive lands between the Mississippi river and the Rocky Mountains by agents
of President Jefferson in 1803, also served to produce a 'frontier' spirit and attitude of mind which remains a factor in any
national election even today, when the frontiers of the United
States are relatively fixed. In 1960 it was possible for a candidate
for the United States Presidency, John F. Kennedy, to fight a
successful campaign on the slogan 'The New Frontier', and in
1964 for an unsuccessful Presidential candidate, Barry Goldwater, to allow himself to go on record as believing that the
country would be better off if 'we could just saw off the Eastern
Seaboard and let it float out to sea'. Many citizens in the United
States have strong regional ties and loyalties which in turn affect
the political process.

The Economic Environment of the United States

The United States spans a continent and with Hawaii extends
into the Pacific. It encompasses a great diversity of geographic
conditions, containing 'mountain' states, 'desert' states, 'plains'
states and states with very contrasting climatic conditions. It has
also expanded across a continent blessed with vast resources of
raw materials whose rapid utilisation have served to make the
United States the wealthiest and most economically self-
sufficient nation in the world. The United States is the fourth
largest and fourth most populous nation in the world, and a
country of this size with such a population provides massive
problems of political organisation.

The United States has become the country with the highest
average standard of living through the exploitation of natural
and human resources, but the benefits have been distributed unevenly. Thus, while output per worker in the United States is
much higher than in Britain, so is the average rate of unemployment.[5] The United States government spends a lower percentage of the total Gross National Product than does the British
government and employs a smaller percentage of the working-
age population It also spends proportionately less on social

[5] See P. Deane and W. A. Cole, *British Economic Growth 1688–1959*,
Cambridge: Cambridge University Press, 1962.

security, but substantially more on defence, than its counterpart in Britain.

Other contrasts are also significant. Though the United States has the highest percentage of enrolment in higher education and the highest number of radios and automobiles per 1,000 people of any nation in the world, the United States lags behind the U.K. in the number of hospital beds available per thousand people and the number of physicians per head of population. The United States also has a less equal distribution of income both before and after taxation than in the U.K., plus a higher rate of infant mortality and a higher incidence of death from group violence.[6]

The United States had reached a high economic level in the 1920s, but the rapidity of economic expansion can be seen by comparing contemporary evidence with that for 1939. In 1939 just over 50% of the population lived in an urban or suburban environment. By 1966 this had become approximately 75%. In 1939 the average industrial worker paid no income tax at all and the federal budget totalled only $9 thousand million. Between 1940 and 1945 the Gross National Product doubled and in twenty-five years the Gross National Product and national income became seven times greater and the federal budget over $100 thousand million, and annual defence expenditure, which in 1939 was a thousand million dollars, had become fifty times as great.[7] However, such economic development has not eliminated poverty in the United States. At the turn of the century, Robert Hunter estimated that in fairly prosperous years almost one-eighth of the population were underfed, underclothed, and poorly housed, while in 1963 almost one-fifth of the population (some 34.5 million persons, 15 million of them children) were in families with income insufficient to purchase a minimum budget. It is estimated that at least three-tenths of the working population receive proportionately less personal income before tax than in 1910. Of the 7 million families with incomes below the poverty line in 1963, about 2 million were non-white (Negroes, etc.). Non-whites constituted a much larger

[6] See B. Russett et al., World Handbook of Political and Social Indicators, New Haven: Yale University Press, 1964, especially p. 298.

[7] For a more detailed analysis of these changes, see J. Brooks, The Great Leap, London: Gollancz, 1967.

proportion of the chronically poor, including 40% of those families with substandard incomes for two successive years.[8] The apparent failure to link economic wealth with social welfare is in part a consequence of the very rapid expansion of economic growth in the United States, and the social ethic of *laissez-faire* which underpinned such growth.

This level of poverty is, however, relative to the overall high standard of living enjoyed by many Americans. Salaries are generally high by British standards, and the poverty line employed by the Council of Economic Advisers in 1963 of a cash income of less than $3,000 in 1962 prices for families of two or more persons (approximately £1,000 in British income terms) is still very high in comparison to income levels in Britain at the same time. Comparisons of salaries of similar levels of professional occupations would also demonstrate the higher real income level obtained in the United States. Yet, despite a decline in the number of persons classified as poor in the 1960s, pressures on governmental welfare budget expenditures increased, and despite public opposition to such public expenditure it has risen, but not in the same way as in the U.K.[9]

It is difficult to compare the economic growth of the United States with new or developing nations, but it is possible to assess the effects of economic growth and a stable political tradition on the position of the United States in the world. In 1914 the United States was one of perhaps eight powers who could be described as great powers – the others were Britain, France, Germany, Austria-Hungary, Russia, Japan, and Turkey. Of these nations the United States was potentially the most powerful, but its geographic isolation kept it outside the complex of forces which produced two World Wars. The post-1945 world became a bipolar one dominated by the U.S.A. and Russia, as the following table indicates.

[8] For more detailed information, see R. Hunter, *Poverty: Social Conscience in the Progressive Era*, New York: Macmillan, 1904, also Harper & Row, 1965; and H. P. Miller (ed.), *Poverty, American Style*, Belmont, California: Wadsworth, 1966. In 1970, 8% of all families were still living in poverty.

[9] For comparative evidence of the growth of public expenditure in the U.K., see A. T. Peacock and J. Wiseman, *The Growth of Public Expenditure in the U.K.*, London: Oxford University Press, 1961. For more detailed information regarding the United States, see F. C. Mosher and O. F. Poland, *The Costs of American Governments*, New York: Dodd Mead Co., 1964.

Table 1:1

INDICES OF RELATIVE G.N.P. IN STANDARD PRICES (U.S. = 100)

	1938	*1950*	*1963*
United States	100	100	100
Russia	47	34	49
Germany	34	13	19
Great Britain	30	19	16
France	24	15	18
China	24	18	20

G.N.P. Index

Source: B. M. Russett, *Trends in World Politics*, London: Collier–Macmillan, 1965, p.4.

The Russian figures exaggerate the gap between it and the United States, and underestimate the gap between it and other major European states, because it enforces a low level of consumption on its populace. The 1950 figures illustrate the severe effects of World War II on the European countries, and this was increased in the cases of France and Great Britain by the loss of colonies in the 1950s. In the post-war world of nuclear weapons the United States was preponderant, but by the late 1950s Russia had lessened this, and the two powers became clearly preponderant over the rest of the world. Indeed, Britain and France became almost entirely dependent on the U.S.A. for their security. In recent years the predominance of the U.S.A. has continued to diminish, as Russia's G.N.P. improved, and Communist China has also made rapid advances. The dominance of both the United States and Russia over their respective 'blocs' has weakened, and a substantial number of smaller and poorer nations have sought to maintain a neutral status.[10] Because of these post-1945 developments the political system in the United States has been subject to a series of cross-pressures over international questions which have often caused severe strains such as those engendered by continued American involvement in the Vietnam war.

Contrasts between the relative paths of economic growth of

[10] For a more comprehensive treatment of these matters, see B. M. Russett, *Trends in World Politics*, London: Collier–Macmillan, 1965, especially Chapters 1 and 8. Chapter 7 also gives a valuable, if rough, indication of changes in levels of economic inequality between countries, indicating that the predominance of the United States in terms of wealth is likely to decline.

Russia and the United States are useful if not entirely reliable. W. W. Rostow has argued that Russian economic development over the past century has been similar to that of the United States, with a lag of about thirty-five years in the level of industrial output and about fifty years in *per capita* output in industry.[11] The reasons for this lag appear to be a consequence of internal factors, with Russia having to overcome a traditional society with overpopulation on the land, problems of land tenure, and a culture which placed a low premium on modern economic activity. The United States, with no strong feudal tradition, an ample supply of men with commercial attitudes, and a social and political system (outside the South) responsive to industrialisation, had by 1860 already left behind the problems of becoming industrialised.[12]

The equality of pace between Russian and American industrialisation has been achieved by a higher proportion of Russian investment in the heavy and metal-working industries. Russia also allocates a far larger percentage of her G.N.P. to military purposes and the persistent fear of a Russian breakthrough in terms of weapons – the conquering of the so-called 'missile gap' – places additional pressures on the American political system regarding the allocation of economic resources. Despite these problems, however, the United States has succeeded in maintaining a high mass-consumption society along with massive expenditures on defence. If the internal distribution of the fruits of economic growth leaves something to be desired, the United States is nevertheless likely to remain for some time the richest major country in the world.

Demography and Immigration

By comparison with Great Britain, the United States is not densely populated. In 1970 the United States contained approximately fifty-eight people per square mile, and Britain some 585 people per square mile. However, the rapid increase in popula-

[11] See W. W. Rostow, *The Stages of Economic Growth*, Cambridge: Cambridge University Press, 1960, Chapter 7, pp. 93 ff.

[12] See D. C. North, 'Industrialisation in the United States 1815–60', in W. W. Rostow (ed.), *The Economics of Take-Off into Sustained Growth*, pp. 44–62, London: Macmillan, 1963.

tion in the United States, linked with a massive industrial revolution, has transformed society from a rural to an urban and suburban base and has provided many political problems.

In 1787, when the American Constitution was drawn up, a handful of citizens, largely white Anglo-Saxons, dotted the eastern seaboard of a vast continent. As the country expanded territorially, so also began the rise in population stimulated by periods of massive immigration. Table 1:2 indicates the rate of

Table 1:2

GROSS POPULATION FIGURES:
U.S.A., U.K., AND ENGLAND AND WALES 1800–1972

	United States			*United Kingdom*	*England and Wales*
	Population	*Area*		*Population*	*Population*
		(sq. miles)			*(in thousands)*
1800	5,308,483	(888,811)	1801	10,500,956	9,061
1830	12,866,020	(1,788,006)	1831	16,261,183	13,994
1860	31,443,321	(3,022,387)	1861	23,128,578	20,119
1890	62,947,714	(3,022,387)	1891	33,028,172	29,086
1920	105,710,620	(3,022,387)	1921	42,769,192	37,932
1950	150,697,361	(3,615,211)	1951	48,854,303	43,815
1972	208,000,000+	(3,615,122)	1971	55,346,551	48,593

Sources: Statistical Abstract of the United States, 1972, p. 5; British Census, 1951; British Census, 1971.

population expansion since 1800, in comparison with that of Great Britain. In thirty years between 1860 and 1890 the population of the United States doubled, a period marked by the assimilation of great blocs of Germans, Britons, Irishmen, Italians, Slavs, Russians, Scandinavians, and even Canadians into the United States. According to the 1860 census, out of a total population of 31·5 million, only some 4 million were foreign-born. Between 1860 and 1890 over 10 million immigrants arrived, and between 1890 and 1914 a further 15 million, largely drawn from Austria-Hungary, Italy, Russia, Greece, Rumania, and Turkey, but also from Far Eastern countries such as China and Japan. Immigration from Mexico also began on a large scale in 1900 and increased in later years, as did immigration from Puerto Rico.[13]

[13] See M. A. Jones, *American Immigration*, Chicago: University of Chicago Press, 1960.

The coming of steam engines and steamships in the mid-nineteenth century facilitated immigrant movement into the United States for the peoples of the entire European continent. It also facilitated swifter movement within the North American continent with the development of the railroads. The western lands were populated initially by native Americans, but many groups of immigrants settled in distinctive geographical areas. Minnesota became a state dominated in the centre and south by immigrants from Denmark, Sweden, and Norway, and from Finland in the north. States like Wisconsin and Michigan developed pronounced concentrations of Germans, and the Pacific Coast states received an influx of Far Eastern immigrants, while immigrants from Mexico settled especially in Texas, Arizona, and California. Religious groupings also began to show well-defined geographic concentrations, notably Lutherans in the northern part of the Middle West, and Catholics in urban areas of the North-East. In consequence, the American culture developed as a blend of the cultures of many millions of immigrants with different languages, colours, religions and mores, spread unevenly across a vast expanse of territory.

Many immigrants, however, resided in the cities. As early as 1860, in cities like New York, Chicago, Cincinnati, Milwaukee, Detroit, and San Francisco, foreign-born residents constituted almost half their populations. With the expansion of industry, so more people began to move to the cities and a higher percentage of immigrants sought work in manufacturing or mining. Increased industrialisation also led to a considerable movement of population. In 1900 the United States population was around 76 million and the combination of immigration and natural increase was so great as to allow western lands to be settled while the city population also expanded. As many people moved westward, others, especially Negroes, moved from the rural South to the industrial areas of the North-East. In the 1960s California displaced New York as the state with the largest population. Yet there has also been a continued and significant population movement towards the urban centres. At least 70% of the population now lives in an urban or urban-fringe environment which covers only 6% of the total area of the country.

Despite this shift, however, only 42% of the population live in metropolitan areas of over 50,000 population, and rural or small-town values still tend to dominate the thinking of many of these new 'suburbanites'. Moreover, since 1940, there has been a decline in the absolute numbers of those living in cities of over a million people, indicating a significant movement of population from the city centres to the suburbs.[14]

The influence and effect of these environmental factors has required of the political system a flexibility and adaptability unknown, and probably unnecessary, in other democracies. The concern of the framers of the American Constitution in 1787 with creating a network of governmental institutions of separate authorities sharing powers, diffusing governmental authority and seeking to protect minority interests, proved fortuitous. It served to provide stable, though not always effective, government for a vast, highly industrialised nation with an increasingly large, mobile, and heterogeneous population unevenly distributed throughout the country.

The pluralism of American society is also significant in producing a vertical pattern of divisions in the United States, in marked contrast to the more horizontal divisions based on class in British society. Vertical divisions based on religious, regional, or racial identity have generally provided a substitute for the class struggle. Such divisions are the consequence of a polyglot population which has imposed upon the class structure a peculiar and complex status system. This has made the achievement of a full American identity a recurrent problem, and has had profound political effects. It has, for example, led to a predominant emphasis on consensus by those seeking to win control of government, involving the need to appeal in general terms to a wide range of distinct social groups in order to forge an electoral coalition capable of winning political power, along with the need to compromise with rival political forces in order to make government work. In political terms, racial and ethnic groupings in the United States still have significant force.

This situation has made it more difficult for a permanent or traditional ruling élite to establish itself, though it has not

---

[14] See *Statistical Abstract of the United States:* 1972, Washington, D.C., U.S. Bureau of the Census, 1972, Section I, pp. 1–46, for tables supporting this analysis.

prevented the existence of a series of 'aristocracies'.[15] Groups have been forced to coalesce as political coalitions after initial competition, and religion has often played an important part in this, especially for groups of Jewish, Irish, or Italian background. Though racial distinctions in the United States are broad (the British not being considered a 'mixed' race, whereas the offspring of a Scottish – English marriage might be considered 'mixed' in Britain itself), certain racial groups such as Chinese–Americans or Mexican–Americans have been less fortunate and exercise political influence only as weak members of a larger political coalition. Moreover, while the political system in the United States has demonstrated an ability to absorb new groups and new peoples (such as those of Irish, Italian, German, or Polish background), and allow them to occupy influential positions in the political arena, no group has found it more difficult to obtain political and social equality than the Negro. Despite limitations on immigration, not all groups have been successfully assimilated.

The political process has, however, served as an effective means of giving status and authority to many immigrants in the cities. The political coalition which produced this began to develop at least as early as 1928, when Al Smith became the first Catholic to challenge for the Presidency. The New Deal 'revolution' of the 1930s (ironically presided over by a Protestant patrician, President Franklin Delano Roosevelt), laid the foundations of an urban-based political force which served to make the Democratic party the normal majority party in the United States until 1972.[16] In 1960, John F. Kennedy became the first Roman Catholic President and ended the domination of the political process by a rural-based white Anglo-Saxon Protestant tradition.

The impact of religion on politics in the United States has also been of persistent importance. While the United States began as a predominantly Protestant nation there was a great deal of

[15] See E. D. Baltzell, *The Protestant Establishment, Aristocracy and Caste in America*, New York: Random House, 1964. For a useful complementary analysis and critique of the theory of democratic élitism in the United States, see P. Bachrach, *The Theory of Democratic Elitism*, Boston: Little, Brown, 1967.

[16] For evidence of the diverse impact of ethnic and religious factors on politics in America, see N. Glazer and D. P. Moynihan, *Beyond the Melting Pot*, Cambridge: M.I.T. and Harvard University Presses, 2nd edit., 1970.

religious diversity with innumerable Protestant sects and denominations. The diversity within Protestantism that characterised the early years of the Republic, and the diversity of faiths that characterises contemporary American society, means that the direct influence of religion in politics has been less than in countries such as France, but this does not mean that it has not produced political difficulties. In order to ensure ratification of the American Constitution a Bill of Rights consisting of ten amendments was added to it in 1791, and one of the major provisions of the First Amendment prohibited the creation of an established religion and prohibited laws designed to limit the free exercise of religion. This separation of church and state has served to protect religious freedoms but has also created political problems.

Certain states, where a large majority of the population is of one religion, have had severe political conflict, such as over anachronistic anti-birth control statutes in Massachusetts and Connecticut. Sects such as the Jehovahs Witnesses have had a series of clashes with political authority over matters like the distribution of literature without consent, and their refusal to allow their children to participate in the mandatory flag-saluting ceremonies in state schools. Questions such as the constitutionality of spending government money on religious schools, and the refusal of parents of differing religious beliefs to allow their children to participate in certain types of 'official' prayers in state schools, have also provoked the type of acute political controversy rare in countries such as Britain which possess an established state church.[17]

Group distinctions emphasised by immigration patterns have been a source of political tension, but the impact has been mixed. The rationale for migration to the United States from other countries was often linked with expectations about the nature of American democracy, and served to produce in many immigrants a strong sense of personal political loyalty and

[17] For studies of the interaction of religion and politics in the United States, see P. H. Odegard (ed.), *Religion and Politics*, Rutgers, New York: Oceana Publications, 1960; and M. S. Stedman, Jr., *Religion and Politics In America*, New York: Harcourt, Brace and World, 1964. For a history of the legal struggle of the Jehovahs Witnesses over the question of flag-saluting, see D. Manwaring, *Render Unto Caesar*, Chicago: University of Chicago Press, 1962.

commitment. This has, in certain circumstances, promoted an irrational excess of nationalism or 'super-patriotism' in response to events outside the country. In World War II, demands for the relocation of Japanese communities in the United States to avoid possible treason or sabotage, led to over 110,000 'Japanese', aliens and American citizens alike, 'voluntarily' accepting evacuation to camps guarded by troops in the interior 'desert' states. To many other Americans the best demonstration of their patriotism was their acceptance of such evacuation and relocation.

A combination of demands for the protection of the rights of minorities, and pressures forcing individuals to demonstrate that they are 'true' Americans, made imperative a political system which contains elements of a unifying nature along with a considerable degree of diffused or decentralised authority. The original states reflected many of these tensions and hence the basic framework of American government was designed, in part, to reconcile these problems.

The essence of the structure of the American political system has been its flexibility. The reconciliation of diverse interests in a country expanding in territory and population has not always been successful, as was demonstrated by the Civil War in the middle of the nineteenth century, but in general those responsible for the political compromises in 1787 were aware of the possibility of environmental changes and of the need for the governmental system to respond to such changes in the future.

Chapter Two

CONSTITUTIONALISM AND CONSTITUTIONAL ADJUDICATION

The American political system is designed to provide a process whereby some of the wants of members of the society may be realised to some extent through political decisions. This requires a stable context for political activity and competition, and this context may be described as a constitutional order which involves a set of fundamental rules and customary procedures designed to resolve political differences and make political decisions legitimate. When members of a society believe that governmental directives are legitimate they will obey without coercion, for what is legal is not necessarily legitimate, legality being determined by judicial action and legitimacy by the values and attitudes which comprise the political culture of a society.

The physical size and social diversity of the United States in 1787 required a series of compromises about the division of governmental authority both within and between different levels of government. Such compromises involved the principles of constitutionalism and federalism. A written constitution served to legitimise political actions as well as define the powers of the different branches of the national government – the executive (the President), the legislative (Congress), and the judicial (the Supreme Court) – in such a way that policies of major importance cannot be enacted and implemented by one branch of the national government alone. The national government itself possesses limited authority in a federal system where state governments possess a high degree of autonomy to determine for themselves their own governmental structure.

Along with the written constitution, which has proved to be a flexible instrument, subject to interpretation and capable of amendment, went the view that individual rights might best be protected by extending the sphere of national governmental authority. As James Madison argued in *Federalist 51*, writing in defence of the new constitution he had helped to construct in 1787, 'in the extended republic of the United States, and among the great variety of interests, parties, and sects which it embraces, a coalition of a majority of the whole society could seldom take place on any other good principles than those of justice and the general good . . . the larger the society, provided it lie within a practicable sphere, the more duly capable it will be of government. And happily . . . the practicable sphere may be carried to a very great extent by a judicious modification and mixture of the federal system.'[1]

Constitutionalism and the Framing of the Constitution

The American constitutional system is founded on the principles of the Declaration of Independence. The struggle for independence by the American colonies promoted an initial sense of cohesion and integration, but this was not maintained under the Articles of Confederation. The fault lay in the individual states themselves rather than in the Articles as a system of government. The union created was a confederation – a union of states rather than people.

The effective working of the Confederation depended upon the co-operation of the states, and difficulties began to arise. States failed to honour requisitions and to abide by treaty obligations, encroached on each other's commerce, issued their own paper money, and loosened the obligations of contract by allowing debts to be paid in depreciated currency.

This situation promoted a certain amount of pessimism as to whether popular government was feasible. Others, however, believed in the necessity for a stronger national government. As early as 1780, Alexander Hamilton, James Madison, and others had made such recommendations. The gathering at Philadelphia in 1787 was called for the express purpose of revising the Articles of Confederation, and was the culmination of practical dissatisfaction with existing arrangements and philosophical speculation as to the best form of constitutional government.

[1] See *The Federalist Papers*, introduced by C. Rossiter, New York: Mentor, 1961, p. 325.

The Founding Fathers were influenced by several different arguments and theories about the nature of government. Many were aware of the writings of John Locke, who argued that, in the past, people had reached an agreement in a contract to create government in order to protect their natural rights of life, liberty, and property. Citizens would obey the state as long as their leaders adhered to the contract, but if they did not perform their tasks properly they could be overthrown legitimately by the people. Because all individuals enjoyed equal rights, political decisions should rest on the base of majority rule. The writings of Montesquieu also affected the thinking of delegates. Montesquieu was less optimistic about the virtues of majority rule, and feared governmental interference with individual rights. He believed that government should be based on the principle of the separation of powers, with one branch of government checking the other, and the division of government into independent legislative, executive, and judicial branches would preserve liberty. Delegates were also influenced by experience of particular types of institutional organisation. Two-house legislatures and an independent judiciary and executive had existed as governmental institutions in the colonies. Government had been limited and had operated on the basis of powers which were clearly enumerated. Since 1776 many states had accepted and implemented the principle of the separation of powers and had also come to accept the need for some form of checks and balances.[2]

At Philadelphia, Madison in particular sought to emphasise the importance of linking these ideas. Separation of powers in itself would not provide security if different branches of government were unable to check and balance others. In Madisons' words: 'Ambition must be made to counteract ambition'.[3] Government must be given responsibilities but it must also be limited, and it must be able to limit itself to ensure that it acts responsibly. The two doctrines, which appeared to be in conflict

[2] For a careful analysis of these early experiments, see M. J. C. Vile, *Constitutionalism and the Separation of Powers*, Oxford: Oxford University Press, 1967, Chapter 6, pp. 119–52.

[3] See *Federalist Paper 51, op. cit.* For analysis of the documents and notes relating to the Convention, see M. Farrand (ed.), *The Records of the Federal Convention of 1787*, 4 vols., New Haven: Yale University Press, 1937.

became interdependent and provided the major principles around which the Constitution was constructed. Conflict did ensue, however, about how strong such checks should be, and what form they should take.

The framing of the American Constitution involved the enunciation of a set of basic values and the creation of institutions by which these values would be implemented and maintained. The Constitution served to institutionalise these values and attitudes, and marked the beginning of the steady growth in the United States of ideas and institutions favourable to popular representative government.

The final result reflected the desire for limited yet balanced authority. The states remained as basic units in a federal system. The national legislature, consisting of one branch based on popular representation and the other on equal state representation, was given specific but limited legal powers, with legislators forbidden from holding any executive office. The President would be elected for a fixed term independent of the legislature, though the legislature might impeach him. He would possess definite but limited legal authority and could veto laws passed by Congress, though Congress could override this veto. The judiciary was to be independent of both President and Congress, appointed by the President with the consent of the Senate, and given specific responsibilities. Amendments to the Constitution required the approval of both the national legislature and the states.

The major compromise involved the division of governmental powers between the national and state governments. Most delegates were in favour of some form of a federal system, but they did not agree on details. One group sought a specific increase in the powers of the national government, which would have legal authority over individual citizens and would represent citizens as well as states, and derive its authority from the people of the United States. Others sought to keep the national government strictly limited and dependent on the state governments.

Most delegates agreed that the states should be preserved as vital elements in a federal system, though Alexander Hamilton would probably have been content to see the states abolished. Many delegates had doubts that a republic could function effectively over an extensive area. It should be remembered also that many of the opponents of radical change never attended the Convention, though they were active in trying to prevent ratification of the Constitution.[4] This was, in part, why those seeking a strong national government in a federal system appeared to do well. The new Congress was given a series of defined legal powers – to lay and collect taxes, duties, imposts, and excises; to pay debts and provide for the common defence and general welfare; to regulate commerce with foreign nations and among the several states; to coin money and regulate its value; to declare war and to raise and support armies (Article 1, Section 8). Also Congress was allowed 'to make all laws which shall be necessary and proper for carrying into execution the foregoing powers, and all other powers vested by this Constitution in the government of the United States' (Article 1, Section 8, paragraph 18). The Constitution was also affirmed as the supreme law of the land (Article 6).

The creation of the Presidency was the product of compromise. Some delegates suggested a plural executive, but most states had a single executive and it was generally accepted that this system would prevail. Hamilton alone was prepared to accept the notion of a monarchy, but there was considerable conflict over the term of office, and after extensive debate a four-year term was agreed upon. The method of electing the President, however, caused much confusion. Some delegates wanted him to be elected by the legislature. Others sought direct popular election, but this proposal was heavily defeated. After protracted discussion the matter was referred to a committee who suggested that each state should appoint (in a manner directed by its legislature) a number of electors equal to their representation in Congress who would choose the President by ballot. This electoral college system was accepted, and it allowed for the transfer of the election to the people in each state in due course without creating a direct popular national election.

The President was given, by Article 2 of the Constitution, an electoral base and constitutional powers independent of Congress, and a fixed term of office to which he could be re-elected.

[4] For a collection of documents illustrating the arguments of opponents, see M. Borden (ed.), *The Antifederalist Papers*, East Lansing, Michigan: Michigan State University Press, 1965.

Article 2 also defined the powers and responsibilities of the President. He was, among other things, required to 'take care that the laws be faithfully executed', and could be impeached for 'treason, bribery, or other high crimes and misdemeanors' (Article 2, Sections 3 and 4).

The specific character of the new federal system was resolved after the basic differences about the Congress and the Presidency were settled. The methods of election to these branches of government reflected the need for national authority along with responsiveness to state and sectional interests. The federal system became a part of the checks and balances by which the national government and its separate institutions were to be controlled.

There is little doubt that the Convention intended the national sphere of government to be limited, as was indicated by the enumeration of specific powers for Congress. While the Convention delineated the pattern of the new federal system it did not make a decisive disposition of the locus of sovereignty. The national government was given only limited and enumerated powers, with the residue of sovereignty left by implication with the states. Certain prohibitions were placed on state governments alone (they could not enter into treaties, coin money, or lay duties on exports or imports) and on both state and national governments (no titles of nobility to be granted and no bills of attainder or *ex post facto* laws passed). However, within its sphere, the national government was a sovereign national authority operating directly upon individuals, and with its own administration, executive, and courts to execute its will. The Constitution sought to define the ground rules of government and divide governmental power in a manner which would exploit the virtues of both national unity and state diversity. The national government possessed authority, but this was divided among those responsible for decision-making so that no single branch of government could act and bind the nation without the approval and support of another branch.[5]

The Constitution also sought to effect certain compromises

[5] For comprehensive discussion of the Constitutional Convention and the internal compromises and conflicts, see especially A. N. Holcombe, *Our More Perfect Union*, Cambridge, Massachusetts: Harvard University Press, 1950; also A. H. Kelly and W. A. Harbison, *The American Constitution; Its Origins and Development*, New York: W. W. Norton Co., 1965.

which reflected conflict between the northern and southern states. Each section was apprehensive that the new national government might advance the economic interests of the other at their expense. It was therefore agreed that an absolute prohibition be placed on export taxes. Southerners were also anxious that slaves be counted as population in determining the number of representatives to which a state would be entitled in the House of Representatives. It was finally agreed that three-fifths of the slaves would be counted in determining a state's quota of seats, and its quota whenever a direct tax was levied by the national government. The slave trade was also allowed to continue until 1808.

An important compromise concerned the question of the admission of new states. Some delegates felt that new states might reflect the radical interests of debtor and small-farmer classes and sought to restrict the admission of new states and provide for their entry into the Union with an inferior status. This was not accepted, and Article 4, Section 3, of the Constitution allowed Congress to decide the terms on which new states might be admitted.

The Constitution rested on the twin pillars of constitutionalism – limited and responsible government defined by a written Constitution – and federalism – sovereignty 'divided' between the national (or federal) government and state governments. A separation of powers within the national government supplemented by a system of checks and balances linking the different branches of government, was designed to create built-in conflict as well as co-operation within the national government. The Constitution did not, however, provide a solution for all the political problems of the period, nor did it serve to prevent conflict in the future over matters dealt with by the Constitution and others ignored by it.

No Bill of Rights was included in the original Constitution. Some argued that this was because civil rights were reserved to the people and so outside the control of government. Madison felt that the checks and balances and limits placed on governmental actions should be sufficient protection and so a Bill of Rights was unnecessary. Opponents of the Constitution, however, attacked the omission of a Bill of Rights.

The framing and ratification of the Constitution was a political act establishing a new governmental system grounded on popular approval. The struggle for ratification was, however, a bitter one. Hostility developed among different economic groups, fed by propaganda, but the Founding Fathers fought vigorously in the states to get approval. The struggle for ratification in New York led Hamilton, Madison, and Jay to publish in the local press a series of essays later known as *The Federalist Papers*, expounding the principles of the new Constitution and its advantages over the Articles of Confederation. Seven states (Delaware, Connecticut, New Jersey, Maryland, South Carolina, Georgia, New Hampshire) ratified by large margins, but in the large states of Pennsylvania, Massachusetts, Virginia, and New York voting was very close. Two states – North Carolina and Rhode Island – only ratified once the new government was established.

Ratification was only obtained in return for the addition of a Bill of Rights, which became the first ten amendments to the Constitution in 1791. Since then only sixteen more amendments have been added, though changes have come through judicial interpretation, especially by the federal judiciary.

As Robert Dahl has indicated, the Philadelphia Convention did not decide that the United States was to be a democratic republic. 'A democratic outcome depended upon widespread acceptance among Americans of the legitimacy of a democratic republic as a system of government for Americans.'[6] The new Constitution sought to provide a framework for political integration; the joining together of groups sharing or prepared to share common political attitudes. American constitutionalism in its contemporary form consists of an amalgam of laws, ideals, and customs, in which the Constitution provides the basic structure and foundation of governmental authority, limiting governmental action yet also giving it form and substance.

The Development of American Constitutionalism

The original form of American constitutionalism has been changed by both formal and informal processes, either to remedy problems which did not exist in 1787 or were not provided for

[6] See R. A. Dahl, *Pluralist Democracy in the United States: Conflict and Consent*, Chicago: Rand McNally Co., 1967, p. 298.

by the original Constitution.[7] Formal changes have been made by constitutional amendment, many of them, especially some recent ones, of a relatively trivial nature.

The first ten amendments can really be regarded as part of the original Constitution, and the 10th Amendment is of particular significance in that it later became the main constitutional support of those demanding a strict limitation of the powers of the national government to those powers enumerated in the Constitution. It has been the source of a series of important constitutional conflicts. The 11th Amendment in 1798 reversed a Supreme Court decision of 1793 allowing states to be sued in federal courts by citizens of another state. The 12th Amendment was adopted in 1804 to adjust the election procedure for the Presidency. The rise of political parties produced a deadlock for the Presidency in 1800 between two Republicans, and the final choice was made by the House of Representatives. The 12th Amendment requires state electors to vote for different candidates for the President and Vice President.

The second group of constitutional amendments came as a consequence of the Civil War. The 13th Amendment forbade slavery and freed all slaves. The 14th Amendment extended citizenship to former slaves, states are forbidden to abridge the privileges or immunities of U.S. citizens, or deny due process of law or equal protection of the laws to any individual, and Congress can enforce these provisions by law. The 15th Amendment forbids states denying voting rights to U.S. citizens on the basis of race, colour, or previous condition of servitude. While these amendments were primarily concerned with protecting and providing guarantees for the rights of Negroes, certain clauses of the 14th Amendment were long used to protect individual rights of property against attempts by states to legislate to regulate certain economic activities.

Later amendments have come in the period since 1913. The 16th Amendment instituted a federal income tax, and the 17th Amendment provided for the direct popular election of Senators. The 18th Amendment prohibited the sale of liquor and followed a lengthy crusade, but in 1933 the 21st Amendment repealed this after it became clear that this policy was a failure.

[7] See E. S. Corwin, *The Constitution and What it Means Today* (12th revised edition), Princeton, N. J.: Princeton University Press, 1958.

The 19th Amendment in 1920 provided for women's suffrage, and in 1933 the 20th Amendment changed the dates for the Presidential inauguration and the convening of Congress. In 1951 the 22nd Amendment was passed preventing any person from being elected President more than twice. Any man, such as Lyndon Johnson, who served less than two years of a term to which he was not elected, would, however, be able to seek election twice. This was designed to prevent a recurrence of the situation which allowed Franklin Delano Roosevelt to serve as President for three full terms and to be re-elected for a fourth in 1944. In 1961, the 23rd Amendment permitted electors in the District of Columbia to vote in Presidential elections. In 1964, the 24th Amendment placed a ban on the use of poll taxes to prevent voting in national elections. In 1967, the 25th Amendment set out the procedure for the Vice-President to serve as acting President whenever the President is disabled and cannot perform his duties. In 1971 the 26th Amendment reduced the minimum voting age to 18. Other amendments have been proposed by Congress but never ratified by the states, and some have been initiated by states but have not been adopted by Congress. They have included proposals to change the Electoral College, limit the powers of the Supreme Court, lengthen the term of Representatives to four years, or require Senate approval of executive agreements made with foreign nations.

Constitutional amendments have helped the American political system to adapt to social and political change, but changes have also been made by statute and by custom. The United States Congress is given the task of lawmaking, and many statutes are passed every year. Some shape or change the structure of the national government, creating new administrative departments or reorganising the bureaucracy in general. Statutes have also affected the organisation and jurisdiction of the federal courts. The Judiciary Act of 1789 was the first of many statutes designed to determine the functions and form of the federal judiciary.

Legislation has also been passed to deal with the effects of social change, guaranteeing economic and civil rights or providing social welfare benefits. Many of these have been the subject of bitter political conflict. Legislation has also been passed to provide for the internal reorganisation of the procedures through which the Congress operates and makes decisions.

Some changes are the result of custom or apparent need, and have come to form part of the procedures whereby political offices are filled and political decisions made. The Constitution makes no mention of political parties, yet they have come to play an important role in the political process. There is some evidence that the Founding Fathers viewed the possible development of parties or factions with concern. However, Madison and Jefferson were among the first to recognise that party organisation was necessary if not wholly desirable, and the 1796 Presidential election saw the real beginning of factional competition which by the 1800 election led to a bitter campaign between the Federalists and anti-Federalists. The anti-Federalists won, and the dire predictions of the Federalists that Jefferson and his supporters would destroy the Constitution proved to be incorrect. The parties began to develop diverse interests, uniting different state party organisations, and became vital instruments in the process of resolving conflicts between the national and state governments.

Each institution of government also began to develop procedures and processes not contained in the Constitution. The growth of the powers of the Presidency led to the development of a formal Cabinet and also the existence of a special group of personal advisers to the President; the increased volume of the tasks of the Congress led to the creation of a formal committee system and a host of informal rules and procedures governing debate and legislative activity. The expansion of the suffrage also served to make the political process more responsive to popular demands and control, and led to the creation of specific electoral practices such as party primary elections to seek to guarantee maximum popular participation in all aspects of political activity. This led in turn to the rise of private associations organised to promote particular or group interests and seeking to stimulate interest in, and debate on, matters of public interest. Interest groups have provided an extensive network of communications and a major link between public opinion, the political parties, and the institutions of government at all levels.

Major changes have also been made by interpretation of the Constitution by the judiciary. The Constitution to some extent sought to establish political competition and conflict within the national government, and between the national government and state governments. Such conflict required settlement. Thomas Jefferson believed that within the national government each branch would settle such conflicts in terms of its own pledge to obey the Constitution. The creation of a separate judiciary also sworn to obey the Constitution led to the development of judicial interpretation of the Constitution, and the exercise of judicial review by the United States Supreme Court, as head of the national judiciary. Judicial review is the power of a judicial body to hold void a law, or an action based on it, that it believes to be in conflict with the Constitution, which is the supreme law of the land. The assertion of such power by the Supreme Court made it a political as well as a legal instrument, and gave it an important adjudicating role in the development and maintenance of constitutionalism in the United States.

The Supreme Court and American Constitutionalism

In Britain an Act of Parliament is superior to all other forms of law and there are no legal limits upon the legislative power of Parliament (or more precisely, the crown-in-Parliament) in constitutional matters. British courts have the power to interpret legislation, but not declare it void, and they are not required to act as guardians of the Constitution.

The American Constitution does not grant such formal authority to the U.S. Supreme Court. Article 6 made the Constitution, and the laws of the United States made in pursuance thereof, the supreme law of the land, and under Article 3 'the judicial power' of the United States was vested in a Supreme Court, and such lower courts as provided by Congress, and the specific nature of this judicial power was defined. No clear reference, however, was made to the exercise of judicial review by the Supreme Court.

It should be noted, however, that two distinct types of judicial review are practised by the Supreme Court. One, federal judicial review, involves determining whether acts of a state government conflict with the national Constitution, and such federal judicial review may be justified by the wording of Article 6 of the Constitution, and by the specific terms of Section 25 of the Judiciary Act of 1789. The other involves declaring on the constitutionality of acts of co-ordinate branches of the national government, and nothing in the Constitution specifies that they possess such power, nor do the records of the Philadelphia Convention indicate, without doubt, that the Founding Fathers definitely intended to give the Court such power. However, the power given the Court by Article 3 of the Constitution to determine 'all cases, in law and equity, arising under this Constitution', and the implication in Article 6 that federal laws made 'in pursuance' of the Constitution are the supreme law of the land, may be used to support such judicial review as an inevitable consequence of the constitutional system.

It has, however, been a matter of academic and legal dispute rather than political reality whether the exercise of judicial review of acts of the national government was intended by the Founding Fathers. Robert Dahl suggests that a great many delegates did not have precise ideas regarding the powers of the judiciary, but that it can be reasonably inferred that a majority of the delegates accepted the notion that the federal courts would rule on the constitutionality of state and federal laws involved in cases before them, but rejected the notion that judges should participate in policy-making.[8] E. S. Corwin also asserted that the great majority of the most influential members of the 1787 Convention thought the Constitution secured to the national courts the right to pass on the validity of acts of Congress, though he also claimed that the legitimacy of judicial review existed wholly apart from any search for the intent of the Founding Fathers, in the historical 'higher law' tradition embodied in the Constitution, which is superior to any laws made by men.[9] The decisions of the Supreme Court under Chief Justice Marshall in *Marbury* v. *Madison* in 1803 and *Martin* v. *Hunters Lessee* in 1816, however, established the power of the Supreme Court to make judgments on the constitutionality of acts of the national government and acts of the state governments respectively.

While the exercise of judicial review has brought the Supreme Court into a policy-making position with a direct involvement in the political process, there are many functions the courts as a

[8] See R. A. Dahl, *Pluralist Democracy in the United States, op. cit.*, pp. 147–8.
[9] See E. S. Corwin, *Twilight of the Supreme Court*, New Haven: Yale University Press, 1934, pp. 103–4.

whole perform which are political, and others which do not affect the political process. As long as law is the most common means of formalising public policy, the judicial office in the United States will be concerned with political power. Judges are required to decide disputes between individual litigants by interpreting constitutional clauses, executive orders, and statutes. The meaning of these legal documents may have an important effect on basic economic and political matters in the society, and such decisions may be as important to society as a whole. In settling disputes, judges are a part of the policy-making process, because that is part of their function. Judges make their decisions in terms of the law, and in many instances the decision is clear. Where there is serious contention, or where the language of the law is broadly phrased, they have the opportunity to exercise considerable personal discretion. As J. W. Peltason has said, 'the law becomes the judges conclusion, not his starting point'.[10]

The federal judiciary, and especially the Supreme Court, performs a major role of constitutional adjudication. Such adjudication may involve acting as umpire in deciding conflicts between the state and national governments over the constitutional division of power, or as protector of the individual citizens against the violation of his constitutional rights by the actions of government or of other individuals. The performance of these functions is, however, hedged about by a variety of political, institutional, legal, and ethical limitations.

To the extent that the Court has a major political responsibility, it is to protect the fundamental guarantees and determine the specific limitations of the Constitution. How it does this is affected by the legal and political attitudes of its nine members. Without support, like any other branch of the national government, it can do little to influence the course of policy-making, though it may define the constitutional limits of the policy-making powers of other political institutions. As well as legitimising the actions of the dominant national political coalition it must also defend the constitutional guarantees of the individual against governmental encroachment. The performance of both these functions requires consideration of the legal, social, and

[10] J. W. Peltason, *Federal Courts in the Political Process*, New York: Random House Inc., 1962, p. 4.

cultural aspects of political action, of what is legally permissible as well as culturally acceptable. It also involves performing its functions in a manner accepted as legitimate by those political decision-makers responsible for their actions to the people.

A history of the constitutional decisions of the Supreme Court is in fact a history of the political group conflict of American domestic affairs, though the Court has rarely had the last word on most of these conflicts. Between 1790 and 1860 the Court issued important decisions on fundamental political issues such as the rights of states over matters of taxation and the regulation of commerce, property rights and contracts, and the legal status of slavery in the Union. Between 1865 and 1920, the Court made vital decisions on matters relating to Reconstruction and the rights of the Negro, the governmental regulation of business enterprise, labour-management relations, and civil liberties in time of war. Between 1930 and 1937 it ruled on major questions relating to industrial recovery from the Depression, social welfare, and the extent of national governmental regulation of economic affairs. Since 1937 the Court has considered important questions such as segregation and racial discrimination, church-state relations, Congressional investigations, legislative apportionment, capital punishment and freedom of the press. In each period the Court, in considering the Constitution and its requirements in terms of political and socio-economic changes, has often aroused protest, and indeed it has often had many severe internal conflicts.

Prior to 1937 the Court often used its powers of judicial review to protect property or economic rights, and criticism of the use of this power came from 'liberals'. Since 1925 and the case of *Gitlow* v. *New York*, when the Court ruled that freedoms guaranteed by the 1st Amendment against actions of the national government were included in the due process of law clause of the 14th Amendment to limit actions of state governments, the Court has moved toward a concern for the protection of individual rights by the use of judicial review. This development was emphasised in 1938 by the comment of Justice Stone in the case of *U.S.* v. *Carolene Products Co.*, that judicial intervention was legitimate when relief was not provided by other branches of the political process. The earlier protests of 'liberals' that the courts were challenging the development of representa-

45

tive government and protecting special interests has become the cry of 'conservatives' in the 1950s and 1960s. It is because the American constitutional system has to balance the need for governmental authority and the need for restraints upon such authority that the adjudicating functions of the Court place it squarely within the process of group political conflict in the United States.

Constitutionalism and Political Stability

A political process is more than simply random behaviour. It possesses a pattern which is often consistent and stable and conforms to certain explicit or implicit rules. The essential function of a constitutional tradition is to emphasise the importance of such rules and the need to provide an orderly process within which political decisions are made. The provision of restraints was felt to be important in the framing of the American system of government and these restraints were embodied in a written constitution.

The American Constitution was fashioned to provide the ground rules of political action, but it is also clear that James Madison and others sought also to fashion these rules to reflect existing social realities. The conflict of opinions at the Constitutional Convention, for instance, indicates the social implications involved in deciding even procedural questions such as whether the President should have a veto power and what form the veto should take, or how the Constitution should be amended.

There are limits to the controls which a written constitution can exert on a political system, but the American Constitution has served to define the scope of authority exercised by particular institutions. It exercises a limiting influence on the President and Congress, and on state governments, irrespective of the actions of the Supreme Court.[11] The history of the American political system reflects the interaction of constitutional and political institutions with social forces and movements. A heterogeneous and democratic society with diverse interests has required the support of a Constitution to help determine the

[11] For an analysis of the responsibility of Congress to deliberate on constitutional issues, see D. G. Morgan, *Congress and the Constitution*, Cambridge, Mass.: Harvard University Press, 1966.

'rules of the game' within which political competition may operate. Specific limitations may be overcome and a degree of discretionary authority made possible only if backed by the potential check of constitutionality. A President may extend his authority to meet political crisis but this extension can be controlled. It is in this regard that the Supreme Court acts as a continuous constitutional convention.

Maurice Vile believes that constitutionalism helps to provide the necessary control and co-operation required in a representative democracy. In contrast to Britain, however, America places stronger emphasis on effective control than effective co-ordination. As he indicates, 'America is still only self-consciously a nation; one part of the country is still unsure of what another part will do, and still has interests which distinguish it sharply from others'.[12] The role of the Supreme Court has been to help to provide the degree of control necessary and the type of co-ordination acceptable to allow a union of many states to remain a cohesive unit. In seeking to do this it has often made law as well as stated authoritatively what the law is. If this has meant that minorities have sometimes succeeded in thwarting the majority coalition by demanding a strict interpretation of the original Constitution, it has also meant that some minority rights have at times been ignored. Yet constitutionalism, as expressed in the decisions of the Supreme Court, has been the vehicle for the defence of majority as well as minority rights. An imperfect and often vulnerable instrument has thus provided a sense of stability and integration for an expanding and pluralistic union of states. The significance of constitutionalism lies less in what has been achieved, than in what may have been prevented. In Britain, perhaps mistakenly, such controls have not been considered necessary, but in a society where the people believe they are sovereign but fallible, and that the American Constitution protects their rights, such controls become vital.

[12] See M. J. C. Vile, *Constitutionalism and the Separation of Powers*, *op. cit.*, Chapter 12, p. 335.

Chapter Three

THE NATURE OF AMERICAN
FEDERALISM

In 1787 federalism seemed a necessity if the United States was to obtain a viable central government, and the need to specify the powers of the national government made a written constitution an inevitable corollary. American federalism was a political expedient designed to foster unity in a society which sought to encourage diversity, and many aspects of the federal relationship were left undetermined in the original Constitution. Each generation of Americans has been forced to work out its own version of this federal relationship.

The basic principle on which American federalism rests is the division of governmental power between two distinct levels of government, each having the use of its powers as a matter of right and each acting on the same citizen body. James Madison, in seeking to explain the nature of the new Constitution, argued that it was partly federal and partly national. The major structural features of the American federal system include the following: a written constitution regarded as the supreme law of the land, the union of several autonomous states for common purposes, the division of the sum total of legislative powers between a national government and state governments, the power of judicial review, and an elaborate method of constitutional amendment in which the states have a co-equal role.

It has therefore been necessary to maintain the division of governmental power against national pressures towards centralisation and local pressures for fragmentation, and to ensure that power is mobilised to make effective government possible at both the national and state level. The task of making government effective enough to meet the demands placed upon it, while maintaining individual liberties by avoiding majority tyranny through the consolidation of power in the hands of those removed from popular control, has not been achieved without tensions and crises.

The Impact of Dual and Co-operative Federalism

The American federal system has never been a neat system of distinct governmental activities and functions. From the very beginning some aspects of national administration have required the mediation and co-operation of the states before they have affected individuals. The Constitution did not create rigidly independent administrative establishments in both national and state government. In many instances co-operation between the national government and the states was assumed from the outset. State and national laws were often brought into alignment with each other and with the Constitution in the period up to 1800. States also engaged in interstate compacts. Before 1800 the national government made its first grants-in-aid in the form of land grants, and the national government and the states developed a substantial division of revenue resources. The national government also gave relief to the states by assuming certain state debts. State and national officials also co-operated in a formal or informal capacity to perform joint or related activities.

In the nineteenth century, despite an early trend within the judiciary to extend national power at the expense of the states, there was also a strong judicial tendency, led by Chief Justice Taney, to create a pattern of dual federalism. This involved the carving out of separate fields of authority for the national government and the states. This attempt led to a struggle for power between the national and state governments because the theory emphasised tension and competition rather than co-operation between the different levels of governmental authority. Studies, however, indicate that this dual system did not supplant the co-operative idea, and there existed a system of separated and a system of interlocking governments. While the dual federalist position continued to be expounded by the courts, examples of co-operative federalism existed and expanded as the financial responsibilities of the national government increased considerably.[1]

Constitutional amendments in the nineteenth century tended to increase national power at the expense of the states despite the important role which the states played in the amendment process. The interpretation of the commerce clause of the Constitution also involved basic questions of national and state governmental authority. In 1824 Chief Justice Marshall, in *Gibbons* v. *Ogden*, defined the national power regarding the regulation of commerce as sovereign and complete. The states could only fully regulate intra-state matters. Gradually, however, this principle was eroded to provide the opportunity for state governmental regulation in the absence of national regulation, and this allowed for emphasis of the reserved powers of the states. By 1918, in *Hammer* v. *Dagenhart*, the Supreme Court was prepared to declare unconstitutional an act of Congress which prohibited the interstate transportation of goods whose manufacture involved the use of child labour. Interstate commerce could be regulated by the national government in terms of commercial activity, but not to affect activities only incidentally concerned with commerce. The ability to regulate the traffic of commerce did not include regulation of the production of such goods. The conflicting nature of such a decision created tensions within the political system. The dual federalist argument, in delineating the powers which the state or the national government could exercise, succeeded in creating an area where no governmental authority could exercise any regulatory influence.

Throughout the era of dual federalism the different levels of government in the American federal system maintained close administrative and fiscal collaboration. Through land grants and grants for services from the national government, state governmental activities expanded. The national government also relied on the resources of state and local government to help carry out its responsibilities. State militia became an important part of the armed forces of the nation, and state governments gave administrative and other help to national programmes of

[1] See D. J. Elazer, *The American Partnership*, Chicago: Chicago University Press, 1962; and M. Grodzins, *The American System*, Chicago: Rand McNally Co., 1966.

reclamation, highways, and homesteading. Administrative co-operation was often supported by Congressmen concerned about consitituency matters. The grant-in-aid system (begun by land grants in 1785 and the Northwest Ordinance) de-veloped because the policy of the national government came to be one of making the states the principal beneficiaries of the sale or use of public lands. The land grant became a cash grant which in turn often became an annual grant based on national tax powers. Sometimes the states were required to match federal funds with a smaller financial contribution of their own.

One source of co-operation which in recent years has caused a good deal of controversy involved legislation concerning elec-tion procedures. The Constitution provided that Congress could at any time make or alter regulations prescribed by the states for holding national elections. In 1842 an act of Congress declared that members of the House of Representatives should be elected on the district plan, and other legislation and court cases involved the question of the national influence on the or-ganisation of elections by the states. Attempts at regulatory co-operation for welfare or economic purposes also often ran foul of a Supreme Court anxious to uphold dual federalism, but legislation such as the Interstate Commerce Act of 1887 led to co-operation between state and national officials.

The problem of slavery, however, raised fundamental ques-tions about the nature of the federal system, and the rights of individual states. From the beginning of the American federal system, doctrines of states' rights have been invoked by minori-ties to challenge the legitimacy or constitutionality of national laws. Such attacks in the name of the rights of individuals or states were expressed by liberal individualists in the Virginia and Kentucky Resolutions of 1798–99 and the declaration of the Hartford Convention in 1814, and by economic conserva-tives in the South Carolina Resolutions in 1828, the Ordinance of Nullification in 1832 and South Carolina's Declaration of Secession in 1860. Though the basic question about the nature of the union between the national and state governments was ultimately resolved by civil war, the doctrine of states' rights continues to be used as a political argument. It survived in many Southern states as a thin disguise for white domination, as was reflected in the revival of pre-Civil War arguments to justify resistance to the decision of the Supreme Court in 1954 to demand racial integration in public schools.

Despite the divisive effects of the dual federalist principle, the powers of the national government, as defined by the Constitution, have been extended. As early as 1819, in *McCulloch* v. *Maryland*, Chief Justice Marshall set out the doctrine of 'implied powers' which in essence asserted that the existence of certain enumerated powers of the national government necessitated the use of certain additional 'implied' powers if such enumerated powers were to be used effectively.

Recurring national crises in the twentieth century have changed the role of government in the United States. Urbanisation, war, and depression demanded the response of government at all levels to many matters previously considered to be outside their sphere of influence. In 1913, when total national expenditure totalled only $700 million and state and local expenditure about $2 thousand million, the national government was empowered to create an income tax which would channel many millions of dollars into the national treasury. At the same time an extensive agricultural grant programme expanded the fiscal and administrative co-operation between the national and state governments. The Depression of 1929 heralded the beginning of a massive emergency aid programme by the national government to states and localities. This programme was extended by the New Deal in the 1930s. Co-operative federalism became of vital importance in this period, though it was not a new phenomenon. The Social Security Act of 1935, old-age assistance, aid to dependent children, and unemployment compensation, all involved a massive extension of the federal grant-in-aid. The Tennessee Valley Authority was established as a regional multi-purpose programme which inaugurated a new system of national-state-local relations. In the 1930s both state and national governments increased the scope of their functions and the size of their financial expenditures. The regulatory laws of the national government provided for co-operation between state and national agencies, while states themselves also used interstate compacts to expand their activities.

All of this was achieved despite political opposition which sought to limit the extension of governmental authority at any level, under the guise of seeking to protect the powers of state governments, by limiting the scope of national governmental authority. Yet by the end of the 1930s the Supreme Court had begun to accept the concept of co-operative federalism, and the extension of state and national governmental authority. This was only achieved after a struggle between President Roosevelt and the Court in the mid-1930s, but by 1942, as the case of *Wickard* v. *Filburn* demonstrated, the Court was prepared to allow the commerce power of the national government to be used to regulate extensively activities taking place within a state.

By 1942, total national expenditure exceeded $35 thousand million, and by 1946 had reached almost $62 thousand million, and state and local expenditure exceeded $9 thousand million in 1942 and had increased again by 1946. Such rapid growth of governmental expenditure occurred at all levels, but an increasing percentage of national governmental expenditure was being spent by state and local government through co-operative federalism. Table 3:1 indicates the general pattern of such expenditure and the changing roles of different levels of government.

Table 3:1

PERCENTAGES OF DIRECT GENERAL EXPENDITURES,
BY LEVEL OF GOVERNMENT

Spending Level	1902	1922	1927	1938	1948	1954	1962
National	34%	40	31	44	62	67	58
State	8	11	12	16	13	11	14
Local	58	49	57	40	25	22	28

Source: F. C. Mosher and O. F. Poland, *The Costs of American Governments*, p. 44.

Since 1945, attempts to reorganise the federal system by governmental commissions seem to have shown little recognition that the sharing of functions has been a major tradition of American federalism.

The American federal system is not simply a three-layer system of government with the institutions and functions of each level operating separately. As Morton Grodzins has shown, it rather resembles a marble or rainbow cake. 'No important activity of government in the United States is the exclusive province of one of the levels, not even the most local of local functions, such as police protection and park maintenance.'[2] The need to undertake many public welfare responsibilities demonstrates the sharing of functions – the national, state, and local governments together administer public assistance programmes, the national government alone administers social security, the national government and the states (plus local business groups) administer employment security, the states and local goverments handle general assistance, and all three branches administer child welfare services.

The Federal System and the States

Despite the growth of the responsibilities of the national government, the potential role of the state governments has also increased. However, some observers believe state governments either do not or should not exercise a partnership role in the governmental system in contemporary America. Yet the fact remains that they exist and are likely to continue to exist as more than mere administrative units. This is not simply because the states' rights argument still has a powerful appeal in the United States. They remain viable 'because they exist as civil societies with political systems of their own'.[3] In this respect they are more permanent than local authorities in Britain. They also remain viable as reflectors of sectional and regional differences in a continental nation, as experimenters and innovators (though many of them have been slow or reluctant to play this role), or as training and recruiting grounds for national political leaders.

The contribution of state governments as partners in an effective system of government in the United States has, however, been erratic. In this respect the structural attributes of

[2] M. Grodzins, *The American System*, *op. cit.*, p. 8. See also M. Grodzins, 'The Federal System', in *Goals for Americans*, Englewood Cliffs, N.J.: Prentice-Hall Inc., 1960, pp. 265–82.

[3] D. J. Elazar, *American Federalism: A View From the States*, New York: T. Y. Crowell Co., 1966, p. 215; also C. R. Adrian, *Governing our Fifty States and Their Communities*, New York: McGraw-Hill, 1963.

federalism have been more successful than the functional. The notion of a division of governmental power has served to check and control government. It has also allowed national governmental authority to increase but not overwhelm the states. However, the part played by the states in using governmental authority is likely to be increased following the attempt by President Nixon to reduce the scope of national governmental responsibility and through revenue-sharing give states more opportunity to develop their own programme priorities.

The sharing of national and state functions varies from programme to programme. In some areas state governments, however willing, are unable to cope with certain problems without help from the national government. Major highway construction, water pollution control or unemployment insurance, are examples where state action requires financial and administrative assistance from the national government. In some areas of public welfare where state governments prove unwilling or unable to act, the national government has used federal grants to stimulate the creation of state participation in programmes operating with minimal national standards and requiring modest financial participation by state governments. Resistance at the state level has been based on both ideological and political grounds, for many of these schemes lessen political control of state patronage and weaken the basis of support for well-established political organisations at the state and city level.

The constitutional status of the states in the federal system is affected by several factors: provisions in federal and state constitutions limiting or guaranteeing state powers *vis-a-vis* the national government and the interpretation of these provisions by the courts, constitutional provisions giving the states a role in the composition of the national government, along with unwritten constitutional traditions which have gained formal recognition. States cannot be divided without their consent, cannot be sued by citizens of another state or a foreign nation, are protected against invasion and domestic violence, and possess reserved powers. States have specific powers which are guaranteed by the Constitution. They are also subject to certain limitations and constitutional prohibitions. The basic pattern of political organisation has remained territorial, and in the nation as a whole state law is the basic law. As Elazar indicates, federal law is limited in scope, and the common law is interpreted on a state-by-state basis.[4] Federal statutory law fills the gaps left by the existence of fifty different state legal systems. A dual court structure exists, with a separate state and federal court system, with the federal courts interpreting federal law, reviewing the work of the state courts, and often enforcing state laws in cases coming under federal jurisdiction.

The United States Constitution requires federal-state co-operation in areas such as the administration of elections, and also gives both governments certain concurrent powers. Acts of Congress have generally given states a specific role in effecting many national domestic programmes, even in areas where the national government could claim exclusive jurisdiction. The supremacy of the fiscal powers of the national government has in general served to stimulate state activity even though state and local expenditures exceed national expenditures for domestic purposes. Annual state governmental expenditures of California and New York, the two states with the largest populations, exceed $4 thousand million. The most characteristic device of co-operative federalism has been the cash grant-in-aid, but informal co-operation and collaboration exists in many areas along with contractual relationships and interdependent activities.[5] Cash grants-in-aid began before 1900 but have become more and more common since the 1930s. They have been of three kinds. Flat grants which give each recipient government an equal sum regardless of local conditions and usually have not required that state governments provide any money beyond paying administrative costs. Proportionate grants made to recipient governments depending upon the size of their own contributions to the particular programme (national highway and education grants are often of this type, the first national highway programme being launched in 1916). Percentage grants are allocated like proportionate grants but recipient governments make a fixed contribution (public welfare grants or state grants to local school districts). There are other variations

[4] D. Elazar, *American Federalism: A View From the States*, *op. cit.*, p. 49.

[5] See Jane P. Clarke, *The Rise of a New Federalism*, New York: Columbia University Press, 1938. For a complete summary of federal grant-in-aid programmes, 1803–1962, see W. B. Graves, *American Intergovernmental Relations*, New York: Charles Scribner's Sons, 1964, Appendices A and B.

of the grant-in-aid principle. In most instances local recipients receive national funds from the state government and not direct, though programmes such as urban renewal often involve direct national-local contact despite state governmental opposition.

The key to the acquisition of national funds is, however, intensive state activity. The more a state is prepared to develop programmes, the more it is likely to receive national funds or contracts. There are really two levels of conflict – the intra-state battle for grant funds to be used for public services and the inter-state struggle for national contracts or direct grants. Grants-in-aid have increased the degree of intergovernmental sharing, as have variations of this such as tax offset or tax-sharing devices. Local governments still retain almost complete financial responsibility for a few local functions, but most of the important functions are shared with other levels of government. Periods of national emergency have led to increased centralisation of government expenditures but, apart from wars and related costs, the principal centralisation has been in the relations between the states and the local governments rather than between the national government and the others, especially during the 1930s.[6]

The bulk of direct spending on education remains local, though the states are bearing an increased share, and the national government is likely to increase its share in the future. States spend most directly on highways, but direct spending on public welfare remains primarily a state and local matter with the national government increasing its spending through the states. The national government is also increasing its direct expenditure on health and hospitals and on natural resources. In 1958, national government expenditures to aid state and local governments totalled $4·9 thousand million; in fiscal 1968 it was some $17·8 thousand million (about half of which was for highways and public welfare) and constituted about 15% of total state-local general revenue.

Despite charges of excessive centralisation of government made by states' rights advocates, as far as direct expenditure is concerned there is a good deal of decentralisation. In 1962 the national government was still responsible for over half of all

[6] See F. C. Mosher and O. F. Poland, *The Costs of American Governments*, *op. cit.*, pp. 44–5.

public expenditures, but this was below its position for 1954 and even lower than its figure for 1948. Moreover, with regard to domestic expenditure in the period 1948–60, national government expenditure increased less than twice, whereas state and local expenditures more than tripled.[7] Moreover, localities carry a heavy burden of expenditure. In 1960, of the $52 thousand million spent directly by state and local governments (excluding grants-in-aid and other intergovernmental payments), local governments spent $34 thousand million.[8]

The state governments occupy a sort of intermediary position, spending money they do not collect and collecting money they do not spend. Receiving a substantial proportion of their general revenue from the national government, they pay out even more to local units of government, especially for education.[9] State administrative patterns have been little affected by federal grant programmes, and differences in state responses to federal programmes have tended to reflect differences in political culture and political organisation among the states.[10] In general, attitudes can be divided into those favouring the federal system as a co-operative organisation, and those favouring the dual federalist view of the need to maintain and emphasise the conflict and tension inherent in the division of governmental authority between the national government and state governments. The latter tend also to see the need for the restriction of governmental authority at any level and oppose the extension of the political bureaucracy and demand a high degree of organisational efficiency where it exists. Sectional and regional differences, urbanisation, and economic factors, all exert their influence on the attitudes of state governments quite apart from specific political factors.

Some states have sought to resist or have chosen to reject the development of co-operation with the national government. Yet co-operative grant-in-aid programmes do provide states with a high degree of flexibility once minimal national requirements

[7] See H. Kaufman, *Politics and Policies in State and Local Governments*, Englewood Cliffs, N.J.: Prentice-Hall Inc., 1963, Chapter 1.

[8] Kaufman, *ibid*, p. 27.

[9] See F. C. Mosher and O. F. Poland, *op. cit.*, pp. 54–6.

[10] See I. Sharkansky, *The Maligned States*, New York: McGraw-Hill, 1972.

are met. Large states also exert influence on the national government when their members in Congress unite to uphold state demands.[11]

Many states engage in interstate co-operation which promotes integration but does not involve the national government. Probably the most important of these activities are interstate compacts which enable two or more states, with the consent of Congress, to organise together for joint action. A good example of this is the Port of New York Authority. It was created in 1921 by a compact between the states of New York and New Jersey and allows the two states to make combined efforts to promote the commercial development of the Port of New York. The Authority has grown into a considerable undertaking, with a staff of several thousand headed by an appointed board of twelve commissioners, and operates and administers a vast network of airports, piers, terminals, tunnels, bridges, warehouses and other facilities serving the metropolitan area of New York. A new innovation has been the interstate compact which includes states and the national government as equal partners. An example of this type of co-ordination is the Delaware River Basin Compact which became operative in 1962. It includes the national government, the states of Delaware, New Jersey, New York and Pennsylvania as well as the cities of New York and Philadelphia, in an attempt to deal with the problems of a river valley on a regional basis.

The role played by state governments in the maintenance and viability of the American federal system remains significant. It has been affected by social change and it has led to extensive and continuous reorganisation of state governments. There has been a continuing increase in the states' supervision of local governmental functions and in the expansion of state revenues and expenditures, but the states have often been reluctant or unable to cope with many of the complex problems created by the development of metropolitan areas which may cross state boundaries. Yet the states remain managers of massive pro-

[11] See J. H. Kessel, 'The Washington Congressional Delegation', *Midwest Journal of Political Science*, February 1964, pp. 1–21; also A. Fiellin, 'The Functions of Informal Groups: A State Delegation', in R. L. Peabody and N. W. Polsby (eds.), *New Perspectives on the House of Representatives*, Chicago: Rand McNally Co., 1963, pp. 59–78.

grammes in areas such as higher education. Several states support higher education systems with larger enrolments than that of the United Kingdom, and California supports a higher education system with more students than in France, Great Britain, West Germany, and the Benelux countries combined.[12]

The decentralised nature of American party politics has strengthened to some extent the position of the states, and the federal system as a whole is sustained because it provides the multiplicity of competing interests in the United States with adequate access to the political process at every level. There are, however, points of tension within the national-state partnership which can serve to weaken the influence of the states. Morton Grodzins refers to these as 'squeak points' in the system, and suggests that these include lack of co-ordination between agencies and programmes of the same government, interagency competition at all levels, the ability of local communities to bypass hostile state governments and appeal to national authorities, and conflicts between states.[13] Conflict is also created as a consequence of differences between national and state budgetary practices. Smaller states also find themselves dominated by national programmes and sense the danger from the increase in national agencies to handle new national programmes and the pressures to promote nationwide conformity in administering programmes, thus reducing state discretion. State administrators, however, tend to be less critical than state politicians of national programmes. Despite political demands for less encroachment by the national government, states have not always been keen to undertake many responsibilities themselves.

Metropolitan America and Creative Federalism

It is necessary to appreciate the constitutional difference between the national-state and state-local relationship. The latter is a unitary rather than a federal relationship, and, in principle at

[12] See D. Elazar, *American Federalism: A View From the States, op. cit.*, pp. 201–2.

[13] See M. Grodzins, *The American System, op. cit.*, pp. 327–31. See also M. Grodzins, 'Centralization and Decentralization in the American Federal System', in R. A. Goldwin (ed.), *A Nation of States*, Chicago: Rand McNally Co., 1962, pp. 1–23.

least, like the relationship between national and local government in Great Britain. Yet the localities, and especially the major cities, have succeeded in acquiring an independent voice in the political process, and some degree of national-local or national-city relations existed even in the nineteenth century.[14] All local governments are, however, in a legal sense political sub-divisions of the state, though the adoption of home rule charters allow cities to obtain full control over all local matters subject to state government intervention in matters of state-wide concern. It is the large metropolitan centres who have been most insistent on gaining a maximum of independence from state control as their problems have become more complex with the transformation of the United States towards an urban or metropolitan society.

The major problems of the large cities include the following: the physical blight of the city centres, problems of urban transportation caused by the 'flight' of city workers to the suburbs, problems of water and air pollution, and problems of substandard housing, juvenile delinquency, unemployment, crime, or education which is the result of central city areas becoming ghettos of poor immigrants to the cities. The need to adjust city government to cope with these problems and the impact on state and national governmental authority has produced significant changes in the American federal system. The practice of co-operative federalism brought the cities within the orbit of the federal system, and the increasing size of the major cities increased their influence within their respective states and their political strength in national politics. As a result of this, especially after the 1960 election, which was won by a Democratic candidate heavily dependent on the urban vote, the national government has tried to alleviate many of these urban problems. In May of 1964 President Johnson formally inaugurated a new type of federal co-operation, known as creative federalism, between the national government and the leaders of local communities.

The need for such formal action followed as a result of two factors – the reluctance or inability of many state governments

[14] See D. J. Elazar, *The American Partnership*, *op. cit.*, Part 2; also R. C. Martin, *The Cities and the Federal System*, New York: Atherton Press, 1965, Chapter 5, and W. B. Graves, *op. cit.*, Chapter 24.

to solve city problems, and the administrative and financial inability of city governments to tackle many of their own problems.[15] Many state governments are limited in the scope of their authority by their constitutions, and for many years state legislatures tended to over-represent rural interests, while state governors often have relatively weak powers, and state revenue systems have often failed to adjust to changing requirements. Roscoe Martin argues that 'the states' concern for the vast new problems of metropolitan America, as measured by monetary contributions toward their alleviation, is quite casual', and they have not appeared in the past to see them as any more than limited state responsibilities.[16] They have also been grudging in granting permission for city participation in programmes aided by national funds, and have often required that such funds be channelled through state agencies. State government has too often reflected a rural and provincial attitude and a philosophy of *laissez-faire*, anti-governmental action, and support for the *status quo* in the past.

The increase of national government payments direct to local governments from 1932 to 1963 largely consisted of programmes such as the Federal-Aid Airport Programme, the Slum Clearance and Urban Renewal Programme and the Low-Rent Public Housing Programme, and the major source of co-operation was the cash grant-in-aid. After the statement of President Johnson in 1964, an extended pattern of creative federalism was soon established. The major aim of creative federalism was the concentration on the enunciation of the vital domestic problems which need governmental action, using whatever organisations seemed the most efficient and prepared to tackle these problems. This involved the revitalisation of state and local governmental bodies, and improved co-ordination both within different branches of government and between these branches.

Creative federalism lacked clear design or rigid application, and did not lend itself to precise definition. In application it has

---

[15] See E. C. Banfield and J. Q. Wilson, *City Politics*, Cambridge, Mass.: Harvard University Press, 1963; W. S. Sayre and H. Kaufman, *Governing New York City*, New York: Russell Sage Foundation, 1960; R. C. Wood and V. Almendinger, *1400 Governments*, Cambridge, Mass.: Harvard University Press, 1960; and S. Greer, *Governing the Metropolis*, New York: Wiley, 1962.

[16] R. C. Martin, *op. cit.*, p. 75.

involved a variety of programmes using different administrative forms of co-operation, but the major features included the restructuring of the national government bureaucracy to make it more responsive and efficient in its relations with state, local and non-governmental organisations. It also involved the redirection of federal grant-in-aid programmes, with less emphasis on national requirements governing the spending of the funds, and more concentration on help to specific areas, including the use of non-governmental bodies if necessary to implement programmes. Central to the concept was the view that it was possible to expand national, state, and local authority at the same time, along with new organisations, and stressed the importance of local initiative and local solutions to local problems.

The new concept constituted a major challenge to state governments to seek to solve the problems of poverty and racial tension evident in the cities in partnership with local organisations, or accept the fact that the national government would bypass them and work directly with organisations at the local level. In 1966, the Annual Report of the Advisory Commission on Intergovernmental Relations warned the states of the diminution of their authority if they did not participate in the new programmes set out by the 89th Congress. The U.S. Congress laid the foundations for President Johnson's 'Great Society' programme with the passage of the Economic Opportunity Act of 1964 (and the creation of the Office of Economic Opportunity), the Elementary and Secondary Education Act of 1965, the Housing Act of 1965 (along with the creation of a new Department of Housing and Urban Development), and the Demonstration Cities and Manpower Development Act of 1966. All these legislative programmes concerned specific problems in the cities and involved federal grants-in-aid. Almost without exception they produced great controversy, and their implementation raised real conflicts within the federal system. In some instances they involved the bypassing of both existing state and local authority and resulted also in demands from state governments for increased responsibilities in the programmes. These demands were often challenged by city mayors, who in turn then sought direct co-ordination with national authority and made strong protests at being bypassed themselves when some funds were allocated to local community groups.

The Economic Opportunity Act was a good example of the strains created by attempts to develop a new federal pattern, in this case to fight poverty in the cities.

The initial bill contained little reference to the states, and the Office of Economic Opportunity was given maximum flexibility in dealing with the states, but for work-training, work-study, and community action, there were some provisions for equalising fund distribution among the states, and state governors were given some measure of veto power over projects in their states. In part this decision was deliberate and was supported by local political forces, but local forces in turn opposed the creation of independent community action agencies at the local level who could obtain national funds to set up programmes at the local level. Of the 600 agencies founded in the first year the vast majority were non-profit, non-governmental organisations, but they did have the tacit co-operation of local governmental and political officials. Initially, control from the Office of Economic Opportunity was small, but political pressure led to increased control being exercised.

Attempts to implement the poverty programme goals also revealed the multiplicity of governmental and quasi-governmental organisations within the framework of the federal system which produce major problems of co-ordination. Such acts also revealed the conflicts implicit in seeking to bypass traditional sources of governmental power at the state and local level in order to spend national governmental revenue to achieve specific goals in the most effective way.[17]

The major significance of the development of creative federalism was as a new attempt to solve the crucial problems facing American cities. In doing so it revealed a series of conflicts which highlight the major problems facing the development and efficiency of American federalism and its ability to solve problems of poverty and race relations.[18] At the national level it prompted administrative reorganisation and the use of im-

[17] See Senate Committee on Government Operations; Sub-committee on Intergovernmental Relations, *Hearings on Creative Federalism*, 89th Congress, 2nd Session, Part 1, Washington, D.C.: U.S. Government Printing Office, 1967.

[18] See D. J. Elazar, 'Urban Problems and the Federal Government: A Historical Inquiry', *Political Science Quarterly*, December 1967, pp. 505–25.

proved methods of budgeting designed to increase the efficiency with which public resources devoted to public purposes are used.[19] At the state level it required state governments and politicians to decide what role they were to play in the task of solving the problems of their cities, and to seek to reorganise their administrative procedures to cope with increased responsibilities if they were ready to co-operate. This also forced those supporting state governments to sharpen their arguments and intentions in order to justify their role in programmes such as the administration of sections of the Elementary and Secondary Education Act of 1965. At the local level it stimulated opposition from entrenched political interests often more used to distributing perquisites and patronage than sharing power, but it equally forced attempts to make city governments more efficient if they were to work with the national government to solve city problems.

One example of this may be shown by the actions of the County Board of Supervisors in Albany, New York State, who rejected national anti-poverty funds for two years because they feared they might surrender patronage power to outside bureaucrats. They also delayed implementing other programmes because the required city matching fund would have to be financed in large part through tax increases on real-estate. Until the regional headquarters of the Office of Economic Opportunity bypassed local political opposition and channelled funds for adult education through public-service, charitable, and social-action groups, Albany remained the largest metropolitan area in the United States not participating in the anti-poverty war.

In 1966 the principle of creative federalism was applied to the question of combatting crime and lawlessness in the cities. Recommendations were made which would make the national government a financial partner in the modernisation of city and state police forces and their approach to crime control. National grants would be used to encourage new techniques which would strengthen community police forces and would avoid the possibility of creating a national police force.

At all levels of government the implementation of legislation based on the broad principles of creative federalism led to

[19] See D. Novick (ed.), *Program Budgeting: Program Analysis and the Federal Budget*, Washington, D.C.: U.S. Government Printing Office, 1966.

political controversy, and strong criticism. Specific programmes like the War on Poverty failed ultimately for lack of money but also in part suffered from administrative inadequacies.[20] Though the impetus for expansion of creative federalism waned with the defeat of the Democrats in the 1968 Presidential election it remains an important attempt to adjust the workings of the American federal system in order to deal with the problems and share the burdens of a changing urban society, where poverty and race relations remain grave problems.

The New Federalism and the Future

The accession of Richard Nixon to the Presidency in 1968 was followed by a new attempt to change the balance of the federal system. Nixon placed strong emphasis on the role of the states and sought to lessen the direct activities of the federal government and its departments and agencies, and strengthen the financial resources of the state governments. Nixon's 'new federalism' was initially expressed in his revenue-sharing proposals which he presented to Congress in 1969 as an investment in renewing state and local government and to make these governments more creative and responsive by shifting power from the federal level to levels closer to the people. The proposals met strong opposition in Congress. The basic provision of these proposals was to earmark a small but growing proportion of federal revenues annually to be returned to state and local governments almost without restrictions on its use.

Evidence that many states and localities were close to financial crisis led the Nixon Administration in 1971 to press again for revenue-sharing. The basic programme sought to share a growing portion of federal revenues with state and local governments without any restrictions, sharing additional federal revenues for use by state and local governments as they chose in special broadly defined areas of national concern, with no matching fund requirements, and maintaining only those existing grant programmes for which there was a clear, continuing national requirement. State and local governments would also

[20] For a critical appraisal, see D. P. Moynihan, *Maximum Feasible Misunderstanding: Community Action in the War on Poverty*, New York: Free Press, 1969.

work out any intrastate distribution of their funds. Despite strong support from state and local governments, it was not until October 1972 that a modest five-year programme was approved, involving some $30 thousand million, about one-third to go to the states and two-thirds to the localities.

In his second term Nixon sought to link the new federalism with a wider approach to domestic affairs. This involved developing 'decision rules' defining a new division of responsibilities between the different levels of government. Income transfers to citizens would be a national responsibility, with heavy emphasis on the use of cash payments, foodstamps or housing assistance for the poor. Human services would be primarily state and local functions, with wide discretion for policy-making at the local level in areas such as education, manpower or public health. Community services such as police or transportation would be basically state-local responsibilities, but broad inter-area matters like air pollution control or national parks would require some national rule-making and specific financial spending. In areas primarily state and local in responsibility, national grants might be used initially to stimulate local initiatives, but national involvement would be one largely of setting priorities.

Mayors and governors, while lamenting budget cuts, in particular grant programmes, gave qualified support to the general development. Evidence on the actual use of revenue-sharing funds by cities was mixed, some simply reducing property taxes, others financing new services.[21]

This brief account of new developments confirms that the national government's role in the federal system need not be an expanding one, in the face of pressures for decentralisation, and that state and local governments remain important. American federalism in the future, as in the past, is likely to remain a flexible, pragmatic and imperfect process.

[21] For more detailed analysis, see M. D. Reagan, *The New Federalism*, New York: Oxford University Press, 1972; also D. G. Stolz, *Revenue Sharing*, New York: Praeger, 1974.

Chapter Four

THE DEVELOPMENT OF THE
POLITICAL CULTURE

Writing just before the American Revolution (though not pub-
lished until 1782 in England), the French immigrant John de
Crèvecœur first sought to answer the question, 'What is an
American?' For Crèvecœur this 'new man' was 'neither an
European nor the descendant of an European; hence that strange
mixture of blood, which you will find in no other country. I
could point out to you a family whose grandfather was an
Englishman, whose wife was Dutch, whose son married a
French woman, and whose present four sons have now four
wives of different nations. *He* is an American, who, leaving behind him all his ancient prejudices and manners, receives new
ones from the new mode of life he has embraced, the new government he obeys, and the new rank he holds. . . . The American is
a new man, who acts upon new principles; he must therefore
entertain new ideas and form new opinions.'[1]

Most Americans then, as now, accepted certain basic values,
beliefs, and traditions about themselves and their political system, and it is the sum of these which constitute the political
culture of the United States. Some level of agreement about this
political culture is necessary if the governmental system is to
remain stable, and therefore basic values in American society
have often been broadly defined.

The American political culture has been affected by both
pragmatic and utopian considerations. The American Revolution in 1776 provided the opportunity for the American people
to create a stable political system based on values and traditions
very different from those dominant in eighteenth-century

[1] J. H. St. John de Crèvecœur, *Letters from an American Farmer*, New York:
Signet Edition, 1963, pp. 63–4.

Britain. By the mid-nineteenth century Alexis de Tocqueville saw American society as egalitarian and competitive, placing a heavy emphasis on personal achievement, and in 1910 James Bryce also emphasised the reputation America had as the land of equality, and agreed with Tocqueville that it possessed an egalitarian style which distinguished it from other societies.[2] By contrast, Walter Bagehot saw British society in the nineteenth century as deferential and élitist, with a strong attachment to aristocratic values, and contemporary studies of the British political culture indicate the continuation of such influences.[3]

The opinion of Tocqueville was something of an oversimplification, and Bryce in fact found inequalities of wealth and education existing in the United States by the beginning of the twentieth century. Indeed, élitist and inegalitarian traits have always existed in American society, with the commitment to equality usually taking the practical form of equality of opportunity. Extensive study by Robert Lane indicates that the commitment to equality in an ideal sense may have been held more strongly by professional groups in the United States rather than by the commercial or working classes. Lane argues that potential class conflict may have been assuaged by the emphasis on opportunity and consumption rather than equality, about which working-class Americans express some apprehension.[4]

However, politicians in the United States have always recognised the importance of the common man. Though not all the leaders of the American Revolution were democrats, the United States became in time more and more committed to a society where the lot of the common man would be improved and similar opportunities made available to all. If this ideal has not always been adhered to in practice it has given American poli-

---

[2] See A. de Tocqueville, *Democracy in America* (Philipps Bradley edition), New York: A. A. Knopf, 1946; and J. Bryce, *The American Commonwealth*, New York: Macmillan, 1910.

[3] See W. Bagehot, *The English Constitution* (Collins edition), London, 1963. For a contemporary analysis, see R. Rose, *Politics in England*, London: Faber and Faber, 1965, Chapters 2 and 3; and R. Rose (ed.), *Studies in British Politics*, London: Macmillan, 1966, Chapter 1.

[4] See R. E. Lane, 'The Fear of Equality', *American Political Science Review*, March 1959, pp. 35-51.

tics a distinctive style evident in comparing the composition and attitudes of the U.S. Congress with Parliament. It can also be seen by reference to political leaders who were historical contemporaries in Britain and the United States – Andrew Jackson and the Duke of Wellington, Palmerston and Lincoln, or Baldwin and Franklin Roosevelt.

Contemporary American society primarily consists of many different sub-cultures, whose views may be heard within the political system. The political system is also designed to protect the rights of individuals and particular sub-cultures as well as maintaining those features in the society which comprise a common national culture. Sub-cultures reflect special patterns of thought and identity which display remarkable tenacity and continuity, but sub-cultural conflicts can be intense. Issues such as the use of government revenue to help finance religious schools raise basic questions about rival ways of life or fundamental notions of freedom. The decision to prevent by law the segregation of races in public schools in 1954 was seen as conflicting with the established way of life in many Southern states and provoked strong political and social resistance.

Dominant American values and attitudes have, however, been determined by white Americans, rather as basic values in the United Kingdom have generally been determined by Englishmen, and the following seem of special political significance: a commitment to the notion of equality of opportunity, an ability to utilise and exploit natural resources and a desire for the economic plenty this may bring, a recognition of the desirability of social and physical mobility, an acceptance of the inevitability of pluralism in society and the elevation of this as a political virtue, and a recognition of the need to promote a sense of national identity and mission (as well as encourage individualism) if unity is to be maintained. All of these characteristics have promoted among white Americans the following paradoxical personal traits: a cosmopolitan manner which often conceals small-town attitudes, individualistic tastes and conformist pleasures, reflectiveness mixed with restlessness, an awareness of change with the certainty that change means progress, and a sceptical ambivalence towards politics and politicians yet a pragmatic and experimental approach towards the solution of problems through the political process.

The Creation of a Political Culture

In order to achieve national self-determination through revolution a decisive break was made with the past. Though many of the inhabitants of the American colonies were conditioned by British traditions they had the opportunity to set up a new kind of state. Yet the colonies were separate communities with distinct cultural patterns. The revolutionary movement provided a thread of unity between the colonies, and the Declaration of Independence in 1776 provided a vital foundation for a permanent political arrangement. Richard Merritt suggests that by the early 1770s the American colonists were sufficiently different from their English contemporaries that they comprised a distinct, if embryonic, American political community. Through analysis of the colonial press and its use of terms and the type and character of their news coverage between 1735 and 1775, Merritt traces the discontinuous development of an increased propensity to pay attention to American events, an increasing willingness to refer to Americans as a single group, and the increasing use of terms identifying the colonists as Americans rather than as members of a British political community.[5] This sense of community among the colonists preceded a demand for the functional amalgamation of their political institutions, yet the Revolution was only the beginning of the process of American community development. Particularistic sentiments and loyalties remained, and therefore the initial governmental structure took the form of a weak confederation, with individual states retaining a high degree of autonomy.

The American Revolution was revolutionary only in the destruction of political ties external to the colonies with a political system in which they had no direct representation. However, it paved the way for new political institutions reflecting the attitudes of the leaders of the new states. The Articles of Confederation set up in 1781 indicated the initial fear of executive power and the reluctance to establish new executive authority. Under the impact of assertions of local sovereignty and the end of external controls, post-revolutionary politics developed centrifugal tendencies.

[5] See R. L. Merritt, *Symbols of American Community 1735–1775*, New Haven: Yale University Press, 1966.

In some of the thirteen state governments the general impetus was toward the recognition of the individual rights of the common man. The suffrage was expanded in several states, bills of rights were obtained, and in all states legislative power gained at the expense of the executive and judicial. In 1779, for instance, Massachusetts held a constitutional convention which was to set up a constitution deriving its authority from the explicit consent of all adult male citizens, a wider suffrage than that authorising ordinary legislation. The preamble to the new constitution emphasised that governmental authority was based on a social compact, and a detailed and elaborate procedure allowed the people of Massachusetts to approve or reject the constitution as a whole, and at town meetings discuss each article separately and state their objections. Though such democratic procedures could be applied to state constitutions, there was opposition to the creation of any strong national authority. Freedom from unconstitutional taxes and domestic interference, however, also meant the end of British protection against foreign powers.

While there remained considerable distrust of executive authority, there was also scepticism about the virtues of popular government. Leaders of the new American political community still lacked the courage of their convictions, but practical commercial problems, and fears that the Articles of Confederation as they stood left the new nation vulnerable to external aggression, led to plans to strengthen the authority of the national government. A meeting in Annapolis in 1786 of representatives from five states to consider trade problems led to recommendations that states send delegates to Philadelphia to consider revisions in the Articles of Confederation.

The convention which met in 1787 in Philadelphia had no popular mandate to devise a new framework of government, and delegates were not elected directly by the people. At times they seemed anxious that the people at large should know little of their deliberations until they were completed.[6] Their view of

[6] For analysis and interpretation of the political ideas and motives of the Founding Fathers, see D. G. Smith, *The Convention and the Constitution*, New York: St. Martins Press, 1965; and R. Hofstadter, 'The Founding Fathers: An Age of Realism', in *The American Political Tradition*, New York: Alfred A. Knopf, 1948.

a new 'federal' union really implied the drawing together of sovereign states, but they also had reservations as to whether republican government could function over a large area and were uncertain about the effects of applying the principle of government deriving its authority directly from the people.[7]

The framing of the new Constitution did, however, involve the explication of a set of values and the establishment of political institutions through which such values could be guaranteed and protected. The principles on which the Constitution was based were not necessarily acceptable to everyone – had they been so, three of the leading architects of the new constitution would not have felt it necessary to embark on a vigorous propaganda campaign (of which *The Federalist Papers* provide a notable documentary record) to ensure that it be ratified. Nor would writers in the future such as Charles Beard have sought to construct theories emphasising the economic origins of the Constitution.[8]

It is nevertheless possible to identify certain preferences already rooted in American society and in existing political institutions which the new Constitution attempted to affirm. The Constitution sought to establish an effective national authority which would provide economic and other protections and integrate the new community of states, and also allow for territorial expansion. This national authority was, however, subject to substantive and procedural restraints of the type already in existence in state governments, and shared authority with state governments. National governmental action would be made legitimate because it was limited by the Constitution, and decision-makers would be subject to periodic re-election or appointment. Not all branches of the national government were directly dependent on the consent of the people, nor were speci-

[7] See J. P. Roche, 'The Founding Fathers: A Reform Caucus in Action', *American Political Science Review*, December 1961, pp. 799–816; and M. Diamond, 'Democracy and the Federalist: A Reconsideration of the Framers' Intent', *American Political Science Review*, March 1959, pp. 52–68.

[8] See C. A. Beard, *An Economic Interpretation of the Constitution*, New York: Macmillan, 1914; also F. McDonald, *We the People. The Economic Origins of the Constitution*, Chicago: Chicago University Press, 1958. For an attack on such interpretations, see R. E. Brown, *Charles Beard and the American Constitution*, Princeton, N.J.: Princeton University Press, 1956.

fic guarantees embodied in a Bill of Rights, and the latter had to be added to the Constitution in order to obtain ratification. The Constitution, in fact, reflected the traditional paradox of American society, a strong moral commitment to the creation of a political system guaranteeing full personal and corporate liberty and freedom, a government of laws and not men, based on popular consent, along with a latent scepticism as to the effects in reality of the full realisation of such demands. James Madison reflected this dilemma in *Federalist 51* as follows: 'But what is government itself but the greatest of all reflections on human nature? If men were angels, no government would be necessary. . . . In framing a government which is to be administered by men over men, the great difficulty lies in this: you must first enable the government to control the governed; and in the next place oblige it to control itself. A dependence on the people is, no doubt, the primary control on the government; but experience has taught mankind the necessity of auxiliary precautions.'[9]

Once accepted as legitimate, the new political system had to be made to work, and this in itself affected cultural attitudes. Initial developments were favourable, but the compromises made by the Founding Fathers were soon to create political tensions, and they reflected disagreements about values and traditions. In the period from 1787 to 1820 the major conflict was over the scope of the power of the new national government, and centred around the political struggles of the Federalists or Hamiltonians and the Anti-Federalists or Jeffersonians.

Just as many of the leaders of the American Revolution were the instigators of the new Constitution, so many of the Founding Fathers were responsible for making the new political system work. Men such as Alexander Hamilton, who would have preferred a stronger national government to guarantee community stability, were sceptical about human nature and so about popular government, but preferred a new constitution to none at all. It is not surprising that such views clashed with those of Thomas Jefferson, who took a more optimistic view of individual potential for goodness, feared the diminution of individual rights by governmental authority, and so emphasised the virtues of limited government and localism in political life.

[9] *The Federalist Papers, op. cit.,* p. 322.

It is easy to oversimplify such attitudes by seeing them as reflecting urban-rural or commercial-agricultural, or even élitist-democratic conflicts. They are important in that they were both rooted in distinctively American traditions and attitudes which the political system was designed to accommodate. The initial victory was gained in 1800 by the Anti-Federalists, and Jefferson became President. Yet such victories have rarely been complete because the political system is one of divided political power, allowing rival attitudes to find expression and influence political decisions by controlling some branch of government. Thus the nationalising ambitions of the Federalists could still find expression through a vigorous Supreme Court led by Chief Justice Marshall.

Perhaps more than any other single individual, the first President of the United States, George Washington, served to institutionalise and formalise cultural attitudes towards the political system. As the symbol of responsible national executive authority, Washington re-established American faith in government. His dignified and responsible leadership also demonstrated that the new nation could remain a cohesive unit while retaining considerable diversity in local traditions and attitudes.

Equality and the Political Culture

Commentators such as Louis Hartz have argued that because the United States was 'born free', it has no tradition of Parliamentary government, and has neither a permanent revolutionary tradition nor a permanent tradition of reaction.[10] But not everyone in the United States in 1800 was born free, for of a total population of just over 5 million, one-fifth were Negro, almost all of them slaves. In the Southern states in 1800 one out of every three persons was Negro and a slave, and the ratio remained the same in 1860. As a result, while a host of European observers in the United States all testified to the high degree of political, social, and economic equality among white Americans in the first half of the nineteenth century in contrast to the situa-

[10] See L. Hartz, *The Liberal Tradition in America*, New York: Harcourt, Brace and World, 1955; also C. Rossiter, *Conservatism in America*, London: Heinemann, 1955.

tion in Europe, a large percentage of the population in the Southern states remained in bondage.

The triumph of Jeffersonian attitudes in the early part of the nineteenth century came in a society still largely rural, and it left permanent political influences. The nation as a whole moved towards greater political equality, if not full political participation for all citizens. By 1845, over twenty years before the Second Reform Act in Britain, property restrictions on the right to vote or hold office were almost extinct, many elective offices were created, the electoral college which elected the President was democratised, and state constitutional conventions were popularly elected and their recommendations ratified by popular vote. By 1836, when the Chartists in England were considered dangerous radicals for demanding universal manhood suffrage, the secret ballot, a short Parliament and pay for its members, such rights were already accepted or close to acceptance in the United States.[11] While Chancellor Kent in the 1820s still clung to notions that office-holding and voting should go to those with an economic stake in society, practical men such as Daniel Webster recognised that widespread property ownership and the emergence of new states in the West made greater political equality inevitable. By 1840 the Whigs, having replaced the Federalists, recognised the fact that birth in a log cabin had been the passport to victory for their Presidential candidate, Harrison. Not until 1840, however, did the Whigs fully realise that they had a good deal in common with this democratic spirit. The eclipse of the Federalists and the rise and fall of the Know-Nothing party (a nativistic, anti-Catholic, anti-immigrant group in the 1850s) indicated that political parties in the United States, in order to be successful, needed to be populist in tone and supporters of equality of opportunity. No party could survive simply as the organ of the better classes, as a minority of younger Federalists had recognised before 1815, but could not save their party.

This emphasis on egalitarianism also marked the end of an

[11] For detailed accounts of the development of the suffrage in the United States, see J. R. Pole, *Political Representation in England and the Origins of the American Republic*, London: Macmillan, 1966; and C. Williamson, *American Suffrage from Property to Democracy 1760–1860*, Princeton, N.J.: Princeton University Press, 1960.

era of government dominated by the Founding Fathers, men distinguished by education and to a lesser degree wealth, and led to the rise of a new type of political leader more attuned to mass sentiments and the techniques of mass leadership and seeking to encourage the common feeling that popular will should control the choice of public officers and the formulation of public policy. This movement was led by Andrew Jackson, a peculiar brand of war hero, pioneer, and aristocrat from Tennessee. Jacksonian democracy began as part of the fight against political privilege, with a strong emphasis on militant nationalism and equal access to office, an offspring of the results of democracy. It blossomed, in response to the underlying tensions produced by the development of industrialisation in the North and West, into a fight against governmental support of economic privilege, and demanded equality before the law and the restriction of government to the guaranteeing of equal economic opportunity for all citizens. The movement towards political democracy proved also to be a movement towards the liberty of economic *laissez-faire*. The age of egalitarianism generated greater psychic and social conflict than any period since the Revolution, as the power of the majority increased and gravitated towards control of the national government through executive power. Jackson, with strong charismatic appeal, became the symbolic mirror of the ideals of many Americans at the time and he extended the potential power of the President because of his mass support. The Jacksonians, however, while able to provide the equality of economic opportunity demanded by citizens, remained unaware of the implications of changing economic realities.[12]

The equality demanded was perhaps less utopian than Jackson recognised, for at the same time there were already forces in existence likely to increase social stratification and the emergence of an aristocracy based on wealth. In achieving political

[12] For a valuable analysis of the different facets of the Jacksonian period, see E. C. Rozwenc (ed.), *Ideology and Power in the Age of Jackson*, Garden City, New York: Doubleday Inc., 1964. See also J. L. Blau (ed.), *Social Theories of Jacksonian Democracy*, New York: Harper, 1947; and Richard Hofstadter, *The American Political Tradition*, *op. cit.*, chapter on Andrew Jackson. For a study indicating the heterogeneity of political attitudes, see L. Benson, *The Concept of Jacksonian Democracy: New York as a Test Case*, Princeton, N.J.: Princeton University Press, 1961.

equality, the use of political authority to provide economic opportunity served to promote social inequalities. Such inequalities only became significant after the Civil War, but the seeds were sown in the period between 1830 and 1860.[13] In a republic where every citizen had an equal chance and was free to become as unequal as he could, the poor seemed to have a vested interest in such equality since every citizen might become rich. Yet no man could blame anyone or anything (lack of birth or education) for his lack of material success. In this respect the acceptance of a meritocracy, of competition for social status based on achievement, had an early effect on American political culture. The frontier provided new opportunities and challenges to individuals, and the industrial revolution new possibilities for economic abundance. In the long term the effects of the drive towards political equality served to guarantee economic opportunity and had a permanent influence on many of the political and social attitudes of contemporary America.

The emphasis on achievement in the period before the Civil War was a valid one while there remained a scarcity of labour and an abundance of land, but the costs of this became more apparent after the Civil War. The new wealthy showed little sense of social or political responsibility. By the end of the Jacksonian period there were signs indicating the existence of an urban industrial proletariat in cities such as New York, consisting largely of new immigrants. However, many of these immigrants had been attracted to the United States because it seemed to be a classless land of plenty where the individual could be master of his own destiny. This was indeed possible for those who created frontier settlements, populated with immigrants of their own background, and they demonstrated a remarkable ability to forget old political traditions and become 'democrats' in their new role of pioneers.[14] For the city immigrant, adjustment was not so easy. Utopians from Britain, such as Robert Owen, foresaw the possible ills of industrialism, but they had little direct impact on the political and social attitudes of the time.

[13] See D. T. Miller, *Jacksonian Aristocracy: Class and Democracy in New York, 1820–60*, New York: Oxford University Press, 1967.

[14] For an example of such a community, see N. Iverson, *Germania, U.S.A.*, London: Oxford University Press, 1967.

It is ironic that the American Civil War was fought against the attitudes of a Southern planter aristocracy by a Northern society already developing a wealthy plutocracy dependent on the economic exploitation of many immigrants. The only real distinction was that the opportunity to join the Northern plutocracy was open to all with the will, and luck, to succeed. Yet it became more difficult to rise from rags to riches, but the myth prevailed and prevented class differences from developing into political conflict. The democratic, agrarian, society of the Jacksonians rapidly gave way to a hierarchical, urban, industrial society in the North, dominated by an aristocracy of wealth which challenged the democratic principle of 'no privilege'. The effects of immigration and industrialisation in these areas ultimately served to fashion a new set of values in a pliable society.

Much of the United States, unlike Britain, was already egalitarian and democratic in spirit before industrialisation. The major exception, however, was the existence of slavery in the Southern states where cotton-growing was heavily dependent on keeping the Negro population as slaves. In a society where equality of opportunity was preached, slavery was an anomaly impossible to justify, and tensions developed over the question of the continuation and perpetuation of this 'peculiar institution' as the United States expanded in size and population. The issue had been a controversial one at the Constitutional Convention in 1787 and a temporary compromise had been reached. By the 1830s it was the question in the minds of every politician but about which few wished to argue. 'That strange mixture of blood' to which Crèvecœur referred did not apparently include the Negro.

Moreover, as the Southern population became more and more a minority (in 1800 they constituted about 50% of the total U.S. population, by 1860 only just over one-third), there began attempts to construct arguments justifying both democracy and slavery. John C. Calhoun, the chief political theorist defending the attitudes of the South, reflected the cultural dilemma. In his early political career Calhoun had been a nationalist and was closely allied with capitalist interests, but his desire to see the Southern states dominate the national government led him to seek to create an alliance between the

agrarian South and West against the commercial and industrial North-East. This initial alliance ended in disaster, because
of his preoccupation with Southern interests and the right of
states to nullify acts of the national government they believed
unconstitutional. Increasing evidence of the decline in the influence of Southern attitudes as Northern industrialisation expanded, and new states were brought into the Union where 'free'
labour existed, forced Calhoun to a defence of a system of élite
rule behind a façade of Jeffersonian ideas regarding the rights
of states and minorities, backed by economic arguments which
sought to prove the inevitability of conflict between labour and
capital and the common interest Northern capitalists therefore
had in preserving slavery in the South.[15]

Unfortunately the conflict between capital and the Southern
planter aristocracy came first, as the expanding 'free' society in
the North succeeded in meeting the impact of working-class
discontent. The total abolition of slavery, since this involved a
revision of the Constitution, and a rejection of nullification or
secessionist claims, was not supported by a majority of Northern-
ers, but a series of compromises obtained by Southern politicians, who themselves reflected a minority view, still could not
resolve the problem. When the Supreme Court in 1857, in the
Dred Scott case, rejected attempts to bar slavery from the new
territories and refused to recognise Negroes as citizens, fundamental questions were raised about the authority of the national
government to act on behalf of majority attitudes in the nation,
and the rights of state governments to secede from the nation if
their minority rights were not respected. The issue of slavery
now became inextricably linked with the question of maintaining the unity of the nation and avoiding secession by certain
states.

In 1860, the victory of the new Republican party, exclusively
a Northern and Western party, and its Presidential candidate,
Abraham Lincoln, led to the state of South Carolina seceding
from the Union, followed by other Southern states. The refusal
of Lincoln to allow these states to secede led to civil war. While
the Civil War did lead to the end of slavery by constitutional

---

[15] See G. Capers, *John C. Calhoun, Opportunist: A Reappraisal*, Gainesville,
Florida: University of Florida Press, 1960; also R. Hofstadter, *The American
Political Tradition*, *op. cit.*, Chapter 4.

amendment, and the passage of further amendments intended to protect and guarantee individual and citizen rights, especially those of the freed Negro, later developments suggest that the Civil War was more a conflict over rival views of the nature of the political system than the result of a strong cultural commitment by a majority of Americans to guarantee full equality to all citizens.

The occupation of the defeated Southern states after the Civil War proved to be expensive, and continuation of it too high a price to pay to ensure full political and other rights to the freed Negro. After the Compromise of 1877, and the withdrawal of federal troops from the South, the patterns of the old Southern culture gradually began to be reasserted. The rest of the country acquiesced to this sacrifice of the Negro in order to avoid further sectional conflict, a weakness which Southern white politicians continued to exploit in the future. By 1896, slavery had been replaced by segregation, legislation designed to guarantee the civil rights of Negroes had been declared void, and the Supreme Court of the United States in *Plessy* v. *Ferguson* tacitly accepted the segregation of races on the grounds that 'legislation is powerless to eradicate racial instincts'. Segregation or racial separation was therefore permissible if the facilities provided were equal, a doctrine which was accepted until 1954. By the turn of the century few, if any, Negroes in the Southern states were able to vote.[16]

As a consequence, a century or more after becoming citizens, the Negro struggle to obtain full political, social, and economic equality in the United States has produced major political conflict. The notion of equality of opportunity in the American political culture has always been a pragmatic one, but the commitment to equality has rarely been more than a recognition of the responsibility to provide an environment in which groups could compete in relative equality (some being clearly more equal than others) for political and economic benefits.

[16] For an extensive treatment of the development of segregation in the South, see C. Vann Woodward, *The Strange Career of Jim Crow*, New York: Oxford University Press, 1957.

The Impact of Industrialisation

The combined influence of increased industrialisation and the growth of an immigrant population in the cities, had a specific effect on the American political culture after the Civil War. The political system was dominated by the Republican party who identified the national interest with the interests of an expanding business community. Virtues and traditions associated with the rural pioneer existence were translated into a desire for economic plenty. Cultural and political attitudes were dominated by capitalists who made economic success and progress the goal of the American dream, and catered openly to the acquisitive impulses of the 'classless' American. Reward was based on individual economic achievement, and humanitarian values were explained away by the morality of the search for individual material prosperity. The style of politics aped the style of business, and the political process allowed business enterprise to flourish unchecked, and was used to aid and protect it when necessary.

Rapid social change, however, did pose certain problems. The social effects of industrialisation forced into consideration the grounds and scope whereby the political process might intervene in the arrangements of economic and social life. Social Darwinists, led by William Graham Sumner, exercised a powerful influence and advocated an evolutionary theory of *laissez-faire* which involved a severely limited role for the political process and maximum freedom for individual economic enterprise.[17] Others, however, continued to insist on the use of political power to restructure social relationships, and supported social equality in its widest sense. The Social Darwinists found a strong ally in the Supreme Court, which used its authority to interpret the Constitution to reject political attempts at both the state and national level intended to control the social effects of unchecked economic development. The domination of political authority by those demanding economic individualism was made possible by the lack of cohesion between groups in society

[17] For commentary on the impact of these theories, see R. Hofstadter, *Social Darwinism in American Thought,* Boston: Beacon Press, 1955; and R. G. McCloskey, *American Conservatism in the Age of Enterprise,* Cambridge, Mass.: Harvard University Press, 1951.

who opposed them, and such groups were also hampered by the need to operate and argue within the American liberal tradition or face charges of being 'un-American'.[18]

Writers such as Henry George and Edward Bellamy, arguing for social reform, and pointing to the inequities of an industrialised society, were widely read but had little direct political impact. In this regard they were like the Transcendentalists such as Emerson, Thoreau, or Whitman, whose writings emphasised a high-minded individualism and spiritual nationalism above economic materialism or political authority. Emerson's emphasis on the moral basis of democracy served to modify the frontiersmanship of the Jackson period and the economic individualism of the Social Darwinists which was to follow. In a more general sense, however, the common suspicion of government and politics evident in the Transcendentalists provided an effective rationalisation of non-political activity for an increasing number of apolitical members of American society in the latter part of the nineteenth century.[19]

The Progressive movement, and to a lesser extent the Populist movement, did ultimately break through the barrier and came to exercise a permanent influence on the political process and on social values. The Populists found organised expression in the agrarian protest movements of the 1890s which rose to challenge the political success of the Republican party who, after preserving the Union, had succeeded in 'holding together East and West, magnate and factory worker, homesteader and banker, in the great enterprise of continental unification, development and exploitation'.[20] They advocated a mixture of economic and political reform along with an undercurrent of nativism, and sought the use of political power. They demanded the free coinage of silver, government ownership of railroads, universal governmental control of utilities, the abolition of

[18] For development of these arguments, see L. Hartz, *The Liberal Tradition in America, op. cit.,* Chapters 8 and 9.

[19] See D. Minar, *Ideas and Politics. The American Experience,* Homewood, Illinois: Dorsey Press, 1964, pp. 237–50. See also Y. Arieli, *Individualism and Nationalism in American Ideology,* Cambridge, Mass.: Harvard University Press, 1964.

[20] V. O. Key, Jr., *Politics, Parties and Pressure Groups,* 5th edition, New York: Crowell, 1964, p. 168.

national banks, tariff reductions, and other measures to improve the credit position of the farmers. The Progressives emphasised the need for the sovereignty of the people to be reflected in government action. They believed the plight of the farmers to be a consequence of manipulation and control of the political process by Eastern bankers and industrialists.

The Progressives were instrumental in forcing important political changes in the states where they became a strong political force, and they sought to take popular sovereignty to its furthest logic. They resisted the control of the electoral process by party organisations and provided for direct primary elections where electors could vote to choose the candidate a particular party would run in the general election, and sought direct popular checks on elected officials through the use of devices such as the recall or referendum which could be used between elections. They also effected a degree of municipal reform. At the national level the Progressive movement had some effect on the campaigns which led to the passage of the 17th and 19th Amendments to the Constitution, providing for the direct election of Senators in 1913 and suffrage for women in 1920, and on the Pendleton Act of 1883 which established a federal civil service. Other changes such as the 16th Amendment in 1913, which allowed Congress to collect an income tax, and legislation such as the Sherman and Clayton Acts, along with the passage of state legislation on wages and laws and the regulation of business affected with the public interest, all came as a consequence of the political challenge of the Progressives.

Progressive writers also sought to demonstrate that the political system had become an economic instrument wielded by privileged classes, especially property holders, at the expense of the interests of other people. Many of these writers believed that the closing of the frontier, and the increase in social injustice created by an industrial society, had produced a situation where democracy must be asserted against privilege. To achieve this, institutional and procedural reforms were necessary.

The 1896 election, however, marked the last full-throated attempt of the American farmer to dominate a national government he had not wholly controlled since Jackson, and had not really controlled at all since the end of the Civil War. William

Jennings Bryan, a Westerner, became the Democratic Presidential candidate with a platform which allowed the Republicans to portray the Democratic party as the party of agrarian radicalism, and persuade voters that what was good for business was good for the country and for employer and employee alike. The Democrats were branded as sectionalists unconcerned with the problems of industrial America. The defeat of the Democrats allowed the virtues of business enterprise to prevail, checked only by governmental action which often protected economic interests as much as the public interest, and which reached its apotheosis in the Republican administrations of Harding, Coolidge, and Hoover in the 1920s. On the eve of the Great Depression, President Hoover still enunciated the virtues of economic enterprise and rugged individualism.

The success of the cultural impetus for unregulated economic enterprise is shown by the failure of any strong socialist movement to emerge in the United States following industrialisation, comparable to that which developed in Britain. The fact that the political process was democratised before the society became urbanised, and the absence of any real sense of class solidarity in a society where labour developed strong bourgeois attitudes and a commitment to individualism, provided no strong political base for a socialist movement. The loose structure of the political process and the nature of elections also created structural obstacles to the establishment of a socialist party. As a social movement it has served to add to the demands for social reform, especially in the period 1900–14, and in the 1930s, despite modest electoral successes, but its effect upon the political culture of the United States has been marginal.

Industrialisation did, however, lead to the assimilation into American society of the many immigrants who came and settled in the cities. The diffusion of political power and the provision of universal white male suffrage allowed political party organisations in the cities in the latter part of the nineteenth century to exploit the numerical strength of the immigrant. Political organisations became a means of acquiring individual wealth and status for those prepared to put their energies into it in the cities. For the Irish–American, and later the Italian–American, city politics provided an opportunity to obtain some stake in

American society, though their national political influence did not develop until after the Great Depression of 1929.[21]

The Great Depression, however, shattered the confidence of the people in an unregulated economy, and ended the reign of economic *laissez-faire* and the political dominance of the Republican party. It led to a more sympathetic and realistic view of governmental regulation of the economy in order to recover and then maintain .economic abundance. It is no longer assumed that government should stay out of economic affairs, though a belief in the virtues of the capitalist system remains a part of the American culture. Nevertheless, pressure for government action has led the national government to take responsibility for promoting the general health of the economy. Since the Employment Act of 1946, it has also promoted maximum employment, production and purchasing power, and presents annual economic reports, and has become responsible for maintaining a high rate of economic growth and price stability. The national government has also become involved in industrial relations, and since 1926 six important acts have been passed concerned with labour-management relations.

Since the 1930s, the national government has also been responsible for a limited amount of public enterprise, though not on the scale of that undertaken by the British government since 1945. Atomic energy is now a government monopoly under a special Commission, and the national government supports farm prices through commodity loans to farmers organised by the Commodity Credit Corporation. Perhaps the single most controversial enterprises of the national government have been in the generation and sale of electric power, beginning in the 1930s with the creation of the Tennessee Valley Authority.

Yet such actions by government are still a matter of political controversy and have not gained full cultural acceptance. The inheritance of an abiding faith in the virtues of individual responsibility in financial and economic affairs in order to achieve abundance, leads to demands for stern fiscal responsibility on the part of government, requiring seeming frugality in public

[21] For an example of the political career of a 'hyphenated' American, see A. Mann, *La Guardia. A Fighter Against His Times, 1882-1933*, Philadelphia: J. P. Lippincott Co., 1959.

spending and a balanced budget. Many state constitutions contain prohibitions against deficit financing by state governments. Yet these views conflict with demands for more and better public services by citizens and the constitutional demands placed on the national government 'to provide for the common defence'. The need to make government spending seem responsible has led to an annual symbolic fiscal ritual in which the U.S. Congress scrutinises and checks the annual spending of government departments and their annual requests for spending in the future.[22] Public expenditure as a percentage of the Gross National Product has, however, risen from 7·7% in 1902 to 11·6% in 1927, to 31·7% in 1962. Public spending for defence purposes has grown at a more rapid rate than general domestic expenditure and has become the largest single item of public expenditure, a trend indicated in Table 4 :1.

Table 4 :1

ALLOCATION OF THE BUDGET DOLLAR 1927–72

	1927	1938	1948	1954	1962	1965	1972
National defence and defence-related	18	12	48	52	37	61	46
Domestic and other Public Enterprises	82	88	52	48	63	39	54

Sources: United States Bureau of the Budget, *The Budget in Brief*, fiscal 1965 and fiscal 1972. F. C. Mosher and O. F. Poland, *The Costs of American Governments, op. cit.*, Table 7:1, p. 103.

Note: The 1972 figures are estimated percentages. The decline in the overall percentage of the budget spent on defence still left it as the largest single item.

Increased public spending on defence has had significant effects on the structure of American industry. In 1961, 95% of employment in the aircraft and missile industry was in defence work, as was 60% of shipbuilding and boatbuilding employment, while 40% of radio and communications equipment was

[22] For consideration of the cultural significance of such symbolic exercises, see T. Arnold, *The Symbols of Government*, New Haven: Yale University Press, 1935, Chapters 1 and 4.

produced for defence purposes.[23] In 1959, 82% of all factory employment in San Diego, California, was in the production of aircraft and missiles. States such as California, Alaska, Hawaii, and Georgia, are heavily dependent on defence spending for employment and economic wellbeing. Since 1960 the United States has also become committed to an extensive programme of public expenditure on space research and development.[24]

In contrast, public spending for internal domestic services has only begun to rise since 1945. Willingness to spend more public money on education is, however, much less than individual willingness to increase personal spending on automobiles, speedboats, or golfing equipment. Public spending on highways and airports is at least as great as that on public welfare, and, while public spending on health and hospitals has increased, the financing of hospital and related services for the elderly through the social security system was only achieved in 1965 after a prolonged political struggle, and the acceptance of any scheme as comprehensive as the National Health Service in Britain seems remote.

Cultural resistance to government beneficence is partly a consequence of initial economic abundance through industrialisation based on individualism and private enterprise, but it is also linked with an innate scepticism about the efficiency of enterprise backed by governmental funds and administration, especially in domestic affairs.

Nationalism and the American Sense of Mission

The political culture in the United States has been affected by the need of the nation to find solace in nationalistic emotionalism in order to emphasise its uniqueness and maintain its unity. The conquest of the frontier and a continent, and the emergence of the United States as an industrial nation unrivalled in the world, was achieved by a single-mindedness which took the Farewell Address of Washington literally and sought little involvement in affairs outside the continent. Yet the creation of a

[23] See U.S. Arms Control and Disarmament Agency, *Economic Impacts of Disarmament*, January 1962.

[24] For a political analysis of this development, see V. Van Dyke, *Pride and Power*, Urbana: University of Illinois Press, 1964.

viable democracy which embraced a vast number of immigrants also led to the rise of a moral impulse to extend the virtues and protection of their unique political system to nearby territories suffering under the colonial yoke. This sense of mission began in 1898 following a popular protest against the Spanish treatment of Cuba, and the United States succeeded in 'freeing' Cuba and Puerto Rico and annexing Hawaii. During the Presidency of Theodore Roosevelt this sense of mission continued.

The outbreak of war in Europe in 1914 indicated, however, that American opinion was divided between those who sought non-involvement with Europe and the rest of the world and those who now wished America to play a world role, but with 'no entangling alliances', since the virtues and mission of America should remain unique. The initial policy of neutrality was based on the argument that immediate national interests were not threatened. However, the fall of France, the sinking of American ships by German submarines, and the economic stake in an Allied victory due to the great volume of war orders which stimulated the American economy from a Britain already involved in the war, forced a reconsideration of American policy. For President Wilson the war in Europe slowly became a struggle between authoritarianism and democracy, and in 1917 he asked Congress to declare war.

The internal effects of the war on American attitudes indicated that in time of stress individual rights were subordinate to nationalism and national purpose. Strong legal and other sanctions were taken against any individuals felt to be 'disloyal' and there was a rise of militant anti-German feelings and activities. The Espionage Act of 1917 provided heavy penalties for any activities designed to obstruct the war effort.

The end of the war produced internal political conflict over the conduct of foreign affairs (in this instance negotiations over the peace provisions and the Treaty of Versailles) by the President. Lack of political foresight and latent opposition to entangling foreign alliances led the Senate to refuse to ratify the Versailles Treaty (and thereby to reject the League of Nations), and the United States remained outside the League of Nations.

American attitudes between 1918 and 1945 included multilateralists who now felt that the national interest was best served by a policy of active international co-operation providing security through alliance with other democratic nations, uni-lateralists who, in the 1920s, wished to return to a policy of non-involvement in affairs outside the hemisphere, and isolationists who, in the 1930s, were prepared to abandon major parts of traditional foreign policy and seek the total insulation of the country even from a neutral role in foreign wars.[25]

In the latter part of the 1930s the unilateralist and isolationist viewpoints appeared dominant, as was shown by the passage of Neutrality Laws between 1935 and 1937, though they were not shared by President Roosevelt. Before the Japanese attack on Pearl Harbor made American involvement a fact, he had sought to persuade the American people that they had some obligations to other democratic nations such as Britain when they were forced into war. In September 1940 he made an agreement to transfer fifty American destroyers to the British government in return for bases in Newfoundland and the West Indies. Later, after directly identifying the security of the United States with the continued survival of Britain, and assert-ing that the United States should be 'the great arsenal of demo-cracy', he got Congress to accept a lend-lease plan designed to allow the transfer, loan, or lease of any article of defence potential to countries such as Britain whose defence was con-sidered vital to the security of the United States. Other mea-sures were taken which brought America closer to direct in-volvement in the war, but at every step there was opposition from powerful elements in American society.

The experience of the United States in World War II, how-ever, changed cultural attitudes. By 1950 the United States had cast off deeply-rooted traditions of foreign policy, aban-doned neutrality and isolation, and became the self-appointed leader of a 'coalition of free nations' whose mission was to lead the struggle against the threat of international communism. In 1947, faced with the increasing intransigence of Communist Russia in a Western Europe weakened by the economic and

[25] For a study distinguishing these different foreign attitudes in a contem-porary setting, see C. O. Lerche, Jr., *The Uncertain South – Changing Pattern of Politics in Foreign Policy*, Chicago: Quadrangle, 1964. See also D. K. Adams, *America in the 20th Century*, Cambridge: Cambridge University Press, 1967, Chapter 3; and U. Schwarz, *American Strategy: A New Perspective*, London: Heinemann, 1967.

physical cost of war, the 'Truman doctrine' of American military aid for free people resisting attempted subjugation by outside pressures, and the Marshall Plan of economic aid to Europe, were accepted by Congress and the American people as vital to American security and the containment of Communism.[26] In 1949 this commitment was extended with the signing of the North Atlantic Treaty, a military alliance which committed the United States to a firm defence of European security. Nor could the United States avoid commitments in the Far East. In 1950 U.S. troops, under U.N. mandate, intervened militarily to help South Korea against invasion from North Korean forces backed by Communist Russia and China.

The United States has thus become involved in a series of costly international commitments, and the impact of this 'internationalism' extended to all reaches of American political life. Not all of these commitments had the unqualified support of all sections of American society. The Korean War provided a great deal of disagreement, especially following the dismissal of General Macarthur by President Truman, and it was a key issue in the 1952 Presidential election which was won by the Republican candidate Eisenhower, former supreme commander of Allied forces in Europe. The new international role proved to be a costly one, and the need to justify many of the commitments by dramatising the threat of international Communism produced severe social strains which were exploited politically, notably by Senator Joseph McCarthy. The 'cold war' situation exposed the latent insecurity of many Americans, and led to the need to reassert and demand loyalty and conformity to the basic ideals of American society, and condemn those who might undermine this inside or outside government. Thus, by a familiar American paradox, the high degree of freedom existing in the United States allowed Senator McCarthy to lead a witch-hunt against individuals in government 'believed' to be Communists and to deprive them and others of basic rights and freedoms guaranteed by the Constitution.[27]

[26] See J. M. Jones, *The Fifteen Weeks*, New York: Viking Press, 1955.

[27] For more detailed analysis of the impact of McCarthyism on American society, see R. H. Rovere, *Senator Joe McCarthy*, London: Methuen, 1960; also D. Bell (ed.), *The Radical Right*, Garden City, New York: Doubleday Inc., 1963.

The new international responsibilities also added an important new dimension to the powers and responsibilities of the President, and made his tasks more complex. The President had become the leader of a coalition of free nations, a role which makes the election of an American President a matter of more than purely domestic interest. Potential Presidential candidates find it necessary to demonstrate their experience and knowledge of foreign affairs and their ability to create a good impression with foreign allies. The American people have been forced by circumstance to accustom themselves to the burdens of this international role and to accept as a fact that decisions of their government can have a profound influence on the lives of many in the world.

The overall response of the American people to this is ambivalent. It is often easy to exaggerate the extent to which the average voter is concerned about matters of foreign policy and has a clear understanding of the issues involved. Mood rather than fact tends to influence attitudes which in turn may only be expressed when a foreign policy issue reaches crisis dimensions.[28] Small-town values and beliefs help to provide a latent scepticism and opposition to foreign alliances and the spending of taxpayers' money except where it is seen to be directly and successfully combating the rival ideology of Communism, and is appreciated by recipients. Many Americans still find it difficult to adjust to the psychological pressures of international situations such as the fighting of 'limited' wars of attrition with only a fraction of the military potential of the country. Characteristic values of success and achievement, individualism, and national pride, are not ideally suited to guaranteeing a rational approach towards the complexities of international relations in the contemporary world.

Survey evidence obtained in 1956 also indicates that there is no relationship between individual attitudes towards domestic and international affairs. An interventionist attitude in foreign affairs is as likely to be taken by a domestic conservative as by a domestic liberal, and the relative isolationist is as likely to

[28] For an analysis of the cultural effects of foreign policy attitudes in American society, see G. A. Almond, *The American People and Foreign Policy*, New York: Harcourt, Brace and World, 1956. See also R. Dahl, *Congress and Foreign Policy*, New York: Harcourt, Brace and World, 1950.

favour increased governmental spending on social welfare as oppose it. In the era prior to 1952 the Democratic party was more closely identified with support for programmes involving governmental activity both in domestic social welfare areas and abroad. In a study done in 1952, Republicans tended to choose isolationist attitudes, whereas Democrats were more likely to be internationalist in outlook. However, in 1956, people who tended to adopt internationalist attitudes were no more likely to express identification with the Democratic party than with the Republican party, but they did tend to be more informed and involved politically and to be more effective participants in politics.[29] A further study by Robert Axelrod indicates that the clearest dimension of consistent attitude consists of a form of 'populism', reflected in support for governmental action to improve social welfare but opposition to current tax levels, civil liberties, and foreign involvement. Such attitudes, however, are most distinct for non-voters.[30]

The war in Vietnam exposed the fact that there are many conflicting attitudes about America's role in world affairs. Former 'internationalists' doubt whether the United States has the resilience and nerve, apart from the economic resources, to continue to commit itself to the protection of the integrity of small nations against Communist or other subversion. Others, inside and outside the country, question whether the United States has the right to intervene in the internal affairs of other nations, and assert that it is necessary to concentrate on domestic affairs where changes in traditional values and attitudes are necessary if increased tensions in the cities and racial hostility is not further to weaken the stability of the political system. By 1972, more and more Americans seemed ambivalent about support for any continuation of an 'imperial' mission for the United States.

[29] See A. Campbell, *et al.*, *The American Voter*, New York: John Wiley, 1960, pp. 198–201; also A. Campbell, *et al.*, *The Voter Decides*, Evanston, Illinois: Row, Peterson & Co., 1954, pp. 118 ff.

[30] See R. Axelrod, 'The Structure of Public Opinion on Policy Issues', *Public Opinion Quarterly*, Spring 1967, pp. 51–60.

Liberty and Social Attitudes

Central to the development of the political culture has been a tradition of liberty. The United States sought to institutionalise many liberties and freedoms in the Bill of Rights. Yet contemporary commentators have indicated that liberty and freedom in post-industrial society in the United States rest on a different institutional footing to that in pre-industrial times.[31] The individual liberty of early American society was a function of the openness and pluralism of society at the time, rather than the result of any centralised libertarian ideology. It rested in the diversity of opinion evident in an open society where no one establishment achieved complete hegemony. The Constitution sought to preserve liberty from tyranny and anarchy, and liberty became almost a by-product of conflict and balance rather than a positive creation of public policy. Individual liberty could be threatened by the oppression of government or the conformist demands of dominant groups. Madison, the framer of the Bill of Rights, believed freedom could exist when no individual or group interest could be institutionalised as the public interest, and the protection of liberty lay in diffusing the power to oppress. The governmental system could be arranged to maximise freedoms by inaction, with a pluralist society led by a neutral government allowing the Constitution to provide the rules. The freedoms the Constitution guaranteed were designed to prevent centralised authoritarianism.

This original design was not completely satisfactory. The Jeffersonians found that the Federalists could get all three branches of the national government to accept the Alien and Sedition Acts of 1798, and the South found that when its views on slavery became those of a sectional minority, not even the Constitution could protect them. In 1833 the Supreme Court ruled that the guarantees of the Bill of Rights did not extend to state governmental actions. The ability to move to new parts of the expanding nation provided the major protection for certain religious minorities against the wrath of direct democracy at the local level. In rural America, freedom seemed to be

[31] See J. P. Roche, *The Quest for the Dream*, London: Macmillan, 1963. See also 'American Liberty: An Examination of the Tradition of Freedom', in J. P. Roche, *Shadow and Substance*, New York: Macmillan, 1964.

heavily dependent on the 'openness' of society and the mobility of many citizens to escape an oppressive environment.

In American cities, social if not physical protection has tended to come from the impersonal nature of suburban and city living. The diffusion of religious and group conformity established in the immigrant ghettos has led in turn to the rise of new conformist tendencies on the part of many second and third-generation Americans who have moved to the suburbs. This may have served initially as a form of protection for individual liberties, since it involved a relative decline in the cohesion of many sub-cultures and their distinctive attitudes,[32] but it has had other contemporary effects. Fearing freedom and individuality the individual seeks social acceptance through conformity. David Riesman argues that many middle-class Americans look to others for a guide to the values and attitudes they adopt rather than to a set of individual attitudes or traditional values.[33] This development, while it may have lessened conflict and promoted stability by providing for the predominance of certain shared cultural characteristics which the lack of a common past made necessary, has also had some unfortunate political repercussions. The Englishman, secure on a solid basis of tradition, can afford the luxury of tolerance, but many Americans feel they must demonstrate that they are true Americans and require others to do the same. Hence the pressures of a competitive urban society and the tensions caused by new external pressures have led in many instances to demands for patriotic loyalty to 'American' ideals and customs and to support for governmental restrictions on individual liberties for the common good.

In this situation it becomes increasingly important for minorities that the Bill of Rights appears to offer some protection against legislation based on short-term emotional majority demands. The desire to maintain and extend certain values in American society has often been at the expense of others, and the Supreme Court has increasingly taken on the task of main-

[32] This phenomena has been explored by anthropologists. See M. Mead, *And Keep Your Powder Dry*, New York: William Morrow Co., 1942, especially Chapter 3.

[33] See D. Riesman, *The Lonely Crowd*, New Haven: Yale University Press, 1950. For a slightly different interpretation, see R. E. Lane, *Political Ideology*, New York: The Free Press, 1959, Chapters 3 and 27.

taining individual liberties and the rights of minority sub-cultures against majority demands.

Emotions and Symbols

The political culture in the United States is also influenced by a variety of emotions and symbols which affect the attitudes and beliefs of individuals. All people react to symbols and make use of them. An individual who has little knowledge about, or interest in, the political process may not be able to discuss the democratic traditions of the United States, yet he may feel a positive emotional response to the national flag, the national anthem, the President, or the American Constitution. Such symbolic attachments are important in maintaining support for the authority of governmental decisions. Political institutions possess sacred and secular, as well as dignified and efficient functions, and the office of the President and the Supreme Court as a body both perform necessary symbolic functions.

The President must perform a variety of symbolic functions as Head of State. He must attend a large number of ceremonial functions usually reserved in Britain for the monarch. He is a symbol of moral leadership in the nation, and his residence, the White House, is an effective substitute for a palace. He and his family take on many of the responsibilities and attributes performed by royalty in other societies. Children in America often are first aware of political matters through an awareness of, and a diffuse attachment for, the President, and the President serves as a common symbol of popular identification.[34] Many of the functions that religious symbols perform in integrating other societies are performed in the United States by central political symbols. The absence of an aristocratic or monarchic tradition, the secularisation of political life and a latent suspicion of political leaders, does not mean that the political system lacks elements of religious symbolism.

The Presidential inauguration ceremony involves the symbolic authority of the President and reinforces his political authority. It is an investiture of power and duty, is attended by the outgoing President, and the Inaugural Address is often a per-

[34] See F. I. Greenstein, 'The Benevolent Leader: Children's Images of Political Authority', *American Political Science Review*, December 1960, pp. 934–43.

sonal appeal by the President to the patriotic feelings of the people. The office of the President symbolises for many citizens the unity of the American nation. The assassination of President Kennedy in 1963 emphasised the significance of this symbolism. It was necessary, for instance, that the Vice-President should be seen legally to assume the position of President as quickly as possible. In this situation the televising of the oath-taking ceremony by which Johnson became President was a practical as well as symbolic act. The news of the assassination generated a climate of confusion and fear as well as grief across the nation, and this 'crisis' situation was relieved by the visible and swift assumption of Presidential authority.[35] Political partisanship also declined for a period after the assassination, and public sentiment for the dead President was much stronger than his personal popularity had been immediately prior to his death. Studies of the effects of a Presidential assassination on the political culture indicate that a complicated and pluralistic society may well be held together less by a common sense of democratic values than by a diffuse emotional commitment to the political system which reveals itself clearly only in 'crisis' situations.[36]

The Supreme Court performs a symbolic function in consequence of its role as guardian of the Constitution. Though research has indicated that the American people view the Court rather as they do other political institutions, and not in any special light, the Court as a body seeks to act in a dignified way, consistent with this symbolic role.[37] The nature of symbolic support for the Court is linked closely with the Constitution and individual reverence for the document. Because of this, direct

[35] Those wishing to linger on the emotional impact of the Kennedy assassination, see W. Manchester, *The Death of a President*, London: Michael Joseph, 1967.

[36] See B. S. Greenberg and E. B. Parker (eds.), *The Kennedy Assassination and the American Public*, Stanford; Stanford University Press, 1965, especially S. Verba, 'The Kennedy Assassination and the Nature of Political Commitment'.

[37] See K. M. Dolbeare, 'The Public Views of the Supreme Court', in H. Jacob (ed.), *Law, Politics, and the Federal Courts*, Boston: Little, Brown,1967; see also J. H. Kessel, 'Public Perceptions of the Supreme Court', *Midwest Journal of Political Science*, May 1966, pp. 167–91, and W. F. Murphy and J. Tanenhaus, 'Public Opinion and Supreme Court; The Goldwater Campaign', *Public Opinion Quarterly*, Spring 1968, pp. 31–50.

challenges to the authority of the Court by other political institutions may conflict with latent support for the values and symbols of an 'independent' judiciary. In 1937, despite massive popular electoral support at the 1936 election, President Roosevelt could not mobilise this support and pass legislation to change the composition and jurisdiction of the Court.

The formal procedures of the Supreme Court help to evoke symbolic and emotional support for itself and reverence for the Constitution. The atmosphere of the Court as it conducts its business is sober, the nine black-robed Justices refer to each other as 'brethren', and each Justice has his own individual seat. The Supreme Court building itself also helps to engender an air of dignity and solemnity to deliberations.

The influence of symbolic attachments is also illustrated by public response in 1967 to a wave of anti-Vietnam war demonstrations, in which the burning of draft cards and the American flag became a temporary method of direct protest. Such actions were widely publicised through the mass media and produced strong public condemnation resulting in Congressional activity to consider passing legislation which would make desecration of the flag a federal crime. State laws were already in existence but had not been enforced. A local judge felt the need to assert that the normal protections of due process of law might be set aside to ensure that people accused of such actions received immediate trials and severe punishment if found guilty!

The symbols of patriotism provide strong emotional support for the political system. Almond and Verba, in a comparative survey, show that Americans are likely to give greater pride of place to their political and economic systems than Britain, as is shown in Table 4:2. Yet Americans tend also to be sceptical of politicians, and popular attitudes towards Congress as a symbolic institution tends to be less than the symbolic influence of Parliament in Britain, though this may simply be because of the more important 'efficient' role performed by Congress *vis-à-vis* Parliament. Certainly the American bureaucracy receives less deferential respect (and the public demands more accountability of its actions) than the British Civil Service. In part this seems to be a factor of tradition, so that in the United States there is less differentiation at all levels between the ability of the citizenry to determine political and administrative compe-

Table 4:2

PRIDE IN ASPECTS OF NATION

Attribute	% Naming	U.S.	U.K.
Government, political institutions		85	46
Economic system		23	10
Social legislation		13	18
Characteristics of people		7	18
Position in international affairs		5	11
Physical attributes of country		5	10
Spiritual virtues and religion		3	1
Contributions to science		3	7
Contributions to arts		1	6
Other		9	11
Nothing or don't know		4	10
Total % of responses (over 100% because of multiple responses)		158	148

Source: G. A. Almond and S. Verba, *The Civic Culture*, p. 102.

tence than in Britain. Americans therefore tend to believe that both politicians and administrators should be responsible to their demands and that they are equally competent to affect both.[38]

To summarise briefly, symbolism and emotion in the American political culture tend to reflect the more idealistic elements in American society. These are in turn a consequence of historical factors – revolutionary beginnings, the impact of a written Constitution, the effects of a frontier tradition and a liberal ideology. Political symbolism is often direct and emotional rather than intellectual in content. It can include such things as the personality of the President (the youth of a Kennedy or the father-figure image of an Eisenhower), or the salute of the national flag in schools and its presence on public buildings. At the state level similar symbolic political associations often hold strong attachments for many people. In a society of immigrants the rites of acquiring citizenship involve heavy emphasis on patriotic symbols, and Americans worry more about the loyalty and patriotism of their fellow citizens than do the British.

A good example of the importance of patriotic symbols is the

[38] See G. A. Almond and S. Verba, *The Civic Culture*, Princeton, N.J.: Princeton University Press, 1963, Chapters 7 and 8, and pp. 440–68 for contrasts between the civic cultures of Britain and the U.S.A.

fact that American public holidays are not drawn from a church calendar but rather from the secular calendar of God's chosen people. Hence Americans celebrate the birthdays of Presidents Washington and Lincoln, remember their revolutionary colonial heritage at Thanksgiving and Independence Day, respect those killed in the Civil War on Memorial Day, and have their own version of May Day on Labour Day (begun in 1882), along with Christmas and New Year's Day.

The electoral process also has a symbolic as well as practical importance, and even political parties find it necessary to uphold and pay lip-service to certain political and patriotic symbols. The position of the United States in the world is of considerable symbolic importance to many citizens. In a society of diverse sub-cultures many private organisations (Veterans Associations, Daughters of the American Revolution, even the American Civil Liberties Union) perform largely symbolic functions, and also indirectly serve to divert primary group loyalties based on religion, ethnic background, or race, toward a recognition of the obligations of national citizenship.

Political Culture and the Political System – an Overview

For most Americans their collection of political beliefs are rarely as clearly defined or their sources as distinct as has been indicated here. They are affected by the day-to-day statements of political leaders, politicians, and friends whose opinions they respect (or hate), the newspaper opinions they read and the television programmes they absorb. Few Americans, however, seek to be involved actively in politics, yet they generally accept the view that governmental authority should be limited and governmental officials checked. They tend to support the dispersion of political power except in what they believe are 'crisis' situations, though they are not averse to the use of the political process to achieve practical and agreed goals if the scope of such power is clearly defined. Elections have their drama and increase interest in political activity, even if they normally lack the significance of elections in other countries, where class issues or the retention of the existing political institutions may be at stake.

How do the distinctive cultural characteristics outlined, and the paradoxes they present, affect the operation of the American political system? On the surface they do not provide a solid or coherent system of values. A belief in equalitarianism has masked the existence of enormous inequalities; a belief in individual liberty, yet a denial of this to some citizens in practice; a belief in a liberal tradition which has embraced doctrines ranging from extreme *laissez-faire* and rugged individualism to. radical collective action, and has allowed racism and reaction to flourish alongside socialism. The creation of a national government designed to reconcile divergent interests and prevent permanent unchecked majority rule has often given permanent minorities an effective veto on swift governmental action backed by majority will.

National characteristics have established goals and objectives to which the political process has been forced to respond. Over the long term, government has demanded the consent of the governed, though not all have had an equal share in this. Equal political rights, at least for white citizens, have been obtained and guaranteed in a more systematic way than social rights. There has been a continuous commitment to the notion of limited government, even if at times capitalism and property rights have transcended individual rights, and government has exercised a selective authority to aid the interests of certain groups while ignoring the demands and rights of others.

A series of idealised but often highly moral national goals have served as guides to social activity, though they have rarely ever been achieved. Some commentators have attached importance to the desire to achieve rather than the expectation of achievement, and see this as a fundamental quality of American democracy.[39] Yet many of these goals have been contradictory, even self-defeating, but they have succeeded in unifying a diverse and often divided society during periods of rapid change, in the absence of established or traditional loyalties. The commitment to democracy has been maintained despite a disinclination to extend governmental authority, and an equal disinclination on the part of many to participate directly in checking its activities.

In the United States, even more than in Britain, limited government took shape in a society characterised by geographic

[39] See W. Riker, *Democracy in the United States*, London: Collier–Macmillan, 1965.

isolation, local and personal self-sufficiency and independence, and the absence of a large professional military. The desire for stable government required the creation of a formal and defined political structure capable of reconciling divergent interests. In a complex modern society dominated by industry, science, and technology, with a large and expensive military and heavy international commitments, it is doubtful if the political culture of the United States is sufficiently flexible to cope with the full range of contemporary problems. For too long the desire to accommodate divergent interests allowed Southern 'exceptionalism' to maintain an unrepresentative political influence. American beliefs in an international mission has led them to ignore their own history of nationalism when dealing with smaller and 'newer' nations, while the resolution of complex urban problems may have to wait for changes in political and social attitudes. The legitimacy of political action depends in large measure on the degree of cultural support for such action, and despite sophisticated challenges to the assumption that a system of competing élites would produce effective decisions, cultural support for new forms of political decision-making has not as yet been achieved. An understanding of dominant cultural attitudes is therefore of prime importance to any assessment of the likely success of political responses to social and other changes in the contemporary United States.

Chapter Five

POLITICAL SOCIALISATION AND RECRUITMENT

Englishmen rarely need to learn how to become loyal Englishmen, but in the United States children and even their parents have often needed to be taught how to become loyal Americans. Englishmen may well be too secure as regards their identity, but Americans have always been insecure about their identity as individuals within their own nation. Because of this, political socialisation is of considerable importance in the United States, and has two major functions. The process of political socialisation induces support for, and loyalty to, the nation, and also inculcates particular values in an individual so as to combine general support for the political system with specific personal attitudes about political events and institutions which the individual may seek to influence by some kind of political participation. The stimulation of political attitudes as a basis for political participation is of special importance in a society whose governmental system depends on popular participation.

Political socialisation is a continuous and cumulative process of learning. Voting behaviour and political attitudes are the product of a wide variety of influences, some of them in existence before an individual is born, and are transmitted to the individual by parents, childhood friends, and early education. This socialisation process may continue throughout the life of an individual. Early socialisation influences help produce latent support for the system in individuals who have a minimal interest in political affairs, and provide individuals with information regarding their duties and rights in a society and the role they are expected to perform in the political system, and in the United States such socialisation is linked with citizenship education.[1]

[1] See F. Patterson, *The Adolescent Citizen*, Glencoe, Illinois: The Free Press, 1960.

The recognition of the need for such a process, and of the need for political analysts of democratic representative government to study the impact of human nature on political institutions, is not new.[2] However, only in recent decades has this aspect of political activity been studied in depth in the United States, often using the techniques of the sociologist or psychologist. An important assumption of democratic government is that members of the society will come to feel able to make an effective contribution to political activity, and feel that they are effective politically. An important part of this is the desire for political participation, at the lowest level as a voter and at the highest as a competitor for the major political offices of government.

The Process of Political Socialisation

We are concerned here with tracing the impact of different environmental influences on individual political attitudes and beliefs. Much of the analysis is based on a broad range of studies and is general and tentative in its conclusions. It is impossible to identify particular influences as being responsible for particular attitudes, because so much depends upon the individual – on personality traits, educational capacity and opportunities, and the intensity of interest in political affairs. It is also difficult to assess which influence is likely to be the most significant in determining party identification, or policy attitudes, or a desire to participate directly in political affairs.[3]

Research has established that children in the United States acquire a wide range of feelings and attitudes about various aspects of political life at a very early age. Much of this appears to take the form of an emotional frame of reference or a very

[2] See W. Bagehot, *op. cit.* For a pioneer study in Britain, see G. Wallas, *Human Nature in Politics*, London: Constable, 1908. See also J. C. Davies, *Human Nature in Politics: The Dynamics of Political Behavior*, New York: Wiley, 1963.

[3] For general analysis, see L. A. Froman, Jr., 'Personality and Political Socialisation', *Journal of Politics*, May 1961, pp. 341–52. See also L. A. Froman, Jr., 'Learning Political Attitudes', *Western Political Quarterly*, June 1962, pp. 304–13.

loose set of attitudes about the relationships between individuals and political authority, and this initial awareness increases as the child becomes older and develops an individual personality. Children learn to like government before they really understand what it is. As Easton and Hess indicate, by the time children have reached the age of seven 'they have learned that they are Americans, and that, in a way they find difficult to define and articulate, they are different from members of other systems'.[4] Such responses occur long before they have the capacity to rationalise political orientations.

Children with greater intellectual qualities, and from better economic backgrounds, seem more likely to acquire such attitudes early and maintain a positive feeling towards them. Parents of such children are more likely to participate directly in political activities, and so the child is likely to grow up used to a home environment where political problems are discussed and political activities take up time. There is little evidence of differences between boys and girls in terms of emotional responses to early political socialisation, though women tend to develop weaker political attitudes and patterns of political participation and interest as they grow older.[5]

It is important to assess what is learned early in life about the political system, since it is argued that such attitudes are more difficult to displace than attitudes acquired later in life.[6] However, adult socialisation is important in determining what form such participation may take, especially in the case of individuals seeking to become elected officials. It is also necessary to differentiate between the importance of political socialisation as a means of maintaining support for the political system, and its

[4] See D. Easton and R. D. Hess, 'The Child's Political World', in E. C. Dreyer and W. A. Rosenbaum (eds.), *Political Opinion and Electoral Behavior*, Belmont, California: Wadsworth, 1966, pp. 151–64. For a study using comparative material indicating that education, class, and family patterns affect the development of political attitudes in different countries, see R. D. Hess, 'The Socialisation of Attitudes towards Political Authority: Some Cross-National Comparisons,' in E. C. Dreyer and W. A. Rosenbaum (eds.), pp. 463–78.

[5] See F. I. Greenstein, 'Sex-Related Political Differences in Childhood', *Journal of Politics*, May 1961, pp. 353–71.

[6] See O. G. Brim, Jr., and S. Wheeler, *Socialisation After Childhood*, New York: Wiley, 1966.

significance in stimulating political participation. The former is especially important for the political system, in that it may provide a reservoir of diffuse support in normal times which can be of crucial importance in times of crisis. [7]

Childhood socialisation involves consideration of matters such as regard for law, or understanding of the nature of political authority and of the role of the individual citizen, and this is affected by family attitudes and environment, and by formal education. Children appear to have positive attitudes towards, and a high positive regard for, the President at a very early age. Much of this initial regard for the President is emotional as well as political, and only later do they come to discriminate clearly between the position of the President and the political and personal attributes of the current incumbent. Their initial image is affected by the personalisation which mass media, especially television, allows, but the President is the first and most important point of contact between the child and the political system in the United States, and the reaction is a positive and political one. This latent attitude is important, since it may allow political dissatisfactions in later life to be generated towards the individual occuping the Presidency and not towards the Presidency as a political office, or towards the political system as a whole. It is not, however, held uniformly, and evidence indicates that positive attitudes may not be developed by children in certain sub-cultures such as the relatively poor, rural Appalachian region where parental influences are often atypical.

As children get older, however, they are inclined to lose some of the emotional faith in the President and see him in a more realistic light. Yet for many citizens the President remains an idealised 'father-figure'. [8] In later years institutions, such as the Supreme Court, may take on some of the qualities characteristic of the President. The formative years of political socialisation in the United States seem to be between three and thirteen, and

---

[7] See D. Easton and J. Dennis, 'The Child's Acquisition of Regime Norms: Political Efficacy', *American Political Science Review*, March 1967, pp. 25–38.

[8] An interesting example of this is the type of personal letters received by Presidents from individuals. See L. A. Sussman, *Dear F. D. R.*, *A Study of Political Letter-Writing*, Totowa, N.J.: Bedminster Press, 1963.

by the age of seven many children are firmly attached to the political community.

Family Influences

The political opinions of American children are most directly influenced by parents, probably by the father. The first training in political socialisation they receive is from the family, and so political attitudes often tend to reflect those of the parents. The child learns to act as a member of a family group and to share and assume values and attitudes characteristic of the family. Studies show that attitudes toward the political community tend to be supportive and to reflect symbolic and emotional instincts, and are closely linked with the way a child views his relations with the family.

These instincts often exist before the child begins school. Study indicates that boys who see their own fathers as dominant in the family often have a less positive image of political or other authority. A child may learn to respect and admire political authority, but often sees it as parental authority writ large. A child may also idealise authority because of his own insecurity, though parents also often talk to children about the Presidency and political institutions in idealised terms, in an attempt to avoid disillusioning the child about politics in general. Girls may even be 'protected' from this by little or no reference to politics by parents in conversation with them, even though the parents may have strong political attitudes and participate in partisan political activities.[9] Similar protective attitudes were found to be prevalent in parental discussion with children over the assassination of President Kennedy in 1963.[10] Parents tended to idealise the sordid realities and to explain the assassination in terms likely to evoke support for the system. The older the child the more practical was the explanation, with more historical

[9] See R. D. Hess and D. Easton, 'The Child's Image of the President', *Public Opinion Quarterly*, Winter 1960, pp. 632–44.

[10] See K. Orren and P. Peterson, 'Presidential Assassination: A Case-Study in the Dynamics of Political Socialisation', *Journal of Politics*, May 1967, pp. 388–405. See also Roberta S. Sigel, 'An Exploration into Some Aspects of Political Socialisation: School Children's Reactions to the Death of a President', in M. Wolfstein and G. Kliman (eds.), *Children and the Death of a President*, Garden City, New York: Doubleday Inc., 1965.

and political information and less idealism, especially by parents whose own political knowledge was extensive. Younger children were also more inclined than older to see the assassination as the act of an individual and to approve of the murder of the assassin.

There is some difference of opinion about the reason for the positive image evoked by children about the President. Studies by Easton and Hess stress the security provided by the President as a symbol of political authority and the links between this and attitudes to parental authority,[11] while a study by Jaros suggests that such positive images may reflect latent authoritarian traits in children which are a consequence of anxiety traits because of conflict in home or general environment, and this leads them to see the President as a source of strength, demanding obedience rather than benevolence. Family influences may be of less direct significance than other factors in consolidating partisan loyalties in this situation.[12]

Most studies, however, support the view that children have a positive image of the President which can be affected by family environment. Some children, even in families where parental influence is poor, may still have an optimistic view of the realities of social and political life by the time they reach adolescence.

Strong ties of affection to one's country may, of course, be the basis for less stable attitudes in later life in particular political situations, and may lead to irrational forms of super-patriotism. It may also serve to provide an excessive idealisation of existing political institutions, thus making reforms of the political system difficult to achieve.[13] Yet early idealism need not prevent the development of a capacity to criticise, and even disobey, political authority as many American children grow older.

The impetus to hold certain political attitudes is often affected by family behaviour. A child brought up in the South whose

[11] See, in particular, R. D. Hess and D. Easton, 'The Child's Image of the President', *op. cit.*

[12] See D. Jaros, 'Children's Orientation Towards the President: Some Additional Theoretical Considerations and Data,' *Journal of Politics*, May 1967, pp. 368–87.

[13] See E. Litt, 'Civic Education, Community Norms, and Political Indoctrination, 'American Sociological Review, 28, 1963, pp. 69–76. On this and more general questions, see F. I. Greenstein, *Children and Politics*, New Haven: Yale University Press, 1965.

parents have strong segregationist views concerning Negroes may well grow up to share their attitudes. Adults in a family are themselves affected by the existing political system, and as generation and group needs change, so too may their values. Families with different origins are also likely to stress different values.

American children develop partisan tendencies at an early age, and these are heavily influenced by parental attitudes. They often identify themselves with a political party in the same way as they accept the religious beliefs of their family. The impetus towards political participation is likely to be affected by family attitudes towards partisan politics.[14] If parents agree on which party they support, the child is likely to adopt the same party. If neither parent expresses strong, consistent, support for a party, the child is likely to adopt an 'independent' position. Where father and mother support different parties the child is likely to be influenced by general preferences for one parent or the other.

While the influence of the class attitudes of parents affects the type of attitudes held by children, family influence in the United States appears strongest in determining party support rather than attitudes towards political issues.[15] Before reaching high school, the average American child is likely to identify with a political party, and if parents are interested in politics and tend to agree on issues and party support and to discuss such matters, the child is likely to reflect this party support and attitudes towards particular issues. (See Table 5:1.)

Rebellion against parental attitudes towards politics need not be linked with a general rebellion against the values and attitudes of parents. The intelligence of a child, education, and contact with peer-groups and others (people or friends outside the immediate family) all affect attitudes and dilute the direct influence of parents. The closer a child is to his parents the less likely he is to rebel. If parents have little interest in politics, then other influences may provide the major stimuli to political

[14] For an excellent analysis of the effects of parental influences on the party identification of children, see H. Hyman, *Political Socialisation*, New York: The Free Press, 1959, pp. 40–100.

[15] See A. Campbell, *et al.*, *The American Voter*, *op. cit.*, Chapters 7 and 17.

Table 5:1

INTERGENERATIONAL RESEMBLANCE IN PARTISAN ORIENTATION –
POLITICALLY ACTIVE AND INACTIVE HOMES, 1958

Party Identification of Offspring	One or Both Parents Pol. Active			Neither Parent Pol. Active		
	Both Dems.	Both Reps.	No consistent Partisanship	Both Dems.	Both Reps.	No Consistent Partisanship
Strong Democrat	50%	5%	21%	40%	6%	20%
Weak Democrat	29	9	26	36	11	15
Independent	12	13	26	19	16	26
Weak Republican	6	34	16	3	42	20
Strong Republican	2	37	10	1	24	12
Apolitical	1	2	1	1	1	7
	100%	100%	100%	100%	100%	100%
Number of cases	333	194	135	308	187	199

Source: A. Campbell, *et al.*, *The American Voter*, p. 147.

partisanship.[16] The consensual nature of American politics and society, however, normally permits intense political disagreements between fathers and sons without creating severe alienation within a family.

Education

American education, unlike British, seeks to emphasise equality. There are no distinctions between types of state schools and no fixed times when the type of future education of the child is determined. State schools provide education for the bulk of students at the elementary and secondary levels, and at the university level public institutions are becoming increasingly predominant in every part of the country outside the North-East. While there are real differences in the quality of education provided, these are largely a factor of geographical location or colour rather than distinctions between students on the grounds of intelligence or social status. State laws usually require child-

[16] See R. E. Lane, 'Father and Sons: Foundations of Political Belief', *American Sociological Review*, 24, 1959, pp. 502–11; and R. Middleton and S. Putney, 'Political Expression of Adolescent Rebellion', *American Journal of Sociology*, 68, 1963, pp. 527–35.

ren to attend school from the age of six or seven until the age of fourteen or sixteen, beginning in elementary schools, and then moving on to junior high school and then to high school. In 1965, over 54 million Americans were enrolled in elementary, secondary, and higher education. Two-thirds of all American youth graduate from high school, and at least one-third receive some form of higher education in some 2,000 institutions of higher learning, though they are not necessarily the best qualified for such education.

The education system in the United States encourages community and national loyalty, and the responsibilities of citizenship. The nature of such indoctrination, however, varies. Edgar Litt studied schools in three communities in the Boston metropolitan area, and found that students in each community were being trained to play different political roles and to respond to political phenomena in a different way. In a predominantly working-class community, where political involvement was low, civics education at school provided training in basic democratic procedures, but there was little emphasis on political participation. In a lower middle-class community, where political life was moderately active, training in the elements of democratic government was supplemented by an emphasis on the responsibilities of citizenship. Only in the more affluent community (where political activity was high) were insights into political processes and the functions of politics passed on to those who (given their socio-economic and political environment) might later take up positions of political influence.[17]

In American schools, courses in civics are compulsory, just as Gaelic may be compulsory in certain schools in Scotland or Ireland. The nature of such courses varies, but the general emphasis is on history with perhaps an elementary understanding of the Constitution and the political institutions. Much emphasis is given to the beginnings of America (the Declaration of Independence, the American Revolution, and the Founding Fathers) and the democratic values upon which the society is felt to be based. Emphasis is also placed on the virtues of early American Presidents such as Washington and Jefferson, or Lincoln.

[17] See E. Litt, 'Civic Education, Community Norms, and Political Indoctrination', *op. cit.*

The type of textbooks used in civics courses and the material in them has given rise to some concern, especially in the South. James Silver has demonstrated how, in Mississippi, school textbooks seem designed to fortify Southern white attitudes concerning the Negro.[18] Negro civil rights' leaders, such as Floyd McKissick (speaking in his capacity as director of the Congress of Racial Equality), have attacked the American system of public education and its emphasis on civics because they believe that it often perpetuates rather than combats racism.

Many black children remain ignorant of the culture and identity of their race in the United States because their civics textbooks and classes make little reference to the Negro in American history, while white children are provided with a view of the development of American society which may reinforce rather than weaken social and racial prejudices.

In general, however, the effects of education appear to be more positive with regard to political attitudes and responsibilities. Education often modifies traditional political attitudes based on family beliefs, and also serves to encourage a sense of political effectiveness and civic responsibility which may increase political involvement, as Table 5:2 indicates.

Table 5:2

RELATION OF AMOUNT OF FORMAL EDUCATION TO DIFFERENCES
IN POLITICAL INVOLVEMENT
(Figures based on data from 1952 and 1956 election samples)

| Involvement | Non-South | | South | |
	High Schools	College	High Schools	College
High	32%	48%	28%	47%
Medium	46%	43%	40%	42%
Low	22%	9%	32%	11%
	100%	100%	100%	100%
Number of cases	1,213	405	378	160

Source: A. Campbell, et al., The American Voter, p. 479.

Studies of students obtaining secondary education in high schools suggest that participation in social and other activities

[18] See J. W. Silver, Mississippi: The Closed Society, New York: Harcourt, Brace and World, 1964.

at school is not in itself indicative of a high level of interest in political issues and activity, but the sense of being integrated in the informal status system of the school can lead to a sense of social trust which is often linked with positive political attitudes. This feeling may even extend to students who do not belong to this status system but feel they could enter it if they wished. A school environment of students from different classes often leads to lower-class students becoming affected by the values and attitudes of those students from the middle or upper classes.[19] University or college education provides a further influence on attitudes and behaviour patterns, and thus effects political attitudes. University teachers may also act as agents of political socialisation. Universities in the United States, however, differ considerably in size, and in the quality and nature of their education, and different universities may have a very different impact on the political attitudes and the degree of political interest of students.[20] Students whose opinions and attitudes were formed in a 'conservative' environment entering a university whose faculty tends to hold 'liberal' views backed by concern about social affairs, may be exposed to influences which endure in later life.[21]

The impact of university education on student political behaviour is, however, complex. Students with passive political attitudes may be influenced by the positive political attitudes of fellow students. Such interpersonal relationships act as cross-pressures on initial sources of political socialisation. Robert Lane suggests that the motivations of some 'liberal' students in their attitudes towards certain issues indicates underlying social

[19] See D. Ziblatt, 'High School Extracurricular Activities and Political Socialisation', in R. Sigel (ed.), 'Political Socialisation: Its Role in the Political Process', *The Annals of the American Academy of Political and Social Science*, 361, September 1965, pp. 20–31. See also K. P. Langton, 'Group and School and the Political Socialisation Process', *American Political Science Review*, September 1967, pp. 751–58.

[20] See E. Litt, 'Education and Political Enlightenment in America', in R. Sigel (ed.), *op. cit.*, pp. 32–39.

[21] See 'Attitude Development as a Function of Reference Groups: The Bennington Story', in T. M. Newcomb, *et al.*, *Readings in Social Psychology*, New York: Holt, 1958, pp. 265–75; also A. S. Adelstein, 'Since Bennington: Evidence of Change in Student Political Behavior', *Public Opinion Quarterly*, Winter 1962, pp. 564–71.

anxieties and affects their attitude towards the role of government.[22]

For many American youths, a university environment can heighten political interest and sharpen political attitudes. Campuses as different as the University of Mississippi and the University of California at Berkeley experienced violence and riots in the 1960s which were often the direct result of 'political' events, and few university campuses have escaped 'direct' political action, whether it be anti-Communist demonstrations by 'conservative' groups such as the John Birch Society or the Young Americans for Freedom, civil rights' demonstrations by members of militant groups like the Student Non-Violent Coordinating Committee, or anti-Vietnam war demonstrations by the Students for a Democratic Society.

James Silver, in discussing the emotional response of students at the University of Mississippi during attempts to enrol a Negro, James Meredith, as a student, reflects pessimism about the influence which a university has in changing political attitudes based on family and home environment.[23] Yet, by contrast, other students at the University of North Carolina, having failed to eliminate racial discrimination by peaceful demonstrations, resorted to illegal acts and faced imprisonment for their actions.[24] Though the experience of a university environment often has a liberalising effect on individuals, student radicalism and alienation from American values appears to influence only a small but vociferous minority of students. Seymour Martin Lipset has argued that most university students in the United States are fairly passive and conformist, though he indicates that domestic tensions occasioned by war may show themselves most strongly in a university environment.[25]

[22] See R. E. Lane, *Political Thinking and Consciousness*, Chicago: Markham, 1969.

[23] See J. W. Silver, *Mississippi: The Closed Society, op. cit.*

[24] See J. Ehle, *The Free Men*, New York: Harper and Row, 1965.

[25] See S. M. Lipset, 'Student Opposition in the United States', *Government and Opposition*, April 1966, pp. 357–74; see also S. M. Lipset and S. S. Wolin (eds.), *The Berkeley Student Revolt. Facts and Interpretations*, Garden City, New York: Doubleday Inc., 1965, and S. Hyman, *Youth in Politics*, New York: Basic Books, 1972.

Group and Generational Influences

The social climate in which an American grows up can also affect his attitudes. Young Americans reaching adulthood during the difficult times of the early 1930s were affected as a group by the current social environment of the New Deal which also affected their political attitudes.[26] Changing political events can change political attitudes, though values and attitudes are often relatively fixed by the end of adolescence, especially political partisan identification. However, according to Angus Campbell, 'the Great Depression swung a heavy proportion of the young electors toward the Democratic Party and gave that party a hold on that generation, which it has never fully relinquished'. Moreover, among older voters, the association of the Republican party with economic depression remained strong a quarter of a century later.[27] Political attitudes and preferences are affected by the historical era in which a person reaches voting age.

The taking of a job, moving to a new environment, or getting married, all affect the community and governmental attitudes of young Americans. Improvement of social or economic position among young American adults has been shown to lead to a change of party but not attitude, while a worsening of position leads to changes in attitudes but not party.[28] A young adult with a better job and more affluent friends than his father often becomes an 'independent' in order to avoid the conflict between parental beliefs and the political attitudes of his new social group.

Marriage also affects the political attitudes of American women. They are often prepared to abandon the traditional attitudes of their parents (especially if their interest in politics is small) and support the same party as their husbands and rely on them for information and guidance about political activity. Young people are also influenced by individuals of their same generation with whom they work or live, and at this time politi-

[26] See M. L. Levin, 'Social Climates and Political Sociology', *Public Opinion Quarterly*, Winter 1961, pp. 596–606.

[27] A. Campbell, *et al.*, *The American Voter, op. cit.*, p. 155.

[28] See E. E. Maccoby, *et al.*, 'Youth and Political Change', *Public Opinion Quarterly*, Spring 1954, pp. 23–9.

cal attitudes and identification with a particular party become established, and after this period such attitudes and identification becomes less susceptible to permanent change.[29]

Early voting studies in the United States emphasised the stability of the party preferences of individuals, which is fortified by a social environment in which the individual is rarely exposed to conflicting political attitudes. The more complex the social environment the more complex politics may seem to the individual.[30]

The common experiences of youth can impart a similar outlook to a generation which may distinguish it from the generation of its parents, and such experiences often provide the impetus for political change and have a considerable effect on the nature of political competition and the policies of the major political parties.

Mass Media Influences

Political socialisation depends upon face-to-face communication between individuals or groups, and is affected by the nature of such communication. However, in a developed society like the United States, many citizens are also influenced by the communications provided by the mass media (newspapers, radio and television) about matters affecting the political system, especially around the time when elections are to be held.

The impact of the mass media on political attitudes in the United States is difficult to assess, especially the extent to which they shape political behaviour.[31] Robert Lane indicates that for those interested in governmental affairs, the mass media offer 'an abundant, but "thin" and repetitive supply of news, some

[29] See J. Crittenden, 'Aging and Party Affiliation', *Public Opinion Quarterly*, Winter 1962, pp. 648–57. See also R. E. Renneker, 'Some Psychodynamic Aspects of Voting Behavior', in E. Burdick and A. J. Brodbeck, *American Voting Behavior*, Glencoe, Ill.: The Free Press, 1959, pp. 399–413.

[30] See H. W. Riecken, 'Primary Groups and Political Party Choice', in Burdick and Brodbeck, *op. cit.*, pp. 162–83; also H. McCloskey and H. E. Dahlgren, 'Primary Group Influence on Party Loyalty', *American Political Science Review*, September 1959, pp. 757–76.

[31] See J. T. Klapper, *The Effects of Mass Communications*, Glencoe, Ill.: The Free Press, 1960; also W. Schramm (ed.), *The Process and Effects of Mass Communication*, Urbana, Ill.: University of Illinois Press, 1954.

opinion, but little serious analysis', and argues that for a majority of the American people they offer sufficient information to stimulate political argument and maintain different political attitudes, and for the many who are disinterested in politics they ensure a minimum awareness of events.[32]

The press in the United States plays a significant role in affecting attitudes towards the political process in general, though its influence on specific political events such as elections may be less than that of television. The 'national' press, and in particular the Washington press corps, provides an important source of information regarding political events and a link between the governed and the governors.[33] About 1,750 daily, English-language, newspapers exist in the United States and reach about 80% of adult Americans. Many newspapers enjoy extensive local monopolies, and much of the press tends to be inclined towards supporting Republicans. In 1964, however, for the first time for many years the majority of newspapers in the United States supported the Democratic Presidential candidate.[34] Certain specific sectors of the press (a few magazines and daily newspapers) play a special role in providing large quantities of political comment and information, and command the attention of those with a high degree of interest in politics. They act as a special communication link between major political leaders and political activists as well as between political leaders. The use of the press by the President, through the holding of press conferences, as a means of communication to political activists, is also important.[35]

While radio has probably become less influential as a medium affecting political attitudes, it continues to remain important. Candidates at elections still spend a considerable amount of their campaign finances on radio electioneering, and, in the days before television, Presidents like Franklin Roosevelt exploited the radio as means of communication with the electorate. By the 1960s, however, television established itself as the public's

[32] See R. E. Lane, *Political Life, op. cit.*, Chapter 19, p. 277.

[33] See D. Cater, *The Fourth Branch of Government*, New York: Vintage, 1965.

[34] For a comprehensive analysis of the role of the press as an agent of political socialisation, see V. O. Key, Jr., *Public Opinion and American Democracy*, New York: A. A. Knopf, 1961, Chapter 15.

[35] See R. Fagen, *Politics and Communication*, Boston: Little, Brown, 1966, pp. 52–63.

primary source of news, and also the most believable source of news. This was especially so among younger people. At the national level, television has become the primary source of information about political candidates.[36] Despite this, however, politics analysts are less certain as to how much television has effected a basic change in the nature of political communication, and whether it has raised the level of political interest in the American electorate by broadening public information about political issues and events. There is evidence to suggest that in the 1930s radio did serve to increase political participation, but there is less evidence that television has greatly affected the willingness of Americans to go to the polls. Television may well have greatly extended the purely visual dimension of political communication, and there is also evidence that the television debates between the Presidential candidates in 1960 did affect public opinion and probably lessened the opposition to Kennedy on religious grounds among Protestant Democrats, but there is less evidence of any greater depth of understanding of political issues than existed before television. People who follow the election campaigns most closely on television appear to be also those who read most about them in the press or listen to radio broadcasts.[37]

Though the influence of television on the process of political socialisation does not appear to be a unique one, television has in certain instances clearly affected the political attitudes of many Americans. The assassination of President Kennedy provides an example where the mass media, especially television, influenced political responses from all levels of the community. Study has indicated that the opportunity to obtain information about the assassination and its immediate effects helped to allay initial reactions of fear about the effects of the crisis on the political system. Many people praised the way in which television provided a 'great public service' in reporting directly on the immediate events which followed the assassination. As well as mobilising latent resources of support for the political system, television appeared to allow people to acquire

[36] See E. Roper, 'The Public's View of Television and Other Media', in E. C. Dreyer and W. A. Rosenbaum (eds.), *op. cit.*, pp. 309–17.

[37] For more detailed analysis, see A. Campbell, 'Has Television Reshaped Politics?', in Dreyer and Rosenbaum, *op. cit.*, pp. 318–23.

a balanced and rational view of the implications of the assassination for the future of the country, providing reassurance by showing the existence and continuity of political institutions and values.[38]

While mass media affect the political attitudes of Americans, and are a source of potential political socialisation, it is easy to exaggerate their effects. Critics on the Left argue that many Americans are lulled by the mass media into accepting the values of the prevailing ideology, especially those of personal success and private property, and this serves to protect the position and influence of certain élite groups. Critics on the Right, however, see the media as major instruments through which 'liberal' intellectuals seek to obtain a dominance over American political attitudes and institutions. While it may be true that there is little opportunity provided through the mass media for the expression of views clearly hostile to the prevailing ideology of the political system, it seems clear that the media serve to strengthen and reinforce attitudes and values already latent or well-defined in individuals. Those people most susceptible to the positive influence of the mass media are also those who pay least attention to the media. The mass media in America, as in Britain, appear to reinforce existing institutions, and political attitudes, but their political influence is complex.

Political Socialisation and the American Negro

Attitudes towards the political system are also affected by many secondary types of association. Ethnic, religious, and racial differences in America make such sub-community associations significant. The identification by political analysts of the Catholic, Jewish, or Negro vote in particular national elections indicates that such secondary associations affect general attitudes towards the political process in America.[39] The integration of many immigrant groups into American society in the large cities has also been the result of a close connection between social and political organisation. William Whyte, in his classic study

[38] See B. S. Greenberg and E. B. Parker (eds.), *The Kennedy Assassination and the American Public, op. cit.*, Part 2.

[39] See L. S. Dawidowicz and L. J. Goldstein, *Politics in a Pluralist Democracy*, New York: Institute of Human Relations Press, 1963.

of rival groups of young people in an Italian slum community in an Eastern city, demonstrates the close links which developed between these organisations and local political activity, and the minimal influence exerted on their political and other attitudes by American society in general.[40] While sub-community attitudes have become less of an influence and a barrier to political socialisation among distinctive ethnic or racial groups in general, a single important exception is the American Negro.

It is difficult to discuss the political socialisation of the American Negro in the same terms as those used for the general impact of political socialisation on white American citizens, because for so long and in so many different ways American Negroes have occupied an inferior status in American society. Protest, alienation, apathy, and violence are more relevant criteria by which to analyse individuals who have been excluded from the dominant political culture of their community and country, and have been denied many of its rewards but have not been excused their responsibilities. A special Negro sub-culture exists, but it varies greatly in the South from that in the North, and in the rural and urban areas, and is also undergoing important changes which have already affected the present generation of young Negroes. The history of Negro exclusion, nationally and locally, from active participation in the normal processes of governmental activity has also had a strong effect on the political socialisation of the Negro, quite apart from the effects of social discrimination.

The particular nature of the Negro family in the United States indicates that the early influences of Negro family life as slaves still exercise a strong influence on individual attitudes. The pattern of family life for many Negroes remains either one dominated by the mother, or by disorganization.[41] Education opportunities have often been poor, in segregated schools or in schools providing a minimum of civics education and using textbooks where the inferior status of the Negro is implicitly, if not specifically, stated. White attitudes have also served to strengthen this view of Negro inferiority.

[40] See W. F. Whyte, *Street Corner Society*, Chicago: University of Chicago Press, 1943.
[41] See E. F. Frazier, *The Negro Family in the United States*, rev. ed., Chicago: University of Chicago Press, 1966.

The prejudices and animosities experienced because of their racial distinctiveness are probably more influential on the political attitudes and views of Negroes than the effects of family or education, or other influences. Socio-economic disabilities, along with the lack of a stable family, educational, or job background, mean that for many Negroes political socialisation is often slight, and this is reflected in attitudes towards political authority. A report based on material obtained from the 1960 National Opinion Research Centre survey of national opinion in the United States revealed that only 49% of the Negro sample believed that government officials were likely to give them 'equal treatment' in matters like housing regulations or taxes (in contrast to 90% of a white counterpart group), and when asked about 'equal treatment' from police only 60% of the Negroes gave a positive response (in contrast to 85% of the white group). Moreover, only 44% of Northern Negroes in the sample, and only 18% of the Southern Negroes, expected agency officials to take their viewpoint seriously; only 47% of the Northern Negroes expected equal handling by the police, and only 29% of the Northern Negroes expected the police to listen to their story.[42]

Matthews and Prothro, in their study of the Negro in the traditional, 'underdeveloped', ascriptive society of the rural South, paint a grim picture of the influence of mass communications on the Negro. Exposure to the mass media provides an image of a different life which in turn may lead to the recognition that there are alternatives to the traditional mode of life, that individual circumstances can be improved, and that politics and political participation is a 'good thing' and may be one way of improving one's lot in life. The cost of political participation for Southern Negroes, however, is still unusually high, and the opportunity to participate is new for most Southern Negroes, since it has been virtually non-existent for them for so long. For most Negroes in the South, exposure to any of the recognised processes of political socialisation appears to be minimal. As Matthews and Prothro observed: 'Given their individual social and economic attributes, the "normal" condition for most Southern Negroes is political inactivity. In the southern

[42] See D. Marvick, 'The Political Socialisation of the American Negro', in R. Sigel (ed.), *op. cit.*, pp. 112–27, p. 118.

political environment, the factors that depress political activity among other populations depress Negro activity even more.'[43]

For the Negro in the metropolitan cities outside the South the situation is somewhat different. Organisations such as the Urban League and the National Association for the Advancement of Coloured People were conceived as channels through which the Negro élite might mobilise the Negro masses to an awareness of their political rights, but there was little recognition of the need to use the political process to guarantee these rights. Until the 1930s Negro adults in both the North and South were politically socialised only in a local sense. Few actions of the national government affected the ordinary Negro American emotionally, or stimulated him to desire to participate in political activity. For the Negro poor, politics was the business of the white man.

Gunner Myrdal,[44] in his massive study of Negro life, indicates that Negroes have passively accepted white domination of the political process in the United States, and made only limited political demands. Many Negroes were poor, passive, apathetic, and unable to protest effectively. It was not that they were disenchanted with American democracy but rather that the leaders in their communities were prepared to negotiate for local improvements outside the political process and did not seek to compete politically, or mobilise support among fellow Negroes to maintain political competiton and to seek their democratic rights. The potential political power of the Negro was often bargained away outside the political process by Negro leaders prepared to defer to white political authority.

In the Northern metropolitan centres, the creation of Negro ghettos produced Negro professional politicians prepared to accept the nature of political life laid down by rival white ethnic groups. The rise of Negro political machines, linking voting power with political demands, did lead to a situation where Negroes need not acquire the trappings of political socialisation and concern themselves with political attitudes, but simply learn

[43] D. R. Matthews and J. W. Prothro, *Negroes and the New Southern Politics*, New York: Harcourt, Brace and World, 1966, p. 95. For detailed comment of Southern Negro attitudes towards politics and political participation, see especially Chapter 4 and Chapters 9–11.

[44] See G. Myrdal, *An American Dilemma*, New York: Harper Bros., 1944.

how to vote. In Chicago, Representative William Dawson sought benefits for his voters and in return delivered the Negro vote to the city Democratic organisation. In New York City, Adam Clayton Powell served as a symbol for other Negroes of all that American society had denied them in the past; and also demonstrated to many Negroes that the white political game could be played successfully by a Negro.[45]

It is not implausible to suggest that much of the growth of political militancy of the American Negro is the result of an increased political awareness on the part of many Negroes in the cities and a consequent change in the leadership styles of many Negro political leaders. The more a Negro learns about the existing political system and the values and beliefs which support it, the more he recognises how badly he has been treated, and the less he is prepared to support the existing system unless his own position changes. In order to achieve this he is more and more likely no longer to compare himself with other Negroes, but with his opposite number in white society. He is likely to become more aggressive politically and to demand changes and seek their achievement by methods involving direct action. For many Negroes, learning about political life is learning about political reality, just as many white Americans are taught about a political environment that is 'unreal'. If Negroes in the past had fully understood the aims of the American 'dream' and wanted it for themselves, they would have been militantly alienated and disenchanted long ago. Instead, only in recent years has a new generation of Negro youths, in many respects better educated than their parents, been able to afford the luxury of asserting through political action their rights as Americans. Other Negroes, such as the Black Muslims, reject these rights and assert the need to maintain a separate black culture and identity.

The recognition of political reality by many Negroes whose families have for generations been socialised into accepting their inferior status from the day they were born, produced severe social conflict in the United States in the 1960s, both in the South and in the Northern cities. This resulted in massive political demonstrations and violence in the South, but it also

[45] For a systematic account contrasting Dawson and Powell, see J. Q. Wilson, *Negro Politics*, Glencoe, Ill.: The Free Press, 1960.

led to the Voting Rights Act of 1965 and increased political participation of Negroes in the South, and the election of more black officials at all political levels, especially where they are in the majority. In the Northern cities it also led to summers of riots and insurrections and demands for 'black power'. The new political socialisation of many blacks has provided a direct challenge to white American society to adjust cultural norms and come to terms with such changes without further violence or resistance.

Political Socialisation and Political Leadership

Political leaders, and those who take an active part in party political activities, are often subject to a wide range of socialising influences. Political leaders at the national level are not a representative sample of the population, and leadership positions are generally occupied by individuals from upper-income groups, well educated and with high social status.[46] Given an electorate with limited interest and information about political leaders in a society where 'getting ahead' is valued highly, social status is often linked closely with political worth.

Personality factors in turn often influence individuals to compete for political leadership positions, and political activists usually have a long record of political interest and a relatively high level of political understanding. Lawyers rather than artists, for instance, seek to move into positions of political leadership, and in the United States even more than in Britain a law career is often seen as a stepping-stone to an intended political career.[47] Civic responsibilities, such as representing a group of citizens over some matter of local politics, can often lead to an individual being drawn directly into the competition

[46] See D. R. Matthews, *U.S. Senators and Their World*, Chapel Hill: University of North Carolina Press, 1960, pp. 11–46. For information on the social background of state legislators, see J. C. Wahlke, *et al.*, *The Legislative System*, New York: Wiley, 1962; and on administrators, see W. L. Warner, *et al.*, *The American Federal Executive*, New Haven: Yale University Press, 1963, Part 2.

[47] See H. Eulau and J. Sprague, *Lawyers in Politics: A Study in Professional Convergence*, Indianapolis: Bobbs-Merrill, 1964, especially pp. 31–53. See also J. Barber, *The Lawmakers*, New Haven: Yale University Press, 1965, Chapter 3.

for political office. Such 'overexposure' to public affairs is an important influence on political activism,[48] and may be more important than early political experiences in affecting political roles as elected officials at the local, state, or national level.[49]

Political leaders, especially elected national officials, are also affected by the institutions in which they serve. The United States Senate, through the prestige conferred upon its members and the symbolic importance of its procedures, can effect its own particular brand of political socialisation upon new members, while the Supreme Court also often has an influence upon a new Justice which is often reflected in the contrast between his views and philosophies as expressed in his judicial decisions as a Justice of the Supreme Court, and his previous political or other attitudes in another position of political or judicial prominence.

Class, Social Status and Political Partisanship

Social class is not as closely related to political attitudes and behaviour in the United States as it is in Great Britain, nor are the political parties in the United States clearly distinguished by their class support. American social structure has many dimensions, of which class is only one. The enormous size of the country, high social mobility and the absence of a permanent landed class, high ethnic and religious diversity, all serve to reduce the significance of national class divisions.

However, many Americans vote in terms of their own perceived interests and see one party as broadly supporting these interests. The major parties are perceived within a class-related frame of reference, and derive varying degrees of support from particular classes. The decentralised party system may reflect the pluralist character of American society, yet this does not prevent some individuals from voting on occasions in terms of their own class interests and seeing a particular political party

[48] See K. Prewitt, 'Political Socialisation and Leadership Selection', in R. Sigel (ed.), *op. cit.*, pp. 91–111.

[49] See K. Prewitt, H. Eulau, and B. H. Zisk, 'Political Socialisation and Political Roles', *Public Opinion Quarterly*, Winter 1966–7, pp. 569–82. See also A. Kornberg and N. Thomas, 'The Political Socialisation of National Legislative Elites in the U.S.A. and Canada', *Journal of Politics*, November 1965, pp. 761–75.

as broadly supporting such interests. This is indicated by Table 5:3.

Table 5:3

CLASS VOTING 1952–62

Index of class voting

	Mean	Lowest	Highest	Nos. of Surveys
Great Britain	40	35	44	8
Australia	33	27	37	10
United States	16	13	23	5
Canada	8	−1	17	10

Index computed by subtracting the percentage of non-manual workers voting for 'Left' parties from the percentage of manual workers voting for 'Left' parties.

Source: R. Alford, *Party and Society*, p. 102.

Class voting has had a recurrent effect on American politics, and may be more evident in certain situations. Class voting tends to rise when economic issues are important and to drop when matters such as foreign policy become more important.[50] It declined to some extent in the 1952 and 1956 Presidential elections when the Republican candidate Eisenhower was successful, but this appears to have been a temporary shift.[51] In 1956, however, a majority of the American working class supported a Republican Presidential candidate. There is little evidence, however, to indicate that there has been a decline in class voting in the United States since the 1930s, only minor fluctuations around a fairly stable class base.[52] Some observers believe that class voting is likely to increase as one-party dominance declines in particular regions, especially to the extent that many of the Southern states (where the Democratic party has been dominant for many years) become more competitive.[53] The

[50] A. Campbell, *et al.*, *The American Voter*, *op. cit.*, pp. 356–61.

[51] See H. Eulau, *Class and Party in the Eisenhower Years*, New York: Free Press of Glencoe, 1962.

[52] See R. Alford, *Party and Society*, Chicago: Rand McNally Co., 1963, Chapter 8.

[53] See D. S. Strong, *Urban Republicanism in the South*, Birmingham, Ala.: University of Alabama, Bureau of Public Administration, 1960.

impact of religious and ethnic identity on class and status voting varies depending on the issues and candidates. In 1960, for instance, Kennedy lessened the appeal of class among Catholics but strengthened the effect of party identification among many Protestant Democrats.[54]

The United States is not a classless society, and many of the political attitudes of American voters reflect class or economic considerations, though class identity is relatively weak. People with lower incomes tend to vote Democratic and by and large support Democratic candidates, despite the fact that in the 1960 Presidential election only 60% of the unskilled workers who voted did so for the Democratic candidate, as did only 64% of trade union members. Low income predisposes a person to vote Democratic, high income to vote Republican, and the tendency to vote Republican increases with rising income. Political participation also tends to increase as individuals improve their social class.

Robert Lane suggests that the lower degree of political participation and interest among groups with low economic and social status is a consequence of less economic security and feeling of control over their political environment, and (especially for the women) less leisure time for political activity. Lower-status individuals can affect and benefit socially from government action by group activity and membership, yet they often avoid such contact and prefer to defer to others with higher income or status or withdraw interest. Individuals with higher incomes and status can influence and benefit from government action, and so have a higher incentive to participate, while high status and education sometimes leads to attitudes of social and civic responsibility.[55]

The increasing general affluence of American society does not appear to have produced a massive change of class identification on the part of voters, but a decline in class awareness may well have taken place.[56] Relationships between social status or

[54] See P. E. Converse, 'Religion and Politics: The 1960 Election', in A. Campbell, et al., Elections and the Political Order, New York: Wiley, 1966, pp. 96–124.
[55] See R. E. Lane, Political Life, op. cit., Chapter 16.
[56] For a contrasting view, see R. F. Hamilton, Class and Politics in the United States, New York: Wiley, 1972.

class membership and political participation tend to become closer at election times in periods of economic crisis (as in the 1930s). Available election study evidence indicates, however, that the majority of the skilled and unskilled workers in the United States have been Democrats since at least 1928, but of these some occasionally vote outside the party, as in the Presidential elections in 1952 and 1956. Defectors, however, have tended to maintain their Democratic party support at other levels. Business and professional groups, white-collar groups, and often farmers, historically have identified themselves with the Republican party, though there have been defectors to the Democratic party who have not returned. In 1940 the parties were about even in terms of the percentage of strong identifiers, but by 1960 strong Democratic identifiers outnumbered strong Republicans by more than three to two. Accounting for the greater political apathy of Democrats, there appears to be a 'normal' Democratic majority of about 54%, though the effects of current issues and candidates give any national election in the United States a high element of uncertainty.[57] Tables 5:4 and 5:5 give a general indication of party affiliations, and the percentage of votes cast by groups in Presidential elections from 1952 to 1968.

Table 5:4

PARTY AFFILIATIONS OF THE PEOPLE

	Rep.	Dem.	Ind.
	%	%	%
1973	27	42	31
1967	27	46	27
1966	27	48	25
1965	25	49	26
1964	25	53	22
1960	30	47	23
1950	33	45	22
1940	38	42	20

Responses to the question, 'In politics as of today, do you consider yourself a Republican, Democrat, or Independent?'

Source: National surveys by the Gallup Poll in the years indicated.

[57] See P. E. Converse, 'The Concept of the Normal Vote', in A. Campbell, et al., *Elections and the Political Order*, *op. cit.*, pp. 9–39.

The gross figures of party identification do demand from the Republican party careful thought regarding their choice of Presidential candidate, since they are in a 'minority' position.[58] Between 1960 and 1964 all major social groupings became more Democratic than Republican for the first time, yet the Repub-

Table 5:5

PERCENTAGE OF VOTE BY GROUPS IN PRESIDENTIAL ELECTIONS –
1952–68

(Estimated from National Survey by the Gallup Poll)

	1952 D	1952 R	1956 D	1956 R	1960 D	1960 R	1964 D	1964 R	1968 D	1968 R	1968 AIP
	%	%	%	%	%	%	%	%	%	%	%
NATIONAL	44·6	55·4	42·2	57·8	50·1	49·9	61·3	38·7	43·0	43·4	13·6
Men	47	53	45	55	52	48	60	40	41	43	16
Women	42	58	39	61	49	51	62	38	45	43	12
White	43	57	41	59	49	51	59	41	38	47	15
Non-white	79	21	61	39	68	32	94	6	85	12	3
College	34	66	31	69	39	61	52	48	37	54	9
High School	45	55	42	58	52	48	62	38	42	43	15
Grade School	52	48	50	50	55	45	66	34	52	33	15
Prof. and Bus.	36	64	32	68	42	58	54	46	34	56	10
White Collar	40	60	37	63	48	52	57	43	41	47	12
Manual	55	45	50	50	60	40	71	29	50	35	15
Farmers	33	67	46	54	48	52	53	47	29	51	20
21–29 years	51	49	43	57	54	46	64	36	47	38	15
30–49 years	47	53	45	55	54	46	63	37	44	41	15
50 years and older	39	61	39	61	46	54	59	41	41	47	12
Protestant	37	63	37	63	38	62	55	45	35	49	16
Catholic	56	44	51	49	78	22	76	24	59	33	8
Republicans	8	92	4	96	5	95	20	80	9	86	5
Democrats	77	23	85	15	84	16	87	13	74	12	14
Independents	35	65	30	70	43	57	56	44	31	44	25
East	45	55	40	60	53	47	68	32			
Mid-west	42	58	41	59	48	52	61	39			
South	51	49	49	51	51	49	52	48			
West	42	58	43	57	49	51	60	40			

Source: The Gallup Poll.

[58] See G. O. Jones, *The Republican Party in American Politics*, New York: Collier-Macmillan, 1965, especially Chapter 4.

licans chose a Presidential candidate who represented a minority within a 'minority' party, with disastrous electoral results.[59]

There are also indications that the class differences in the United States are of lower intensity than Britain and so political competition and partisanship has tended to decline as American society has become more affluent. Robert Lane intimates that the intensity of concern for the outcome of national elections was less in the 1960s than in the 1930s. While party identification remained a basic source for individual political participation, people were changing the meaning attached to their party membership, and coming to feel that the opposition was not so dangerous as they once thought. Such a movement towards a politics of consensus can lessen the significance of class as an indicator of political partisanship.[60]

The effects of class and social status on political attitudes and participation is also weakened by the fact that people with similar class and social status are not united in their attitudes towards political events or problems. Overlapping loyalties tend to inhibit the polarisation of political attitudes along economic and social lines. The result is that the major political parties in the United States seek to create an electoral coalition consisting of people with similar views on some issues but divergent views on others. The voter in America is also more likely to respond to appeals to party loyalty than appeals on the basis of social class or status.

Class or social status can, however, affect direct political participation in party organisation. Upwardly mobile people attempting to improve their class status may become active in politics.[61] Higher income people are also more likely to be prepared to take up active positions within a party organisation. Labour unions have also been successful in mobilising some of their members for political action, and many union members believe that participation by the union in politics is legitimate,

[59] See P. E. Converse, et al., 'Electoral Myth and Reality: The 1964 Election', American Political Science Review, June 1965, pp. 321–36.

[60] See R. E. Lane, 'The Politics of Consensus in an Age of Affluence', American Political Science Review, December, 1965, pp. 874–95.

[61] See D. Marvick and C. Nixon, 'Recruitment Contrasts in Rival Campaign Groups', in D. Marvick (ed.), Political Decision-Makers, Glencoe, Ill.: The Free Press, 1961, pp. 193–217.

yet the effect of such activity on national political elections is not as dramatic in the United States as in Britain.[62]

Conclusion

Most Americans are aware, or come to believe by the time they reach voting age, that if democracy is to flourish, citizens should be interested in, and informed about, politics. A major value in the American political culture stresses the importance of popular participation in government and governmental responsibility to an informed citizenry. Almond and Verba see the American political culture, in contrast to Britain, as predominantly a participant culture, where the role of the participant is highly developed and individuals are frequently exposed to politics, engage in political discussion and involvement in political affairs, have a sense of obligation to take an active part in community affairs, and possess a strong sense of competence to influence the government.[63]

Yet this optimistic view is not always reflected in studies seeking to analyse the level and intensity of political participation in the United States. Greenstein, in discussing the citizen base of the American political system, shows that in the three Presidential elections between 1952 and 1960, almost 40% of American adults were non-voters, and in off-year congressional elections in this period less than half the adult population went to the polls. He also indicates that active political participation – financial contributions or personal efforts to get a candidate elected – involved fewer than one individual out of nine, and his analysis of public opinion polls suggests that the level of political information of American citizens was not high, and many revealed a surprising lack of knowledge about elementary political facts, including the names of prominent political leaders.[64] Rasmussen, citing evidence based on survey research

[62] See F. Calkins, *The C.I.O. and the Democratic Party*, Chicago: Chicago University Press, 1955; see also J. D. Greenstone, 'Party Pressure on Organised Labor in Three Cities', in M. K. Jennings and H. Zeigler (eds.), *The Electoral Process*, Englewood Cliffs, N.J.: Prentice-Hall Inc., 1966, pp. 55–80, and V. Vale, *Labour in American Politics*, London, 1972.

[63] See G. A. Almond and S. Verba, *op. cit.*, pp. 440–1.

[64] See F. I. Greenstein, *The American Party System and the American People*, Englewood Cliffs, N.J.: Prentice-Hall, Inc., 1963, Chapter 2.

study of the 1960 and 1964 Presidential elections, estimates that only 3–5% of the adult population are active in party affairs or electoral campaigns.[65] Eldersveld also indicates that, on the basis of an intensive study in 1951–52 of political affiliation in metropolitan Detroit, 'only 7% of all voters in the area are consistent Democrats who work in campaigns for the Democrats', and 'less than 3% of all voters in the area are consistent Republicans who work in campaigns for the Republicans'.[66]

American adults are also somewhat suspicious of politics. In 1944 only 18% of a national sample of the National Opinion Research Centre said they would like to see their son enter politics as a career, and politics as a career ranked well below that of semi-skilled labourers in their esteem. Of a sample of the electorate in Wayne County, Michigan, in 1956–57, only 13% of adult respondents said they would encourage sons who were 'thinking of going into politics', 28% said they would discourage them, and 55% said they would make no suggestion. From the reasons given, many people seemed to feel party politics to be a parasitic occupation. In the face of such negative or neutral public reaction to a career in politics, it seems clear that only a minority of Americans can be socialised positively for politics during the years of development into adulthood, and they are more likely to be protected from party careers than urged to pursue them.[67]

The level of voting participation by American citizens in elections is also only moderate. Turnout at Presidential elections was consistently high in the latter part of the nineteenth century (in 1876, 85·8% of adult enfranchised males voted), but in the early 1900s it declined, dwindling to 44·2% in 1920. Even in the 1930s and 1940s it never reached 60%, and has only rarely exceeded that percentage in recent decades. Even fewer people vote in congressional elections, especially those when no President is to be chosen.[68] Yet this portrait of an electorate

[65] See J. S. Rasmussen, 'Party Responsibility in Britain and the United States', *Journal of American Studies*, October 1967, pp. 233–56.

[66] S. J. Eldersveld, *Political Affiliation in Metropolitan Detroit*, Ann Arbor: Bureau of Government, University of Michigan, 1957, p. 157.

[67] See S. J. Eldersveld, *Political Parties. A Behavioral Analysis*, Chicago: Rand McNally Co., 1964, p. 168.

[68] See W. D. Burnham, 'The Changing Shape of the American Political Universe', *American Political Science Review*, March 1965, pp. 7–28.

apparently ill-equipped to control its political leaders and demonstrating a low level of political participation is incomplete, though it is reflected in other stable, democratic, political systems such as Britain's. Some commentators, notably the late V. O. Key, have argued that the American electorate is more responsible than the raw voting figures suggest.[69] Others suggest that low voter participation is a consequence of a high level of consensus in American society, or blame the major political parties for failing to provide genuine alternatives, and so a significant number of people do not vote.[70] Whatever the reasons, the fact remains that many citizens in the United States fail to live up to the classic democratic prescription of the informed participant elector.

[69] See V. O. Key, Jr., *The Responsible Electorate: Rationality in Presidential Voting 1936–60*, Cambridge, Mass.: Harvard University Press, 1966.

[70] See E. E. Schattschneider, *The Semi-Sovereign People*, New York: Holt, Rinehart and Winston, 1960.

Chapter Six

THE ROLE OF INTEREST GROUPS

From colonial times, interest groups in the United States have sought to prompt and also prevent the exercise of governmental authority. Full recognition of the diversity of opinion in American society, and that the peaceful adjustment of such differences was a major task of government, is reflected in the discussions by Madison in *The Federalist Papers*. Madison saw conflict between groups as axiomatic in society, and warned of the possible effects of the influence of factions and factional conflict. It was therefore necessary to create a governmental structure of strength and flexibility which would allow for a multiplicity of interests but would minimise the danger that any one of them might assume such control of the governmental process as to threaten the rights of the larger community. Madison was correct about the number and variety of interests, and about the link between political organisation and the influence of such groups, but was not correct in assuming they would form only temporary coalitions. National political parties and nation-wide interest groups have grown up as relatively stable alliances of political interests, but they have been affected by the diffused structure of power within the political system.

The Scope of Interest Group Activity

David Truman has defined interest groups as those groups possessing shared attitudes and making claims on society.[1] He considers those groups that make claims upon or work through government as 'political' interest groups, and it is these groups which seek to mobilise public support in order to influence governmental decisions.

[1] See D. B. Truman, *The Governmental Process*, New York: A. A. Knopf, pp. 33–43.

In a nation of many million people, the individual cannot expect to exercise much influence on governmental policy acting alone. To achieve his objectives an individual may choose to work through a political party, and if such a party stands for a definite set of principles this approach may be rewarding. In the United States, however, the major political parties seem to be loose coalitions of interests whose primary concern is with winning elections and exercising governmental power. If the individual wishes to influence the political process he is more likely to find it expedient to join forces with others of like mind in interest group activity.

Interest groups in the United States have more ideological cohesion than political parties, but the existence of a large number of groups with overlapping memberships means that the intensity of individual support for group demands may not be uniform. It may be easier to distinguish interest groups from political parties in the United States than in Britain, but the nature of their influence on political decisions is more complex. In part this is because of the greater number of access points within the political process available to interest groups in the United States than in Britain. The lack of formal party discipline in Congress, and within the parties as a whole, provides the opportunity to exercise influence over individual political decision-makers, and also makes them more vulnerable to such influences.

Moreover, in contrast to Britain, major interest groups do not seek to maintain formal links with one or other of the major parties. The American Federation of Labour–Congress of Industrial Organisations, the American counterpart of the Trades Union Congress in Britain, does not formally ally itself with a national political party, yet this does not prevent it from exercising considerable influence over governmental decision-making. At the state level, however, where party organisation is more cohesive, in states like Michigan[2] or New York, certain individual unions may heavily influence or control the Democratic state party organisation. Some interest groups are also prepared to give help at elections to candidates supporting their views, but groups may support a party on one issue and

[2] See J. Fenton, *Midwest Politics*, New York: Holt, Rinehart and Winston, 1966, Part 2; also S. Eldersveld, *Political Parties. A Behavioral Analysis, op. cit.*

oppose it on another. At the same time that the American Medical Association fought to prevent a Democratic Administration obtaining the adoption of medical insurance legislation for the aged in the period 1961–63, it sought also to work with the Democrats to obtain federal aid for medical education. The U.S. Chamber of Commerce and the American Farm Bureau Federation, frequent opponents of the Democrats, both supported the Kennedy Administration in 1962 and its efforts to obtain a Trade Expansion Act.

A real concern for the opinion of individuals or groups in the local constituencies is characteristic of the American political system, and this concern leads legislators and executives at both the national and state governmental levels to consider shades of opinion and listen to the views of interest groups. Different levels and branches of government become interest groups in themselves in seeking to influence the policies of the national government. The U.S. Conference of Mayors, a congressional delegation from a state, even a particular city, may seek to exercise a permanent and direct influence on certain specific decisions of the national government. The separation of powers within the national government diffuses the influence of interest groups but also allows groups to play off one branch of government against another.

Many interest groups become concerned with political decisions only in response to the rise of particular political issues. Many engage in political pressure in response to rival groups who begin to mobilise support or opposition to a particular piece of legislation. Other groups, such as the American Farm Bureau Federation, while concerned initially with legislation directly affecting their interests, have established permanent organisations to influence political decisions, and often take stands on issues which have a marginal effect on their members. The American Medical Association, having been drawn into the political process over issues affecting its members, supports the interests of other groups in return for their support on issues important to A.M.A. members.

Groups seeking to influence political decisions in the United States may organise campaigns designed to obtain public support, or may seek to lobby politicians by direct contact. Direct lobbying is often performed by paid professional lobbyists operating at all levels of government on a particular deci-sion-maker. Such direct communication varies and is affected by institutional and individual factors. The organisation of campaigns to obtain public support is often expensive, and large, wealthy, well-established groups are more likely to do this. However, small groups may also do this on a modest scale. In 1967, for example, the American Humane Society continued an intensive letter-writing campaign to extend measures obtained in a 1966 bill requiring research institutions to observe humane conditions in feeding, housing, and caring for animals used by them. The 1966 measure was passed after a heavy mail campaign to Congressmen by constituents.

Direct or indirect lobbying may be used by groups either to prevent legislation or to promote efforts designed to obtain changes in the existing political environment. Some groups also conduct general, long-range campaigns designed to create a favourable image of themselves, with no reference to immediate demands or objectives.

Interest groups in the United States are more numerous and diverse than in Great Britain, especially those engaging in political influence. At the national level it is estimated that between 1,500 and 2,000 national associations exist with substantial, continuous, political interests, and with an organisational structure to support them. There may be eight to ten times as many located, or principally active, in the fifty states. In the larger states, as many as 400 associations or concerns may register as employers of lobbyists in a typical legislative session.[3] The scope and expense of such activity is also greater, although it should not be assumed that the size of expenditure is related to degree of success. In 1964 it was estimated that 288 organisations reported spending over 4 million dollars to influence the U.S. Congress on legislation. While the 1946 Federal Regulation of Lobbying Act requires organisations to file lobby spending reports if they solicit, collect, or receive money for the principal purpose of influencing Congress on legislation, many major organisations such as the National Association of Manufacturers and the U.S. Chamber of Commerce do not file reports because they claim they do not obtain money principally to lobby

[3] See E. Lane, *Lobbying and the Law*, Berkeley and Los Angeles: University of California Press, 1964, p. 7.

Congress; nor do the figures reported represent the total amount spent by groups on all types of lobbying.

Table 6:1

TOP 15 GROUPS LOBBYING CONGRESS, 1970. DECLARED EXPENDITURE

Organisation	1970	1969
Veterans of World War 1, U.S.A. Inc.	$341,244	$9,955
National Association of Letter Carriers (A.F.L.–C.I.O.)	277,125	265,970
United Federation of Postal Clerks (A.F.L.–C.I.O.)	228,325	250,827
Council for a Livable World	214,626	112,603
A.F.L.–C.I.O. (national headquarters)	197,493	184,938
American Farm Bureau Federation	163,553	146,337
American Hospital Association	153,241	69,925
National Association of Home Builders of the United States	151,605	138,472
United States Savings and Loan League	149,794	126,421
Citizens Committee for Postal Reform Inc.	138,545	83,951
Record Industry Association of America	123,286	115,334
Disabled American Veterans	117,134	15,368
National Committee for the Recording Arts	99,886	139,726
Livestock Producers Committee	96,945	7,255
American Medical Association	96,064	91,355

However, the list of the top fifteen spenders for 1970 in Table 6:1 does reveal the range of organisations involved in direct lobby activities, and the amount of money spent is often related to the type of legislation before Congress.[4] The major spender in 1970, Veterans of World War I, U.S.A. Inc., sought a separate pension for the 1·4 million World War I veterans. The group claimed that it had reported its total budget, and that only some $9–10,000 was actually spent on attempts to influence legislation. Passage of a Postal Reorganisation Act was the major goal of the National Assocation of Letter Carriers, the United Federation of Postal Clerks and the Citizens Committee for Postal Reform Inc. The Council for a Livable World was a citizen group concerned with legislation on arms control, military construction and Defence Department appropriations, and other defence issues, while the major interest of the A.F.L.–C.I.O. in 1970 was the Occupational Safety and Health Act.

[4] See Congressional Quarterly Weekly Report, August 6th, 1971, pp. 1680–2. Washington, D.C.: Congressional Quarterly Inc., 1971.

The list of top spenders includes well-established groups such as the A.F.L.–C.I.O., or the American Farm Bureau Federation with a nation-wide organisation engaging in direct lobbying of governmental decision-makers as well as extensive public propaganda campaigns on a range of public issues. It also includes organisations such as the National Assocation of Letter Carriers concerned with a specific piece of legislation and not usually engaged in lobbying activities.

Of the 289 organisations reporting lobby spending for 1970, 137 were business organisations, 62 citizen organisations, 25 employee and labour organisations, 20 farm organisations, 7 military and veterans organisations, and 18 professional organisations. The amount of money spent or reported as having been spent, however, bears little relationship to the success or failure of an interest group campaign.

There are many different kinds and categories of political interest groups in the United States, and within different categories there are often competing groups. Business groups may differ and may find themselves ranged on different sides of an issue. Large businesses and trade associations are generally represented by the National Association of Manufacturers, or the Chamber of Commerce; professional management in big business by the Committee for Economic Development, and small businesses by groups such as the National Federation of Independent Businesses. When general issues of union or government power come before Congress these groups will unite, but the National Federation of Independent Businesses strongly supports government aid to small business and does not always support the N.A.M. over questions involving the increasing concentration of economic power. Business groups lack the ideological unity achieved in general by labour groups, but are generally more successful in obtaining legislation favourable to them.[5] Agricultural groups provide the best example of the diversity of interest groups representing similar interests. In contrast to Great Britain, where most farmers are members of one organisation, American farmers have no monolithic organisation. Three major organisations represent farming interests. The largest is the American Farm Bureau Federation, with a

[5] See R. J. Monsen, Jr., and M. W. Cannon, *The Makers of Public Policy*, New York: McGraw-Hill, 1965, Chapters 2 and 3.

claimed membership of over a million and a half coming from the South and the corn-hog areas of Indiana, Illinois and Iowa. Despite its close connections with the Department of Agriculture and early governmental legislation, it is the most conservative of the three major farm groups, though a new group, the National Farmers Organisation, has grown up in the 1960s which is even more conservative. The National Grange, with close to a million members, is the second largest general farm organisation, has its principal strength in the North-East and Ohio, and is generally middle of the road in its attitudes. The National Farmers Union claims to have close to 300,000 members concentrated in the Middle West and North-West (especially in wheat-growing areas) and represents a more militant liberal group which often allies with the A.F.L.–C.I.O. on general matters. In a political system where agricultural interests are declining, farm interest groups remain divided.

In 1961 the Kennedy Administration sought to pass supply adjustment legislation to stabilise agricultural production, and give additional powers to the Secretary of Agriculture and farm commodity groups to determine farm policy. This was opposed by the A.F.B.F., but supported by the Farmers Union and the National Grange. After failure to obtain congressional approval the programme was put to a national referendum in 1963. All the interest groups waged an intense campaign to persuade farmers to support or oppose the programme. When the farmers finally voted they rejected the administration programme. Under 50% of the 1·2 million votes cast supported the programme – far less than the two-thirds majority required. The American Farm Bureau Federation gained a notable victory and immediately sought to introduce an alternative farm bill into Congress. The divisions between agricultural interest groups to some extent reflect regional and crop differences, but they serve to weaken the overall influence of agricultural groups on legislation, and waste some of the potential support for such interests within Congress. The existence of many access points of influence for interest groups in the United States does not mean that organised minorities are therefore more successful than similar groups in Britain.[6]

[6] See J. R. Pennock, 'Agricultural Subsidies in England and the United States', *American Political Science Review*, September 1962, pp. 621–33.

Interest groups in the United States also find it more difficult to obtain support for, and passage of, legislation than to oppose legislation. The political process, with its checks and balances, and in particular the nature of the legislative process in Congress, provides ample opportunities to amend or defeat legislation and a series of difficult obstacles for promoters and supporters of legislative change, as was illustrated by the problems encountered in obtaining the passage of the Civil Rights Act of 1964, the Elementary and Secondary Education Act of 1965, or the Trade Expansion Act of 1962.[7]

At the state level, some groups take advantage of state laws allowing popular initiative and referenda to try to overrule previous legislative action, and such actions may be binding on a state legislature. In 1964, the California Real Estate Association succeeded in using the initiative procedure to get voters to approve a state constitutional amendment which would overrule legislation forbidding discrimination on any grounds in the rental or sale of housing.[8] Such direct action by interest groups provides a challenge to political authority, but often serves to distort the democratic process. Initiative campaigns to negate legislative actions may stimulate interest among opponents of the effects of such legislation, while electors who support the legislation are often unaware of the need for them to vote on the matter. The final result is therefore not necessarily representative yet it can limit the authority of elected officials.

[7] See R. Bendiner, *Obstacle Course on Capitol Hill*, New York: McGraw-Hill, 1964; and F. J. Munger and R. F. Fenno, Jr., *National Politics in Federal Aid to Education*, Syracuse, New York: Syracuse University Press, 1962. On the Trade Expansion Act, see R. A. Bauer, *et al.*, *American Business and Public Policy*, New York: Atherton Press, 1964.

[8] See A. Holtzman, *Interest Groups and Lobbying*, London: Collier–Macmillan, 1966, Chapter 6.

The Nature, Structure and Operation of Interest Groups

The resources, membership, funds and life of interest groups in the United States may vary tremendously. At least nine distinctive types can be said to exist.

1. *Economic groups* constitute the largest single group, though the range, size, and extent of the activities of such groups are very varied. Not all such groups are large, wealthy, or have a large membership. Examples of such groups include the National Association of Manufacturers, the A.F.L.–C.I.O., the American Farm Bureau Federation, or the Teamsters Union (similar in size to the Transport and General Workers Union, and not affiliated to the A.F.L.–C.I.O.).

2. *Professional groups* – represent specific interests with large but specialised membership – American Bar Association, the American Medical Association, or the American Federation of Teachers.

3. *Reform groups* – usually small membership, often concerned with specific matters relating to 'good government' – League of Women Voters.

4. *Patriotic groups* – often a large membership with a wide range of interests – American Legion, American Coalition of Patriotic Societies.

5. *Civil Rights groups* – moderate-sized membership, often low funds – American Civil Liberties Union, National Association for the Advancement of Coloured People, Congress of Racial Equality.

6. *Quasi-political groups* – moderate-sized membership and funds, operating mainly on the political parties directly and indirectly – Americans for Democratic Action, John Birch Society, Young Americans for Freedom, Students for a Democratic Society, National Rivers and Harbours Congress.

7. *Short-term, single-interest citizen groups* – Washington Home Rule Committee, Committee for Time Uniformity, Society for Animal Protective Legislation.

8. *Religious groups* – National Catholic Education Association, American Jewish Committee.

9. *Long-term citizen groups* – Liberty Lobby Inc., American Automobile Association, American Cancer Association, National Rifle Assocation, Common Cause.

There are also organisations or individuals representing foreign governments who lobby at the national level and seek to influence legislators and administrators, especially over issues such as foreign aid, while a new type are environmental groups.

Political interest groups in the United States are federal, unitary, or confederate in structure. It is important for a group to preserve internal unity in order to maximise its influence on legislation. The federal structure of the American Farm Bureau Federation has at times weakened its position. Within the Federation, geographic constituent units reflect diverse agricultural interests and weaken the authority of the national federation. When the Federation sought in Congress to kill the Farm Security Administration, leaders of the Ohio branch testified in support of this agency. The A.F.L.–C.I.O. is also a federation. Confederation demands a high quality of central leadership and close co-operation with independent groups. The National Council for a Permanent Fair Employment Practices Commission in 1943 failed to maximise its potential influence because of an inability to obtain the necessary co-operation between the leadership and co-operating independent organisations.[9] Almost all of the major political interest groups are oligarchic, with a small number of individuals making decisions and speaking on behalf of the group. Often the leadership has to communicate to its members in order to obtain their support for both direct and indirect political action. Many members of an organisation may give only moderate support to the activities of their leadership. In 1952 the unions sought advocacy of the repeal of the Taft-Hartley Act of 1947. The Act had been debated in the 1948 election and talked about up to 1952, yet 41% of a sample of respondents in blue-collar households with a union member had no opinion on the issue in 1952.

9 See A. Holtzman, *Interest Groups and Lobbying*, *op. cit* , pp. 27–9; also L. C. Kesselman, *The Social Politics of F.E.P.C.; A Study in Reform Pressure Movements*, Chapel Hill: University of North Carolina Press, 1948.

In discussing the operations of political interest groups at the national level it is necessary to dispel assumptions that most of this activity is directed at Congress and Congressmen and that a good deal of it is unscrupulous, even corrupt. Certainly Congress may be vulnerable to the influence of lobbyists, and there have been dramatic situations such as in 1956 when Senator Francis Case of South Dakota announced in the Senate, a few days prior to a vote on an important natural gas bill, that a lobbyist for the natural gas interests had approached his campaign manager in South Dakota and left $2,500 as a contribution to his political campaign. Such instances are rare and have little real effect on final legislative decisions.

Professional lobbyists do not spend all their time in direct contact with Congressmen. Of the nineteen representatives of a variety of industrial companies who participated in 1958 in a round-table discussion of their jobs, only one spent the bulk of his time on legislative matters, and most of them spent a considerable amount of time dealing with individuals in executive agencies.[10] The use of professional full-time lobbyists, however, using direct techniques on political decision-makers, is almost uniquely American. In Britain, much formal lobbying is also attempted with administrators rather than legislators, but it is hardly on the scale of that in Washington.

The use of professional lobbyists by interest groups differs widely. Some groups employ full-time lobbyists (A.F.L.–C.I.O. or the N.A.M.) who lobby solely for one group on a variety of issues. Other groups employ a professional lobbyist (who may have other clients with very different interests) for a short period to lobby on a single issue. Some groups or private organisations do not employ a professional lobbyist but have one of their legal representatives permanently in Washington to deal with political or administrative matters when the interests of the organisation are affected. Many private companies do not employ lobbyists but use the services of organisations who provide them with daily information regarding all political and administrative developments in Washington, and decide on the basis of these reports whether and how to present their views to decision-makers if a matter arises which may affect their interests.

[10] See P. W. Cherrington and R. L. Gillen, *The Business Representative in Washington*, Washington, D.C.: Brookings Institution, 1962.

Such professional lobbyists are frequently as much involved in lobbying executive agencies, and even the Executive Office of the President, as they are with Congressmen. Legislative lobbying is often only one part of an effort to affect executive actions, and executive lobbying involves constant attempts to influence the implementation of legislation. No single official is as much the target of influence as the President, and he and his advisers face a barrage of opinion and comment designed to persuade him to support certain legislation or seek to amend existing legislation. In 1965, President Johnson responded to demands by labour interests and sought unsuccessfully to obtain repeal of Section 14B of the Taft–Hartley Act which allowed states to enact 'right-to-work' laws. Helping a President to be elected, or giving strong support to his policies, may strengthen the potential influence of a group, but the President also has ample authority at his disposal to ignore group demands if he chooses. Mobilisation of public opinion may force a matter to the attention of the President, and a group seeking major innovations needs his backing. He, in turn, may seek to co-ordinate the activities of friendly interest groups to help him persuade Congresss to accept his legislative demands.[11]

The relationship of interest groups and executive agencies at both the state and national level is, however, one of mutual co-operation and dependence rather than hostility. They are often dependent on each other for information and services. Unlike Britain, the party controlling the executive is not an integrated and unified organisation. Administrative departments are vulnerable to legislative attack and may also face conflict with other departments. Agency or department heads often feel the need to develop special relations with interest groups whose members may be affected by their decisions.[12] The A.F.L.–C.I.O. acts as a clientele group for the Department of Labour, and relations between the National Rivers and Harbours Congress and the Corps of Engineers are close since they both have a vested interest in public works, especially flood control legislation. The American Legion is also influential in the activities of

[11] See R. A. Bauer, et al., op. cit., Part 4, regarding the mobilisation of interest groups in support of the Trade Expansion Act of 1962.

[12] See W. Boyer, Bureaucracy on Trial, Indianapolis: Bobbs-Merrill, 1964, pp. 22–5 and 53–67.

the Veterans Administration, and education interest groups seek to maintain special relations with the U.S. Office of Education. Executive agencies may encourage such co-operation in order to gain interest group support in their battles with Congress to obtain funds to implement programmes, since they are not allowed to use funds to lobby on their own behalf in Congress beyond testifying before committees. Some agencies, as in Britain, appoint representatives of private groups to sit on advisory committees to the agency. Many groups have as a major objective their establishment as a formal part of the process within which political decisions are made.

Attacks upon an agency may also originate from within the administration, and may involve reductions in the size and duties of the agency or the transfer of the agency to the jurisdiction of another department. Agencies therefore seek to obtain maximum support from friendly interest groups to try to persuade the executive not to make such changes. Agencies may also consult interest groups and ask for advice before they begin implementation of some legislation, or they may use their cordial relations with interest groups to obtain some feedback concerning reactions to the implementation of legislation.

The need for clientele support for the financial requests of administratives agencies places interest groups in a stronger position than groups in Britain seeking to influence administrative departments. Some groups will, however, use the conflict between the executive and legislature to undermine legislation which they oppose. Groups such as the Liberty Lobby, who oppose foreign aid legislation, seek to maintain cordial relations with Congressmen on committees dealing with these matters whom they know share their views, and take advantage of opportunities provided to testify against foreign aid before such committees. The lack of a strong private group supporting foreign aid legislation makes it more difficult to obtain requests for foreign aid funds from Congress, but does not prevent such legislation from being accepted. In contrast, the U.S. Corps of Engineers finds a valuable ally in the National Rivers and Harbours Congress, who have Congressmen from both parties on their executive, often from the Congressional committees considering public works appropriations and authorisations.[13] Some departments possess Congressional liaison officers who also seek to work with interest groups to determine the necessary strategy to adopt in working for the success of department bills in Congress.

The incorporation of interest groups in this way coincides with the need of interest groups to have some voice in executive affairs. Interest groups politically close to the party leadership in the executive may be able to exercise influence over certain administrative appointments. During the Eisenhower Administration, representatives of the American Farm Bureau Federation were given some important posts in the Agriculture Department, and when the Democrats took over in 1960 the National Farmers Union received similar opportunities. The needs of interest groups coincide with the wants of many agencies. In some respects members of executive departments are more vulnerable than legislators to interest group politics, yet they do have the ability to control the extent of the influence an interest group may have. A department head may have his own communication links with Congressmen and may prefer to do without the support of friendly interest groups.

In contrast to Britain, interest groups also seek to influence the judiciary, to the extent that the Supreme Court is a political as well as a judicial body with powers to overrule legislative and executive action and interpret state and national constitutions. Interest groups are very active with regard to the selection and nomination of federal judges,[14] especially the American Bar Association. The A.B.A. has succeeded in becoming an integral part of the federal recruitment process through its Committee on the Federal Judiciary, and can at least expect to be consulted regarding the desirability of a particular nomination. Its influence is small but it is not insignificant, especially if an appointment is controversial. It is also more direct and visible than the influence of legal organisations such as the Inns of Court in Britain.

[13] See A. Maas, *Muddy Waters*, Cambridge, Mass.: Harvard University Press, 1951; also H. Zeigler, *Interest Groups in American Society*, Englewood Cliffs, N.J.: Prentice-Hall Inc., 1964.

[14] See D. Danelski, *A Supreme Court Judge is Appointed*, New York: Random House, 1964; also J. B. Grossman, *Lawyers and Judges: The A.B.A. and the Politics of Judicial Selection*, New York: John Wiley, 1965.

Interest groups often link broad interests in society to individual parties of interest in bringing cases to the Supreme Court. Since 1909 the National Association for the Advancement of Coloured People has improved the legal status of Negroes by victories won through Supreme Court decisions. The first Negro Supreme Court Justice, Thurgood Marshall, began his legal career as special counsel for the N.A.A.C.P. Legal Defence and Educational Fund. Groups whose lobbying fails to defeat legislation may continue opposition by litigation.

Interest groups may also seek direct access by filing special briefs to the Supreme Court, where a case involves interests concerning them. These briefs may help the Court decide the case and affect its thinking not only on the immediate decision but on future cases. Not all groups, however, have equal access, and access through the filing of special briefs usually depends on whether a group can show they have an interest directly affected by the case. In the Steel Seizure case of 1952, which concerned the constitutionality of an action by President Truman, the C.I.O. was permitted to file a brief but the American Legion was refused permission.[15] On other occasions interest groups have encouraged the executive to support them and file a special brief.

Groups such as the N.A.A.C.P., in the face of continued opposition by Congress to civil rights legislation, turned to the courts in the 1940s and 1950s, and in a series of test cases succeeded in eliminating certain legal barriers to the equal rights of Negroes. Such an approach was expensive, but the 1954 Supreme Court decision outlawing school segregation proved to be an important step in stimulating such groups into more positive pressure to secure civil rights legislation. The American Civil Liberties Union also uses legal procedures to publicise its demands, and the success of its litigation in 1962, questioning the power of New York State to write a prayer for use in state school classrooms, represented a political victory as substantial as defeating a bill in Congress. Indirect lobbying of the judiciary may also occur through the writing of articles in legal journals which are

[15] See A. Holtzmann, *op. cit.*, p. 136. See also C. E. Vose 'Litigation as a Form of Pressure Group Activity', in R. E. Wolfinger (ed.), *Readings in American Political Behavior*, Englewood Cliffs, N.J.: Prentice-Hall Inc., Chapter 8.

likely to be read by Justices, or the writing of personal letters to members of the Supreme Court.

Lobbying of Congressmen has received most attention from observers and attracted much adverse comment, especially the activities of the professional lobbyist. In fact, however, the lobbyist is only an intermediary link in a massive network of communications between legislators and electors. Empirical study has revealed the existence of a pattern of communication between Congressmen and lobbyists which is more formalised and controlled than some commentators have suggested. Freshmen Congressmen may be more vulnerable to the attentions of interest groups while they are 'feeling their way' around Capitol Hill, but their votes are unlikely to have a major effect on the fortunes of a piece of legislation. Most Congressmen, however, welcome lobbyists, and indeed expect them. They find them useful in providing general information, or research data or speech material, and if they are prepared to comply with certain 'rules of the game' they are encouraged to maintain direct contact. Lester Milbrath, in his study of Washington lobbyists, shows that 80% of his respondents preferred direct methods and indicated the types of approaches which would be the most effective. A poll of Senators and Representatives in 1957 found that the 122 legislators answering the poll agreed they received valuable information on complicated issues from lobbyists, felt little unreasonable pressure from them, and knew a good deal about the lobbyists they talked to.[16]

Congressmen meet many people every day and are used to dealing with a variety of individuals urging them to listen to their views, be they fellow Congressmen, liaison men from the White House, or constituents. They also develop a pattern of behaviour heavily influenced by the procedures and problems involved in legislative decision-making, and lobbyists are likely to be more effective if they comply with these behavioural norms. Congressional respondents indicate they prefer lobbyists who are sincere, enthusiastic, energetic, understanding, and confident, and resent aggressive or antagonistic approaches. The lobbyist must convince the Congressman that he has some-

[16] See L. W. Milbrath, *The Washington Lobbyists*, Chicago: Rand McNally Co., 1963, Part 3, especially Chapter 11. See also Congressional Quarterly Service, *Legislators and the Lobbyists*, op. cit., 1965.

thing at stake and must demonstrate how an issue is likely to affect his constituents. The lobbyist must also have a strong case and also give the impression that he appreciates the arguments of an opponent. He must also be succinct and to the point, since time is precious to a Congressman. Above all he should not threaten a Congressman with direct opposition if he refuses to support the position of the group he represents. Lobbyists must also be prepared to work with the senior staff members of a Congressman, provide them with information and keep in close contact. Sometimes a lobbyist may prefer to use the opportunity to testify before a committee of Congress rather than approach individual Congressmen.

Many lobbyists are ex-Congressmen who may work for one or several different groups. More than 100 ex-Senators and Representatives registered as lobbyists at one time or another between 1946 and 1970. Such lobbyists have the advantage of knowing the problems of Congressmen and of being able to exploit previous contacts and friendships made as Congressmen. Being an ex-Congressman may, however, also be a liability, if an individual obtained a poor reputation as a Congressman and also made many enemies. Interest groups vary in their views on the desirability of employing ex-Congressmen and generally prefer to recruit lobbyists who have experience of government service, as administrators or Congressional staff members. Some Congressmen, like M.P.s, are members of interest groups and work directly to help these interests in Congress.

One of the major dilemmas facing lobbyists is the need to approach Congressmen who are indifferent or hostile to their position. Such Congressmen are less likely to be willing to listen to the lobbyist, yet failure to communicate with these legislators means that the influence of the lobbyist will be minimal. Most lobbyists ignore those legislators they know to be opposed and concentrate their attentions on Congressmen who are indifferent or wavering. Such Congressmen are also likely to be approached by rival lobbyists, so a careful strategy of approach must be worked out. Indirect lobbying by stimulating constituency responses must be done with care, for most Congressmen are experienced at distinguishing spontaneous constituency reaction from reactions stimulated and aided by interest groups. A wavering Congressman is unlikely to treat a visiting lobbyist as cordially if he has just received that morning 1,000 letters from constituents almost identical in content and language, and clearly the result of stimulation by the interest group which the lobbyist represents. Congressmen, as is indicated later, like to get some feel of constituency attitudes but also like to feel they can make up their minds on legislation, with constituency attitudes being only one of a number of factors influencing their decisions.

It would be wrong also to infer that interest groups and lobbyists are highly organised and can conduct a smooth and highly professional job of mobilising their members and other supporters in a concerted campaign. Study of the background to the Trade Expansion Act of 1962 provides a picture of interest groups often lacking in internal unity and co-ordination of effort and often simply counteracting the efforts of rivals. As the authors of the study comment: 'groups which we observed were more inept than we had anticipated', and add significantly that 'Congress as a body can to a great extent be its own boss'.[17] The influence of any single group is minimised by the efforts of rival groups to exert similar influence, and by the ability of Congressmen to listen to their appeals by viewing them as only a part of the evidence they consider before making a decision. There is no doubt that, when voting on an issue is close, the ability to gain access to several Congressmen who may be indifferent to the issue and persuade them to vote their way may determine the final result of the vote. However, this is rare and is likely to be at only one stage of the legislative process, and other decisions will have to be taken which will affect the issue.

Interest Groups and Medicare Legislation

On July 30th, 1965, President Johnson signed a Social Security health-care-for-the-aged bill into law. The legislation followed a bitter political dispute which began in 1935 over the proper role of the national government in the provision of health care for the general population. Organised labour, many Northern Democrats in Congress, organisations of the elderly, and many liberal organisations supported broad national responsibility. In the 1940s they supported proposals for a compulsory

[17] R. A. Bauer, *et al.*, *op. cit.*, pp. 486–7.

national health insurance system financed by a national payroll tax. Such proposals failed to win enactment, despite the support of President Truman, largely because of the strong opposition of the medical profession. In 1957, a limited proposal for a compulsory national health insurance programme for the health care of persons over sixty-five was opposed by President Eisenhower, insurance industry representatives, and other groups as well as the medical profession. Despite the support of President Kennedy, such a plan was defeated in 1960 and 1962 in the Senate by a coalition of Republicans and Southern Democrats, and in 1964 was rejected by the House of Representatives after passage in the Senate. In 1965, the 89th Congress finally accepted Medicare legislation and ended the battle.

Throughout this period the Social Security health care issue produced a massive amount of lobbying of Congress and extensive public propaganda appeals.[18] The major organisation responsible for this was the American Medical Association and its Political Action Committee. The A.M.A. opposed legislation because it might lead to 'socialised' medicine and because they believed legislation to be unnecessary and likely to bring about bureaucratic interference in the practice of medicine, and so reduce the quality of medical care in the United States.

In June 1965 the A.M.A. had more than 200,000 dues-paying members (over two-thirds of the country's doctors, but only about 0·1% of the population), receiving several free journals concerned with A.M.A. activities. The A.M.A. exerted pressure through activity at the local level (at local community gatherings and local medical society meetings), and maintained a staff of 900 persons at its headquarters in Chicago. There were also twenty-three in a Washington office which possessed four full-time registered lobbyists working to defeat Social Security health care legislation. The 1964 budget of the A.M.A. was $23 million, almost half coming from advertising in its publications. A large portion of this money was spent on publicity attacking Medicare legislation.

[18] See S. Kelly, Jr., *Professional Public Relations and Political Power*, Baltimore: Johns Hopkins Press, 1956; and E. Feingold, *Medicare: Policy and Politics*, San Francisco: Chandler Publishing Co., 1966, Part 3. For comparative analysis, see H. Eckstein, *Pressure Group Politics: The Case of the British Medical Association*, London: Allen and Unwin, 1960.

In addition to direct lobbying in Washington, several other methods were used to stimulate opposition. Members were urged to write to Congressmen and to urge other local people to write opposing the bill. Several groups were created to try to set up improved voluntary schemes to improve health care for the aged and so make legislation unnecessary. The Political Action Committee received voluntary contributions which were used to support congressional candidates who supported the A.M.A. position on the medical care bill and on other legislation, especially Congressmen on important committees dealing with the bill. A national publicity campaign was conducted in newspapers, and on radio and television. In 1962 the A.M.A. spent over $83,000, and in 1961 almost double this figure, on congressional lobbying. For the first quarter of 1965, the A.M.A. filed a lobby spending report (required of all Congressional lobbyists) of almost a million dollars, of which over $800,000 was for press, radio and television campaigns.

Supporters of the legislation were heavily engaged in pressure activities. The major group supporting passage of Social Security health care proposals was the American Federation of Labour-Congress of Industrial Organisations. In 1965 it had 129 affiliated national and international unions with a total membership of over 13 million, several newspapers and other publications, a large headquarters in Washington with a large staff of lobbyists, and an extensive network of paid officials across the country. Union publications were used to urge members to write to Congressmen, send local delegations to meet Congressmen, or persuade city councils or state and local government bodies to pass resolutions demanding congressional action on the bill. Union radio shows were used to publicise the issue along with direct lobbying in Washington, while public statements by union leaders attracted wide press coverage. The Committee on Public Education (a political branch of the A.F.L.–C.I.O.) conducted strong campaigns in congressional elections from 1958 to defeat opponents of the Social Security health care bill. Another organisation supporting legislation was the National Council of Senior Citizens. Formed in 1961, its chief objective was to obtain passage of the medical care bill, and it sought to publish pamphlets, organise public rallies, and present radio and television shows in support of the bill. It also organised petitions and letter-writing campaigns to Congressmen and supported Congressmen favouring legislation. In 1963–65 it had an annual budget of over 150,000 dollars, some of this coming from donations from the Democratic party and the A.F.L.–C.I.O. It did not seek to lobby Congressmen directly.

The overwhelming Democratic victory in Presidential and Congressional elections in 1964, together with the support of President Johnson for a Social Security health care bill, helped to make possible the passage of legislation in the 89th Congress, but it did not get through the 1965 Congress without considerable negotiation and opposition. The A.M.A. maintained its high expenditure on advertising and other forms of publicity against the bill, and also sought to obtain popular support for an alternative bill offering fuller medical coverage, but only available to those who could pass a means test. This bill would be voluntary in nature and operated by state governments. When passage of the initial bill by the House of Representatives seemed likely, several state medical societies passed resolutions of non-compliance with any future Medicare law. The A.M.A., however, warned against such action because of its possible effect on public opinion. Senate attempts to alter the bill served to expand the benefits for older people, and the bill passed the Senate, with eight Southern Democrats opposing it. Differences between the House and Senate versions of the bill were quickly reconciled and Congress passed the bill without further debate.

Groups working actively for and against the legislation reflect a wide range of interests, small and large. In support of the legislation were the A.F.L.–C.I.O. and several independent unions; the National Council of Senior Citizens; the Group Health Association of America (representing community group health service plans); the Senior Citizens Council of the National Farmers Union; the National Medical Association (an organisation of Negro doctors); the American Nurses Association; the Social Welfare Council of the National Council of Churches; the National Conference of Catholic Charities; the National Social Welfare Assembly; the American Public Health Association; the American Public Welfare Association; Americans for Democratic Action, and a host of other small or *ad hoc* organisations. Leading opponents of the bill were the American Medical Association; the U.S. Chamber of Commerce, state chambers of commerce, and junior chambers; state associations of manufacturers; several drug companies; the American Farm Bureau Federation and the National Grange, and insurance organisations including the Health Insurance Association.

This case-study demonstrates the nature of the influence exerted by groups in the American political process, and indicates the type of conditions where the decision-making process is subject to direct influence. Despite the massive expenditure of money and maintaining an intensive campaign at all levels of influence, the A.M.A. clearly had a difficult task in the 89th Congress in seeking to prevent the passage of Medicare legislation. While they delayed the passage of legislation a few years, and supplemented the efforts of those decision-makers opposing legislation, their efforts failed to halt the gradual shift of public and political support away from their position.

The Overall Impact of Interest Groups and Lobbying

The picture of interest group activity presented here is not a clear-cut one. It does, however, reflect the general impact of interest group and lobbying activities. In a pluralist society with a diffuse political system dependent on popular control, interest group activity has become a necessary part of political activity. At times it has given considerable concern, as is reflected by legislative attempts at both the national and state level to regulate and control such activities. The Federal Regulation of Lobbying Act of 1946 has had little real effect beyond giving some modest indication of the extent of lobbying activity directed at Congress, and many state laws are also weakly enforced and exercise little real regulation.

In 1966 legislation was passed amending the Foreign Agents Registration Act of 1938 to strengthen requirements that individuals, acting on behalf of foreign governments or principals and engaged in political activities designed to influence political decisions, should register with the Department of Justice and disclose expenditures. This legislation followed allegations of dubious lobbying and propaganda practices on the part of some of these representatives on Congressmen, along with factual misrepresentation to their principals about matters relating to decisions on foreign aid legislation. Attempts to obtain congressional reform in the 90th Congress included provisions designed to strengthen the 1946 Federal Regulation of Lobbying Act. Major regulation, however, has come from the political process itself. Interest groups themselves can exercise a form of countervailing power on each other, though not all groups have equal resources to compete on an equal basis, nor are all interests in society represented by interest group activity. Middle and upper-income groups are better organised and large areas of the population may be outside the system of private organisation.[19] In 1968, for example, even after the assassination of two major political figures, strong lobbying by the National Rifle Association and representatives of the arms trade made it difficult to obtain passage of comprehensive legislation to control the sale of firearms, and there was little evidence of the existence of a strong permanent lobby in support of such legislation.

Interest group activity, however, is only a part of a complex process by which conflict is resolved and decisions made by the political process. Decision-makers find interest group activity useful in aggregating, defining and communicating specialised opinions, but they have also developed a range of techniques to control the extent of their influence while permitting groups to provide a contribution to the welter of information and attitudes they need to consider.

Information from congressional staff or administrative specialists can also provide a countervailing influence on certain types of lobbying. The contribution of interest groups to the political process is very different from that in Britain, and is affected by the particular structure of political institutions and the process of decision-making. A great deal of effort is 'wasted' in terms of concrete returns for resources expended by individual interest groups. However, given the existence of certain formal and informal controls on their activities, such groups may supplement rather than distort the process within which political decisions are made. The political institutions of the United States were designed to accommodate the claims of a diverse range of interests and groups. As long as the demands of small constituencies or interests do not become so institutional- ised as to distort attempts to evaluate the public interest and pre-

[19] See E. Schattschneider, *The Semi-Sovereign People, op. cit.*, Chapter 2.

clude those elements in the political process, such as the parties and the Presidency, from reflecting national interests and seeking to achieve such objectives, groups reflecting special interests are likely to play a legitimate role in the American political system. Nevertheless there remains the danger of interest groups becoming too institutionalised or formalised within the political process, because they may therefore be able to overcome or avoid the hurdles and obstacles which can refine and dilute their influence on decision-making. Evidence of this in particular situations, as reflected by the concern expressed at the influence of the so-called 'military-industrial' complex in the 1960s, has led to the emergence of 'public interest' groups, of which Common Cause is the most notable as a group, and the varied activities of Ralph Nader in the areas of consumer and environment questions the most distinctive as an individual. Increasing technology may also change the nature of interest group activity in the United States but such activity by groups is likely to remain significant and to continue to be affected by the institutional and cultural framework within which they operate.

Chapter Seven

POLITICAL PARTIES AND THE POLITICAL SYSTEM

The major national political parties in the United States appear to be loose coalitions of state and local party organisations united by a common desire to win control of the Presidency. More clearly than major British parties, they operate as electoral coalitions of interests rather than cohesive organisations. They are, in part, the products of the structure of American government. The federal system helps to maintain the 'independence' of state party organisations, and party structure at the national level is based on geographic representation which at best lacks unity and at worst can be intensely parochial. Both major parties are affected by interest groups, but groups rarely affiliate with either party on a permanent basis. They do, however, seek to influence the national party platforms of both the major parties (the A.F.L.–C.I.O. submits platform proposals to both parties at their national conventions) and may work with a party to obtain the election of certain candidates. Because the parties need to form coalitions of disparate political organisations in order to win Presidential elections, their major concern is to build and maintain such coalitions, which are often based on sectional, ethnic, historical or economic factors. The simple fact that the major parties hold national conventions every four years just before the Presidential election campaign begins, rather than annually as in Britain, illustrates their concern with winning elections rather than debating policies.

Political Parties and the Political Process

If the political process affects the structure of the two major parties, it has also affected other parties seeking to compete in national elections. The electoral process is controlled primarily by the states, and this helps to explain why, since 1860, every Presidential election has been won by a Democrat or a Republican, and in only five of these has another party ever won a single state. Because all the electoral votes of a state go to the Presidential candidate with the largest popular vote in the state, plus the fact that it is this electoral college vote and not the popular vote which decides the Presidential election, it is difficult for minor parties to compete and attract support since the electoral system weighs so heavily against them. Some minor parties have difficulty in getting their candidate on the ballot in Presidential elections in some states because of the state electoral laws. The election of Representatives and Senators on a winner-takes-all basis in district or state-wide elections means that, except in areas where support is concentrated, they are unlikely to succeed even if they increase their overall vote.

Furthermore, minor parties competing in Presidential elections who are, in effect, former factions of the major parties who have split away, tend to do better than permanent minor parties. In 1948 the Dixiecrat party, who split from the Democrats and sought to prevent any Presidential candidate from getting the necessary majority of electoral college votes, polled only approximately 12,000 more votes than the Wallace Progressives but obtained 39 electoral college votes. The Progressives, with over a million votes polled, won no electoral college votes. As in Britain, the electoral process works in favour of the two major parties.

There are, of course, many other reasons why minor parties in the United States have failed to compete nationally. In part it is due to the inability of parties of broad ideology, such as the Socialist, Socialist Labour, and Socialist Workers parties, to prevent ideological differences from further weakening their organisation. The lack of strong class identification among blue-collar Americans, the prior existence of party organisations in large cities which were not based on ideological considerations, restrictions on immigration, and the failure of trade unions to evince any interest in co-ordinating with them to obtain political power, have all conspired to make it impossible for such parties to compete effectively in national elections. Traditional and stable voter allegiance to the two major parties, and a general political culture that seeks to link political support with political success, also work against minor parties.

This does not mean that minor parties have not affected the major political parties and the political process. Minor parties have succeeded in effecting political reforms (the Anti-Masonic party was the first to use the national convention to choose Presidential candidates in 1831, and the Progressives forced the introduction of state-wide direct primary elections in certain states in the early 1900s). Interventions in the Presidential elections of 1892, 1912, 1924, 1948, and 1968 led the major parties to adjust their tactics and seek to integrate such opposition into their respective coalitions. In each instance the general result was to push 'liberals' toward the Democratic party and 'conservatives' in a Republican direction.

Minor parties have also had a direct electoral effect. In 1884, 575 votes in New York State taken from Democrat Grover Cleveland and given to Republican James G. Blaine would have given Blaine all the electoral college votes in the state and made him President. The Prohibition party polled 25,006 votes in New York State, mostly taking them from the Republicans. In 1916 the 13 electoral college votes in California which determined the final Presidential outcome went to the Democrat Woodrow Wilson by a margin of 3,806 votes. The Prohibition Party polled 27,698 votes in the state at this election.[1] In 1912, Theodore Roosevelt, as the candidate of the Progressive party, which had split away from the Republican party after the nomination of Taft, gained more popular votes and considerably more electoral college votes than Taft.

The decline of the impact of minor parties has coincided with an increase in two-party competition at all levels. Though the Democrats and Republicans have dominated national campaigns since 1860, they have often been very weak indeed at the state level in some areas, and at the national level one party tends to dominate Congressional and Presidential elections for long periods. In the Southern states, the Democratic party has dominated state and national politics since the Civil War and many Democrats have been elected unopposed until the 1960s. In elections for the House of Representatives between 1952 and

[1] See S. Petersen, *A Statistical History of the American Presidential Elections*, New York: Ungar Publishing Co., 1963.

1962, the Democrats won 436 seats without opposition and the Republicans 21 seats, and in the Senate elections in this period 19 Democrats and 1 Republican were unopposed.[2] While the number of uncontested seats is diminishing – in 1952, 92 House seats were uncontested, by 1970 this was reduced to 63 – it is still markedly different from the situation in Britain.

Leadership groups in the major American parties can be considered as special kinds of interest groups. Individuals may have either issue or patronage motivations for being party activists. It is possible to distinguish three main types of state party systems: issue-dominated two-party states, traditional job-dominated two-party states, and one-party states. In some one-party states, party organisations of the weaker party may exist only to contest Presidential elections in order to obtain the patronage available if their candidate is successful. The amount of patronage at the disposal of successful parties is much greater than in Britain, while the opportunity to win elections and put into effect specific policies is more difficult. The electorate which determines the Presidency is a different one from that which chooses the Congress, and this division is duplicated at the state level. Patronage-motivation may well be stronger than issue-motivation on the part of some political activists but this depends on the nature of the state political system.[3] However, the task of the political parties and their leaders has often been to act as political brokers drawing interests together, and this task may be better performed by the individual whose motivation is one of jobs rather than issues.

Control over nominations and policies of parties is diffused and decentralised to state and local organisations, though this does not mean more democratic control. Senatorial nominations are determined at the state level, and Representatives are nominated at the local level. In contrast to the procedures in Britain, the choice of party candidates is determined by party primary elections. This procedure was begun around the beginning of the present century as a substitute for the caucus and convention methods of choosing party candidates. A primary

[2] See C. O. Jones, *The Republican Party in American Politics, op. cit.*, p. 77.
[3] See T. Lowi, *At the Pleasure of the Mayor*, New York: Free Press, 1964; also D. P. Moynihan and J. Q. Wilson, 'Patronage in New York State 1955–1959', *American Political Science Review*, June 1964, pp. 286–301.

election is really little more than a none-assembled caucus designed to return party nominations 'to the people'. Control of nomination machinery moved from the party to the state, all parties choosing candidates on the same day under the supervision of public election officials. Wisconsin in 1903 was the first state to establish compulsory primary elections for all state elective offices. Primary elections are of two types, partisan and non-partisan. In both types, candidates normally qualify for a place on the primary ballot by securing a required number of signatures of qualified voters on a petition. Non-partisan primaries are usually for municipal or state judicial elections.

The partisan primary, where the party affiliation of candidates appears on the ballot, may be open or closed. An open primary is open to any qualified voter regardless of his party affiliation. In a closed primary the voter must be registered as a member of the party in whose primary election he votes. Closed primaries are most common, and the primary elections in some states where one party tends to dominate may include a run-off primary. This is common in Southern states where the Democratic party primary has, until very recently, often been more important than the general election. In this situation, when no candidate wins an absolute majority, a run-off election is held between the two candidates receiving the most votes in the first primary, which is won by the candidate obtaining a majority of the vote.

Some states have party conventions before the primary to choose an endorsed slate indicating the candidates which are the choice of party leaders. This partially negates the original purpose of party primaries but is believed by the parties to provide some party cohesion along with popular involvement in the final choice. Reformers also urged that voters should have some influence on the nomination of Presidential candidates, and over twenty states provide Presidential primaries or some form of Presidential preference poll. There are two major types – those where voters choose state party delegates to the national party conventions, and those where voters indicate preferences among candidates who have chosen to enter the contest in that state. A few states provide both processes, though in most states the party delegates to the national conventions are chosen by state or district conventions or by party committees.

While the primary election is the major method of party nomination in the United States, it has proved a mixed blessing. The average voter does not consider the party primary election to be very important, and often resents having to disclose his party preference in order to participate. The costs of primary elections often discourage candidates, and in general the parties still exercise considerable control over nominations. Primaries also emphasise personality rather than policies and discourage party responsibility, while encouraging intra-party rather than inter-party conflict. However, party primaries are likely to long remain the mechanisms by which many of the actual decisions in the selection of persons for public offices are made. Differences in party structure and election procedures in different states reflect the political environment in each state. Primary elections were initially advocated on idealistic grounds, but they have often been adopted for practical political reasons by those who believed they would increase their political power, and changes in the procedures of primary elections are likely to reflect such political realities.

The institutional division between the President and Congress, the fixed nature of elections, and the different constituencies to which the President and Congress are responsible, all conspire to make it difficult to maintain party discipline at the national level. The President is nominated by the national party and is elected in a nation-wide election, while Congressmen are nominated at the state and local level and elected by voters in individual states or districts, not always at the same time as the President (Representatives must be re-elected every two years along with one-third of the Senate). The reluctance of parties in Congress to impose sanctions on Congressmen who refuse to support a President of their party emphasises the relative inability of the national parties in the United States to guarantee the implementation of their policies even when in control of both the Presidency and Congress.

Strong state and local party organisations exist which profit from the patronage obtainable from electoral success at the national level, yet they seek to remain self-sufficient and dominant at the state level and resist attempts by the national party leadership to limit their discretion. A party leader who sought to centralise policy-making and candidate selection would challenge the authority of entrenched and powerful state party officials, and such efforts would be bitterly resisted. However, though party discipline and unity in voting are less evident in the House of Representatives than in the House of Commons, careful analysis of formal roll-call votes in Congress indicates that party pressure may still be the most important single influence on congressional voting, and party the most reliable indicator of voting intentions, despite significant deviations over some issues.[4] Party cohesion is also often strong on some committees in Congress. In some state legislatures, notably Connecticut, Rhode Island, Pennsylvania, and Michigan, party discipline is important, and party cohesion is more evident in state party systems where issues rather than patronage motivates party activity and where competition between the two major parties is keen. In some modified one-party states (Louisiana, perhaps, or Tennessee) the dominant party is divided into two well-organised and cohesive factions.

While the ideological differences between the major parties in the United States are slight, since they share an agreed commitment to certain American traditions such as the separation of church and state, free public education, or privately owned business, there are important differences in programmes and policies. These differences, however, may sometimes be obscured in the desire to appeal to as many voters as possible at national elections, though they become clearer at certain elections such as in 1964 and 1972. The differences can also be seen in the party platforms adopted at national conventions and also in the statements of party leaders in Congress.[5] One Republican Congressman aptly stated the philosophic distinction between the two major parties in the simplest terms as follows: 'They tell people what they are going to do for them, we tell them what we are keeping the government from doing to them.'[6]

[4] See J. Turner, *Party and Constituency: Pressures on Congress*, Baltimore: Johns Hopkins University Press, rev. ed. 1970: D. B. Truman, *The Congressional Party*, New York: Wiley, 1959. For party activity in state legislatures, see the contribution by T. Dye, in H. Jacob and K. N. Vines, *Politics in the American States, op. cit.*, pp. 184–200.

[5] See K. H. Porter and D. B. Johnson, *National Party Platforms 1840–1964*, Urbana: University of Illinois Press, 1966.

[6] See C. L. Clapp, *The Congressman: His Work as He Sees It*, Washington, D.C.: The Brookings Institution, 1963, p. 19.

The parties do not lack ideological views, but the similarity of ideological perspective shared by most Americans means the existence of successful parties who are similar in ideology, and this in turn reinforces the similarity in ideological perspective on the part of voters. Each party obtains votes from every section of the population, but many sections vote consistently in greater numbers for one party rather than the other. Party success in Presidential elections tends to go to the party able to combine the support of its strong identifiers with a significant number of electors from all the major sections of the population. For over a century the Republican and Democratic parties have at least succeeded in achieving the former, with the single and unusual exception of 1912. Even in the worst years both parties have succeeded in attracting around 30% of the vote for the President. In spite of a disastrous defeat in 1964, the Republicans still obtained 38·5% of the popular vote and won several important elections for state governors.

Since 1932 the Democrats have been able to dominate elections to national offices. The slow long-run shift to the Democrats, accompanied by a long-run strengthening of support among specific groups such as Negro voters, has been limited only by short-term fluctuations in mid-term congressional elections and a short-run surge in 1952, heavily influenced by personal factors, which allowed the Republican party to win the Presidency in 1952 and 1956, but not maintain more than temporary control of Congress. The permanent realignment of voters with the Democrats in the period 1932–36 was not matched for the Republicans in 1952–56. The Presidential elections of 1952 and 1956 represent examples of deviating elections, with large numbers of 'Democrats' voting solely for the Republican Presidential candidate and not changing their basic party loyalty. The 1960 Presidential election won by the Democratic candidate was an example of a reinstating election with a return to traditional voting habits by many Democrats, and this was maintained and consolidated in the 1964 election, but in 1968 the Republicans narrowly won control of the Presidency but not of Congress,[7] and in 1972 won a landslide Presidential victory but few gains in Congress.

[7] For development of this analysis of types of Presidential elections, see A. Campbell, *et al.*, *The American Voter*, *op. cit.*, Chapter 19.

The Major Parties as Organisations

The Republican and Democratic parties are different organisation structures from General Motors, the Teamsters Union, or the American Farm Bureau Federation, because their functions in the political system are different. The parties are oriented towards their clientele and are open at most organisational levels to new recruits prepared to work for the party. The American parties are also more open at the top than British parties, if such a strategy will help the power aspirations of the party.

In 1952, for example, General Eisenhower was nominated as Presidential candidate by the Republicans and became President without ever having held elective office or having been a Republican activist for very long (in 1948, in fact, a group of Democrats had approached Eisenhower enquiring if he would like to seek their Presidential nomination). American party organisation is permeable and adaptive, not susceptible to strong managerial control, and given to factional pluralism. Within the parties there are identifiable sub-coalitions based on geographical boundaries (Democratic Congressmen from the Deep South, Republican Congressmen from the Middle West), organisational strength (party delegations from the large states at national conventions), demographic or ethnic categories (Irish Catholic Democratic organisations in the Eastern cities) or broad ideology (the John Birch Society or Goldwaterites within or supporting the Republican party, and New Deal Democrats or the Americans for Democratic Action within or generally affiliated to the Democratic party). Some organisational entities are quite self-reliant and there may often be disagreements between the general goals of the party and the specific demands of a sub-coalition.

Samuel Eldersveld, on the basis of an intensive empirical study of the Democratic and Republican parties of Wayne County, Michigan, within which the city of Detroit is located, argues that party organisation in American metropolitian society is a mass organisation attracting and recruiting activists and followers from the lowest social classes, from minority racial and ethnic groups, and from those with established and traditional social status.[8] Such organisations are not led by a social élite but by a diverse coalition of careerists from all segments of society. Both parties are prepared to seek support where they can, and perform important social as well as political functions. In more general terms, the picture of party organisation that emerges is one of a moderately efficient structure closely linked with the social and economic environment, influencing the voter but having a strong impact on those activists willing to occupy organisational positions. The parties appear as open structures at all levels, preoccupied with the recruitment of new support from individuals in economic and social groups more normally identified with the other party, and prepared to reward such individuals by giving them positions of influence in the party. Their command structure is diffused and rarely élitist, with power proliferating to different strata of organisation representing different sub-coalitions which have equal status and importance within the party. There is no recognised hierarchy of authority or of organisational efficiency. An individual in a prominent position in the party (a state or county chairman) may have little knowledge of the operational strategy of the state party, while a lone organiser at the local level, isolated from élite associations, may be both efficient organisationally and conscious of general strategic considerations. There is no formal pathway to power within the state party organisation.

Ideological attitudes are often muted. Leadership is recruited which is realistic and concerned with democratic goals. The party organisations also contribute to citizen interest in public affairs and to party loyalty, and are not directed by a handful of leaders, maintaining themselves in power by recruiting new careerists with élite attitudes. It is 'an open, stratarchical, sub-coalitional, and pluralised leadership structure'.[9]

This picture of party organisation and competition is valuable, but other studies have produced different evidence. It does, however, provide some qualification to the image of the large cities in the United States dominated by Democratic political machines, patronage-oriented and concerned with maintaining political power. Eldersveld's analysis is of a situation of two-party competition in a state where the party organisations

[8] See S. Eldersveld, *op. cit.*, p. 525.
[9] S. Eldersveld, *op. cit.*, p. 528.

tend to be issue rather than patronage-based. A wider study of the political parties in Pennsylvania, where the parties are competitive at the state level but patronage-based, indicates how constituency expectations can also shape the nature of the parties, and dictate the characteristics of party candidates.[10] The party system in Pennsylvania is decentralised and localised. Although the parties generate discipline in the state legislature, this discipline tends to be the result of local constituency pressures. 'In the state legislature, Democrats and Republicans represent areas of differing political cultures, as well as of differing interests.'[11] Legislators of each party represent distinct clusters of local interests, personal characteristics and values, and varieties of political and party experiences, and these distinctions help to promote party discipline.

The parties reflect an inarticulate ideology based on the common goals of similar constituencies from which they obtain their strongest support. The strong distinction between urban and rural constituencies is shown in the type of party organisation. In the towns and cities of Pennsylvania, party organisation for both Republicans and Democrats is affected by the environment and develops 'machine' tendencies – consistent full-time committee work, patronage-motivated, with internal party discipline and centralisation of authority. In the rural areas both parties have much looser organisations but again party activity is based on patronage. As the Democrats tend to dominate elections in the cities and the Republicans in the rural areas, the nature of the constituency rather than prospects for party victory determines the type of party organisation. Party power at the local level is put at the service of the constituency, and party success is associated with political culture rather than any particular type of party organisation.

What the political party in the United States at the state level is, and what it does, seems to depend less on the wishes of party leadership than on local political attitudes, values and expectations. Its roots lie in the muted conflict and diversity of culture which characterise a pluralistic society. In states where one

[10] See F. J. Sorauf, *Party and Representation*, New York: Atherton Press, 1963; see also E. F. Cooke and E. G. Janosik, *Pennsylvania Politics*, New York: Holt, Rinehart and Winston, 1965.

[11] F. J. Sorauf, *op. cit.*, p. 149.

party has dominated for a long period this analysis will be less applicable, for internal party organisation may lead to intra-party factional organisation based on geographical area or individual candidates, or attempts to control the dominant party by disciplined machine organisation similar to the machine operated by the late Senator Harry Byrd in Virginia, relying heavily on patronage and low electoral turnout. However, party institutions at the state level often differ markedly in form from the national parties, and they are not miniatures of the national party system.

Though the major parties possess a national organisational structure it is based primarily on state party organisations, which in themselves differ in organisation and function, but few possess effective control and co-ordination of local organisations. In only a handful of states do local party leaders and their followers submit to the authority of the state party chairman or even the governor. The national party committees and chairmen also lack the authority and direct influence given to similar party organisations in Britain.[12] Unlike Britain, the basic organisational structure of the major parties at the national level and in particular states is almost identical.[13] This is primarily because state election laws often specify certain organisational requirements. In Michigan, for instance, these requirements help to give district chairmen a good deal of independent authority within the county organisation.

Party organisation in the states is affected greatly by a host of environmental factors, institutional as well as social and polical. At the national level, however, the major parties are concerned to maintain an organisational pattern which will allow them to compete for national political office, rather than with providing a structural mechanism for the discussion and enunciation of policies.

[12] See C. P. Cotter and B. C. Hennessy, *Politics Without Power: The National Party Committees*, New York: Atherton Press, 1964.

[13] See the diagram in J. H. Fenton, *People and Parties in Politics*, Glenview, Ill.: Scott, Foresman Co., 1966, p. 17. For a comparison with the pattern of British party organisation, see J. Blondel, *Voters, Parties and Leaders*, London: Penguin, 1963, Chapter 4, especially pp. 114–17.

National Two-party Politics

It is impossible to analyse closely every facet of the activities of American political parties. We have been concerned here with analysing the role of the political parties as organised groups in the political process. We have seen how, in contrast to British parties, the two major parties are very similar in basic organisation. As managers of government, political parties cannot avoid reflecting in their own organisational structure the structural components of the governments they manage. So the Republican and Democratic parties have become as federal as the nation and as divided at the national level as the different branches of government. Observers have even argued that within the two major national parties exist two distinct parties, the congressional and presidential, the former involving competition between the 'conservative' wings of both parties for control of Congress and the latter involving competition between the 'liberal' wings for the Presidency.[14]

While this may be true in an organisational sense (though it was not the case in the 1964 election), the national parties also serve as vital 'communicators' between men of like mind in the various branches and levels of government. This is so despite the fact that in both major parties there exist a multitude of semi-autonomous groups capable of engaging in the crucial party function of institutionalising conflict over control of political decision-making. Each party agency concentrates on a different aspect of the political process and often engages in competition with other party groups in party primary elections.

Changes in the party system since 1945 have, however, led to a gradual, though not always apparent, deterioration in the independent strength of state and local parties. This is partially the result of the increase in issue-based rather than patronage-based party competition at the state level.[15] State party competition has also increased in areas formerly dominated by one party, the most notable area being in the South.

In 1964 the increase of issue-dominated party competition

[14] See J. M. Burns, *The Deadlock of Democracy*, Englewood Cliffs, N.J.: Prentice-Hall Inc., 1963.

[15] See J. Q. Wilson, *The Amateur Democrat*, Chicago: University of Chicago Press, 1962.

was reflected in particular at the Republican convention, which was dominated by militant conservative Republicans who did not consider themselves representatives of a state party and were not concerned with jobs. They sought to nominate a candidate, Barry Goldwater, who would represent their policy views, and were not concerned with uniting with other factions within the party once they had obtained the nomination. By a strange paradox, a convention which attacked the expansion of the powers of the national government also perhaps heralded the decline in the independent influence of state parties. The Democratic party, since 1952, has also held national conventions dominated by delegates of issue-based state parties concerned about national problems and policies as well as jobs, and their influence has been one of gradually changing the character of Democratic national conventions.

Yet the national party organisations lack effective sanctions over state and local parties and their authority is still diffused. Some attempts were made in the 89th Congress to purge disloyal Southern Democratic Congressmen who did not support Johnson in the 1964 election, but the results were modest. Outside the South, Democratic Congressmen in the 89th Congress tended to support presidential programmes and identified themselves with the national presidential party. Dissension in the Democratic party in Congress comes largely from Southerners, but elections since about 1962 have indicated that party competition is increasing in the South, and this will affect Democratic party cohesion in the long term. The passage of a large amount of legislation in the 89th Congress led to increased discussion of national issues, and the 90th Congress revealed evidence of desires on the part of House Republicans to present positive alternatives to legislation sponsored by a Democratic President, along with an increasing reluctance to ally with Southern Democrats to modify such legislation by coalition voting.

The major political parties in the United States are in a constant process of change, though their primary functions remain the same. Among their activists, practicality and patronage appear to be becoming linked with an increase in idealism and concern for issues.[16] Within state party organisations there has

[16] For an example of this at the state legislative level, see J. D. Barber, *The Lawmakers*, New Haven: Yale University Press, 1965.

been increasing conflict between patronage-motivated activists and groups anxious to emphasise issues and choose candidates supporting particular policies. Study also indicates that there are real differences of attitude between party activists who work for a party and those who vote for a party. A study of Democratic and Republican activists at the 1956 national party conventions[17] indicated that they tend to be distinctive groups who differ sharply on many important issues. They stood furthest apart on issues growing out of group identification and support – labour, minority, low-status and intellectual connections on the Democratic side, and managerial, proprietary and high-status connections on the Republican side. The opinions of these party élites are linked by common party attitudes towards issues.

However, while party leaders diverge strongly, party followers differ only moderately in their attitudes towards issues. Republican followers tended to disagree far more with their leaders than with Democratic party leaders (a presage perhaps of 1964?)! The natural cleavage between leaders was not reflected by the voters. The primary function of winning elections, therefore, serves to force the parties to blur such differences, as does the institutional pattern of national elections, and the existence of a highly pluralistic social and political community. During periods of party or voting realignments, as shown by elections, the real cleavages in society and between the parties may be revealed. In the 1964 Presidential election campaign three major issues, civil rights, the struggle in Vietnam, and governmental welfare benefits, aroused significant contrasting reactions in different sections of the electorate, and on electoral balance strongly favoured the Democratic candidate.

The electorate in the United States is faced at Presidential elections with a choice between parties whose roots and basic values may be very different, but who generally make their appeal in terms of the individual personalities of candidates or appeals to traditional party identification. Activists strive to win the Presidency in order to be able to help a President try

[17] See H. McCloskey, P. J. Hoffman, and R. O'Hara, 'Issue Conflict and Consensus Among Party Leaders and Followers', *American Political Science Review*, June 1960, pp. 406–27. For comparative data, see R. Rose 'The Political Ideas of English Party Activists', *American Political Science Review*, June 1962, pp. 360–71.

to put into practice the policies he committed himself to support in order to win the nomination of his party. Meanwhile the electoral system permits electors to vote for a Presidential candidate, and at the same time a Congressman of the same party who may not support the Presidential candidate on many issues. It also allows electors a further opportunity in the mid-term elections of supporting such Congressional candidates. In order to maximise support and gain Presidential victories the parties are forced to sacrifice party discipline, which is already weakened by the necessities of decentralised organisation. Therefore in order to perform their major functions as mobilisers of interests, channels of communication, and links between the diverse institutions of American government, they become more diffuse and less issue-oriented than the attitudes of party activists would indicate. The need to become complex coalitions of interests means that specific sub-cultural interests within the parties may compete for control of the party, but in order to win Presidential elections they must moderate the specific issue-content of their appeal if they are to obtain the advantages which winning the Presidency brings. In Britain, parties tend to mute intra-party conflict and pretend inter-party conflict on issues in order to win control of government. In the United States, parties often need to obscure the extent of inter-party conflict on issues in order to maximise their chances of Presidential victory.

Political Parties and Presidential Elections

Political parties in the United States are affected by the machinery of elections. The history of American election laws, which are set up largely by state governments, has been a history of attempts by parties or factions to keep or establish procedures likely to preserve their authority or make it more difficult for opponents to obtain power.

In order to be able to vote, individuals must register as voters, and states can determine the qualifications necessary to obtain registration. In some states attempts have been made to set up qualifications such as a literacy test or the payment of a poll tax which on their face do not discriminate but which have been employed by political parties to prevent or discourage certain people from voting. Also each state specifies the way in which the names of the candidates and their parties shall appear on the ballot, and differences in the rules governing the marking of the ballot can affect the way in which an elector casts his vote. Attempts have been made to limit some of the effects of poll taxes and other devices but the absence of any comprehensive national electoral law does make elections confusing for many people.

While there are a multitude of elective political offices in the United States, there are also many elections, some held at the same time, others at different times. The dates for choosing Presidential electors and United States Senators and Representatives are fixed by national law. National elections are held every two years on the first Tuesday after the first Monday in November. The Presidency, one-third of the Senate, and every Representative come up for election at the same time, and two years later the so-called 'off-year' elections involve all Representatives and another third of the Senate. State and local elections need not be held at the same time as the national, but in many instances they are. Local candidates, and their elections, are affected by the national elections, and popular candidates for national office can help to improve the vote for the whole party ticket. Turnout may also be larger, but less predictable, and some states such as New Jersey and Virginia hold state elections in years when there are no national elections to avoid the submergence of local issues and allegiances.

The most important single election is, however, that for the President. The American method of choosing a President is unduly complex and unnecessarily confusing, consisting of a network of elections, nominations, and campaigns. There are two distinct operations involved for any candidate. The first is obtaining the nomination of one of the major parties, the second is conducting a national campaign. The choice of a Presidential candidate is made by the major parties at national conventions held in the summer immediately prior to the November Presidential election. Voting takes place by delegates representing state party organisations. These delegates are chosen by a variety of methods, some by state party committees, some by state party conventions, some by the use of Presidential primary elections, others by a combination of these methods. This takes place between March and July of the election year.[18]

There are strategies which can be employed by an individual in the quest for the nomination of one of the major parties as Presidential candidate, and a great deal depends on the political strengths and weaknesses of a prospective nominee. The first major decision to be made is whether to compete in any of the Presidential primaries or preference polls. In 1972 over twenty states, and the District of Columbia, selected party delegates to the national conventions by primaries held in the spring and early summer before the national conventions. Of these a fair number held primaries in which the delegates chosen were committed to a particular Presidential candidate. However, the performance of a Presidential candidate in these primary elections can influence the selection of convention delegates in states where this is done by party committees or conventions, and so a careful choice is made as to which primaries to contest. This decision is not entirely in the hands of the candidate, for in some states the Presidential preference of a candidate for a delegate position may be indicated on the ballot even if the Presidential candidate has not given his consent. In 1956, Adlai Stevenson found himself running in the 1956 Democratic primary in Florida because well-wishers put his name on the ballot. In some states it is also possible to win a primary without having campaigned in a formal sense, for in ten states it is possible to write-in the names of candidates not officially nominated. In 1964, Henry Cabot Lodge won the first Republican primary in New Hampshire as a write-in candidate, and showed further write-in strength in the Massachusetts, Texas, Illinois, and Nebraska primaries. Yet he refused to resign his ambassadorship to Vietnam in order to come home to campaign. He was later narrowly defeated in the primary in Oregon, and from then on was no longer a serious challenger for the nomination. In 1952, however, strong write-in support for Eisenhower in New Hampshire began a chain reaction which finally led to his selection as Republican Presidential candidate, and to his success in the November election. In 1968, Nelson Rockefeller also obtained a surprise write-in victory in the Republican primary

---

[18] For a summary of this, see N. W. Polsby and A. B. Wildavsky, *Presidential Elections*, New York: Scribners Sons, 3rd edit., 1971, pp. 160–63.

in Massachusetts but did not get the Republican nomination.

In most of the states only registered voters of a party can take part in the primaries. In Wisconsin, however, a voter need not register with one party or the other and can participate in either the Democratic or Republican contest. In some states the preference polls for Presidential candidates are quite separate from the election of convention delegates, and such polls are merely advisory in that delegates need do no more than take note of the fact that various voters prefer certain aspirants. Other states, such as Oregon, make such preference polls binding on state delegates, at least on the first ballot at the conventions. In Oregon the parties may only put up a single slate of uncommitted delegates. The state secretary of state then draws up a list of names of those people he considers are important contenders for the nomination and puts them on the list with or without their consent. Write-in votes are possible, but the winner of the poll is the candidate the convention delegates of each party must support when their conventions open.

In general, primaries are contested by those candidates who feel they need to demonstrate popular electoral support within their own party. An incumbent President wanting another term normally receives little opposition from within his party, and if he does he will seek to avoid any sort of primary contest. Other aspirants seek to avoid the primaries because they feel they are unlikely to do well in them, and that their best chance for the nomination lies at the convention itself. In this respect the strategy adopted by supporters of Senator Goldwater in 1964 is illuminating, not merely because it was unusual, but because it illustrates how individual strategies are often based on, and affected by, external events. This strategy was based on the establishment of Goldwater as a conservative, and obtaining the support of Republican party professionals influential in choosing convention delegations at state party conventions or in state party committees. In 1952, the conservative wing of the Republican party supported Taft for the Presidential nomination, but lost to the moderates who chose Eisenhower. In 1948, the candidate of the moderates also won, but lost the election. Eisenhower, however, was successful, but he failed to maintain a Republican majority in Congress during his tenure as President. In 1960, the conservatives were prepared to accept the protégé of Eisenhower, Nixon, though they were bitterly disappointed on his defeat. In 1964, Goldwater's strategy proved successful and opportune for several reasons.

The first major reason was the weakness of the moderate opposition to Goldwater within the Republican party which was increased by the primaries themselves. The only candidate willing to challenge Goldwater and force him to campaign in the primaries was Governor Nelson Rockefeller of New York. Yet in a situation where personality is often of crucial importance, Rockefeller's private life (his recent divorce and remarriage) weakened his popular support. The refusal of Lodge to campaign to consolidate his early popularity in the primaries further weakened 'moderate' opposition. Rockefeller's defeat by Goldwater in the Californian primary in June 1964 left the attempt by Governor William Scranton of Pennsylvania to unite the Eastern moderates too late to challenge Goldwater. Richard Nixon, whose narrow defeat for the Presidency in 1960 was followed by defeat for the governorship of California in 1962, sought to remind Republicans of his previous experience and of his ability to be acceptable to all wings of the party, but he had no strong basis of support and could only hope that the convention would be unable to agree on any other candidate.

The second reason was related to the internal organisation of the Republican party in 1964, and the current position of the Democratic party. Republican state party organisations were more loosely organised than usual in many states. Lacking coherent party leadership and the unifying influence of patronage (only sixteen states had Republican Governors), many Republican state parties had no strong leadership or committed preference to a particular Presidential candidate. In contrast, the assassination of President Kennedy in 1963 had led to a strong wave of bipartisan support for the new President, Johnson, who had capitalised on this to make the prospects of a Democratic victory in 1964 more probable than might have seemed the case immediately after Kennedy's narrow victory in 1960. Therefore some Republicans probably doubted if any candidate from their party could win in 1964.

The third reason concerned Goldwater's own strategy of building up his support among Republican party professionals. As chairman of the Republican Senatorial Campaign Committee for the 1956, 1960, and 1962 elections he had succeeded in becoming well acquainted with state and local party leaders, which whom he appeared to get on well, both as a personality and in what he had to say. Moreover, alongside this was a deliberate strategy on the part of many conservative political activists to obtain key positions within local and state party organisations and so be able to influence the selection of state party delegations for the 1964 convention. As a result, while national attention was fixed on the primaries, convention delegations were being chosen in state after state composed of supporters of Goldwater and his conservative views. These delegates were less 'professional' in the traditional sense in their view of political realities. They were less concerned with actually winning the Presidency and other elections in 1964 than with gaining control of the Republican party. Goldwater also appealed to professionals because he reflected their views on policies, despite their misgivings as to whether he could win. As a consequence he succeeded in winning the Republican Presidential nomination in 1964 on the first ballot, despite only moderate success in the primaries that he contested.

Few candidates, other than an incumbent President, can afford to ignore the primaries if they are to demonstrate that their claims to the Presidential candidacy must be taken seriously. In 1956, Adlai Stevenson, the defeated Democratic candidate in 1952, despite the fact that he was the titular head of the party, found it necessary to enter several primaries in order to demonstrate the fact that he was still strongly supported within the party. Richard Nixon, in 1968, also recognised the strategic necessity of successful primary campaigns in his quest to obtain the Republican nomination for a second time.

Presidential primary competition is, however, expensive in both time and funds, and requires the creation of a strong personal organisation if success is to be achieved. The financial resources of the candidate are most important at this pre-convention stage, as Hubert Humphrey found in 1960 when his defeat in the West Virginia Democratic primary by John Kennedy was partly due to his lack of funds. His defeat also made it more difficult to obtain further money, and also provided the breakthrough that Kennedy sought.

Some observers indicate that the primaries may be becoming

more significant, especially for the party not in control of the Presidency. The mass media and public opinion polls give the parties early information about the potential popularity of candidates, and also may lessen the actual influence of both primaries and the conventions. Yet primary victories alone cannot guarantee success, as Estes Kefauver found in 1952 when he won more primaries than anyone else but failed to get sufficient delegate support to obtain the Democratic nomination.

Despite impressions to the contrary, the party conventions are serious and important gatherings. They represent the single embodiment of the parties as national decision-making bodies. They also provide the final climax to the preliminary skirmishes which form the first part of an American Presidential election. In this regard the role performed by the national party convention for the parties involves certain hazards as well as advantages, especially for the party not in control of the Presidency. Pre-convention competition for the nominations may well expose differences within one or both of the major parties, and the national party conventions can further expose such differences. Yet, after considerable intra-party debate and conflict, the parties should leave their conventions united in support of the candidates they have nominated to compete for the Presidency and Vice-Presidency. Intra-party competition must be muted if success is to be achieved. In this respect the 1964 Republican convention was unusual in that Goldwater, on winning the nomination, was allowed to choose a fellow conservative as his Vice-Presidential running-mate. The decision seemed calculated to exacerbate party differences, as did certain passages of the speech made by Goldwater when accepting the nomination. Many Republicans left the convention determined not to support the Presidential candidate of their party. This was a marked contrast to the massive demonstration of unity and harmony shown by the Democrats in 1964.[19] However, in 1948 the Democratic convention saw several Southern delegations walk out of the convention, and form the Dixiecrat party to oppose the official Democratic nominee in the general election.

The staging of a national party convention is a considerable feat of organisation. It is attended by large groups of dele-

[19] See M. C. Cummings, Jr. (ed.), *The National Election of 1964*, Washington, D.C.: Brookings Institution, 1966, Chapter 1.

gates, each state delegation being larger than the delegate votes they possess. In 1968 the Democrats had over five thousand delegates and alternates with 2,622 delegate votes, and the Republicans over two thousand with 1,333 votes. The proceedings of the convention are also watched by millions of Americans on television. The national committees of the parties organise the conventions and appoint important convention committees such as the Committee on Credentials and the Platform Committee. The Credentials Committee has the task of approving the credentials of each state delegation. Sometimes rival delegations come to the convention claiming to represent the same state party, and the Credentials Committee has to decide which delegation is legitimate and will be seated and allowed to vote at the convention. This can be important, for such delegations usually support different candidates. At the Republican convention in 1952 an important decision had to be made between rival pro-Taft and pro-Eisenhower delegations from certain states, and at the 1964 Democratic convention rival delegates arrived from Alabama and Mississippi. The latter conflict proved to be a very difficult one. An integrated delegation from Mississippi (known as the Mississippi Freedom Democratic Party), selected at a 'rump' election which followed state statutes and party rules but allowed Negroes to vote, opposed an all-white 'regular' delegation whose attitudes indicated that they might not support the Democratic candidate in the general election. The final decision taken was that the 'regular' Democratic delegation would be seated if each member signed a personal loyalty pledge to support the party candidate when chosen, two of the M.F.D.P. delegates were seated as 'at large' delegates with a vote each, and the remainder of their delegation were welcomed as 'honoured guests' of the convention. All but three of the Mississippi delegates refused to take the loyalty pledge and left the convention, as did many of the 'regular' Alabama delegation when faced with the same decision.

The Platform Committee has the task of listening to a wide range of evidence presented by many spokesmen before deciding on a platform statement to present to the convention. This statement is often influenced by the composition of the committee itself, and though it is not debated in full, it can cause conflict. In 1948, delegates at the Democratic convention voted for an amendment strengthening the civil rights plank of the party platform, at which point delegates from the Southern states left the convention. In 1960, liberal Republicans obtained compromises on the party platform from the chosen Presidential candidate, but failed to obtain similar compromises in 1964. The writing and presentation of a platform does, however, help to find a common ground which may draw party factions together.

The major task of the convention is to select a Presidential candidate. Some candidates, especially incumbent Presidents, are often chosen by unanimous acclamation, without requiring a ballot. Others are chosen on the first ballot, and it is here, or when the selection requires many ballots, that a complex process of bargaining is likely to take place between rival groups of delegates supporting particular candidates. In this situation, those state delegations who came to the convention committed to local 'favourite son' candidates (often their leading party elected official, i.e. Governor or Senator in their state) are likely to be the centre of attempts seeking to persuade them to give their support to one of the leading candidates on the first ballot. Because of this, leading candidates need to set up an elaborate network of communications among staff workers in order to ensure that they know with whom, and when, to take action. In 1960 and 1964, John Kennedy and Barry Goldwater, as leading contenders for the nomination of the party not in control of the Presidency, set up elaborate personal organisations at the conventions to obtain delegate support, even though ultimately both were selected on the first ballot.

On occasions, notably at the Republican convention of 1920 and the 1924 Democratic convention, compromise candidates are finally selected after the conventions become deadlocked. When several ballots are required before one candidate finally obtains the required number of delegate votes, decisions as to whether to hold a further ballot, or adjourn and try again the following day, can be significant, and this power rests in the hands of the convention chairman, who controls the course of the convention. The convention also selects a vice-presidential candidate, but this decision is usually given to the Presidential nominee, and his choice is accepted by convention delegates. In 1956, however, the Democratic candidate Adlai Stevenson allowed the decision to be made by the convention as a whole.

The candidate for Vice-President is usually chosen with an eye to maintaining unity in the party and presenting a strong, 'balanced' ticket. A Governor or Senator from New York state winning the Presidential nomination might well select a Governor from California as his running mate, even if he comes from a rival faction of the party. This action provides electoral strength, unites party factions, and allows the possibility of obtaining support for the ticket from a broad spectrum of electoral opinion. In 1964 Goldwater responded to the geographical aspect of balancing the ticket, but not the ideological, when he chose a fellow conservative Republican from the state of New York. Geographical balance, and the choice of a well-qualified and experienced politician, remain as important as the need to reconcile different factions within the parties in the choice of contemporary vice-presidential candidates.

Such a comprehensive process of selection has produced a wide range of Presidential candidates. Some, like Eisenhower, may be classed as political 'amateurs', others are soon forgotten. Most nominees have been male white Protestants who have held some political office at the state or national level, but there is no recognised path to the Presidency. Not until 1928 did a major party dare to choose a Catholic, and only in 1960 did a Catholic become President. In 1968, however, it was not considered unusual for two Catholics, Eugene McCarthy and Robert Kennedy, to become major contenders for the Presidential nomination. In 1972, a black woman, Representative Shirley Chisholm, was a Democratic contender. However, the major attribute of any candidate is the assessment of their potential to win the Presidential election, and it is in this regard that the Presidential primaries become imperfect but not insignificant indicators of electoral attitudes towards particular candidates. For the party out of office in particular, evidence of popular support within and outside the party is very important, especially if the party activists believe they have a strong chance of winning the election.

The nature of Presidential election campaigns is affected by the personalities and attitudes of the candidates, the issues which surround the election or emerge during the campaign, and the assessment of the electorate made by party strategists. In this regard, any assessment of election campaigns needs to be based on evidence regarding the nature of the electorate and its voting record in elections. Study of available election statistics since 1952 indicate that the voting of the American public demonstrates unusual fluctuations as strong as any in the past century. The movement in a single two-year span from a 42% Democratic vote for President in 1956 to a vote for Democratic candidates for the U.S. Congress in 1958 of close to 57% is a good illustration of this. Since 1948 the average swing has been high both to the Republicans as well as the Democrats. In the Presidential elections of 1952 and 1956 there was a cumulative swing of 10% to the Republicans, in 1960 there was virtual equality, and in 1964 a swing of over 11% to the Democrats.[20] Yet despite such changes, voting studies indicate that there is a high stability of identification with one particular party among American voters, though this does not mean that voters will always support the Presidential candidates of the party with whom they identify, as the 1972 Presidential election indicated.

In the United States, many people have a multiplicity of group loyalties, and such loyalties are not of equal importance at every Presidential election. Some elections may present a clash of loyalties such as faced many low-income Protestants in 1960, with the choice by the Democrats of a Catholic candidate. The social characteristics of many American voters do not form a pattern consistent with the norms of society and this helps to explain the fluidity of the American voter.

A further important factor revealed by studies of voting behaviour which affects the parties and Presidential elections is that, in Presidential elections in which party considerations predominate, the Democrats can expect to win and obtain about 54% of the vote. Yet in every election since 1948 issues can and have won Presidential elections, and two important issues – prosperity versus depression, and war versus peace – have been basic in several of these elections, and such issues are most likely to increase the awareness of voters to issues. This remains so even though only some 15% of the electorate appear to have anything like a wide range of opinions on election issues and some coherent means of assessing policies. As many as 45%

[20] See D. E. Stokes and G. E. Iverson, 'On the Existence of Forces Restoring Party Competition', *Public Opinion Quarterly*, Summer 1966, pp. 159–69.

of voters see issues in terms of group interests and in relation to benefits for a particular group, a further 25% tend to judge politics in terms of the temper of the times and are only indirectly concerned with issues, while the remainder tend to be completely devoid of issue considerations, and many of these may vote totally in response to their attitudes towards specific candidates.

Such factors affect the actions of the parties both with regard to choosing Presidential candidates and fighting the election campaign. In 1952, dissatisfaction with the Democratic Administration and its handling of the Korean War made the choice by the Republicans of a Second World War hero, General Eisenhower, an astute one, especially given the 'built-in' electoral bias to the Democrats and the normal advantage of being the governing party. In 1964, the relative absence of such crucial issues and the choice of a candidate who represented a minority of a party already in the minority, made the Republican campaign strategy of Barry Goldwater, of sharpening rather than blurring party lines, abnormal in terms of party rationality, and disastrous in electoral terms.[21] Any Republican Presidential candidate needs to base his election campaign on the assumption that he can only win by drawing almost monolithic support from Republicans, attracting a majority of 'independents', and obtaining unusual defections among the less committed Democratic identifiers. In turn, the electoral image of a party can be improved by the visible characteristics of the candidate.

Voter behaviour cannot be explained or influenced solely on the basis of group affiliations. While it may be of some significance that a particular aspirant for the Democratic nomination has the support of the leaders of organised labour, or Negro leaders, this does not mean that he or his party can guarantee to obtain the electoral support of all individuals in these groups. The nominating conventions and the election campaigns in 1968 were overshadowed by the effects of the Vietnam War on the electorate, and the issue of the war and the apparent loss of confidence in the Johnson Administration as reflected by the early primary victories of Eugene McCarthy, who directly challenged the policy of a President of his own

[21] See P. Converse, et al., 'Electoral Myth and Reality: The 1964 Election', American Political Science Review, June 1965, pp. 321–36.

party, affected the decisions of the Democratic party in its choice of Presidential candidate and the conduct of the election campaign. Before the 1968 election was underway it became clear that the conduct of the war and its adverse economic repercussions, plus the emergence of the issue of racial violence in the cities, made the outcome of the election uncertain in that there was a visible weakening of the Democratic coalition of support which under normal circumstances would ensure the victory of the Democratic candidate. The recognition by the Republicans that they had an opportunity to effect a realignment of electoral support also influenced the strategies of aspirants for the nomination of both parties, and the thinking of both parties, towards the 1968 election. This was reflected in the dramatic announcement by President Johnson that he would not seek renomination by his party for the Presidency in 1968.

It is necessary to reassert that the American people do not directly elect the President. The votes they cast in November are for electors, and the Presidential candidate obtaining the most votes in a state obtains the whole of the electoral college vote of that state. The electoral college vote of a state coincides with the number of Congressmen in the state, some of the smaller states having only three electoral college votes and large states like California or New York some forty such votes. This means that Presidential candidates tend to be chosen from states with large electoral college votes and seek to win the states with large electoral college votes, especially those states where both parties are strongly competitive. This system also means that it is possible, though unlikely, that a candidate winning a popular majority in the nation as a whole may lose the election in the electoral college. In general, however, the electoral college vote tends to magnify the popular vote margin, since it is possible to win all of the electoral college votes of a state, yet obtain only fractionally more popular votes than an opponent, as John Kennedy did in 1960 in states like Illinois.

It is also possible for no candidate to win a majority of the electoral college vote necessary to be elected. In this event the election is decided by the newly elected House of Representatives, each state delegation having one vote. The strategy of a third party candidate in a Presidential election is often to seek to achieve this situation. It should also be noted that once a President is chosen by the electoral college he does not actually become President until his formal inauguration in January, at least two months after the popular elections.

This brief analysis of the nature of Presidential elections in the United States gives some indication of the complexity of the process and the importance of a variety of strategic considerations which it is necessary for the political parties to consider, though such strategic considerations vary from election to election. The process has also become an expensive one both for the candidates and the parties themselves. In order to obtain the nomination of a party, most candidates must now have a large personal organisation, access to large sums of money outside of funds available to the parties, and an ability to be both attractive and skilful in direct face-to-face contact with voters and in exploiting the facilities provided by the mass communications media for political campaigning. The decision of Richard Nixon, in 1960, during the election campaign, to engage in formal television debates with his Democratic opponent John Kennedy, who at the time was a less familiar and prestigious political personality, had adverse consequences, since Kennedy was able to project an attractive personality as well as emerge from the debates the apparent equal of Nixon.[22]

Total reported spending for election contests at all levels of government in 1968 was approximately $300 million, as opposed to estimated totals of $175 million in 1960, $155 million in 1956, and $140 million in 1952. Major party national campaign costs in 1964 totalled $29·2 million ($17·2 million for Republicans, $12 million for Democrats), compared with $52 million in 1968.[23] In order to gain the 1964 Republican nomination, organisations supporting Barry Goldwater spent over $5 million, as did those for his rival, Nelson Rockefeller. The increasing significance of finance in Presidential elections, and the fact that only 10% of Americans make political contributions, has led to recommendations both to control such party

[22] See B. Rubin, *Political Television*, Belmont, California: Wadsworth, 1967, Chapter 3.

[23] See H. E. Alexander, 'Financing the Parties and Campaigns', in M. C. Cummings, Jr. (ed.), *op. cit.*, Chapter 5. See also A. Heard, *The Costs of Democracy*, Chapel Hill: University of North Carolina Press, 1962.

expenditures and also to lessen the influence of finance on party primaries by the substitution of a national primary election, but there have been few important moves to achieve major reforms beyond tentative debate by Congress. In 1961 President Kennedy established a Commission on Campaign Costs who made certain recommendations in 1962, but these were not then made law. Unlike Britain, there are few formal and enforced limitations in the United States on the amounts that individual candidates may spend in an election campaign.

Attempts to implement more general reforms of the mechanics of the election of the President have been equally unsuccessful. Criticisms of the national party conventions, and of the primary elections as they exist, have led to proposals for a national Presidential primary, but this has been opposed by the parties because it would lessen the influence of state party leaders over the nomination and might also create greater divisions within the parties than is possible at national party conventions. There have also been recommendations for constitutional amendments to change the electoral college system, either substituting election by national popular vote or giving a candidate the percentage of the electoral college vote proportionate to his popular vote in each state. Such proposals have been debated in Congress, but have not gained acceptance, though steps have been taken to try to ensure that the electoral college voters in a state do vote for the candidate winning a popular majority in that State.

The political parties in the United States are vital instruments in an electoral system that often seems cumbersome and confusing. They also play an important role as vehicles for the selection of political leaders.[24] At any Presidential election the American voter is faced with a large number of choices for a variety of elected offices at all levels of government, and for a majority of the electorate the parties provide a significant guide in making these choices and reducing a complex process to the simple assertion and demonstration of the democratic rights and responsibilities of a citizen. Though voting for the candi-

[24] For comparative evidence regarding the nature of political leadership in Britain and the United States, see the chapter by E. C. Hargrove in L. J. Edinger (ed.), *Political Leadership in Industrialised Societies*, New York: Wiley Sons, 1967.

dates of a particular party may often be based on oversimplified, even inaccurate, notions, the parties do provide the vehicles at election times through which important issues can be raised and discussed, new policies formulated and criticised, new political personalities recruited, and new political leaders elected.

However, political developments since 1960 have revived argument as to the relevance and significance of the major political parties and their ability to deal with current crises in American political life. Evidence of increased volatility of voting patterns in national and state elections; realignments in the distribution of electoral support for the parties in certain regions; the nomination of 'ideological', minority candidates by the Republicans in 1964 and the Democrats in 1972 along with the ultimate demise of the old Roosevelt Democratic coalition and of the Democratic party as the normal majority party; the effects of reapportionment, voting rights legislation and the lowering of the voting age on electoral competition, are some of the factors accounting for new demands for party reform and change if they are to retain their accepted role. Some observers have pointed to the development of conditions more favourable to the possible growth of responsible parties,[25] others to the increase in more issue-motivated voting.[26] Criticism has also been made of the archaic nature of current party organisations and the relative lack of genuine citizen involvement in their activities, and their inability to use new techniques available with improved technology to develop as more genuine citizen-based organisations in order to compete effectively with new interest groups, utilising the mass media and rationalising the growth of political consultants as an alternative organisational source to the traditional party organisation.[27]

[25] See, for example, G. Pomper, 'Toward a More Responsible Party System? What, Again?', *Journal of Politics*, November 1971, pp. 916–40. For a useful overall discussion see P. Fotheringham, 'Changes in the American Party System 1948–72', *Government and Opposition*, Spring 1973, pp. 217–41.

[26] See D. E. Repass, 'Issue Salience and Party Choice', *American Political Science Review*, June 1971, pp. 389–400; and a group of articles under the general heading of 'Issue Voting' in *American Political Science Review*, June 1972, pp. 415–70.

[27] See especially J. Saloma III and F. H. Sontag, *Parties. The Real Opportunity for Effective Citizen Politics*, New York: A. A. Knopf, 1972.

Chapter Eight

THE AMERICAN CONGRESS: LEGISLATIVE REPRESENTATION AND ACTION

The formation of the United States Congress was the result of a compromise. The Founding Fathers were sympathetic to new ideas yet many feared the consequences that might follow from the creation of a national legislature chosen directly by the people. It was clear also that the representatives of the small states at the Constitutional Convention in 1787 would not accept any plan which would lead to the domination of this legislature by those states with large populations. The final compromise provided a House of Representatives chosen by the people every two years, and an Upper House or Senate consisting of two Senators from each state to be chosen by the state legislatures to serve for six years, one-third to be chosen every two years. The passage of the 17th Amendment to the Constitution in 1913 allowed Senators to be elected by the people of each state but retained the principle of state representation.

The structure of Congress provided for territorial and popular representation, with the Senate designed as a check on the popular assembly and so maintain balanced government. At first the House tended to overshadow the Senate, but the grant of certain powers to the Senate alone served in time to strengthen its influence and prestige. The Constitution gave to the Senate the power to give 'advice and consent' to the making of treaties by the President and the major Presidential appointments, and these became important as America came to be involved in international affairs, and the executive branch of government increased in size and responsibilities. The House was given the constitutional power to originate all revenue bills and the traditional right to initiate the consideration of bills appropriating

189

money to implement legislation. While these responsibilities have provided sources of influence for House members they have also tended to encourage Representatives to be more parochial in their attitude towards their legislative responsibilities.

Other factors have also helped to make the House in many respects less liberal than the Senate. Representatives must seek re-election every two years and also have a smaller and usually more homogeneous electorate to represent than a Senator. The geographical boundaries of Congressional districts are also determined by each individual state, and this has meant that rural interests have often been over-represented in the House of Representatives. However, the Supreme Court, in a series of decisions beginning in 1962, has taken action to guarantee that Congressional districts be more fairly apportioned, and this has had an effect on the House of Representatives. Yet it remains clear that in many respects the check placed upon the House by the Senate in the contemporary Congress is not the same as that envisaged by the Founding Fathers.

Legislators and their Constituents

The development of representative government in America rests on different values and assumptions to those in Britain. Senators and Representatives alike are expected to be good constituency men who will reflect or be responsibe to the demands of constituents. All Congressional candidates must be residents of the states in which they seek election, and by tradition a Representative must reside in the district he seeks to represent. Constituency loyalty may often be stronger than party loyalty, and it has proved difficult to maintain in Congress the type of formal party discipline which exists in the House of Commons. Voting in the House and Senate may be predominantly along party lines, but this can rarely be guaranteed in advance. Many legislative decisions can be made without requiring a formal vote, but Congressmen need to be very careful when a formal roll-call vote is taken since they may have to justify their formal voting record to constituents.

The formal voting record of a Congressman on any issue is likely to be affected by three major factors; his own policy preferences, his perception of the attitudes of his constituents towards the issue, and the way his party would like him to vote. Contrary to general belief, a Congressman may not always be clear as to the attitudes of his constituents, and fortunately for him they, in turn, may not always be aware of his actual policy preferences. Studies have shown that constituencies vary a great deal, and so do constituency influences, even for Congressmen of the same party. A Negro Representative from New York City responds to very different constituency pressures than a fellow Democrat from a rural constituency in Alabama or Mississippi. Constituency pressures are important, yet it is also clear that 'no single tradition of representation fully accords with the realities of American legislative politics'.[1]

The internal organisation of Congress also allows legislators to perform different representational functions in different situations and on different issues of policy. Miller and Stokes identify several different types of relations between Congressmen and constituents, depending on the policy matters at issue. A Congressman may find himself playing several different roles in the course of his daily round of legislative activities. Robert Dahl has indicated that on foreign policy issues Congressmen may have considerable discretion. Constituency opinion can be influential but 'in many situations, especially in the short run, it is not'.[2] This conclusion is supported by Miller and Stokes, who suggest that Congressmen tend to look to sources other than their districts to help them make up their minds on foreign policy issues. If they are poorly informed on the issues under consideration they may support the position of the President. Over questions of foreign affairs, Congressmen appear to come closest to exercising the type of 'independent' representation so dear to the heart of Edmund Burke.[3] However, over questions of civil rights, Congressmen are more likely to reflect constituency opin-

[1] W. E. Miller and D. E. Stokes, 'Constituency Influence in Congress', *American Political Science Review*, March 1963, pp. 45–56, p. 56. See also C. F. Cnudde and D. J. McCrone, 'The Linkage Between Constituency Attitudes and Congressional Voting: A Causal Model', *American Political Science Review*, March 1966, pp. 66–72.

[2] R. A. Dahl, *Congress and Foreign Policy*, New York: W. W. Norton, 1964 (revised edition), p. 44.

[3] See Miller and Stokes, *op. cit.*, p. 56. For a different view see A. Clausen, *How Congressmen Decide: A Policy Focus*, New York: St. Martin's Press, 1973.

ion and act as delegates, while on questions of social welfare (an area which has been a source of party conflict for many years) party loyalty may be the most important influence.

Constituency influence is, however, both potential and real and can be exercised by party activists who have helped a Congressman win the party nomination and get elected, or by the electorate as a whole. Voting differences between Democrats and Republicans reflect constituency support by appeals to small but important segments of the electorate. Stokes and Miller also argue that over a period of years a Congressman can develop a personal electoral support which extends beyond the support of party loyalists. On some matters he may therefore go against his party because his constituency demands this; on other matters he may vote against his party because he knows his constituency is not concerned as to how he votes. Arguments that Congressmen are tied to the demands of constituents are based on the assumption that electors keep careful track of the voting record of their Congressmen and keep him constantly informed of their attitudes towards policy matters. Election studies and more specific studies by Stokes and Miller, however, reveal that such a high level of interest is maintained by only a very small percentage of the electorate.[4] Many Americans do not know even the name of their Congressman and vote in Congressional elections primarily for party. In Detroit in 1957 only 18% of the people interviewed could correctly name the Congressman from their own district, and only 13% knew the names of both United States Senators from Michigan.[5]

Different representational roles are played in different legislative situations. A case-study of the House Agriculture Committee shows that a Representative can help important constituency interests by being a member of a particular committee, yet may represent party interests by his vote on the final recom-

[4] See D. E. Stokes and W. E. Miller, 'Party Government and the Saliency of Congress', *Public Opinion Quarterly*, Winter 1962, pp. 531–46, quoted in R. E. Wolfinger (ed.), *Readings in American Political Behavior*, *op. cit.*, p. 83.

[5] See D. Katz and S. J. Eldersveld, 'The Impact of Local Party Activity Upon the Electorate', *Public Opinion Quarterly*, Spring 1961, pp. 1–24, p. 20.

mendations of the committee.[6] On separate occasions, in different legislative situations, differing demands may be made upon the legislator, and he must try to reconcile all these demands by his actions.

A Congressman operates in a system which emphasises de-centralisation and the popular representation of interests, and so he must stress the importance of the expressed demands of constituents. He must recognise that whatever kind of Congressman he wishes to be, and how he seeks to evaluate and control outside pressures, he must be accessible to constituents. Many perceptive Congressmen also feel that their constituents are less concerned about policy issues and the way they vote than with keeping open the channels of personal contact with their elected representatives. Diligent service of constituency interests will not guarantee re-election, but it has become an integral part of the duties of all Congressmen. Many Congressmen and constituents alike are suspicious of the federal bureaucracy, and constituents often feel the need to gain the support of their Congressmen in dealing with the bureaucracy. The size of America serves to make Washington seem a remote and unfriendly place for many constituents, and the Congressmen can act as a familiar and powerful link between them and the national government. In a diverse society this social function is important, and the variety of services a Congressman performs for constituents provide an important link between the governors and the governed.[7]

Congress as a whole appears to be increasing its concern with matters relating to the control of the federal bureaucracy at the expense of its powers of legislative initiation, and in this situation Congressmen may consider the service function he performs for constituents to be vital. All members of Congress also have offices and personal staff where such matters can be dealt with efficiently.

The nature of the representational role played by a Congress-

[6] See C. O. Jones, 'The House Agriculture Committee and the Problem of Representation', in R. L. Peabody and N. W. Polsby (eds.), *New Perspectives on the House of Representatives*, op. cit., 1963, pp. 126–7. For information on the degree to which a Congressman can exercise free choice, see R. A. Bauer, I. De Sola Pool and L. A. Dexter, *American Business and Public Policy: The Politics of Free Trade*, op. cit., pp. 406–32.

[7] For examples, see C. L. Clapp, *The Congressman: His Work as He Sees It*, op. cit., Chapter 2.

man depends upon the channels of communications he has with his constituents. The image of his district and his constituents and his interpretation of what he hears does depend also upon the personality of the Congressman and his position in his party and in Congress. His picture of the world inevitably affects his reactions to information and influences his decisions to act.[8] The absence of strong party discipline and the many opportunities available for exercising personal influence in Congress mean that, while a Congressman must be aware of constituency opinion and may have to reflect this more consciously than a Member of Parliament, he has more scope for individual action and has more freedom to determine for himself what his role as a legislator should be, provided he does not neglect the service functions he performs for all constituents.

Successful re-election for a Congressman often depends more on what a Congressman can get by way of appointments, jobs, or contracts for his constituency, or the people in it, than upon his stand on important issues. Edward Kennedy campaigned successfully in Massachusetts in 1962 on the slogan 'Who can do more for Massachusetts?' A Senator such as Senator Fulbright of Arkansas reflects the schizophrenia of the daily routine of a Congressman. Fulbright carefully divides his time and resources between parochial service and constituency work for Arkansas and the resolution of important questions of foreign policy which he must consider as chairman of the Senate Foreign Relations Committee.[9] For Congress as a whole, decision-making is not at the core of its being, but representation is.

The Institutional Structure and Function of Congress

The American Congress, like any legislature, has developed certain formal and informal organisational features designed to help promote effective decision-making and resolve internal differences. The traditional function of the legislature in England – to consider executive proposals, ventilate public criticism and then provide money to support executive programmes – was transplanted in the American colonies, but colo-

[8] See L. A. Dexter, 'The Representative and His District', in R. L. Peabody and N. W. Polsby, *op. cit.*, pp. 3–29.

[9] For other examples, see J. Bibby and R. Davidson, *On Capitol Hill*, New York: Holt, Rinehart and Winston, 1967, Chapter 3.

nial legislatures gradually asserted their power to originate policy. The unicameral legislature under the Articles of Confederation was weak, and while the Constitution established by the Founding Fathers in 1787 provided the executive with strong powers, including a check on the legislature through the veto power, early Congresses operated as policy-makers, with the President a mere administrator of laws. Jefferson found, however, over the question of the Louisiana Purchase in 1803–4, that the executive could act more effectively than the legislature with regard to policy-making. Congress also proved unable to prosecute a war effectively in 1812 or set a policy for peace after the Civil War. While the nineteenth century was sprinkled with dominant legislative figures such as Daniel Webster, John C. Calhoun or Thaddeus Stevens, and Woodrow Wilson in 1885 analysed a Congress which dominated the national government, the twentieth century has seen a decline in the initiating role of Congress.[10] In consequence, Congress has returned to the traditional role of legislative assemblies, that of critic and investigator of the executive. This has occurred because, in a period of tremendous social change in America, Congress has failed to recognise that its position has changed, and internal procedures have failed to respond to these changes. It has permitted the executive to take over many of its responsibilities for the initiation of new legislation. As a result, when Congress seeks to exercise its independent judgment and oppose Presidential recommendations, such action is considered obstructive. Congress is forced to assert its independence by refusing to accept certain legislation, yet by accepting legislation sponsored by the President it appears to be surrendering its authority.

The failure of Congress to respond to political changes is demonstrated by the fact that the elements of internal structure and power analysed by Woodrow Wilson in the 1880s, such as the diffusion of power among congressional committees, remains virtually unchanged. It is an odd irony that the revolt in the House in 1910 against the increased power of the Speaker and the abuse of this power by Republican Speakers Reed and

---

[10] See W. Wilson, *Congressional Government*, New York: World Publishing Co., 1965 (originally published 1885). See also D. J. Rothman, *Politics and Power. The United States Senate 1869–1901*, Cambridge, Mass.: Harvard University Press, 1966.

Cannon, served to increase the diffusion of power within Congress. This continued in the 1920s and was increased by the Legislative Reorganisation Act of 1946, which made committees stronger and more effective and led to the rise of sub-committees, leaving co-ordination and integration within Congress to be achieved by committees and committee chairmen rather than by party leaders. The legislative function of Congress has declined, and the nature of internal organisation along with the growth of the federal bureaucracy has led many 'unofficial' leaders in Congress to emphasise the value of maintaining efficient oversight of the bureaucracy as an alternative role. This can be achieved with little change in existing internal structure. Many Congressmen are prepared to accept this rather than make internal changes which would strengthen the position of Congress as a whole but would also weaken their personal influence on decision-making. Thus Congress has preferred to change its basic role rather than its basic structure.[11] Such a change in role is often easier to achieve than procedural changes which may lead to increased internal conflict and instability. Many Congressmen, however, believe changes should be made through reforms designed to increase party responsibility (at the risk of increasing potential executive control of Congress) and thus help to rejuvenate Congress as a positive initiator of legislation.

Congress has several other functions to perform as well as its legislative function. The Constitution requires Congress to perform a judicial function with regard to the impeachment of civil officers of the United States. The House has the sole power of impeachment and the Senate the sole power to try impeachments. If the President is to be tried, the Chief Justice of the Supreme Court presides over the Senate proceedings. Each House is also the judge of the elections, returns, and qualifications of its members, and is authorised to determine the rules of its proceedings, compel the attendance of absent members, and punish members for disorderly behaviour. Congress also has important fiscal responsibilities constituting the 'power of the purse' conducted by the Appropriations Committees of the

[11] See S. P. Huntington, 'Congressional Responses to the Twentieth Century', in D. B. Truman (ed.), *The Congress and America's Future*, Englewood Cliffs, N.J.: Prentice-Hall Inc., 1965, Chapter 1.

House and Senate, with the aid, since 1921, of the General Accounting Office. The Senate has important executive functions through participation in the treaty-making and appointment processes, treaties requiring the consent of two-thirds of those Senators present and voting. Congress also has a constituent function in that, if two-thirds of those voting in both Houses approve, constitutional amendments can be proposed, and Congress may also have to choose the President if the Electoral College does not produce a candidate with a majority of votes.

Both Houses seek to maintain an appearance of dignified and thoughtful deliberation, helped by an elaborate set of rules and procedures, though the Senate is probably more successful than the House in maintaining such an appearance. The institutional organisation of Congress affects the positions of individual Congressmen, who in turn are subject to external pressures from interest groups or party activists as well as constituents.

Congress can best be understood as a body seeking to reconcile effective representation with the need for decision-making, and to do this requires efficient internal organisation to reduce and refine conflict into agreed decisions. Students of Congress tend to see it either as an arena of conflict and struggle, or as a delicate mechanism of compromise, but all emphasise the need to control internal differences if decisions are to be made.[12]

Any decisions of Congress, however, require the approval and agreement of both the House and the Senate. Formal differences between the two bodies exist and are important. The Senate is a small body, and the fact that only one-third of the Senate needs to be elected every two years makes it a 'continuous' body also. The Senate and its members also appear to have greater prestige than the House. The House of Representatives is very conscious of this and is keen to defend its own activities and assert the importance of its actions. Collectively it is as powerful as the Senate, but it is a bigger institution, debate must of necessity be limited, and freshmen Representatives often feel less secure and more anonymous than their counterparts in the

[12] See B. Gross, *The Legislative Struggle*, New York: McGraw-Hill, 1953; also E. Griffiths, *Congress, Its Contemporary Role*, New York: New York University Press, 1961; and R. Young, *The American Congress*, New York: Harper Bros., 1957. Valuable studies on the role of Congressmen include C. Miller, *Member of the House*, New York: Scribner, 1962, and C. L. Clapp, *op. cit.*

Senate, and see fewer opportunities to become powerful or influential. Representatives tend to be suspicious of the Senate, sensitive to references to it as 'the upper body', and they believe they work harder and are more expert in their specialist areas of interest than are Senators, who often have to serve on several committees. They also believe that Senators need to rely a great deal on the efficiency of their staffs. The House also considers itself to be truly representative of the people and more responsive to their demands.

The House insists that it does superior committee work in such areas as appropriations, and defends its powers granted by the Constitution to originate all bills raising revenue and the tradition of originating bills appropriating money. In 1962 senior members of the Appropriations Committee in the House stated publicly that they were unhappy at the way their Senate counterparts decided on appropriations, and demanded that half of the meetings of conference committees (where differences between the legislative recommendations of the House and Senate are normally reconciled) be held on the House side of the Capitol and chaired by Representatives not Senators. The Senate Appropriations Committee said it would agree to this request if the House in turn would recognise their right to originate half the appropriations bills. This angered the House and resulted in deadlock, with both sides bitterly attacking each other. No conference committee meetings were held for several weeks and appropriations were not made. This created a serious financial problem for some executive agencies who needed funds. A compromise was finally reached, and conferences were held in the old Supreme Court chamber, midway between the House and Senate wings of the Capitol.[13]

This is an illustration of the latent rivalry existing between the House and the Senate which is often obscured by the need to co-operate to reach a final decision on many legislative matters.

The House of Representatives

The actions of the House of Representatives are affected by problems of size, organisation, and party leadership. The sheer size of membership has required the use of certain procedural

[13] See J. L. Pressman, *House* vs. *Senate: Conflict in the Appropriations Process*, New Haven: Yale University Press, 1966.

devices to regulate debate. In such a large assembly, influence on decision-making is not distributed equally. Two types of leadership position exist in Congress: party leaders and committee chairmen. Committee chairmen compete as well as co-ordinate with party leaders in the House such as the Speaker, the majority and minority party leaders, and their party whips. Some Representatives hold both committee and party leadership positions and can exert maximum influence in certain situations.

The workload of Congress is substantial, and there are both individual and institutional demands for specialisation and internal division of labour and responsibility. The rewards and incentives of specialisation to a Congressman, and the increased influence which expertise can produce, create a pattern of mutual deference. A Congressman will defer to the opinions of others he considers expert in a particular area, and in return will find others willing to defer to his expertise. In order to help in developing this expertise and also to perform routine clerical tasks, all Congressmen are given funds to hire personal staff, and are members of committees composed of members of both parties with special committee staff.

A Representative is rarely a member of more than one of the twenty standing committees of the House, and the standing and special committees are the important centres of decision-making. There are also joint committees composed of members of both Houses of Congress. Standing committees of Congress vary in size, but are composed of Congressmen from both major parties according to the ratio of members from each party in either the House or Senate. Bills are referred to standing committees for consideration and they report on them to the House as a whole. Committees hold extensive hearings on important legislation and invite testimony from witnesses representing executive departments, or interests likely to be affected by the legislation. Their decisions are often accepted by the House with little amendment or debate, though controversial legislation may provoke extensive debate and attempts to amend committee recommendations.[14] Committee decisions, however, are

[14] See R. F. Fenno, Jr., 'The House Appropriations Committee as a Political System: The Problem of Integration', *American Political Science Review*, June 1962, pp. 310–24, and J. D. Lees, *The Committee System of the United States Congress*, London: Routledge and Kegan Paul, 1967.

respected in areas such as finance, affording the opportunity for men like Wilbur Mills, of Arkansas, as Chairman of the House Ways and Means Committee, or George Mahon, of Texas, as Chairman of the House Appropriations Committee, to become powerful figures in the House of Representatives.

It is often difficult and unrewarding to challenge committee decisions on the floor of the House even if attempted by a cohesive group of Representatives. Such opposition conflicts with the accepted patterns of behaviour in the House, is generally of moderate electoral value, and can be costly in terms of time, as it is difficult to get precise and accurate information on which to base such challenges. It is much easier to go along with committee recommendations in general. Not all committees, however, have the same prestige and influence, and some can expect considerable floor opposition.

Because of this situation, fiscal committees such as those on Appropriations and Ways and Means are desirable committees of which to be a member, and they have also developed their own methods of controlling the possible consequences of differences of opinion within their committees in order to present unanimous committee decisions to the House as a whole, based on hard and dedicated work in complex areas of decision-making. This makes floor opposition difficult indeed.[15]

The House Appropriations Committee is important because it is given the task of considering many Presidential recommendations for funds to implement legislation. It stands as a 'little Congress' in itself. A new highway programme, health or aid requests, are first authorised by the relevant standing committee, but the programme must receive funds approved by the House and Senate Appropriations Committees before it can be implemented, and Congress as a whole must approve the expenditure recommendations made by these committees. Opponents of legislation have thus an opportunity to limit the scope and effect of legislation if they can obtain support within the Appropriations Committees. Legislation is therefore a two-step

[15] See R. F. Fenno, Jr., *The Power of the Purse*, Boston: Little, Brown, 1966; and J. Manley, 'The House Committee on Ways and Means: Conflict Management in a Congressional Committee', *American Political Science Review*, December 1965, pp. 927–35.

process of authorisation followed by appropriations, and senior members of Appropriations Committees can strike effective bargains with other Congressmen in return for taking certain action affecting funds to implement legislation. The House Ways and Means Committee is powerful because it originates all laws raising revenue, including tax laws and laws regulating foreign trade, complex matters which require a good deal of specialist knowledge.

The House Appropriations Committee has to consider so many requests that it has created an effective division of labour by using sub-committees. This often means that sub-committee decisions by a small group of legislators, working as a non-partisan group, can become the decision of the whole House, and members of such sub-committees find that by reconciling differences within the sub-committee and presenting unanimous recommendations for formal ratification by the full committee, personal and group influence is enhanced greatly.[16]

The position of the committee chairman is of considerable importance, as is the power to determine who becomes a member of a particular committee. A committee chairman is usually the senior member of the majority party with the longest consecutive period of service on a committee, and has a formidable array of reponsibilities. He controls internal committee procedure and decides its agenda and whether and when it will hold hearings on legislation. He can create sub-committees and affect who will be the sub-committee chairmen, what will be the jurisdiction of a sub-committee, and who will be a member. He also chooses, controls and allocates committee staff. Formal position is not, however, everything. Much depends upon the committee and also how well the chairman can control his committee through the distribution of influence to loyal senior committee members, and the checking of dissent by the use of certain sanctions. Co-operation with the most senior minority

---

[16] See G. Goodwin, Jr., 'Subcommittees: The Miniature Legislatures of Congress', *American Political Science Review*, September 1962, pp. 594–604; also C. O. Jones, 'The Role of Subcommittees', *Midwest Journal of Political Science*, November 1962, pp. 327–44; and I. Sharkansky, 'An Appropriations Subcommittee and Its Client Agencies: A Comparative Study of Supervision and Control', *American Political Science Review*, September 1965, pp. 622–8.

party member also helps to lessen opposition. The retention and increase of influence by a committee chairman is often achieved by sharing as well as using his formal powers.

In many respects a sub-committee chairman within the House Appropriations Committee is more powerful than the committee chairman of a minor standing committee such as the Committee for the District of Columbia. He may even be more important than the chairman of the authorising committee whose appropriations requests his sub-committee consider. These facts emphasise the importance of procedures such as the seniority principle and the method of assignment to committees within Congress as a whole.

Committee chairmen usually owe their positions to seniority. Seniority is not mentioned in the House or Senate rules but it exercises a pervasive influence on congressional decision-making. Two types of seniority are important; seniority determined by the length of service in Congress, and seniority based on length of continuous service on a committee. Supporters of the use of the seniority principle to determine committee chairmanships argue that such a standard operates automatically and eliminates the need for bargaining and lobbying for such positions. It helps to preserve a more co-operative and harmonious atmosphere and produces chairmen who are experienced in legislative procedure and in the subject matter of the committee and its relations with executive agencies and departments. Supporters also believe that many of the alternatives suggested (which have included selection of chairmen by the President, or party leaders, or by the senior members of each committee) would increase conflict without guaranteeing a much more representative choice.

Objections to the seniority principle have been general and specific, and its major opponents have been 'reformers' inside and outside Congress seeking less diffusion of power in Congress, increased party reponsibility, and more power in the hands of party leaders. They do not believe that seniority is a fair method of filling important positions, and they also claim that the principle is not always applied strictly in the assignment of members to committees or in assigning chairmen or members of sub-committees, nor in assignment to the delicate bargaining processes determining the final outcome of a bill which take place between the House and Senate at conference committees.[17] The seniority system places too much emphasis on survival and too great an advantage in the hands of members from largely one-party districts, who are often (though not inevitably) 'conservatives', and may be out of touch with the policies of their party and with general shifts in public opinion.

Such opposition reflects a certain frustration at the separation of powers between the executive and the legislature, and the effectiveness of checks and balances within the system, which may allow a party to win control of the executive and the Congress and yet have great difficulty in passing legislation because the seniority system may give congressional power to legislators with different attitudes to those of the President. This was clearly the pattern in the Kennedy Administration, when senior Southern Democrats holding key committee chairmanships, supported by Mid-Western Republicans, formed an effective 'conservative coalition' which succeeded in preventing the passage of a good deal of Kennedy's 'New Frontier' legislation. While the forces of this opposition declined in the face of astute action by President Johnson, especially in the 89th Congress which followed the 1964 election, it seemed difficult to accept that a hardy constitution and a safe seat are the best qualities for committee chairmen to possess,[18] and reform efforts have made chairmen more accountable to their party causes. Before, chairmen did not always apply seniority rigidly in the selection of sub-committee chairmen or members, or in selecting delegations to conference committees, because they liked to delegate responsibility to committee members who tended to reflect their views. In the same way committee chairmen may influence committee assignments and will try to get new members who will work in harmony with other committee members and accept and conform to existing procedures within the committee.

Assignments are decided by party committees, which until recent reforms consisted of small groups of senior party mem-

[17] See G. Goodwin, Jr., 'The Seniority System in Congress', *American Political Science Review*, June 1959, pp. 412–36. See also B. Hinckley, *The Seniority System in Congress*, Bloomington: Indiana University Press, 1971.
[18] See R. E. Wolfinger and J. Heifetz, 'Safe Seats, Seniority, and Power in Congress', *American Political Science Review*, June 1965, pp. 337–49.

bers appointed and influenced by party leaders.[19] Committee chairmen are often in the group or are able to influence their decisions, and seniority may be made the basis of selection, or it can be ignored if required. The way in which this is done has angered many Congressmen, and Senators Clark, of Pennsylvania, and Proxmire, of Winconsin, among others, have protested at this abuse of the seniority system by committee chairmen and others in the 1960s.

Such protests reflect opposition to the extra power which a committee chairman can exercise, yet it is difficult to generalise about committee chairmen. Former Representative Smith, of Virginia, when House Rules Committee chairman, was a prime example of the advantage given to 'conservative' interests by the seniority principle. Smith, and his committee, were the object of a series of executive-inspired moves between 1960 and 1966 designed to lessen their independent influence on the fate of legislation in the House, by changing the size of the committee and the scope of its responsibilities.[20] However, Wilbur Mills, as chairman of the House Ways and Means Committee, though attacked by 'liberal' Democrats for opposing tax increases in 1968, did give President Johnson considerable help on other occasions in getting legislation through Congress.[21] The accession of Mahon to the chairmanship of the House Appropriations Committee in 1964 also helped Johnson check for a time the heavy opposition to foreign aid programmes by the House Appropriations Sub-committee for Foreign Operations, led by Representative Passman, from Louisiana.

A committee chairman can increase his power by having a comprehensive knowledge of the many rules and procedures necessary in a large assembly such as the House which seeks to avoid unlimited delay in making decisions. Clarence Cannon, the former House Appropriations Committee chairman, and Smith, the former House Rules Committee chairman, are good examples of experienced parliamentarians who were able to

[19] See N. A. Masters, 'House Committee Assignments', *American Political Science Review*, June 1961, pp. 345–57.
[20] For analysis of these moves, see R. L. Peabody, 'The Enlarged Rules Committee', in R. L. Peabody and N. W. Polsby, *op. cit.*, pp. 129–64.
[21] See J. Manley, *op. cit.*, and D. Cater, *Power in Washington*, New York: Random House Inc., 1964, pp. 144–9.

translate procedural knowledge and skill into increased power over decision-making.

The Speaker is, however, the most powerful single individual able to utilise his control over procedure to increase personal power. Unlike the Speaker in the House of Commons, this is a partisan position deriving from colonial experience. Along with procedural controls, he has the power to recognise (or fail to recognise) any member wishing to speak, and he can determine whether a quorum is present to allow debate to continue. He also decides, in doubtful cases, which standing committee will consider a bill, appoints special or select committees, and formally chooses conference committee members. The scope of his procedural controls and the element of discretion he possesses give him a reservoir of potential power to affect the course of legislation.

The nature of the process by which legislation is considered in Congress provides many opportunities for individual Congressmen to exercise influence on the fate of a particular bill. A bill must pass both the House and the Senate, and if consideration of it begins in the House, it will be sent by the Speaker for initial consideration to the standing committee which has jurisdiction over the particular subject matter of the bill. The chairman of the committee then has the power to determine how his committee will consider the bill. He may pass it on for consideration by one of his sub-committees or it may be considered by the whole of the committee. He will probably decide to hold committee hearings on the bill, which may be in public or private, and witnesses will be invited to testify before the committee concerning the bill. Such hearings are recorded and printed as evidence to guide committee members, and copies are also later made available to each Representative when the bill is considered by the full House. Witnesses often include senior members of the executive branch, often members of the Cabinet. Following the completion of hearings, which may last for several weeks, the committee will meet in private and decide on the recommendations it will make to the House. These are incorporated in a committee report which is again circulated to all House members and the bill is 'reported out' of committee. It then becomes necessary to decide when and how the bill will be considered by the full House of Representatives. At this stage the House Rules Committee can exercise an important influence on the bill.

The Rules Committee has the task of deciding what rules will apply in the consideration of a bill, and in order to assess this they may also decide to hold hearings on the bill. Following this the Rules Committee will grant the bill a rule which specifies the length of debate and the number and type of amendments that will be acceptable from the floor of the House. It is clear that the Rules Committee helps to maintain an orderly flow of business in the House, and this is necessary since it is impossible to have unlimited debate on all bills because of the size of the House. However, in performing this procedural function, the Rules Committee can and does consider the policy aspects of bills. The chairman and committee members can protect provisions in a bill which they support, but can also make it difficult for other provisions they oppose. They may ask for concessions and revisions to the recommendations of the standing committee, and if these are not forthcoming, they may refuse to grant a rule for a bill, and so exercise a virtual veto over the bill. Some bills such as money bills are privileged and have priority over other bills and do not require action by the Rules Committee. However, sometimes the Appropriations Committee, in violation of House rules, may add 'legislative' provisions to a money bill, and the Rules Committee will often protect such provisions from amendment on the floor of the House. The power of the Rules Committee to refuse to grant a bill a rule can be ended by the use of a discharge petition, signed by a majority of House members, which forces the Committee either to report out a bill with a rule for debate immediately or allow the House to consider the bill without any action of the Rules Committee. A more complicated procedure known as Calendar Wednesday is available, but it has rarely been used to force the Rules Committee to act. Some sessions of Congress have also used a procedure known as the 21-Day Rule which allows a committee chairman on certain days to ask the Speaker to overrule the Rules Committee and bring a bill before the House, if the Rules Committee has not acted within twenty-one days of beginning consideration of a bill. This is a more direct check on the Rules Committee, if the Speaker will co-operate, but it has not yet become a permanent rule of the House.[22]

[22] See J. A. Robinson, *The House Rules Committee*, Indianapolis: Bobbs-Merrill Co., 1963.

The power of the Rules Committee indicates how the procedures of the House provide a series of 'roadblocks' which bills must negotiate and where it may be possible for opponents to delay or defeat a bill. Many bills never get beyond the standing committee stage, or when they do come up for consideration by the whole House they are very different from the original recommendations. It is difficult for legislation to pass the House which does not command almost unanimous support. Legislation sponsored by the President may have to be submitted year after year and face a war of attrition with individuals and groups in Congress opposed to it, and in positions where they can make it impossible for the legislation to pass without amendments or changes. Such a war of attrition took place before the Civil Rights Acts of 1964 and 1968 were passed.

The party organisations in the House find it difficult to overcome this fragmentation of power, where individuals and groups reflecting minority opinions can often use positions gained through seniority to check majority will. They do seek, however, to give some element of central control to House decision-making. They organise to elect their own members to the formal leadership positions in the House, but find it difficult to exercise any permanent discipline of members. Inside Congress, as outside, the parties remain loose and informal groups.

The majority party does, however, meet in caucus to choose the Speaker, the majority leader, and the majority whip. The Speaker is both leader of his party and leader of the House. His formal authority as party leader may not seem extensive but it can be important, as the late Speaker Rayburn, of Texas, demonstrated by a combination of personal respect and skilful use of his personal power. Long periods of one-party control, increased average tenure in office for Representatives, and the institutionalisation of patterns of succession to the Speakership, have contributed to a tendency toward leadership stability in the House of Representatives in the twentieth century. Study of party leadership changes in the period 1955–66 with the Democrats in control, reveal different patterns between the two parties. The Democratic majority was more likely than the Republican minority to resolve the questions of leadership change through non-contested elections or appointments, especially for top positions. An established pattern of succession

(Majority Whip – Majority Leader – Speaker) appeared to have developed. The Republican minority was, however, more prone to intra-party leadership change through contested means, and the longer the party remains in the minority the more it is prone to leadership change through revolt, especially following losses at congressional elections (the best recent example was the revolt in 1965 and the replacement of Minority Leader Halleck, of Indiana, by Ford, of Michigan, which followed the disastrous election results in 1964).[23] However, contests do take place for minor positions of influence within the House Democratic party. At the beginning of the 88th Congress in 1963, House Democrats succeeded, at a party caucus meeting, in defeating one of the nominees of the leadership for vacancies on the House Ways and Means Committee, whose Democratic members formed the Democratic Committee on Committees which determined committee assignments in the House for Democratic Representatives at that time.

The Speaker and the Majority Leader must, however, gain the respect of fellow Representatives and also reflect a high degree of devotion to the House itself. The formal responsibility of the Majority Leader is to control the legislative schedule of the House. He has the aid of a party whip and his assistants, whose main functions are to act as channels of communications between (rather than putting pressure or discipline on) the leadership and the rank and file. New research on the whip organisations in the House indicates that they are becoming more important and successful in increasing party cohesion. Randall Ripley reports on the Democratic party whip organisation: 'the pattern of leadership in 1962 and 1963 was for the Speaker, Majority Leader, whip, deputy whip, and relevant committee chairmen to work closely together in the effort to pass a given piece of legislation.'[24] The importance of the whips depends on the type of leadership exercised by the Speaker or Majority Leader. Speakers such as Rayburn relied on the whips less than others,

[23] See R. L. Peabody, 'Party Leadership Change in the United States House of Representatives', *American Political Science Review*, September 1967, pp. 675–93.

[24] R. B. Ripley, 'The Party Whip Organisation in the United States House of Representatives', *American Political Science Review*, September 1964, pp. 561–76, p. 574.

but they can play an important party role.

Implicit in the formal role of the House Majority Leader to manage the legislative schedule are important questions of strategy in determining legislative priorities, and developing plans about when legislation should be considered. In doing so he will often seek the co-operation of the Minority Leader on certain matters. If his party controls the Presidency he has the responsibility of presenting and defending Presidential legislation. The lack of an effective system of party policy committees means that decisions of party groups are often the result of negotiations and bargaining, but the party leader has a variety of rewards and sanctions available with which to bargain for the legislative support of Representatives who lack seniority and influence.

The House of Representatives is an institution where rules and traditions are of special significance and importance because it is large yet decentralised. Individual specialisation on committees and elsewhere can increase individual influence and provides an effective division of labour. Many of these decision-making patterns exist in the Senate also, but there are other formal and informal processes which are distinctive to the Senate.

The Senate

There are many conflicting views and interpretations of the position of the contemporary Senate in the legislative process, and the nature of its internal organisation and behaviour, but all agree on the importance of the less formal processes of internal organisation in understanding Senate decision-making.[25]

Studies by White and Matthews sought to explain Senatorial power almost wholly in terms of internal, informal, patterns of influence. White argued that while the Senate is no longer, and maybe never was, the most exclusive club in the world, it can

[25] See W. S. White, *Citadel*, New York: Harper, 1956; D. Matthews, *U.S. Senators and Their World*, Chapel Hill: University of North Carolina Press, 1960; and R. K. Huitt, 'The Internal Distribution of Influence: The Senate', in D. B. Truman (ed.), *op. cit.*, pp. 77–101. See also R. B. Ripley, *Power in The Senate*, New York: St. Martin's Press, 1969.

best be understood in these terms. In particular he stressed the importance of the so-called 'Inner Club', consisting of a number of Senators, not all the most senior, who are recognised and accepted as Senate 'types'. Having defined rather arbitrarily what he believes is the real power centre in the Senate, he gives some indication of those intangibles which go to make a 'good' Senator; 'ultimate good faith in what he is about, one of the main criteria of good faith being the absence of petty exhibitionism. An understanding acceptance of the requirement of compromise, and therefore a willingness to abide dissent. A concentration upon the coherent and important and an avoidance of the diffuse and doubtful. A deep skill in sensing what may and may not be done. A gift if not for friendship at least for amicable association with other minds and with the interests of others.' He also stresses human qualities such as sensitivity, discrimination, an 'ardor for life, an *élan vital* that is constant if not necessarily intense, to survive in a trying and hazardous way of life'.[26]

If this seems an excessively subjective analysis, the more intensive study of Matthews (based on interviews with Senators) identified 'folkways' or norms of the Senate which tend to support White. Matthews discusses formal practices such as the seniority system and the rules of comity governing floor debate which restrict individual Senators, but also points to certain codes of behaviour expected of Senators, freshmen or otherwise. These include, for the freshmen, the cheerful acceptance of chores such as presiding over floor debate, making floor speeches only on invitation, seeking advice from senior Senators and getting acquainted with others. For all Senators he emphasises the virtue of becoming a specialist, working hard at unglamorous legislative work, avoiding excessive publicity, ready to do favours for other Senators, speaking well of the Senate as an institution, and keeping one's word.

Many of these behaviour traits could also be applied to the House of Representatives, and while they explain a good deal about Congress they do not tell the whole story. Senators behaving in the expected manner are not guaranteed entry to the 'Inner Club', nor do those who refuse to conform always suffer

[26] White, *op. cit.*, cited in T. Lowi (ed.), *Legislative Politics*, Boston: Little Brown, 1965, pp. 73-4.

or fail to play an effective or legitimate role in the Senate. The Senate has, in fact, demonstrated its tolerance of 'mavericks', an obvious if not entirely happy example being the late Senator McCarthy; another was Senator Morse, of Oregon, who was a Republican, Independent and Democratic Senator! Senator Proxmire, of Wisconsin, has also been regarded as something of an 'outsider', yet he has become an influential Senator. Since 1964, however, there is evidence that many of the old 'rules of the game' of the Senate have been modified, and the 'old guard' Senators have lost much of their earlier influence.

The smallness of the Senate is important, as is its continuity, and the nature of the powers it shares with the executive, especially concerning foreign policy. It is in this respect that the Senate Foreign Relations Committee has often been the most desirable and prestigious Senate committee. All Senators are also accustomed to more deference and respect than Representatives simply because they are Senators. Even the lowliest freshman has the opportunity to exercise some influence, but prestige inside and outside the Senate may be very different, and prestige alone does not bring influence.

The Senate is officially presided over by the Vice-President, but he has little formal power in the Senate, and this is largely a symbolic position. Consequently the party leaders hold the formal positions of power in the Senate, and are helped by whips. Senate committees are vitally important, but Senators must serve on several committees. An influential and senior member such as Senator Russell, of Georgia, in the 88th Congress, was a member of four committees, being chairman of one important committee (Armed Services), an important sub-committee chairman of the Appropriations Committee, a senior member of a Joint Committee, and a member of the Democratic Steering Committee responsible for assigning Democratic Senators to committees.

However, other Senators have become powerful in rather different ways. The late Senator Kerr, of Oklahoma, was never an 'official' Senate leader, but as chairman of the Rivers and Harbours Sub-committee of the Public Works Committee exercised considerable power, and could help Senators by promoting their pet home projects and so obtain a variety of favours in return. Subject-matter specialists can also carve out small but important empires as sub-committee chairmen, examples being former Senator Hill, from Alabama, with the Appropriations Sub-committee for the Departments of Labour and Health, Education and Welfare, and Senator Jackson, of Washington, with his sub-committee of the Senate Government Operations Committee dealing with national security policy machinery. Investigating sub-committees can also give Senators considerable public prominence, as the late Senator Kefauver, of Tennessee, and Senator McClellan, of Arkansas, demonstrated through investigations of organised crime and illegal union activities in the 1950s. The work done by the then Senator Truman as chairman of the Senate Special Committee to investigate the National Defence Programme in 1941–4 helped him become Vice-President in 1944, and he became President on the death of Roosevelt.

The position of the party floor leader in the Senate is difficult and complex. He is at the centre of the party communications network in the Senate, and can control the scheduling of floor consideration of bills and influence party assignments to committees. He is immediately recognised by the Chair if he wishes to speak, and the Majority Leader has the difficult task of trying to control debate and activity in a body where individuals have considerable freedom of action.[27]

The Senate conducts much of its business by unanimous consent, where debate is limited and rules set aside. But if one man objects all this is ended. Because of Senate Rule 22, which allows for the possibility of 'unlimited debate', a determined minority can filibuster or seek to 'talk out' a bill to which they object. This illustrates the latent anarchy which exists in the Senate. Attempts have been made to control debate by applying a closure rule to end such a filibuster, but it is not easy to invoke. It requires a petition of sixteen Senators backed by two-thirds of those Senators present and voting. After cloture has been imposed each Senator has a limited time in which to speak. Senators are reluctant to use this device to curb debate, and it can make the position of the Majority Leader a frustrating one. In times of national emergency, such as in 1932 and the passage of the New Deal programme, he can lead the Senate. At other

[27] See R. K. Huitt, 'Democratic Party Leadership in the Senate', *American Political Science Review*, September 1961, pp. 566–75.

times he may have great difficulty in controlling Senators in his own party. A great deal depends on the type of person chosen as Majority Leader. Observers have contrasted the way in which Lyndon Johnson performed this role in the 1950s with the strategy of his successor, Senator Mansfield of Montana. Johnson was Democratic Majority Leader under a Republican President Eisenhower, and he sought to use his powers of persuasion to the utmost in order to get what he wanted. Mansfield, in contrast, deliberately sought to be a different kind of leader, less assertive and coercive, and with a rather different problem of working for the success of the programme of a Democratic President, though his style changed little after 1968.

In his study of political parties in Congress, Truman claims that the Senate Majority Leader tends to be a moderate within his party who seeks to build a bipartisan coalition in support of bills.[28] Party leaders in the Senate are not without inducements, but how they exercise them depends on the situation and the individual involved.

The internal political organisation of the Senate is controlled but not dominated by a coterie of influential men. The Senate tends to make decisions on a group basis, dividing power and work (not always equally) among almost all its members. Even deviants or 'mavericks' are not without prestige, power, or usefulness. Ties of party, regional interest, and policy preference, along with personal attitudes, produce shifting coalitions who form and regroup as different issues are considered. Party leaders seek to concentrate power in the Senate in their own hands, but in general it has become more decentralised, and the committee system emphasises this decentralisation. As in the House, bills are sent to bipartisan standing committees, where seniority rules. There are almost as many standing committees in the Senate as in the House, and so Senators must specialise and be prepared to defer to the specialist opinion of fellow Senators on substantial questions of public policy. Expertise may be more crucial than formal position and co-ordination is sought through party leadership and appeals to party loyalty. Independence, however, is possible and considered legitimate, as Southern Democrats have shown in their use of the filibuster to oppose civil rights legislation.

[28] See D. B. Truman, *The Congressional Party, op. cit.*, pp. 140 and 242.

The Staffs of Congress

An important if neglected aspect of Congressional organisation is the influence of the professional staffs of Congress. Each Congressman has a separate office and funds to hire a sizable staff, who help him with the heavy burden of legislative and non-legislative tasks he feels obliged to perform.[29] In many ways they become the 'eyes and ears' of Congressmen, especially Senators. They handle mail, see visitors, take telephone messages, as well as perform a variety of research tasks relating to pending legislation and the policy interests of the Congressman.

Professional staffs attached to committees are also important. The Legislative Reorganisation Act of 1946 initiated this legislative 'bureaucracy', and they have proved effective assets to committees in fulfilling their role of oversight and control of executive agencies. Many committees have developed valuable informal channels of communications with executive departments and agencies through their staffs, and they are also useful to committee or sub-committee chairmen at hearings. The increase and establishment of such staffs has raised some problems, in that as the committee chairman has the job of recruiting staff he may use them to strengthen his personal position. Members of the minority party on a committee may be starved of staff, and so there have been demands for partisan professional staffs on committees, with minority staff chosen and responsible to minority party members. This is opposed by some senior Congressmen, who are also reluctant to encourage rapid increases in committee staffs. They believe this may increase disagreement within committees, making them more difficult to control.

While the provision of factual information should help the legislator, some Congressmen fear it might lessen the opportunity for bargaining based on mutual self-interest which exists on many committees. Many Congressmen also see staffs as potential rivals because of the bureaucratic tendencies likely to follow the increase in such staff beyond a certain number. However, so long as Congress continues to emphasise the importance of oversight and control of executive agencies, so the role of the professional staffs is likely to expand.

[29] See K. Kofmehl, *Professional Staffs of Congress*, West Lafayette, Ind.: Purdue University Press, 1962.

Party and Congress

Party cohesion in Congress is generally believed to have existed in the early Congresses, especially in the Jeffersonian era.[30] Recent study has cast doubt on such analysis. It suggests that legislators in this period did not acknowledge party affiliation. While group discipline and preconcerted voting existed, party activity and party discipline did not exist in a formal sense. This revisionist interpretation emphasises the significance of boarding-house cliques and state delegations of Congressmen, often sectional and ideologically factional, in forming the basis of unified voting patterns out of which developed the more conventional partisan politics of Congress in the era of President Jackson.[31] This does not mean that Jefferson as President did not try to exercise influence over Congressmen of his party in the House of Representatives, but that in Congress at this time party members did not elect leaders, the parties had no whips, no seniority leaders, and none of the organisational apparatus which mark congressional parties in the twentieth century. Leaders existed in Congress, and certain Congressmen could be identified as spokesmen for Jefferson in Congress, but Jefferson did not establish a recognised position of leadership of the majority party because Congress did not want such positions. While there is evidence of increased party cohesion in formal roll-call voting in the 1840s and 1850s, the initial sub-division of the congressional community into minority blocs is important because, despite the development of a more formal organisational structure within Congress based on party, the separation of powers and sectional or state differences have consistently allowed groups of legislators the opportunity to act independently of fellow party members within their own body and of a President of their own party.[32]

[30] See N. E. Cunningham, Jr., *The Jeffersonian Republicans 1781–1801*, Chapel Hill: University of North Carolina Press, 1957; also W. N. Chambers, *Political Parties in a New Nation*, New York: Oxford University Press, 1963; and J. Charles, *The Origins of the American Party System*, New York: Harper, 1961.

[31] See J. S. Young, *The Washington Community 1800–1828*, New York: Columbia University Press, 1966; also R. P. McCormick, *The Second American Party System*, Chapel Hill: University of North Carolina Press, 1966.

[32] See Young, *op. cit.*, pp. 126–31, also J. H. Silbey, *The Shrine of Party: Congressional Voting Behavior, 1841–1852*, Pittsburgh, Pa.: University of Pittsburgh Press, 1967.

The creation of a permanent bipartisan committee system also allowed groups of Congressmen to develop a degree of independent authority which may often dilute party cohesion. In 1885 Woodrow Wilson indicated that while national parties were well defined outside Congress, inside Congress they were obscure and intangible, and committees were partially responsible for this.

By 1885 political parties in the Senate 'were still without coherence, exercising only limited influence'.[33] Party organisations had assumed some importance on questions of reconstruction after the Civil War, but party caucus activity and discipline in general was unusual. Analysis of roll-call votes in the Senate between 1869 and 1887 indicate that on most legislation party harmony was minimal. However, by the end of the century the situation had changed. Party ranks stood firm on votes on tariff legislation, and on foreign affairs and appropriations, and in the 1890s party unity became normal on key roll-call votes.[34]

In the House, the strengthening of the powers of the Speaker, begun in 1890 by Republican Speaker Reed, led to increased party responsibility and concentrated majority party leadership. The use of these powers also served to mobilise and strengthen formal opposition, and in 1910 a coalition of insurgent Republicans and Democrats succeeded in destroying the system of party government, party discipline, and majority rule based on the Speaker. Yet between 1910 and 1920 party caucuses succeeded in retaining a good deal of party responsibility in the House, especially during the Wilson Administration.[35]

In the Senate, while this period was one of political change, analysis of formal roll-call votes indicates that the parties remained quite unified, and few Senators crossed party lines to record their votes. On many of the most controversial issues the majority of Senators were able to agree with party colleagues, despite the wide divergencies of constituencies represented. The Republicans rather than the Democrats seemed more anxious to maintain discipline, though the larger the size of the repre-

[33] D. J. Rothman, *op. cit.*, p. 39.
[34] See Rothman, *op. cit.*, pp. 86–90.
[35] See G. Galloway, *History of the House of Representatives*, New York: Crowell, 1961, Chapter 9.

sentation of the majority party, the more prone it was to factionalism.[36]

Between 1918 and 1945, however, the party caucus slowly lost influence, party discipline declined and party government in the House was gradually replaced by loose coalitions of voting blocs with shifting leaderships. Efforts to bind party members to vote for measures designed to carry out election pledges were rarely made. A similar pattern of change occurred within the Senate. Such a situation has considerable implications for the position of a President with a majority from his own party in both branches of Congress.

Evidence suggests that party may have a stronger effect on roll-call voting than constituency in the contemporary Congress, but this may vary depending on particular issues. Julius Turner indicates that despite the importance of the coalition of Southern Democrats and Republicans in opposition to the programmes of President Truman, only 5% of the 1950 House membership voted more often with the opposition than with their own party, but certain issues caused greater cleavages than others.[37] However, this information may be scant comfort to a President. Even with a majority in Congress of his party, he cannot rely on the support of all of them. Fred Greenstein indicates the extent of this problem in demonstrating that in the 1961 session of Congress, only forty-one Democratic Senators out of sixty-four supported President Kennedy more than 60% of the time, and House roll-call voting followed a similar pattern. In both the Senate and the House there were sufficient Democrats, especially Southerners, to join with Republicans to defeat the Administration or obtain a modification of its stand on several important legislative issues.[38]

The importance of the effect of particular issues on party loyalty in Congress can be seen by reference to congressional votes on foreign aid. Leroy Reiselbach has indicated, by reference to roll-call analysis over a period of time, that the degree of party unity over matters relating to foreign aid can vary

[36] See J. M. Clubb and H. W. Allen, 'Party Loyalty in the Progressive Years: The Senate 1909–1915', *Journal of Politics*, August, 1967, pp. 567–84.

[37] J. Turner, *Party and Constituency*, op. cit., pp. 29–32, 70–5.

[38] See F. I. Greenstein, *The American Party System and the American People*, op. cit., pp. 89–90.

considerably, and is affected by a number of external factors. In the 76th Congress (1939–40) the parties in the House were ranged with near unanimity on opposite sides of the question, in the 77th and 80th Congresses a few members of each party broke ranks, and by 1958 the Republicans in the 85th Congress had come to provide a proportionately greater share of their votes to the support of foreign aid, as Table 8:1 indicates. The election of a Republican President in 1952 with an internationalist bent, and the increased fiscal conservatism and isolationism among Southern Congressmen, affected the general question, but party support became much less important as a

Table 8:1

DISTRIBUTION OF REPRESENTATIVES ON FOREIGN AID,
BY PARTY AND CONGRESS

Party and Voting Position	Congress					
	76th	77th	80th	83rd	85th	88th
	%	%	%	%	%	%
Republicans						
Isolationists	81·9	84·0	24·4	36·7	36·8	60·9
Internationalists	0·0	6·2	14·4	55·2	54·9	11·7
Moderates	1·7	8·6	52·4	4·5	5·4	25·7
Democrats						
Isolationists	0·0	4·1	3·1	13·4	29·8	23·2
Internationalists	79·8	89·1	65·6	72·2	47·1	68·0
Moderates	8·4	0·0	20·0	11·1	20·6	2·7

Note: Those who voted infrequently are omitted.
Source: L. N. Reiselbach, 'The Demography of the Congressional Vote on Foreign Aid, 1939–1958', *American Political Science Review*, September 1964, p. 578, and *The Roots of Isolationism*, Indianapolis: Bobbs-Merrill, 1966, p. 197.

determinant of foreign aid voting in 1958 than it had been almost twenty years before.[39] However, in the 88th Congress party affiliation again became the distinguishing feature and the Republican party offered a significantly greater proportion of the opposition to the foreign aid programme.

Different types of legislative issues affect the degree of party cleavage, as do questions as to whether an issue is procedural or

[39] See L. N. Reiselbach, 'The Demography of the Congressional Vote on Foreign Aid, 1939–1958', *American Political Science Review*, September 1964, pp. 577–88.

substantive, or both. Table 8:2 illustrates the differences in party cohesion on different types of matters. The figures are averages for the period 1961–63 on matters of both procedure and substance. The table indicates that in moving from procedural to specific substantive questions, cohesion within the majority party, the Democrats, decreases. Matters such as adoption of rules, conference reports and final passage, which were generally proposed by the Democrats, found Democrats more cohesive than Republicans. However, on Republican proposals of substantive alternatives to Democratic measures

Table 8:2

PARTY COHESION AVERAGES ON ALL CONTESTED HOUSE ROLL-CALLS, BY CATEGORY, 1961–1963

Figures indicate the percentage of Democrats and Republicans voting alike on the roll-calls analysed

Category	Average	Rank	Average	Rank
Election of Speaker	100·0	1	100·0	1
Rules	90·6	2	77·9	6
Miscellaneous Procedure	84·5	4	91·9	2
Final Passage	85·2	3	78·0	5
Recommital motions	84·1	5	87·8	3
Conference Reports	82·6	6	78·1	4
Amendments	76·6	7	77·7	7
	Democrats		Republicans	

Source: L. A. Froman, Jr., and R. B. Ripley, 'Conditions for Party Leadership: The Case of the House Democrats', *American Political Science Review*, March 1965, p. 57.

(motions to recommit to committees, amendments) and on miscellaneous procedures, Republicans were more cohesive than Democrats. Defections seem less likely on motions sponsored by a particular party.[40]

In a comparative study of roll-calls in the House of Representatives from 1947 to 1962 on farm, city, labour and Western issues, distinct differences in the type of party cohesion between the Democratic and Republican parties were found. In voting on each of these sets of issues, Democrats from constituencies

[40] See L. A. Froman, Jr., and R. B. Ripley, 'Conditions for Party Leadership: The Case of the House Democrats', *American Political Science Review*, March 1965, pp. 52–63.

affected by the legislation were more cohesive than Democrats from constituencies indifferent to the issue. The reverse, however, was true of the Republicans. 'Interested' Democrats scored considerably higher in party loyalty than 'interested' Republicans, and were helped on many occasions by Democrats whose constituencies were unlikely to be affected by the legislation voted on. This was even shown by reference to Southern Democrats. While a large number of Southern Democrats had low party loyalty scores, a bloc of Southern Democrats consistently supported party positions on city and labour issues. While the Democratic party sought to operate as a party of 'inclusive compromise', Republicans joined in opposing farm and housing bills, and only a minority found itself on any single issue unable to support the party because constituency interests demanded support for the legislation. Whereas 'interested' minorities in the Democratic party supported each other's programmes, 'interested' minorities in the Republican party stood alone.[41]

The result of this for the Democratic party has been that, when in the majority since 1945, they have required House majorities of different sizes in order to pass legislation to gratify their different minorities, and for city and labour issues this required Democratic memberships of over 280, and this was not achieved until 1964 when the Democrats totalled 294 in the House. The nature of party cohesion in the House means that simple majorities for one party or the other may be insufficient to obtain much legislation for a President of the same party, and for the Democrats the size of this majority determines the type of legislation which will have a strong chance of success. The failure of many attempts to increase party cohesion reflects a simple fact that many Congressmen, unlike M.P.s, do not believe that re-election depends on their strong support for their party. However, if party discipline is weak, party identification is a reality, and cohesive party factions are important.

Congressional Reform

Not all Congressmen accept or are happy with the existing mechanisms of legislative decision-making, and many are concerned at the role played by Congress. The separation of powers guaran-

[41] See D. R. Mayhew, *Party Loyalty Among Congressmen*, Cambridge, Mass.: Harvard University Press, 1966.

tees Congressional influence, and the Founding Fathers built under each branch of government institutional and political foundations to sustain it in the face of political circumstances, and many would like to see Congress reassert its position as a legislative innovator. Younger, aggressive, reform-minded Congressmen, especially from the majority party, often feel frustrated in a situation where prime emphasis is placed on seniority, deference, specialisation and conservatism. Two brief examples demonstrate this.

In the House of Representatives there has developed an organisation known as the Democratic Study Group, containing over 100 northern and western 'liberals'. In an effort to increase their influence within their party and in the House they hold meetings to settle positions on policy issues, organise their own whip system, and have a special staff.[42] They operate rather like a back-bench party committee in the House of Commons. In 1965 they achieved a notable breakthrough, forcing changes in party ratios on the Appropriations and the Ways and Means Committees, disciplining two recalcitrant Southern Democrats, and limiting to some extent the 'independence' of the Rules Committee. The Democratic party leadership has reacted in an ambivalent way to the activities of the group, supporting their requests if they can persuade the House to accept them, but not giving the group any official party status.

They have increasingly sought to strengthen the party caucus as a decision-making body. In 1969 they succeeded in getting the party caucus to 'purge' several Southern Democrats of committee and party seniority because they did not support the Democratic Presidential candidate in 1968. They have also used the party caucus to challenge and change committee assignments made by the Democratic Committee on Committees, and to require committee chairmen to be formally elected by the caucus at the beginning of each session of Congress. In 1962 and 1971, due largely to their pressure at the time of the selection of new Speakers, they obtained some procedural concessions designed to weaken the influences of seniority and the autonomy of committee chairmen.

As a consequence of wider demands and pressures from vocal

[42] See K. Kofmehl, 'The Institutionalisation of a Voting Bloc', *Western Political Quarterly*, June 1964, pp. 256–74.

reformers,[43] a Joint Committee on the Organisation of Congress was created in 1965 to consider questions of Congressional reform. The Committee obtained testimony from a wide range of sources, and its final recommendations were subject to a good deal of opposition. It was not until 1970 that a new Legislative Reorganisation Act was passed. The Act consisted of four principal sections, concerning the committee system and floor procedures, sources of congressional information, legislative oversight and fiscal controls, and general housekeeping. The most important section consisted of a series of proposals known as the committee 'bill of rights', intended to meet some of the major criticisms of standing committee behaviour such as the excessive secrecy and autonomy of many committees, the independent authority of committee chairmen and the advantages accruing to senior committee members. Committees were required to fix regular dates for meetings which might be held even in the absence of the chairman, committee meetings should be open unless a majority of the committee deem otherwise and hearings open to radio and television coverage, and committee reports include all committee votes (with the votes of individuals recorded) and be more readily available before consideration of committee recommendations. The effects and vigour of the implementation of these proposals have been mixed, but in time they could help to eliminate some of the less democratic and anomalous features of the committee system. In 1973 the House of Representatives created a Select Committee on Committees to consider other matters of committee reform.

The 1970 Act also included recommendations designed to speed up the process, involving the use of electronic voting in the House, and encouraging an increase in recorded votes. Rules were also set up limiting the number of committee and sub-committee chairmanships an individual Senator could hold. The Act also set out changes designed to strengthen the ability of standing committees to exercise oversight on admini-

[43] See J. S. Clark, *Congress: The Sapless Branch*, New York: Harper and Row, 1964; J. S. Clark *et al.*, *The Senate Establishment*, New York: Hill and Wang, 1963; J. S. Clark (ed.), *Congressional Reform: Problems and Prospects*, New York: Crowell, 1965; also R. Bolling, *House Out of Order*, New York: E. P. Dutton Co., 1965.

strative implementation of legislation, and to improve the committee and general resources for obtaining information. More changes are, however, likely to be needed if Congress is indeed going to reassert its role of legislative initiator and continue the constitutional challenge begun in the late 1960s to Presidential authority. There is evidence of a significant change in the personnel, attitudes and mores of Congress[44] which may lead ultimately to the development of new patterns of internal influence and procedures and the emergence of Congress as a more responsible and positive legislative force as well as a more effective overseer of the bureaucracy.

[44] See, for example, J. S. Saloma III, *Congress and the New Politics*, Boston: Little, Brown, 1969; also N. W. Polsby, 'Goodbye to the Inner Club', in N. W. Polsby (ed.), *Congressional Behaviour*, New York: Random House, 1971, and J. D. Lees, 'Reorganization and Reform in Congress – Legislative Responses to Political and Social Change', *Government and Opposition*, Spring 1973, pp. 195–216.

Chapter Nine

THE DIRECTION, CO-ORDINATION AND ADMINISTRATION OF POLICY

The American governmental system is a Presidential system. The most important political leader is the President. The Presidential system is also mirrored in the scheme of governmental organisation set out by each of the fifty states. A particular combination of characteristics makes this system unique. In contrast to Cabinet government, the executive in the United States is elected directly by the people and not the legislature. The result is that at times the American President is extraordinarily powerful, at others his powers seem far more limited than any Prime Minister in Britain. The Constitution, the Supreme Court, and historical development, together have given him great potential authority, yet no President can avoid the need to spend a great deal of time bargaining and persuading other political decision-makers in order to get even a fraction of what he wants by way of legislative or administrative action. While performing the major symbolic role in political life in America he cannot avoid the constant demands of partisan politics as leader of a political party. While making important decisions on foreign policy and national security he cannot neglect his responsibilities as superintendent of the day-to-day administration of the operations of the national government and the application and implementation of legislation.

The American Presidency is therefore something of a paradox. The President is head of an administration consisting of over two and a half million personnel which must be controlled and directed, and the major dilemma facing any contemporary President is how best to harness these administrative resources to translate specific goals and plans into effective programmes and policies. The President occupies an isolated position both within the political process and within the executive of which he is head, and the powers of persuasion necessary to obtain the support of other branches of government are also necessary to control his own branch. It is the task of the President to overcome this dual isolation through the help of certain facilities which are at his disposal if he wishes to utilise them.

Presidential Supports as Executive Co-ordinator

The resources available to the President are varied. Some are constitutional powers, others are a product of the development of the responsibilities of the President, and different Presidents utilise different resources, depending on how they perceive their personal role and their evaluation of the utility of particular resources to achieve certain goals.

Constitutional powers are important, but they are not completely under the control of the President. Perhaps the most significant is the President's power of appointment. If the chief executive is to be held accountable for administration of the laws he should have a controlling voice in appointing those through whom he must act in fulfilling this responsibility. By the selection of key administrative personnel in sympathy with his basic objectives, the President can exert a significant influence over government policy in every area. This power of patronage is extensive, and it should be remembered, in contrast to Britain, that while the majority of bureaucrats are career federal employees, the top-level positions in departments are held by personal appointees of the President. In a nominal sense the appointive authority of the President is considerable, though by the Constitution and by law many of these are subject to the advice and consent of the Senate. This limitation does force a President to tailor his nominations to conform to certain political realities.[1] Nor can the President always guarantee that the individual he would like to appoint is prepared to accept the position.

The degree of Senate involvement in the selection process tends to vary with particular offices. The top-level appointments to Cabinet positions which are closely linked with the

[1] See J. P. Harris, *The Advice and Consent of the Senate*, Berkeley: University of California Press, 1953.

President's discharge of his constitutional duties are rarely challenged. Not until 1834 did the Senate reject a Cabinet post nomination, when they failed to act on the nomination by President Jackson of Roger Taney for the post of Secretary of the Treasury. Ambassadorial nominations have been most subject to Senate opposition and rejection, and the Senate appears to take a more independent line over appointments to major independent boards and commissions and may also challenge Presidential nominees to the Supreme Court. Two nominees of President Nixon were formally rejected in 1969 and 1970 respectively. Some lower-level appointments are subject to the limitations of 'Senatorial courtesy' whereby the Senate will confirm nominees only if they are acceptable to the Senator or Senators of the President's party within whose patronage jurisdiction the position is felt to lie.

In short, the President's appointing powers are not unlimited, but they do allow him to choose individuals who are prepared to co-operate with him to occupy the most important positions within the bureaucracy. His power to remove executive officials is limited to some extent by Congress, but it serves as a useful tool to maintain co-ordination and harmony within his administration. He may also invite individuals who are not members of his own party to occupy important positions as heads of major governmental departments. In the Democratic administrations of both John F. Kennedy and Lyndon Johnson, Republicans served as key department heads for lengthy periods, notably Douglas Dillon as Secretary of the Treasury, Robert McNamara as Secretary of Defence, and John Gardner as Secretary of Health, Education and Welfare. The fact that such department heads are rarely professional politicians who normally can be removed without serious political repercussions can help a President in his role as co-ordinator of the executive. The President faces the increasing possibility of conflict within his administration between major departments over policies or funds. Such conflict is political and may often lead to Congressional interference, which in turn may affect the direct relationships between the President and Congress over matters of legislation. Congress may threaten to cut the funds of an agency or department if the President does not take steps to remove its head. The extent of independent removal powers available to the

President is therefore hedged about by political influences and depends upon the political situation and the extent to which he believes he should exercise such authority. He has more flexibility than a Prime Minister in this regard, and there is likely to be less individual political risk involved in taking action, since there are few department heads who build up strong political support which they can use to counter any removal attempts by the President (one possible exception being J. Edgar Hoover, when head of the Federal Bureau of Investigation).

The formal co-ordinating body within the executive is the Cabinet, but, like the modern Prime Minister, the modern President has developed a more personal informal organisation which is directly responsible to him. This organisation was created by executive order in 1939, and is known as the Executive Office of the President. Its principle units are the White House Office, the Bureau of the Budget, the Council of Economic Advisers, and the National Security Council.

A major recommendation of the Committee on Administrative Management, appointed by Roosevelt in 1937, was an increase in the White House staff. The core of this organisation is the personal staff of the President, individuals chosen carefully by the President to reflect his views and attitudes, but also with the opportunity to influence these views on specific issues. It is this latter quality that has made such positions very attractive. The electoral success of John Kennedy in 1960 brought to Washington a group of 'New Frontiersmen' loyal to Kennedy but also with very definite ideas on policies and on the nature of the Presidency, and they had a considerable influence on the Kennedy Administration, and on any historical appraisal of his Presidency.[2] The success of such developments in the United States led to attempts in Britain to provide similar supports for the Prime Minister, operating from 10 Downing Street.

Certain members of the personal staff of the President have defined responsibilities, notably the Press Secretary, whose position has become more important with the development of the

[2] See T. C. Sorenson, *Decision-Making in the White House*, New York: Columbia University Press, 1963; and Richard Neustadt, *Presidential Power*, New York: John Wiley Sons, 1963. See also P. Salinger, *With Kennedy*, London: Cape, 1967.

mass media and the televising of Presidential press conferences.[3] The President is likely to assign at least one of these special assistants for special liaison duties with Congress, to discuss and negotiate with Congressmen and obtain support for the President's policies. Other assistants may be assigned general responsibilities. They help prepare messages, speeches, and communications, analyse and refine problems coming before the President, and advance his purpose with executive departments and subordinates. The potential of the President's personal staff as a Presidential instrument to co-ordinate executive action is considerable, and the range of their activities is as broad as the President wishes to make it.

The existence of such a staff has its hazards as well as its limitations. The major hazard is that such staff may become more than auxiliaries of the President and limit or even usurp his range of choices of action. This depends on the degree of control over such staff exercised by the President. If he likes to delegate authority, as was Eisenhower's practice, he may lose touch with much of the detail of policy processes, and thereby risk becoming less than master of his staff system.

An important tool of Presidential control of the bureaucracy is control of the annual budget, and the Bureau of the Budget provides valuable support for the President. The Bureau was created by the Budget and Accounting Act of 1921, and prior to its creation the President did not review the financial requests of departments and independent agencies. It was initially a part of the Treasury Department, and its head was appointed by the President alone. Until its transfer in 1939 to the Executive Office of the President, it remained a technical instrument of the President. Now as the Office of Management and Budget it seeks to provide a means whereby the President can impose a personal influence on the fiscal demands of departments and exercise an overall control of the administrative budget. While the Prime Minister occupies the position of first Lord of the Treasury, his control over the Treasury and budgetary matters is less than that of an efficient President.

The O.M.B. assists the President in setting general budgetary

[3] See E. E. Cornwell, Jr., 'The Presidential Press Conference: A Study in Institutionalisation', *Midwest Journal of Political Science*, November 1960, pp. 370–89.

policies, allowing for review, approval, and reduction of the annual estimates submitted by departments and agencies. It apportions funds appropriated by Congress, which means it can control the rate at which appropriated funds are spent by particular branches of the bureaucracy. It also reviews the requests of agencies for legislation, in order to determine if they conform to the legislative programme of the President, and legislation passed by Congress which is submitted to the President for his signature. It can recommend to the President that he sign or veto a bill and may even prepare a draft veto message. The O.M.B. also has the important task of studying the organisation and management practices of executive departments and agencies, improving financial management practices (in co-operation with the General Accounting Office and the Treasury) and making recommendations designed to increase the fiscal efficiency of the bureaucracy.

These responsibilities can be used as a valuable instrument for Presidential actions. The budget itself is an important part of the legislative programme of the President, and allows him to set a pattern of legislative priorities based on budget requests. Departments are forced to persuade the O.M.B. that they need certain funds and must demonstrate that they will seek to use such funds (if obtained from Congress) in an efficient way. Having obtained funds from Congress, the O.M.B. can again control the spending of these funds by departments, and may refuse to give funds to departments if their use does not conform to the programme of the President.

The responsibilities of the O.M.B. to increase fiscal accountability within the bureaucracy are also important. One major attempt to improve the allocation of resources within the bureaucracy by the President was the development of the new planning, programming, and budgeting system initiated by President Johnson in 1965. This system was designed to improve the capacity of the executive branch to plan, and through planning, to develop, a budget which represents an effective use of national resources to meet perceived public needs. The passage of the annual budget provides a high degree of conflict between the Congress and the President. Congressional consideration of the Executive budget involves much argument, debate, and discussion on almost every item, and it is always amended and revised by Congress, sometimes drastically. Departments often seek to obtain from Congress funds left out of the Executive budget, and the end product is an amalgam of the priorities of the President modified by the conflicting priorities of Congress.[4]

The increasing exercise of fiscal oversight by Congress on departments and agencies forces increased internal efficiency in the spending of funds. The initial impetus for the development of new techniques of budgetary efficiency followed the attempts by Secretary of Defence McNamara, beginning in 1960, and supported by President Kennedy, to rationalise the structure of the Defence Department in both organisational and fiscal terms. The Bureau of the Budget took up this initiative and after 1965 they sought to extend these budgetary techniques to all departments, but the Nixon administration lessened its use. If employed with sophistication, the budgetary process can be the most effective tool available to the President in controlling the activities of departments. Because of this, the new role of O.M.B., with its large staff of some 300 members, functioning in close alliance with the President, can be an indispensable asset in maintaining administrative responsibility to the President.

The role of the Council of Economic Advisers is rather different, but it is often concerned with matters related to the O.M.B., though it exercises a less powerful influence. Created by Congress in 1946, the Council has become the symbol of the responsibility of the President for the economic welfare of the nation, and a source of specialised economic knowledge. It prepares reports on which are based the annual economic message of the President to Congress. The specialist information, rationale, and advice provided by the three-man team of economic advisers serves to strengthen Presidential political leadership. It increases his ability to take the initiative in controlling departments. The nature of the influence exerted by the Council has been affected by the views and personality of its chairmen, and the Presidents under whom they served.

The passive acceptance of the Council by President Truman, and his coolness toward economics and economists, affected the

[4] See A. Wildavsky, *The Politics of the Budgetary Process*, Boston: Little, Brown, 1964; also J. D. Lees, 'Legislative Review and Bureaucratic Responsibility: The Impact of Fiscal Oversight by Congress on the American Federal Administration', *Public Administration*, Winter 1967, pp. 369–86.

activities of the Council and its chairmen, Nourse and Keyserling. Eisenhower's military concept of staff assistance, and his reliance on them to aid an ailing economy, affected the Council with Burns as chairman. Kennedy's grasp of modern economics and his style of pragmatic analysis shaped the use he made of the Council chaired by Heller and its response to his approach, while the demands of Johnson and his Great Society programme affected the response of the Council chaired by Gardner Ackley.[5] Each Council has served Presidents of very different political persuasions and styles, with different priorities and concepts of office, and different views on the role of the Council. The Council chaired by Nourse and Keyserling, faced with emergencies growing out of the Korean War and domestic inflation, was more activist than the Council chaired by Burns. Under a less active President, adopting a more conservative attitude, the Council operated as a consultant to Eisenhower in a mildly recessionary situation in which minimal governmental direction of the economic life of the nation was a primary political objective. Under John F. Kennedy, Heller promoted a new economic rationale for the New Frontier and exercised considerable influence on the President. The influence of the Council has been more extensive than that of the specialised economic advice provided by advisers appointed to the Cabinet Office by the Prime Minister, or the creation of new economic departments in Britain directly supervised by the Prime Minister.

As well as making important economic decisions, the President has a pivotal role in matters of national security. In 1947, Congress created the National Security Council and gave it the responsibility of advising the President concerning the integration of domestic, foreign, and military policies relating to national security in order to achieve effective co-operation between the military services and other government agencies and departments on such matters. The Council was therefore closely concerned with matters relating to two of the largest governmental departments, the State Department and the Department of Defence.

The Council is formally composed of the President as chairman, the Vice-President, Secretary of State, Secretary of

[5] See E. S. Flash, Jr., *Economic Advice and Presidential Leadership*, New York and London: Columbia University Press, 1965.

Defence, and Director of the Office of Emergency Preparedness (concerned with the emergency use of resources of all kinds including manpower, industry, transportation and other facilities). The President may appoint to the Council, or invite to specific meetings, other officials, such as the Secretary of the Treasury or the Chairman of the Joint Chiefs of Staff (the military advisers of the President). The N.S.C. is rather similar to a Cabinet committee, and its proceedings are top secret. It has been used in very different ways by different Presidents, but its overall utility as an instrument of Presidential power is limited, yet it has served as a means of co-ordination, and achieving some general agreement, between key military and diplomatic advisers responsible for important policy-implementing activities.

Under President Truman, the N.S.C., as initially organised, was influenced by the organisation originally known as the Imperial Defence Council, established in Britain in 1908. Before 1950 President Truman did not preside at meetings of the N.S.C. The Secretary of State presided but the President determined the agenda. After 1950, Truman presided and called on members for their questions, but never stated his own views or took a vote. He made his decisions after the Council meetings. President Eisenhower presided over most of the N.S.C. meetings, which met more frequently than the Cabinet. In his first term the N.S.C. initially reviewed and recommended revisions of existing national security policies of the preceding administration, and then began to prepare recommendations for new national security policies to deal with existing situations. In Eisenhower's second term the primary focus of the Council shifted, at the request of the President, from the consideration and approval of written policy statements to oral discussion of national security policy issues. The President was an active participant in discussion, and encouraged conflict and debate between different members of the Council. Sometimes the President would decide in the course of the meeting on a disputed issue, or would decide later on the basis of a draft formal record of the meeting. Eisenhower liked to use the Council and often held weekly meetings.[6]

[6] See H. M. Jackson (ed.), *The National Security Council* (Jackson Subcommittee Papers on Policy-Making at the Presidential Level), New York: Praeger, 1965, especially pp. 99-140.

The National Security Council proved to be a valuable advisory body to President Eisenhower, providing him with a regular meeting of his principal advisers, and led to some degree of co-ordination in administration as well as to regular exchanges of views among the leading foreign policy agencies. Presidents since Eisenhower have found the National Security Council a less effective body for the integration of overseas programmes and activities. In 1961 President Kennedy decided to rely for co-ordination over national security matters on informal staff procedures worked out by McGeorge Bundy and the State Department. If this procedure seemed defective in terms of effective co-ordination over the abortive Bay of Pigs Invasion, it appeared to succeed brilliantly in helping Kennedy handle the Cuban missile crisis and the 'confrontation' with Kruschev in 1962. The informal approach also appeared to be useful in the management of complex problems relating to the Vietnam War. However, the informal organisation had become large by 1965, and President Johnson gave Maxwell Taylor the responsibility of reviewing these procedures and recommending possible improvements.

In March 1966, President Johnson announced certain changes. The Secretary of State was given specific authority to co-ordinate all interdepartmental matters affecting American policy abroad. To assist the Secretary of State, an interdepartmental committee was established, known as the senior Interdepartmental Group, with the Under Secretary of State as its executive chairman, responsible for seeing that decisions are reached. Other members of the committee included the Deputy Secretary of Defence, Director of the Central Intelligence Agency, the Chairman of the Joint Chiefs of Staff, the Director of the United States Information Agency, the Administrator of the Agency for International Development, and a representative of the White House staff. The committee, once created, met regularly. Below this organisation was created another interdepartmental committee consisting of the Assistant Secretaries responsible for Regional Affairs. President Nixon sought initially to revitalise the N.S.C., but gradually relied more and more on the combined efforts of himself and his personal National Security adviser, Henry Kissinger, who in 1973 also became Secretary of State.

An additional source of Presidential support is the Cabinet. It is not, however, his strongest. To readers familiar with the importance of the Cabinet in the British system of government, this may seem surprising, but it serves to emphasise the singular position of the President. The Cabinet is dependent upon the President. If government in Britain is government by Prime Minister, carried on as though it were still Cabinet government, government in the United States is government by President carried on as if there had never been a Cabinet. While Prime Ministers have made important decisions of policy without referring the matter to the Cabinet or have presented decisions for the formal approval of the Cabinet, Presidents seek only advice about policy decisions from Cabinet members, and make the final decisions themselves. It is not a body whose members feel any strong sense of collective responsibility or mutual obligation, and its members may have had little previous acquaintance with each other or the President. It is at best of limited utility to the President as a source of advice, though some Presidents have used it in a manner which elevated it to a position close to that of the Cabinet as it is supposed to exist in Britain, and its continued existence is a reflection of certain needs of the Presidency.

Richard Fenno has called the Cabinet 'a schizophrenic body' whose personnel can be divided into members of the Cabinet and men of Cabinet rank.[7] It is less institutionalised than the O.M.B. or the N.S.C., though its core personnel constitute an identifiable group holding governmental positions created and defined by statute. Resting on usage and executive convenience, rather than on a statutory foundation, its role in the operation of the Presidency has been a varied one. The President's power to use the Cabinet or not is a final one, and there are real limits to the kind and extent of assistance a President may get from the Cabinet. In time of crisis, however, the existence of the Cabinet may be useful in symbolising governmental stability. The smooth transition following Kennedy's assassination was helped by the loyal support to Johnson given by the members of the Cabinet under Kennedy.

[7] See R. Fenno, Jr., *The President's Cabinet*, New York: Vintage Books, 1959, p. 20. See also, for comparative information, J. P. Mackintosh, *The British Cabinet*, London: Stevens, 1962.

Particular Presidential interpretations of the role of the Presidency also affect the role of the Cabinet. The views of Theodore Roosevelt about the need for vigorous leadership by the President led him to attach little importance to the Cabinet. Historically, elevation of the role of the Cabinet by a President has generally been linked with attitudes and beliefs minimising strong executive leadership. Eisenhower placed a heavy emphasis on the 'team' function of the Cabinet (as did Attlee as Prime Minister), and also had a limited view of the powers of the President. His methods of decision-making also made the Cabinet of greater utility, and he went so far as to create the post of Cabinet secretary to arrange the agenda for Cabinet meetings, circulating it to members, oversee the preparation of Cabinet papers presenting proposals for Presidential action, and recording the results of Cabinet discussion.

In 1970, President Nixon created a Domestic Council to advise him 'on the total range of domestic policy'. Though it included all members of the Cabinet with domestic responsibilities, its executive director was a top personal assistant of the President. In the field of domestic affairs it occupied a position equivalent to the N.S.C. over national security, reflecting the further diminution in importance of the Cabinet meeting as a vehicle for Presidential decision-making and policy planning and formulation, and in efforts to produce a sense of coherence and responsibility in a fragmented and specialised administrative structure.

Presidential Approaches to Executive Responsibilities

The use of the Cabinet and personal advisers by Presidents illustrates the different approaches made by different Presidents to their responsibilities, and the need for a President to be aware of the different options open to him in any major decision. The final decision is made by the President, but the determination of the options or alternatives may be made by advisers of the President. Some Presidents, like Franklin Roosevelt or John F. Kennedy, sought the advice and opinions of trusted advisers but determined their own options from which they made their final decision. President Eisenhower, in contrast, allowed his staff to decide the options and then made the final decisions. Personal qualities also affect the attitudes of a President regarding the manner in which he performs his executive duties. Both Roosevelts exercised Presidential power with vigour and self-confidence, while Truman undertook Presidential authority with a full recognition of the awesome responsibilities of the position and of his own personal inadequacies. Yet he did not flinch from making crucial decisions, and fought hard and successfully to keep the Presidency in 1948.

President Franklin D. Roosevelt presided over a very unconventional but highly personal organisation which some felt violated the then accepted canons of efficient administration. Much of the New Deal programme in the 1930s was administrated by a new and inexperienced bureaucracy. To obtain action, Roosevelt often bypassed department heads and dealt directly with subordinates. By avoiding any formal pattern of decision-making he succeeded in keeping vital powers in his own hands. Lines of authority were blurred, jurisdictions overlapped, and conflict between agencies was encouraged. He used the Cabinet as a sounding board or as a means to put his own thinking on display, but in his later years the only institutional staff of substantial size under his control was the Bureau of the Budget. He gave a minimum of fixed assignments to members of his personal staff and maintained a complicated pattern of rewards and sanctions designed to keep them efficient and loyal. Fixed staff assignments reflected areas of action rather than particular programme areas, and individuals like Tugwell, Corcoran or Hopkins did not become specialists. Assignment activities deliberately overlapped and personalities often clashed. No staff had any fixed assignments involving continuous contact with Congressional leaders or with appointed department heads. He used a host of 'outsiders' (including his wife) as supplementary channels of information and communication. No single aide was ever allowed to become his spokesman.

At the centre of this network sat the President. Even with changes during the Second World War, none of the new aides had exclusive jurisdictions or fixed assignments, though the 1939 recommendations of the Brownlow Committee were generally accepted by Roosevelt. While the staff of 1944 was larger, had better technical resources, a wider range of interests, and more general scope for action, than his staff in 1939, Roosevelt continued to strengthen his personal hold over policy decision-making. During the war Harry Hopkins became Roosevelt's major 'troubleshooter', both at home and abroad. The open arena of peace-time policy-making allowed for the deliberate creation of conflict between leading administrators or personal staff assistants. During time of war it was necessary to be more secretive and discreet. It was also less possible for Roosevelt to maintain his disorderly process of decision-making, but he could still exercise control over the bureaucracy because the war served to minimise tensions between and within political institutions.[8] After the end of the war, organisations were set up at the Presidential level, such as the National Security Council, which were designed to control the type of executive flexibility practised by Roosevelt.

In contrast to Roosevelt's distinctive and personal methods, President Eisenhower formalised Presidential relationships within the executive by a careful delegation of tasks and responsibilities to subordinates. The President would co-ordinate and direct these efforts, and on the basis of short and precise reports by subordinates would make a final decision. Eisenhower made Sherman Adams his Presidential assistant, and he was responsible for maintaining this system. Only the Secretary of State, Dulles, was able to approach the President directly. Adams scrutinised policy proposals, almost always based on staff study and recommendation, and made some decisions without troubling the President. He also had a good deal of control over patronage. It is inconceivable that Roosevelt would ever have created or tolerated such a rival position of influence.

Adams maintained a co-ordinated White House staff which often discussed specific matters with Eisenhower but not broad general matters, and operated as an efficient staff secretariat.[9] The Cabinet meeting became more formalised with the creation of a Cabinet secretary to record the results of Cabinet discussion and meet with senior department officials to discuss the implementation of Cabinet decisions. Secretaries of major depart-

[8] See R. E. Neustadt, 'Approaches to Staffing the Presidency: Notes on FDR and JFK', *American Political Science Review*, December 1963, pp. 855–64. See also L. W. Koenig, *The Chief Executive*, New York: Harcourt, Brace and World, 1964, Chapter 7.

[9] See S. Adams, *Firsthand Report*, New York: Popular Library, 1962.

ments were often given broad initiative and responsibilities, and Eisenhower was swift to defend his department secretaries against political criticism.

The system created by Eisenhower suited his own particular style of individual activity and his conception of the Presidency. It was efficient but not infallible, and its major defect was in allowing the President too little initiative and impact on policy evaluation. It ignored a vital dimension of Presidential activity – the need to use his authority to change the opinions and interests of politicians and administrators. Eisenhower relied too heavily on his staff and left himself with a restricted area of choice in making decisions. It also left him vulnerable if they made an error. The omission of a minor piece of information about an individual by his staff led to government scandals over the Dixon–Yates contract to provide electric power for the Atomic Energy Commission in Tennessee.[10] Too often Eisenhower's staff acted as a tranquilliser for the President, creating a false sense of security, rather than acting as a generator of Presidential initiative and action.

President John F. Kennedy reflected a style akin to Roosevelt, but in a very different administrative and political setting. He wished to distinguish between his personal staff and staff which were necessary for any President. He sought to run his personal staff of special assistants as a small core of specialists in action-spheres rather than in specific policy areas. These general-purpose staff with fixed assignments were supplemented by temporary specialist staff. Kennedy also sought to make decisions in an atmosphere of competition between competing ideas. However, Kennedy also inherited an Executive Office of considerable size. He dismantled much of Eisenhower's staff and cabinet-committee systems, with the major exception of staff for legislative liaison and special projects. Kennedy also sought to make the independent regulatory commissions within the bureaucracy more responsible to himself and the public, and through appointments did begin to affect their decisions and investigations. He sought 'to steer a course between Roosevelt's disorder and Eisenhower's system',[11] keeping in close per-

[10] See A. Wildavsky, *Dixon-Yates: A Study in Power Politics*, New Haven: Yale University Press, 1962.

[11] R. E. Neustadt, 'Approaches to Staffing the Presidency', *op. cit.*, p. 862.

sonal touch with department heads but not at formal gatherings. He also delegated responsibilities to Cabinet members which Roosevelt would have kept to himself. Personal relationships became more important than institutional structure in stimulating bureaucratic action. Kennedy sought to make decisions, not approve them. He opposed interdepartmental committees and supported task forces consisting of personal staff and departmental staff to work on specific problems. Staff members like Arthur Schlesinger or McGeorge Bundy sometimes performed duties handled in the past by departments, and others were responsible for checking departmental proposals for policy or political weaknesses.

Yet this new organisation also made mistakes. Lack of incisive checking and questioning led to the disastrous errors of the abortive Bay of Pigs 'invasion' of Cuba in 1961. The infrequent use of formal Cabinet meetings or meetings of the National Security Council, and the substitution of personal involvement in decision-making for group discussion of alternatives, rested on a view of the executive branch as being a centre of personal Presidential judgment and responsibility, with neither the apparatus nor the formality of collective responsibility as exists in Britain. The maximisation of Presidential involvement in policy decisions and the sense of vitality inspired by swift action was not without its weaknesses. It placed a heavy strain on Kennedy himself, and a reliance on quick, concise, decisions not always backed by a careful analysis and consideration of every alternative by specialist advisers.

President Johnson also developed a special combination of different resources to perform his responsibilities on assuming the Presidency. He linked a preference for the use of formal administrative institutions like the National Security Council with a penchant for seeking advice from individuals outside governmental circles. The implementation of his 'war on poverty' programme was engineered by the director of the Office of Economic Opportunity, which was created within the Executive Office of the President to co-ordinate department activities. Johnson elevated the 'independent' authority of major department heads, especially the Secretaries of Defence and State, and preferred the presentation of material to him on paper before he decided what action he would take to persuade governmental officials of the need to work to implement decisions he intended to make. His particular brand of politics as practised by him when a Senator also affected his methods of operation. His persuasive tactics were often personal and direct especially on Congressmen, and his decisions on domestic policy indicated an acute perception of political realities.

Each of these Presidents thus sought to maintain the type of control commensurate with the size and scope of the bureaucracy, their personal inclination and attitudes towards the role of the President, and their assessment of current political realities. A combination of institutional organisation and personal staff, utilised according to the dictates of the individual President, has been used to control a sprawling, disparate, bureaucracy and to perform the many responsibilities of the President which require attention, tax his diplomatic, political and managerial skills, and demand formal decisions on his part on a massive number of questions.

The Vice-Presidency has, after being dormant for most of the nineteenth century, become a position of greater importance in the twentieth century, and can also provide valuable support to the President in his administrative enterprises. Henry Wallace undertook certain administrative duties in the Second World War as Vice-President under Franklin Roosevelt. In the Truman Administration, Alben Barkley became a member of the National Security Council, as did Richard Nixon under Eisenhower. Nixon also presided over some Cabinet meetings and undertook a range of ceremonial duties to help the President. In the Kennedy Administration, Johnson chaired several interdepartmental committees and undertook assignments abroad, and Humphrey was given several important duties relating to civil rights and poverty legislation by President Johnson. This increase in the general responsibilities of the Vice-President is valuable not simply to lighten the burdens on the President, but also because of the need for the Vice-President to have some awareness of policy decisions and the nature of administrative co-ordination since he may be called to step into the position of President with little or no warning.[12] In a subordinate administrative capacity the Vice-President may streng-

[12] See D. Young, *American Roulette: The History and Dilemma of the Vice Presidency*, New York: Holt, Rinehart and Winston, 1972.

then the overall position of the President rather than simply helping the President perform ceremonial duties. Yet the position of Vice-President is one of frustration and relative impotence in contrast to that of the President.

The President and the Administration

When Washington was President, a few hundred civil servants were sufficient to carry out the administrative tasks of the national government. In 1967 it required the services of over two and a half million personnel (over two-thirds of the total United States population in 1789). The Department of Defence alone spends almost one-tenth of the annual gross national product of the country. This vast administrative bureaucracy provides a continuing problem for the President, who is responsible for controlling its activities. Though centred in Washington, only some 10% of the personnel of the federal bureaucracy actually work in or around Washington.

It is clear that the constitutional requirement to 'take care that the laws be faithfully executed' cannot be performed by the President alone. The constitutional system has created a fragmented bureaucracy which is not responsible only to the President. A combination of legal, constitutional, and political factors shape the kind of authority possessed by the President over administrative agencies and departments.

The creation and structure of administrative departments and agencies are determined largely by statutory authority granted by Congress. With the growth of the bureaucracy, Congress has sought to increase its responsibility to check on such activities. In some respects such action may supplement the authority of the President, but it can also undermine this authority. Attempts by the executive to control bureaucratic independence by centralising decisions about annual budgetary requests of departments in the O.M.B. inevitably produced friction with Congress. Congress also often gives independent authority to subordinate bureaus within executive departments, and the creations of independent regulatory commissions such as the Interstate Commerce Commission or the Federal Communications Commission provides administrative organisations which are 'independent' of the President and of any systematic supervision by Congress as a whole. Such Commissions are intended to regulate certain economic matters and exercise quasi-judicial functions. Commissioners, once appointed to their allotted term, cannot be removed by the President alone.

Some agencies, such as the Tennessee Valley Authority (established in 1933), the Atomic Energy Commission, or the National Aeronautics and Space Administration (created in 1958), are independent of executive departments but come within the scope of Presidential authority. The Civil Service Commission also comes under this category. The reason for the independence of these agencies has been the need for flexibility, and the difficulties involved in trying to fit such organisations into established departments.

The twelve executive departments came under the direct control of the President. The Department of State is the oldest (1789) and probably still the most prestigious, and is responsible for foreign affairs. The Treasury Department is concerned with managing government finances but does not have the degree of authority or prestige held by the Treasury in Britain. The Defence Department is relatively new, and was not created until 1947, when it combined the armed services departments under one Secretary. The Department of Justice was created in 1870 and serves as the law office to the executive. The Post Office Department was created in 1872, and the Postmaster General has been a traditional party patronage position. The Department of the Interior, created in 1849, is concerned with natural resources west of the Mississippi, and also Indian affairs. The Department of Agriculture (1862) and the Department of Commerce (1913) have specific functions, as does the Department of Labour (1913). The Department of Health, Education and Welfare was created in 1953 and its responsibilities have increased considerably in the 1960s, and within it the Office of Education has become very important. The Department of Housing and Urban Development was created in 1965, and reflects the interests of the Democratic party in urban problems, as does the creation of the Department of Transportation in 1966.

The national bureaucracy performs many functions. It provides the expertise that makes possible the provision of complex programmes in a modern society. For the political party winning the Presidency, a part of the bureaucracy is a source of patronage for party workers and a basis of support for a President anxious to control its activities. To interest group leaders, bureaucrats may be seen either as threats to their aims or valuable allies in strategic positions of influence. Until 1883 the federal bureaucracy was recruited almost exclusively on a partisan basis, but the Pendleton Act created the Civil Service Commission, and provided for recruitment by open competitive examination. At the outset this covered only about 10% of the employees on the executive branch, but steady expansion has brought some 90% of federal employees under the competitive provisions of the Civil Service Act or the merit system. Recruitment by patronage involves a relatively small number of posts, but over a thousand Cabinet, sub-Cabinet and other top-level positions remain directly under the control of the President. In marked contrast to Britain, leading administrators are partisan political appointees.

Study of the social and personal characteristics of career federal executives indicates the high degree of importance attached to education beyond undergraduate level. Also a disproportionately high number come from a city background. Foreign-service officers tend to have degrees in the humanities or the behavioural sciences, and their family background patterns are much closer to those of the business élite than other career service executives. Fathers of career civil service executives are well distributed among the different types present in the work force of the country. Almost 25% were skilled workers or mechanics. In broad view, big business and government executives are more alike than not in social and economic characteristics, yet there are differences. Both come more often from the higher occupations, though the range of occupations of their fathers run from the top to the lowest level, and the proportions of federal executives are more evenly spread through all occupational levels.[13] The American bureaucratic élite appears to be rather more specialised in training and education, more

[13] See W. L. Warner, *et al.*, *The American Federal Executive*, New Haven: Yale University Press, 1963. Contrast with British evidence presented in R. Rose, *Politics in England*, *op. cit.*, pp. 94–7. For historical contrasts, see S. H. Aronson, *Status and Kinship in the Higher Civil Service*, Cambridge, Mass.: Harvard University Press. 1964.

of a meritocracy and less affected by formal role socialisation than their counterparts in Britain.

Rank within the Civil Service or career section of the federal bureaucracy depends on the position rather than the person, but the most senior positions also have specific titles. Security of tenure within the civil service, however, is not absolute. Procedures for dismissal are more complicated than in private business, but over 13,000 federal employees are dismissed annually for inadequate performance.[14] The public in the United States, while poorly informed about the functions or procedures of governmental agencies, are often sceptical of the bureaucracy and critical of the high cost of government. Moreover, it seems to be the case that, except for people with low economic status, jobs in private business rate higher than similar jobs in government. Limitations are also placed on the political activities of bureaucrats, and strict precautions taken to weed out 'security risks'.

The combination of patronage and merit for choosing senior administrators allows for stability along with political responsibility. It can also cause friction within departments. The President remains formally in control of the administrative process, but beneath him the head of a department has important responsibilities. No two departments or independent agencies have the same formal organisation, though there are three major types of units – the secretary, and one or more undersecretaries and assistant secretaries responsible for specific sectors of department activities; auxiliary department-wide positions of responsibility such as budget directors; and the major operating units known as bureaus. The latter constitute the basic units of the bureaucracy, and bureaus often become very independent of their parent department and develop considerable internal homogeneity. Bureau chiefs have often been in charge for a long time and are experienced specialists with close and often harmonious contact with Congressmen and clientele groups. It is not always easy for a department head to exercise full control over such bureaus, who may in turn often be in conflict with bureaus in other departments. One good example

[14] See F. P. Kilpatrick, *et al.*, *The Image of the Federal Service*, Washington, D.C.: Brookings Institution, 1964. See also C. R. Adrian and C. Press, *The American Political Process*, New York: McGraw-Hill, 1965, Chapter 17.

of this is the annual hostility and struggle between the Corps of Engineers in the Army Department and the Bureau of Reclamation in the Interior Department, to obtain public works contracts for dam construction and the development of water resources in the far West. The Corps of Engineers is more responsive to control by Congress who therefore look favourably upon its activities.

The positions of assistant and under-secretaries are important, and nearly all are Presidential appointees, sharing with department and agency heads the functions of 'political' leadership. The selection of such men for the second echelon of the executive team of the President reflects many of the basic values and characteristics of the American political system. The process is haphazard: no standard formal procedure exists for locating, classifying, and persuading qualified men to take such positions, nor is there any formal process of preparation for such jobs. Selection is a highly decentralised and personalised process. Department and agency heads are given wide latitude in selecting subordinates. A substantial number of these appointees in the last few decades have had previous governmental administrative experience, and some also possessed prior knowledge of the activities of their respective departments by having been in other appointive positions (see Table 9:1). They are more specialised and professional than leading civil servants in Britain. Appointees are usually well satisfied with their positions, and consider the rewards of service outweigh possible disadvantages. In a survey of such officials, only two of the 108 interviewed wished that they had not served, and the majority leave their appointments for personal reasons related to job tenure, financial loss or career advantage.[15]

Existing appointment procedures reflect political tradition and realities, but the delegation of responsibility for such appointments to department heads, especially during an administration, does not always serve to help Presidental co-ordination. In 1965, President Johnson made the chairman of the Civil Service Commission, John Macey, Jr., also responsible to him as chief personnel advisor appraising potential candidates for political positions in the government, rather in the way the

[15] See D. E. Mann, *The Assistant Secretaries*, Washington, D.C.: Brookings Institution, 1965, pp. 266-7.

head of the Civil Service Commission in Britain advises the Prime Minister on senior appointments.

Table 9:1

ANALYSIS OF THE CRITERIA OF SELECTION FOR REPRESENTATIVE SAMPLE OF SECOND-LEVEL POLITICAL EXECUTIVES, 1945–1961

Criteria of Selection	Truman (1945–52)	Eisenhower (1953)	(1954–60)	Kennedy (1961)	Total
Expertise in a specific area of responsibility	3	7	5	8	23
Expertise plus political factors	2	1	3	1	7
General experience in area of responsibility	20	3	12	4	39
General experience plus political factors	9	8	3	9	29
Party service	3	2	3	2	10
	37	21	26	24	108

Source: D. E. Mann, *The Assistant Secretaries*, p. 92.

The major difficulty in improving Presidential control over political appointments is increased by the general bureaucratic problem of obtaining suitable candidates for political executive office, the relatively brief tenure of occupancy of such positions, plus the low social status and economic rewards accorded to government service as opposed to private business or other activities. However, Presidential co-ordination, both in a political and administrative sense, requires the delegation of responsibility by the President. Unlike the Prime Minister, a President is not free to leave the implementation of policy, once determined, to others. Because of this the choice of personal advisers and 'political' administrators must be made with care by any President if he is to maintain some control over the federal bureaucracy.

There must also be some co-ordination between Presidents when there is a change of administration such as occurred in 1960, when a Democratic President, Kennedy, took over from a retiring Republican, Eisenhower. This involved an extensive change in the senior 'political' personnel in many departments. In 1960, President Eisenhower took a positive and constructive attitude towards the transition and instructed his administration to do the same. President Kennedy responded to Eisenhower's co-operation, but also made extensive preparations by evaluating potential candidates for jobs and formulating policies. He was helped by the fact that the Democrats were returning to power after only eight years. In 1953 the transition was less smooth, for the Republicans had not won the Presidency for over twenty years and Eisenhower had an inexperienced team. In 1961 some of those who had served President Truman returned, while many higher civil servants had been trained in the Roosevelt and Truman Administrations, and easily adjusted to the demands of the 'New Frontier' of Kennedy.[16]

In 1963 the Presidential Transition Act sought to promote the orderly transfer of executive power, maintain maximum continuity, and provide funds to the incoming and outgoing Presidents for this purpose. Future transitions are likely to depend on individual personalities. In 1961 Kennedy retained a certain number of political executives from the preceding administrations and gave certain departments new and important responsibilities requiring speedy action. The take-over by Johnson on the death of Kennedy in 1963 was smooth, largely because of the particular nature of this situation. Many Kennedy appointees stayed on to maintain continuity and stability, though a good many of them, especially personal advisers, were no longer working for Johnson by the time he was elected in 1964. Many observers believe that an efficient and constructive transfer of power is imperative if a contemporary President is to be ready for any contingency or emergency which he may have to deal with early in his administration.

The President, the Supreme Court, and Policy-making

The President is responsible for the administration and implementation of legislation as well as for the making of public policy. In all these areas he is influenced by the actions of the Supreme Court. As constitutional arbiter between the states and the nation, and between the branches of the national

[16] For more detailed evidence, see D. T. Stanley, *Changing Administrations*, Washington, D.C.: Brookings Institution, 1965; also the contributions by L. L. Henry in P. T. David (ed.), *The Presidential Election and Transition 1960–1961*, Washington, D.C.: Brookings Institution, 1961.

government, the Supreme Court may be forced to declare unconstitutional legislation initiated by the President. However, despite the bitter political struggle between President Roosevelt and the Supreme Court in the mid-1930s, after the Court had declared unconstitutional a large amount of Roosevelt's New Deal legislation, the Court is more likely to support (and so help to legitimise) controversial legislation rather than declare it void. At the height of the conflict in 1936, one of the major opponents of the New Deal legislation, Justice Sutherland, gave the majority opinion in *United States* v. *Curtiss-Wright Export Corporation*, which declared that the national government had inherent powers in foreign relations which did not depend on grants of authority by the Constitution, a decision which legitimised the extension of Presidential power in foreign relation.

A prominent Supreme Court Justice argued in support of the authority of the Court as follows: 'The utility of an external power restraining the legislative judgment is not to be measured by counting the occasions of its exercise. The great ideals of liberty and equality are preserved against the assaults of opportunism . . . by enshrining them in constitutions, and consecrating to the task of their protection a body of defenders.'[17] The presence of this restraining power may be a valuable support to the political system, but it can limit Presidential discretion as well as allowing those interests defeated in the executive or legislative process a final opportunity to challenge the legitimacy of a particular policy.

In interpreting federal statutes and executive orders, the Supreme Court may often be required to make policy as well as adjudicate on policy, where the language of legislation is deliberately vague, as was the case with anti-trust legislation such as the Sherman Act of 1890. This provides an additional source of judicial power, and the Court can also use opinions given on cases to influence the political process. The nine members of the Supreme Court make the final decisions in the judicial process, and can exercise considerable discretion in determining which cases they will consider and when to consider them. The Court receives requests to consider over two thousand cases annually, and more than three-quarters of them

[17] B. N. Cardozo, *The Nature of the Judicial Process*, New Haven: Yale University Press, 1921, pp. 92–3.

are dismissed as unworthy of review by the Court. The Supreme Court considers most cases on appeal from lower federal courts or state Supreme Courts, and many of these cases are brought before it by a writ of *certiorari* (asking the higher court if it will inform itself with the proceedings in the lower court), which it is at the discretion of the Court to use. Such petitions are granted only if at least four of the nine judges agree that a case raises issues of special importance. The exercise of this discretion may involve political as well as legal considerations.

Justices are free to write opinions concurring with, or dissenting from, the majority opinion, and in the contemporary Court non-unanimous decisions are often more common than unanimous. It should be noted also that Justices are appointed by politicians and have often had extensive political experience themselves. In particular the position of Chief Justice, whose formal authority consists of his role as presiding officer in court, and at conferences, where the Justices discuss cases and where he assigns the writing of opinions, can be used as a position of political influence, as Chief Justices such as John Marshall, William Howard Taft, and Charles Evans Hughes demonstrated.[18] Marshall, as Chief Justice, used his rhetoric in opinions in cases such as *Marbury* v. *Madison* in 1803 (where he also criticised the President) to influence public and political opinion, and so affect public policy. Other Justices, notably Oliver Wendell Holmes, Louis Brandeis, Felix Frankfurter, and Hugo Black, have used opinions, both majority and dissenting, to seek to influence wider political issues than those considered by the particular case before them. Nor have individual Justices been afraid of seeking to exploit political friendships, especially with the President, to influence policies and judicial or other political appointments, especially men like Taft, Frankfurter, and Fortas in this century.

There are, however, considerable limitations on the exercise of judicial power. While prestige may be a source of judicial

[18] See A. T. Mason, *William Howard Taft*, London: Oldbourne, 1965; also A. T. Mason, *Supreme Court. Palladium of Freedom*, Ann Arbor, Michigan: University of Michigan Press, 1963. See also D. J. Danelski, 'The Influence of the Chief Justice in the Decisional Process', in W. F. Murphy and C. H. Pritchett (eds.), *Courts, Judges and Politics: An Introduction to the Judicial Process*, New York: Random House Inc., 1961, pp. 497–508.

power, popular expectations of how the Court is expected by tradition to behave act as limitations. A judge is required to explain his decisions in terms of constitutional or legal precedents, the 'intent of the Founding Fathers', the 'intent of Congress', or constitutional guarantees or protections. The relationship between the Court and public opinion is complex, yet the two should not be divorced for too long or too often. The Supreme Court may not always need to dutifully 'follow the election returns', but it must be aware of the prevalent views and attitudes of the day. The Supreme Court may be anxious to protect minority rights in the absence of Presidential action, yet it needs to be careful not to alienate the opinions of political activists in the process. Moreover, the protection of 'minorities' by the Court has not always been a distinguished one, since it has included 'privileged' minorities such as shareholders and wealthy financiers as well as Jehovah's Witnesses or Southern Negroes.[19] Individual Justices on the Court have often sought to persuade the Court to exercise judicial self-restraint and avoid conflict with the President and Congress over the making of policy.

In a concurring opinion in the case of *Ashwander* v. *Tennessee Valley Authority* (1936), Justice Brandeis summarised the restrictions the Supreme Court should impose on itself. The Court should avoid if possible the necessity of declaring on the constitutionality of legislation, and should presume constitutionality wherever possible, declaring a law unconstitutional only when such a conclusion is inevitable. The authority of the Court is clearly limited by technical restrictions, institutional factors, and the checks and balances of the political power of Congress and the President.

The Supreme Court, for instance, cannot initiate action. It cannot declare immediately on the constitutionality of an act of Congress or of a state government. It can only exercise influence or policy by deciding individual cases brought by individuals with a genuine personal case and where a genuine controversy exists over which the Court has jurisdiction. As early as 1793 the Court refused to give advisory opinions to the President. Justices are also only supposed to decide the issues raised by the

[19] See R. A. Dahl, 'Decision-Making in a Democracy: The Role of the Supreme Court as a National Policy-Maker', *Journal of Public Law*, 6, 1958, pp. 279–95.

litigants themselves, and their decisions legally bind only the parties to the particular case. A Supreme Court decision that school segregation in Alabama is unconstitutional does not legally require school boards in other states to desegregate, though it does invite other litigants to begin legal action with a strong possibility of success, for this decision would serve as a guide to lower court judges in deciding on future cases.

Examples of Court decisions illustrate these limitations. In 1923 in *Frothingham* v. *Mellon*, a federal taxpayer sued to prevent federal funds being expended under the Federal Maternity Act. Her primary interest lay in the relationship of her tax payments to the expenditure of federal funds. The Supreme Court argued that her interest was so minute and indeterminable as to afford no basis for appeal to the Court. However, in 1947, in *Everson* v. *Board of Education*, a local taxpayer was permitted to question the use of local tax revenue to provide transportation for students to parochial schools.

Litigants must also have exhausted all alternative remedies and the issue raised must be a 'justiciable' and not a political question. The Court has the right to determine this, and it has often been used to avoid controversial questions which may bring them into conflict with other branches of the national government. This can be done by asserting that the Constitution, expressly or by implication, bestowed authority to determine such a question on another branch of government. The distinction is, however, deliberately left imprecise by the Court, though the Court has indicated that certain questions such as the conduct of foreign policy, qualifications of members of the Congress, or ratification of constitutional amendments are beyond their competence. In *Luther* v. *Borden* (1849), the Court also affirmed that the constitutional guarantee to every state of a 'republican form of government' presents a 'political' question. However, external factors can lead the Court to relax its self-imposed limitations over 'political' questions.

One final technical restraint on judicial power, more familiar to students of the courts in Britain, is that of precedent, which can be used as a rationale for judicial decision-making. However, for members of the Supreme Court it is probably a restraint which they can, as individuals, use or avoid, since they may always find in a particular case some special issue which allows them to distinguish it from a precedent they may not wish to maintain. If sufficient fellow Justices can be persuaded of the special nature of a particular case which demands decision in a particular way this can be used as a justification for rejecting the claims of an earlier case as providing a precedent. This type of technique was used with skill by Chief Justice Hughes in seeking to extricate the Court from the political conflict with the President in 1937, so that the Court moved to a position of presuming the constitutionality of legislation without appearing to be reversing itself in the light of earlier decisions declaring New Deal legislation unconstitutional.[20]

Institutional factors also restrict the Court. Any opinion speaking for the Court rather than individual Justices requires the approval of a majority of the Justices. The range of alternative possibilities for decision do not always make it easy to obtain a majority opinion. Moreover, a decision accepted by only five Justices out of nine weakens or casts doubt on the legitimacy if not the legality of a decision. It was the fact that several of the major decisions striking down New Deal legislation in the 1930s were by 5–4 decisions (four Justices dissenting, not always in concert, against the majority) that increased political opposition to the Court and strengthened demands to change the jurisdiction of the Court. In addition, the Justices often have to depend on the co-operation of state and lower federal court judges in implementing their decisions, and this cannot always be relied upon, especially over controversial decisions.[21] Cases generally come to the Supreme Court from lower courts, and reversal of a decision of a lower court may simply involve the sending back of a case to state or lower federal courts with instructions to deal with the matter by further proceedings, taking note of the decision of the Supreme Court. State and lower court judges are often either political appointees or elected officials and may reflect very different values and attitudes towards specific matters than members of the Supreme Court.[22]

[20] See A. T. Mason, *Supreme Court: Palladium of Freedom, op. cit.*

[21] See J. W. Peltason, *Fifty Eight Lonely Men*, New York: Harcourt, Brace and World, 1961.

[22] See W. F. Murphy, 'Lower Court Checks on Supreme Court Power', *American Political Science Review*, December 1959, pp. 1017–31. See also H. Jacob, *Justice in America*, Boston: Little, Brown, 1965, pp. 192–4.

Political checks on the Court are, in principle, extensive. Congress can impeach (or threaten to impeach) and thereby remove Justices, change the number of Justices on the Court, diminish or withdraw its federal jurisdiction, cut appropriations necessary for general Court expenses, pass laws reversing statutory interpretations, or propose constitutional amendments curtailing judicial power. The following are but a few examples. The Eleventh Amendment took away from the Court its jurisdiction to hear suits against states. In 1802 Congress ordered the Supreme Court not to meet again for a year in order to delay a decision in *Marbury* v. *Madison*. In 1804 an attempt to impeach Justice Chase almost succeeded. After the Civil War, Congress withdrew the jurisdiction of the Court over appeals arising under the Habeus Corpus Act of 1867. In 1895 the Supreme Court declared that the income tax was unconstitutional, but this was reversed in 1913 by the adoption of the Sixteenth Amendment. After the Supreme Court decisions in the early 1960s over legislative apportionment, attempts were made in Congress to cut the general appropriations requests of the Court.

A major limitation on the Court is the fact that it is dependent on executive support to implement its decisions. Many Court decisions can only be enforced by an administrative agency. The President can order executive officials to refuse to enforce Supreme Court decisions, can use his position to influence the future composition of the Court, and may encourage congressional or other action designed to limit the authority of the Court. Presidents Jackson and Lincoln blatantly ignored judicial decisions, and some Presidents have encouraged state and local evasion of a Supreme Court decision by their failure to give it strong endorsement. The reliance of the Court on voluntary compliance with their decisions may not prevent the Court from acting but it may limit the extent of their political influence, since it is possible for state and local officials to evade, or refuse to co-operate in implementing a Court decision.[23]

The existence of these limitations, however, may restrain, but need not prevent, the Court from playing a strong role in making and implementing policies, but this role is affected by

[23] See F. J. Sorauf, '*Zorach* v *Clauson*: The Impact of a Supreme Court Decision', *American Political Science Review*, September 1959, pp. 777–91.

the attitudes of its members and by external political circumstances. As Martin Shapiro has demonstrated, the Supreme Court plays a wide variety of roles in the various areas of its jurisdiction. It has also played different roles at different times within the same area of jurisdiction. At times it has sought to limit the power of Congress to regulate commerce and the economy, at others it has given Congress strong support. Over antitrust legislation it has often sought to lead policy, but over matters of taxation it has avoided policy-making. In some areas, such as Congressional investigations, it has sought to limit the scope of such activities and set out specific standards, in other areas it refuses to set out a specific doctrine.[24] On certain matters the Court, through its opinions on cases, can seek to persuade the President to initiate certain policies. It can also declare Presidential actions as unconstitutional, as President Truman found in 1952. On occasions it has sought to direct the administration of policies, either in the face of challenges to such policies or to support political forces anxious to implement such policies. In this regard the Court has often supplemented as well as thwarted Presidential attempts to direct, co-ordinate and administer policy.

The President and the Political System

Commentators have found it useful to distinguish between 'weak' or 'strong' Presidents, depending in part upon the views of Presidents on their role and their performance in office. The view of President Taft, that Presidential power was limited to those powers specifically granted to him by the Constitution and by acts of Congress,[25] has been contrasted with statements made by Presidents such as Theodore Roosevelt and Woodrow Wilson that the President should be a powerful figure undertaking a variety of responsibilities. In the 1960s it is apparent that every President must exercise firm political leadership and must be strong in order to perform his administrative and managerial duties of co-ordination, and his political responsibilities

[24] See M. Shapiro, *Law and Politics in the Supreme Court*, New York: The Free Press of Glencoe, 1964.

[25] See W. H. Taft, *Our Chief Magistrate and His Powers*, New York: Columbia University Press, 1925.

of innovation and persuasion, both within government and out-side. His freedom of choice is limited by a range of factors but his responsibilities are clear.

The federal system has felt the impact of the increase in the scope of Presidential government. Modern Presidents have come to feel less inhibited by the limitations of states' rights and to seek to extend their influence over policy-making into certain aspects of state and local government. In part this is the result of the political significance in any Presidential election of the city vote and the electoral college votes of the large urban states. We have seen that 'creative federalism' involved the develop-ment of national programmes designed to use funds and resources to help solve problems of housing, poverty, transporta-tion, and education in the cities. The success of these pro-grammes rested heavily upon the ability of the President to exercise strong control over fiscal priorities. Americans thus became accustomed to independent Presidential action in many fields, from the federalising of state guards to the use of executive agreements in foreign affairs, if he chose to act.

In the late 1960s a major pressure on the President proved to be fiscal, and a major policy question that of priorities be-tween overseas commitments and domestic crises.[26] Congress had already demonstrated its ability to limit the effective imple-mentation of legislation passed by the 89th Congress following the massive electoral victory of President Johnson in 1964. In 1967 it also rejected Presidential demands for tax increases, and found the increasing financial demands of the war in Vietnam provided an excuse to force economies from the President within the bureaucracy and impress on the President the need to lessen foreign aid commitments and contain the expansion of the implementation of social legislation at home.

However, as a vital political factor, city problems are likely to affect Presidential government in the future if any President is to continue to commit the United States to the goal of broadening equality of opportunity as well as protecting basic freedoms. Presidents need to respond to events, and their pur-poses are affected by events. In domestic affairs the President has become the great initiator and promoter of new ideas and

[26] See J. M. Burns, *Presidential Government: The Crucible of Leadership*, Bos-ton: Houghton Mifflin, 1965.

has come to undertake increased responsibilities, while in foreign affairs he has become the final decision-maker.

Changing economic and social conditions, both domestic and international, have increased the responsibilities of the President within the American political system as a whole. The essential elements of the modern Presidency are the result of increased socio-economic change and interdependence in American society. They are not measured simply by the increase in the volume of activities of the national government. The political system must provide for the negotiation of adjustments and the determination of priorities among alternative lines of action when a society is subject to rapid change. It is the development of such changes that accounts for the actions of President Lincoln in the Civil War period, of Theodore Roosevelt in intervening to resolve the anthracite coal strike in 1902, of Franklin Roosevelt in demanding a negotiated settlement to end the sit-down strikes of 1936, or John F. Kennedy's intervention in 1962 to prevent steel firms raising their prices.[27]

The responses demanded by rapid change have come inevitably from the President because, in a political system emphasising checks and balances, his position is the only one where quick and authoritative action is both possible and legitimate. He can at least initiate activity, and choose between priorities, with a reasonable expectation of these decisions being accepted. President Truman, however, found out in 1952 that while he could act to end a serious steel dispute during the Korean War by persuasion, he could not take over the steel industry without acting unconstitutionally. Yet he was still able to take action as he saw fit. A President's choices may not be adopted, or his actions may be unsuccessful, but he can no longer escape involvement, whether the matter be economic or political. As E. S. Corwin has stated: 'The President's very obligation to the law becomes at times an authorisation to dispense with the law.'[28]

Congress can use a variety of weapons to limit the discretionary authority of the President over domestic affairs. It may change laws, change appropriations, and seek to investigate

[27] See G. McConnell, *Steel and the Presidency, 1962*, New York: W. W. Norton, 1963.

[28] E. S. Corwin, *The President: Office and Powers*, New York: New York University Press, 2nd edition, 1941, pp. 114–15.

and oversee administrators. In practice, however, while the executive power of the President is in itself limited and cannot easily be used to overrule Congress, over domestic matters a President combining the will to obtain and the ability to persuade is likely to be able to defeat Congress in the long run. The President's responsibility for directing American foreign and military policy is limited constitutionally but in fact is far less subject to limitation than domestic responsibilities. In time of military crisis, Presidents have always been able to act with initiative and suffered little opposition. On matters of diplomacy also the President has, with the single exception of the Senate rejection of the Versailles Treaty in 1919–20, a considerable advantage over Congressional opponents. In these areas it has proved difficult for Congress to refuse to accept the actions of the President without appearing to be acting contrary to the national interest, especially in the years since the Second World War.

Many difficulties confront a President in exerting policy leadership and mobilising Congressional support in the general area of foreign affairs. The President is likely to try to develop a consensus, among people inside and outside government, on the basic goals of American foreign policy and the appropriate means of attaining such goals. Congress is an integral part of this national consensus, and the President needs their support, and success depends on an ability to obtain a majority in support of a programme. In order to do this, the President may have to exert direct influence on the legislative process, and the nature of such intervention is important. The President must be exceedingly tactful about such intervention.

A direct method of persuasion may be to try to alter the preferences and perceptions of constituency opinion held by Congressmen. A President may also appeal to specific sub-groups of Congressmen, appealing to one group in terms of party loyalty, or to a committee as a group, or to the opposition in terms of the importance of bipartisanship in foreign affairs. He may also make specific appeals to individual Congressmen, either directly or indirectly. The particular tactics chosen must be used carefully. The powers of the President are sufficient to allow him to be the leader in the making of foreign policy, but he is likely to face sufficient opposition to require careful consideration of strategies to persuade Congress to give him strong support and to ensure bureaucratic efficiency in implementing policy decisions. While his constitutional position provides ample resources to mobilise both public and governmental support, the range of his authority over foreign affairs is by no means unlimited nor is support guaranteed.

Congress has indeed tried to limit Presidential prerogatives in particular situations. Two examples illustrate the problems involved for Congress. In the 1950s, 'conservatives' in Congress tried, through the so-called Bricker Amendment, to restrict the ability of the President to make executive agreements, by making them dependent on Congressional authorisation. Such agreements had been made by Presidents in terms of their executive authority, without requiring the Senate approval demanded for a formal treaty. Later versions of the Bricker Amendment took a broader character, but Senate debate on the proposal in 1954 led to the substitution of a milder version by Senator George of Georgia which required that all treaties and executive agreements be subject to the limitations of the Constitution, and denied to executive agreements any self-executing force. This substitute failed to obtain the necessary two-thirds majority in the Senate by only one vote in February of 1954.

In 1967, following increasing criticism of the escalation of American military involvement in the war in Vietnam, Senator Fulbright, as Chairman of the Senate Foreign Relations Committee, began a campaign attacking Presidential usurpation of authority in making foreign commitments based on a joint resolution of Congress in 1964 known as the Gulf of Tonkin resolution. This resolution gave Johnson unlimited authority to take all necessary steps, including the use of armed force, against aggression in South-east Asia.[29] Fulbright argued that Congress should have considered the requests of the President more carefully, and his Committee passed a resolution demanding that the constitutional powers of Congress to declare war should not be eroded by Presidential usurpation, and that future joint congressional resolutions should be more precise in their delegation of authority to the President. Further resolutions and amendments introduced in Congress sought to limit the use of Ameri-

[29] See J. W. Fulbright, *The Arrogance of Power*, London: Cape, 1966, Chapter 2.

can military forces in South-east Asia, and to restrict Presidential initiatives not backed by Congressional approval. Accompanying this was a strong determination to rectify the imbalance of power in matters of foreign affairs that had developed between the executive and legislative branches of government.[30] While increased public discontent forced President Nixon to end direct American involvement in the Vietnam war, and continued opposition in Congress to his use of war powers led in 1973 to legislation intended to limit Presidential initiatives and reassert Congressional authority, executive discretion in the domain of foreign policy still greatly exceeds that which can be exercised over domestic policy areas.[31] President Nixon faced little formal restraint in his efforts to take significant new initiatives over relations with the Soviet Union and with the Peoples Republic of China, and to change the balance and emphasis of American foreign policy.

Nevertheless, the political trauma of Vietnam provoked comment which was explicitly sceptical as to the necessary virtue of a strong and energetic President, initiating policies at home and abroad, and expressed concern at the decline in the traditional accountability of the executive and in checks on its activities. Some warned of the dangers of undertaking too many responsibilities and initiatives. Others pointed to evidence of the growing insulation and isolation of the President from normal political and party conflict and controls believed to be fundamental to responsible democratic government.[32] One consequence of these developments was the growth of decision-making structures within the White House designed to help the President exercise greater unilateral control over those areas of policy to which he gave top priority, but at the risk of increasing his dependence on a small group of advisors and abandoning accepted methods of consultation and persuasion. The actions of President Nixon in asserting the inherent powers of the President, as exemplified in his claims regarding the scope of executive privilege, his excessive use of impoundment authority

[30] For detailed discussion of this, see F. O. Wilcox, *Congress, the Executive, and Foreign Policy*, New York: Harper and Row, 1971.

[31] On this point, see especially A. Wildavsky, 'The Two Presidencies', in A. Wildavsky (ed.), *The Presidency*, Boston: Little Brown, 1969.

[32] See H. G. Nicholas, 'The Insulation of the Presidency', *Government and Opposition*, Spring 1973, pp. 156–76.

and veto powers, and his attempt to defend any action of his Administration (legal or illegal) as necessary to preserve national security, ultimately produced a constitutional crisis which culminated in his resignation from office in August 1974.

However, the rise of the imperial Presidency was not solely the consequence of the personal attitudes, ambitions and insecurities of Richard Nixon, and the particular political situation faced by his Administration. It was the culmination of a pattern of Presidential activity begun in the Kennedy Administration, consolidated by Johnson with disastrous personal and dramatic political consequences, and consummated after 1968. Its development was tacitly encouraged by many observers of the Presidency, and abetted by the reluctance and inability of Congress, the political parties and public opinion to exercise necessary checks and restraints. While the constitutional process did finally, if belatedly, bring down the edifice created by Nixon, there remained the formidable but necessary task of ensuring the more responsible exercise of executive authority in the future. This requires, at the very least, statutory changes in the financing of Presidential elections. It also requires public recognition that the frankness, integrity and constitutional responsibility of Presidential candidates is at least as important as their policy attitudes, and that the man they elect must earn rather than inherit respect and authority. Congress too must assume and assert more responsible oversight and accountability of the activities of all spheres of the executive branch. Above all the President must be aware not only of the awesome nature of his potential authority but of the necessity for comity and consent if his actions are to be legitimate, and also recognise that how he decides may be as crucial as what he decides in fulfilling his duties under the constitution.

Chapter Ten

POLICY PROCESSES

The patterns of political activity and influence in the United States are complex. The case-studies which follow are designed to illustrate this complexity and provide a series of instances in which different institutions of government interact in response to specific problems or situations which tend to recur in the American political system. Certain questions, such as foreign aid or farm legislation, produce annual conflicts between institutions of the national government. Other questions affecting foreign relations, such as the Cuban missile crisis of 1962, occur as a consequence of political events outside the United States, and often require swift and decisive action on the part of the President. In domestic politics, particular problems such as urban decay or poverty are often taken up by groups and organisations inside or outside the political process and come to require some response, usually by the President, in the form of legislative recommendations.

Problems affecting civil rights and education can arise as a consequence of the federal system and the particular polyglot nature of the American population, and require some political response even if they may not be capable of resolution. Others such as legislative reapportionment arise as a result of changes outside the political process to which the normal channels of political action may not respond. In contrast to questions of policy, such matters are technical as well as substantive, and raise basic questions about the legitimacy of existing institutions, in this particular instance the question of the representative nature of state and national legislatures.

None of these case-studies are unique. Other examples raising the same basic questions about the nature and workings of the American political system might equally have been used. They provide a series of 'snapshots' of the political process in action, illustrating many of the points raised and discussed in earlier chapters. The fact that some of the case-studies may now seem a little 'dated' is less important than the nature of the inter-actions between political institutions and individuals that they illustrate. New issues and problems emerge, new admini-strations reflect different priorities, but the nature of the policy process remains substantially the same.

Before considering the case-studies, it is important to sum-marise the pattern of the law-making process in the American federal system. This formal process is more complicated than that in Parliament. Many bills introduced in Congress will never reach the statute book. There are three major types: public bills (for general legislation affecting citizens as a whole), private bills (for specific legislation affecting named persons or organisations), and joint resolutions. Behind the recommenda-tion of bills may lie a long history of agitation or planning by interest groups or government departments. Many important bills are recommended by the President in formal messages to Congress, but bills can only be introduced by Congressmen, at the request of the President or interest groups or on their own initiative. The framing of legislation is often important because the parliamentarians in either the House or Senate decide, without debate, to refer it to a standing committee which has jurisdiction over the subject-matter of the bill. Every standing committee receives more bills than can possibly be handled, and many bills are 'pigeonholed' and forgotten and are never re-ported out of committee. Those bills in which the committee chairman has a personal interest are generally given prompt attention, and important bills supported by the President usually receive careful scrutiny by the committees who decide on their recommendations at a 'mark up' session where specific points of a bill are discussed by the whole committee. Non-controversial bills may go through committee and Congress quickly, but the normal procedure for most bills is slow and it is often very difficult to force committees to speed up their deliberations. In both houses, bills go on calendars in the order reported, and there are devices available to bring certain bills forward for swift consideration. Certain appropriations and revenue bills are 'privileged' and can be brought up for con-sideration in the House by the Committee of the Whole at almost any time. Others require special rules which are proposed by the House Rules Committee before they are considered. In the Senate there is only one legislative calendar, from which the Majority Leader, after consultation with the Minority Leader and other influential Senators, selects bills for floor action.

Bills are debated on the floor of the House and Senate, where amendments can be offered and formal recorded roll-call votes taken on such amendments and on the bill itself. If a bill is passed in the House, the Speaker signs it and sends it to the Senate, where committee deliberation and recommendations precede the Senate floor debate, which is less restricted than that of the House. Normally, House and Senate versions of a bill differ, and these differences may require conference committee action. Once a compromise bill is agreed to in conference, and is passed in identical form by both Houses, it goes to the President for his signature. After receiving advice on the bill, the President can act in one of three ways. He may sign the bill, thus making it law. He may return it to the branch of Congress from which it originated, with a veto message indicating his objections to the bill, and it can then only become law if it is passed in identical form by both Houses by a two-thirds majority. He may neither sign nor object, and if Congress is still in session on the tenth day (Sundays excepted) after the President received the bill, it becomes law; but, if Congress has by this time adjourned, the bill does not become law and the President is said to have exercised a 'pocket veto' on the bill.

Once a law is passed it must be implemented by the Administration according to the terms of the law. To do this requires the appropriation of funds by Congress, and the need to obtain further Congressional action can mean that certain fiscal and other limitations may be placed on the way in which a law is implemented. The need to obtain funds annually to implement a law may also lead to a situation where a law is on the statute books but is rendered ineffectual because of the refusal of Congress to appropriate adequate funds to implement it. Standing committees of Congress and interest groups also try to exercise careful watch over the implementation of legislation by executive departments, especially on controversial matters, as the initial case-study demonstrates.

Recurring Conflict: the Struggle for Foreign Aid Funds

In the years since 1945, no single aspect of American foreign policy has come under such frequent and critical scrutiny by Congress as the foreign aid programme. Because the assent of Congress is required for almost all such expenditures, foreign aid proposals give Congress a maximum opportunity to influence executive policies. Though aid proposals have in general been accepted by Congress, they have provided a major source of conflict between any President and Congress. Congressional influence has varied with the issue, the party in power, and the individuals in leadership position, but overall such influence has been significant in shaping or circumscribing foreign aid policy.

Basic tension between Congress and the President over foreign aid springs from the fact that Congressmen are often required to appropriate specific amounts of money for general categories of aid but have little control over specific details or projects in the programme. Congress therefore often inserts restrictive amendments into such legislation to strengthen legislative control. Cuts in the foreign aid programme have often come by fiscal action, with Congress initially authorising less money than that sought by the Administration and then appropriating less money than originally authorised, as Table 10:1 indicates. The House in particular has also generally looked more favourably upon military rather than economic aid.

Table 10:1

CONGRESSIONAL ACTION ON FOREIGN AID FUND REQUESTS
Selected Years 1948–68 (in thousand million dollars)

Fiscal Year	Request	Authorisation	Appropriation	% Cut
1948–9	$7·37	$6·91	$6·45	12·5%
1950	5·68	5·59	4·94	13·0%
1955	3·48	3·05	2·78	20·1%
1960	3·93	3·58	3·23	17·8%
1964	4·53	3·60	3·00	33·8%
1965	3·52	3·50	3·25	7·6%
1966	3·46	3·36	3·22	6·9%
1967	3·39	3·50	2·94	13·3%
1968	3·46	2·67	2·30	33·5%

Source: Congress and the Nation 1945–1964, Congressional Quarterly Inc., 1964, p. 185 (amended).

Committee or sub-committee chairmen in particular have been influential in Congress over foreign aid, though the nature of such influence depends in part on position and personal prestige in Congress. One of the most influential Congressmen was the late Senator Vandenberg of Michigan, Chairman of the Senate Foreign Relations Committee in the 80th Congress (1947–8) controlled by the Republicans, who sought to assist President Truman to get his request for Greek-Turkish aid accepted, as a prelude to obtaining Republican support for a European Recovery Programme. Senator Fulbright of Arkansas also used his position as chairman of the Senate Foreign Relations Committee after 1959 to support foreign aid programmes, but in 1966 sought a reappraisal of American economic and military aid programmes in the context of the goals of American foreign policy as a whole. Representative Passman, a Louisiana Democrat, has used his position as chairman of the Foreign Operations Sub-committee of the House Appropriations Committee to mount an annual attack on foreign aid programmes to eliminate wasteful or unnecessary expenditure, especially on economic aid.

The increase in foreign aid programmes after 1945 came in response to demands for economic aid from European countries, and evidence of increased Soviet intransigence in Central Europe. In 1947 President Truman urged Congress to authorise military as well as economic aid on a bilateral basis to Greece and Turkey, and in December of that year sent to Congress a message calling for $17 thousand million in grants and loans over four years to maintain European recovery. This programme, inaugurated in 1948, was begun, despite opposition within and outside Congress, as a result of bipartisan efforts by supporters in Congress.

Following the signing of the North Atlantic Treaty in 1949, Truman asked Congress to authorise substantial amounts of military aid to European allies and certain other countries. This began the development of extensive military and economic aid, and became part of a general Mutual Security Programme. After 1953, however, the pattern of aid changed as the Soviet Union began to take an increasing interest (through offers of aid and technical assistance) in underdeveloped and newly independent countries. In 1961, the mutual security arrangements were ended, and economic aid was administered by a new Agency for International Development, with military aid coming under the Defence Department. By 1966 the foreign aid programme, despite economies by President Johnson, was criticised by former supporters, and also suffered from pressures on funds created by the American commitment in Vietnam.

Foreign aid legislation was one of the most controversial subjects facing Congress in 1966. It was also unusual because it involved a reversal of attitudes by the two branches of Congress. In previous years the House had been anxious to keep the authorisation and funding of foreign aid programmes on an annual basis, while the Senate had been more generous in its attitude towards authorisations. Congress normally accepted a foreign aid programme which contained severe cuts in funds requested by the President, and provided funds on an annual basis, but authorised programmes on a multi-year basis. In 1966, the President got legislation which suffered fiscal cuts and was also restricted to a single-year authorisation.

President Johnson requested a multi-year authorisation and the separation of economic and military aid into two bills. Congress enacted one bill and authorised most programmes for one year only. The result was the most important foreign aid setback encountered by Johnson since becoming President. Yet it was also the first time in the history of foreign aid programmes that Congress authorised more than the amount of funds sought by the President. The struggle with Congress in 1966 indicates how external circumstances, in this case the mounting costs of the war in Vietnam and increased Congressional criticism of the foreign policy of the President, can add a particular twist to an annual confrontation between Congress and the President.

On February 1st, 1966, President Johnson asked Congress to appropriate just under $3·39 thousand million for foreign assistance in fiscal 1967. This was the smallest request in the history of the programme and considerably less than in the previous year. The President submitted two separate requests, one for authorisations covering five years, the other for appropriations for fiscal 1967. The President also argued that separation of military and economic aid would clarify the goals and functions of programmes, while a five-year authorisation would free Congress from the burdens of annual renewal and would indicate the depth of American commitment.

The House Foreign Affairs Committee held hearings from mid-March to mid-June on the foreign aid authorisation requests. Members of the Committee indicated to Administration witnesses, which included the Secretary of State, that they were willing to be convinced of the need for lengthy authorisation, but felt five years to be too long. The Secretary of Defence also testified in support of the military aid requests. On June 23rd, the House Foreign Affairs Committee reported a single bill authorising some $4·1 thousand million in funds for fiscal 1967 and some $4·2 thousand million in fiscal 1968 for both military and economic assistance. The bill was approved by a 28–7 vote of the Committee on June 20th. Military and economic aid was combined into a single bill despite the request of the President, and provided a two-year authorisation for almost all programmes. Specific fund limits were set for every programme in each fiscal year. The Committee added certain policy statements to the bill – among them were statements that the President should keep Congress informed about countries receiving aid which divert economic resources for propaganda directed against the United States, and a prohibition on aid to countries trading with North Vietnam.

Five Republicans opposed the existing aid programme in a minority report, and six other Republicans voiced their opposition to two-year authorisations. On July 14th a foreign aid bill was passed, authorising the appropriations recommended by the Foreign Affairs Committee. Although a multi-year authorisation was approved, it met strong opposition, narrowly surviving a Republican attempt to cut funds and authorise most programmes for one year only. Republican floor opposition was strong, though four Republicans on the House Foreign Affairs Committee supported the multi-year authorisations and provided vital votes, along with five Democrats who opposed the bill but also voted against the Republican action.

The Administration put strong pressure on House Democrats to accept multi-year authorisations, especially the five Democrats who ultimately switched for the crucial vote. The Speaker and the House Majority Leader spoke in the debate on the Republican amendment, a rare occurrence on such a matter.

Before passage, the House adopted several policy amendments, one seeking to prevent funds given to the United Nations from going to Cuba, another seeking to limit aid to countries who might be helping North Vietnam.

The Senate Foreign Relations Committee began hearings in April of 1966 on the President's foreign aid requests. In a speech on the Senate floor, Senator Fulbright, chairman of the Foreign Relations Committee, announced the start of the hearings and criticised existing United States aid programmes for failing to provide sufficient resources to generate growth in underdeveloped countries, and also criticised certain bilateral aid programmes. On April 6th he introduced seventeen amendments to the aid requests. Testimony was heard from Administration witnesses, and the hearings at which the Secretaries of State and Defence testified were televised, and much discussion centred on Vietnam, where a major portion of the economic aid programme was to go. On July 7th the Committee reported a bill authorising less than $2·4 thousand million for foreign economic aid, over $117 million below the request of the Administration. When the Committee met to 'mark up' the bill, several major amendments were made by Democrats. The aid programme was to be extended for one year only and development funds were to be cut. The Committee bill recommended a one-year authorisation for economic aid programmes, and limited the number of countries eligible to receive assistance in order to concentrate aid to fewer countries, and such aid was not to be construed as creating a commitment to use U.S. forces to defend another country.

The Committee report stressed that consideration of the aid programme and some changes of attitude were influenced by the Vietnam war, since many Committee members believed the United States was overcommitted in the world at large. Aid should be concentrated on fewer countries, with greater use of multilateral mechanisms. The report also sought to explain the reversal of Committee support for multi-year authorisations. It stressed that the current world situation had led to a consensus on the Committee against long-term authorisations, though members continued to support the foreign aid programme as a necessary instrument of American foreign policy.

On July 26th, 1966, the Senate passed the foreign economic aid bill after a week of sharp and critical debate. Some twenty-six restrictive floor amendments were accepted, and twenty-seven roll-call votes were taken on the bill. Several amendments cut back fund requests and others affected the implementation of the bill by the Administration. The Senate version was very different from that passed by the House, and from the original requests of the Administration.

The bill was managed on the Senate floor by Senator Fulbright. Contrary to normal practice, he supported several restrictive floor amendments. An amendment by the Senate Minority Leader to reduce the Development Loan Fund by $250 million was accepted by a 59–34 roll-call vote and was supported by Fulbright, but another amendment opposed by Fulbright was accepted, with twenty-five Democrats opposing the Committee recommendations. An amendment to cut supporting assistance by $42 million was accepted, and it was left to a Republican to get an amendment accepted to provide a two-year authorisation for an important programme (the Alliance for Progress). Senator Morse, a Democrat and a member of the Foreign Relations Committee, opposed the amendment, as did Senator Fulbright. Other amendments passed or defeated indicated that the Democrats were divided over specific matters relating to the bill. In general debate, Senator Fulbright outlined his opposition to bilateral aid, and set out proposals for reforming the aid programme, while Senator Kennedy of New York criticised the Senate attack on the bill and the unwillingness of the Administration to defend the bill strongly.

The bill, as passed by the Senate, authorised a two-year programme for the Alliance for Progress and one-year funds for other economic aid programmes. Total authorised appropriations for economic aid were approximately $2·1 thousand million. On July 7th, 1966, the Senate Foreign Relations Committee reported a military aid authorisation of $892 million ($25 million less than the Administration's request) for fiscal 1967, limited to forty the number of countries which would receive grant assistance, and prohibited military aid to any nation failing to prevent its ships or aircraft from transporting goods to or from North Vietnam. The Committee expressed its uneasiness over the existing military programme, and Fulbright indicated his general opposition to the military aid requests.

On July 27th, the Senate passed an amended bill authorising appropriations of $792 million for foreign military aid during fiscal 1967. The cut in the original Committee recommendation followed a roll-call vote accepting an amendment by Senator Church, Democrat from Idaho and a member of the Foreign Relations Committee, to reduce the authorisation for fiscal 1967 appropriations by $100 million. Thirty-two Northern Democrats supported this action, and almost as many Republicans as Democrats sought to prevent this and uphold the President's position. An amendment to make even heavier cuts was defeated, with every Republican who voted voting against the cuts, as did almost all Southern Democrats. Senator Fulbright, though floor manager of the bill, voted for the funding cuts and against the final passage of the bill. This action was very unusual, since the floor manager normally seeks to defend the recommendations of the Committee of which he is a member.

On August 31st, House and Senate conferees presented a conference report resolving the differences between House and Senate versions of the foreign assistance legislation. Two Democratic Senators refused to sign the conference report, as did two Republican Representatives. The House conferees indicated that the conference report did not express agreement between the House and Senate as to the nature and administration of foreign aid. The military and economic aid bills were joined together and an authorisation was made of over $3·5 thousand million total funds for fiscal 1967, almost $120 million more than the Administration had requested. All programmes were limited to one year, except the Development Loan Fund and the Alliance for Progress which received three-year authorisations—the Administration had requested five-year authorisations for all programmes. House conferees preferred bilateral aid rather than through international institutions, while Senator Fulbright wanted the reverse. The conference took a month to resolve the differences between them, and many of their compromises were 'contrived' in order to obtain some sort of agreement. Few conferees seemed happy with the final result. On September 1st, however, the House adopted the conference report, but Representatives (including the Foreign Affairs

Committee chairman) expressed general disappointment with the final measures. On September 7th, the Senate adopted the report by a 33–25 roll-call vote. Senator Sparkman of Alabama managed the floor debate of the conference report, and indicated that authorisations were fixed largely by accepting figures midway between those authorised by the House and Senate, and the House agreed to accept Senate limitations on the length of authorisation in exchange for the Senate accepting a joint bill for both military and economic aid.

Despite limitations on authorisations, the recommended appropriations were in excess of Administration demands. However, funds had still to be appropriated. The Foreign Operations Sub-committee of the House Appropriations Committee considered the fund requests and, as in the past, was not generous. On September 16th, the House Appropriations Committee recommended appropriating less than $3·1 thousand million for foreign aid, almost $300 million below the initial Administration requests, and most sections of the bill were cut. The House, on September 30th, voted to appropriate less than $3·05 thousand million for foreign aid. Before passage, by a 186–163 roll-call vote, the House accepted a motion by Republican Representative Bow, of Ohio, the ranking minority member of the House Appropriations Committee, to recommit the bill with instructions to limit economic aid to a figure 10% below the President's initial request. Only eight Republicans voted against this amendment, and Democratic defections (especially Southern Democrats) proved sufficient to gain its acceptance.

Representative Passman, chairman of the House Appropriations Sub-committee on Foreign Operations, as floor manager of the bill, spoke at length against the foreign aid programme, and for the acceptance of certain amendments restricting Presidential discretion in using funds. He showed that traditional House hostility, as expressed in fiscal terms, remained high. On September 28th, the Senate Appropriations Committee reported a recommendation that less than $3·05 thousand million be granted for fiscal 1967 foreign aid. Two programmes were cut below the amounts appropriated by the House, but certain other items were increased by small amounts. On October 5th the Senate voted to appropriate $2,936,490,500 for foreign aid. They adopted three amendments by Senator Ellender, Democrat from Louisiana and a member of the Senate Appropriations Committee, which involved cuts of some $110 million in three of the foreign aid programmes. It was apparent that the Senate wanted to make further cuts, though debate in general was short. Senator Pastore, of Rhode Island, floor manager of the bill, opposed the cuts, but Senator Fulbright supported cuts in military aid. Several amendments were added, on the lines of amendments in the original Senate authorisation which had been deleted in conference with the House.

On October 6th the House–Senate conferees agreed on a $2,936,490,500 total for foreign aid appropriations in fiscal 1967. On October 7th the House adopted the conference report as did the Senate later. In Senate debate, Senator Fulbright expressed pleasure that the conference had agreed to give the President discretionary authority to transfer some funds to international organisations for multilateral aid purposes, but threatened that if this opportunity was not taken by the President he would oppose bilateral aid bills in the future.

The Administration proposals received a drastic overhaul by Congress. They rejected proposed changes in foreign aid authorisation, and also provided less money than requested by the President. Numerous restrictive amendments also limited the scope of his discretion in using the funds appropriated. The Senate accepted the President's request for separate economic and military aid bills but not for multi-year authorisations, and the House took the reverse attitude. The result was that in order to obtain a compromise and obtain some programme and funds, neither of these proposed changes was accepted. The major issues of the bill were debated against the background of the Vietnam war which divided Congress in support or opposition to the President's policies. The changes in attitude toward foreign aid by former supporters in the Senate such as Senator Fulbright were a consequence of their general opposition to the foreign policy of the Administration. Traditional House hostility toward foreign aid was muted to some extent by uncertainty, with an election near at hand, about the attitude of the public toward the war. Though Fulbright did not lead floor attacks on the bill in the Senate, he encouraged such attacks in committee and did not oppose such attacks by other Senators.

The foreign aid bill in 1966 was affected not simply by the

normal type of conflict between Congress and the Administration, but also by a special internal conflict in Congress, between and within the House and Senate, involving a considerable reversal of roles and attitudes on the part of many influential Congressmen.

The Administration found that old opponents in the Republican party were prepared to preserve parts of the bill against cuts made by traditional supporters of such legislation. Senator Fulbright, a firm supporter of foreign aid, became almost as hostile as a traditional opponent, Representative Passman, but for very different reasons. Administration strategy to divide military and economic aid, in order to obtain more of the latter, might have succeeded in a 'normal' year, but had little chance of acceptance in 1966. The Democrats in Congress were completely divided on the issues involved, and the Administration seemed unable or unwilling to put extensive pressure on them. In the House many Northern Democrats worked to preserve what they could of the original requests, while some Northern Democrats and other traditional supporters in the Senate seemed anxious to embarrass the President and attack many of his requests. Traditional Southern Democratic and Republican opponents of foreign aid on fiscal grounds continued their opposition, but other Republicans in both Houses who tended to agree with the Administration policy in Vietnam supported the military aid requests of the Administration. The Administration, in turn normally reluctant to put strong pressure on Congressmen over foreign aid, in this situation found it even more difficult to anticipate Congressional reactions and actions. External interest group influence was less evident than in previous years, though groups such as the Liberty Lobby continued to testify at committee hearings against the foreign aid programme as a whole.

In 1967, the Administration found Congress even tougher, final appropriations being the lowest in the history of the foreign aid programme. In 1969, Republican President Nixon called for a reorganisation of the entire foreign aid programme, following record-low authorisations and appropriations for fiscal 1969. But in his first term Congress rejected two foreign aid bills outright, and in three of the four years of the 91st and 92nd Congresses final congressional decisions were not reached until the succeeding session, and funding for foreign aid continued to drop. This conflict has, since 1968, become a symbol of the wider legislative-executive struggle over the making of foreign policy decisions, especially following Nixon's efforts to make foreign aid a major weapon in his revamped foreign policy.

Presidential Initiative and Response

1. *The Cuban Missile Crisis of* 1962

The crisis in 1962 was one of a long series involving the United States and Cuba. It was, however, the most dramatic, and provided a crucial test of the ability of President John F. Kennedy to lead the United States in a direct confrontation with the Soviet Union and challenge the Russian installation of offensive missiles in Cuba. The immediate background to the situation was not auspicious. The first major problem in foreign affairs which faced President Kennedy on taking office also concerned Cuba, and it had proved to be disastrous.

The history of Cuba as an independent republic has been a turbulent one. One régime after another came to power with promises of progressive reform only to turn to graft and corruption. The feeling of political frustration and contempt for existing régimes among professional men and intellectuals stimulated the rise of a revolutionary force pledged to implement the liberal constitution of 1940, and provide free elections, civil liberties, and agrarian reform. In 1958, Fidel Castro overthrew the Batista régime and created a new government which by 1959 seemed clearly committed to the establishment of a Marxist dictatorship in Cuba and to serve the ends of Soviet foreign policy. The Castro revolution was very popular in the United States initially, though official policy towards Castro was somewhat confused. Castro, however, appeared to scorn any suggestions of American aid and adopted a hostile attitude toward Washington.

As Arthur Schlesinger has indicated, Cuba was not a new issue for Kennedy in 1960, nor was his view of Castro wholly negative.[1] He had no doubt that Castro had betrayed the ideals of the revolution and made Cuba a communist satellite. In his election campaign he condemned the policy of the Eisenhower Administration towards Cuba, but felt that there was now little

[1] See A. M. Schlesinger, Jr., *A Thousand Days*, London: André Deutsch, 1965, Chapters 9 and 10.

that could be done to get rid of Castro. He had no knowledge, until he had won the Presidential election, that a secret Cuban army of exiles was in Guatemala training, with the help of American members of the Central Intelligence Agency. On November 17th, 1960, Kennedy learnt of their scheme to land in Cuba and lead a revolt against Castro. On November 29th, Kennedy received a detailed briefing on the C.I.A.'s plans to support such activities. His response seemed sufficiently positive for the C.I.A. to continue to make plans. In the interim period between the election and inauguration of Kennedy, such plans were allowed to become more definite, despite press publication of the existence of the exile army in Guatemala.

Immediately after his inauguration, Kennedy was again given details of the plans, and his reactions were cautious. The Joint Chiefs of Staff gave limited approval to certain invasion plans. In early March the President of Guatemala wrote to President Kennedy requesting assurances that the Cuban exiles leave his country by the end of April. The C.I.A. also reported that Castro was about to receive jet aircraft from the Soviet Union, to be flown by Cuban pilots trained in Czechoslovakia. By mid-March it seemed that Kennedy was confronted with a virtual *fait accompli*. A contingency scheme soon became a reality. Kennedy agreed tentatively to allow the plans for the invasion by the Cuban exiles to continue provided there was no direct American military involvement, but he added carefully that he would still make the final decision.

The C.I.A. planners finally settled on the Bay of Pigs as the best invasion area, and continued to indicate that such an invasion would gain an increasing amount of local support. Kennedy, however, remained sceptical, despite support for the invasion by the Joint Chiefs of Staff, but later he made the decision to go ahead on April 17th, provided the operation was entirely Cuban. The invasion proved to be a disastrous failure in which the United States could not escape from charges of involvement. Kennedy immediately accepted sole responsibility and shouldered the burden of criticism of America by other countries, and sought to contain the political consequences of the *débâcle*.[2] Most Americans, however, rallied behind the President

[2] For a detailed account of the invasion, see H. Johnson, *The Bay of Pigs*, New York: Dell, 1964.

in the moment of national crisis. Arthur Schlesinger indicates that by May 3rd Kennedy wryly pointed out that if he had been a British Prime Minister he would have been thrown out of office, but that in the United States failure had somehow increased his charm.[3]

Later Kennedy sought to understand how a rational administration had come to involve itself in so ludicrous an adventure. The invasion was misconceived both technically and politically. Kennedy, above all, blamed himself, though he was also privately critical of his 'inherited' advisers, in particular the C.I.A. and the Joint Chiefs of Staff. Yet he also saw this as an important lesson and set to work to ensure that no such fiasco could occur again. He sought to free himself from the bonds of established experts and attain a position of flexibility in which his personal advisers would be more influential. The Bay of Pigs proved to be a harsh initiation for Kennedy, but it steeled him for the situation which was to develop with the further deterioration of relations between Cuba and the United States, and the actions of Russia in pouring military equipment and personnel into Cuba.

On October 15th, 1962, American U-2 planes returned from reconnaissance missions over Cuba with evidence that Soviet medium-range missiles and missile sites were clearly in place on the island. This revelation set off a train of diplomatic and other events which brought the United States to the brink of nuclear war. Kennedy had some inkling of such developments for several months, but this final evidence required positive action on the part of the United States to call Khrushchev's bluff. In September, Khrushchev asserted that only defensive weapons had been imported into Cuba, and Kennedy had publicly declared that if this were not in fact the case then the situation would be grave.[4]

Kennedy convened the Executive Committee of the National Security Council, which after intensive discussion decided to intensify air surveillance over Cuba. The Committee remained in session while Kennedy continued to perform his normal long-established commitments, which included a meeting with the Soviet Foreign Minister, who reaffirmed previous assurances that Soviet activity in Cuba was purely defensive, and Kennedy repeated his assertion that grave consequences might follow if

[3] A. Schlesinger, *A Thousand Days*, *op. cit.*, p. 265.
[4] See L. W. Koenig, *The Chief Executive*, *op. cit.*, pp. 371–82.

this in fact were not so. The Executive Committee gradually developed a strategy which involved the use of a sea blockade. On October 20th, Kennedy broke off a brief campaign visit to Chicago and returned suddenly to Washington on the pretext of having a heavy cold. On arrival he directed that the necessary preparations be made to impose a blockade, subject to his final word to go ahead the next day. In the evening of the 21st of October, after discussion and briefings with senior Congressmen and members of his administration, Kennedy delivered a public statement presenting the facts of the situation to the people. He blamed the Soviet Union for violating the assurances of its leaders, and said that he had ordered a 'quarantine' on all offensive weapons coming into Cuba. Ships carrying them would be turned back, and, if the preparation of missile sites in Cuba continued, then further action would be taken.

The initial Soviet reaction was a lengthy statement of accusations and warnings about the possibilities of thermonuclear war, followed by a letter from Khrushchev to Kennedy. Reactions from many other countries to Kennedy's statement were positive, though U Thant, Acting Secretary General of the United Nations, called for a suspension of the blockade and of arms shipments to Cuba while negotiations were held. Khrushchev accepted this but Kennedy turned it down. In the first twenty-four hours of the blockade a Soviet tanker was stopped but not searched, and later a freighter from the Lebanon was stopped, boarded, and searched by U.S. Navy personnel.

Khrushchev then sent Kennedy two letters, the first offering to withdraw offensive weapons, supervised by U.N. forces, if the American blockade was lifted. The second letter, however, suggested that the Soviet Union would trade its bases in Cuba for the N.A.T.O. missile base in Turkey. Kennedy chose to ignore the second, and responded by indicating that he would accept the removal of offensive weapons from Cuba in return for ending the blockade. In the meantime, American military forces were mobilised to attack Cuba if necessary, and general military mobilisation was stepped up, and similar action apparently took place on the Soviet side.[5] A single accident or incident could

[5] See H. M. Pachter, *Collision Course*, New York: Praeger, 1963, especially Chapter 1. See also D. L. Larson, *The Cuban Crisis of 1962*, Boston: Houghton Mifflin, 1963.

have begun a war, and almost did. An American U-2 aircraft was shot down over Cuba and another U-2 on a mission from Alaska went off course and flew over territory of the Soviet Union.

However, on October 28th, Khrushchev wrote to Kennedy to say that he had ordered work on the missile sites to stop, and agreed to ship back to the Soviet Union the weapons deemed offensive by the United States, and promised to allow U.N. observers to verify that the sites were dismantled. In return he sought assurances that the United States would not attack Cuba or tolerate attacks on it by others and would discontinue flights over Cuba. Kennedy responded by congratulating Khrushchev on his constructive and statesmanlike decision.

In the months which followed this direct confrontation, both sides treated the Cuban question with great caution. Resistance by Castro made it impossible to obtain U.N. inspection as Khrushchev proposed, and therefore the United States never fully gave a reciprocal pledge not to invade Cuba. However, the direct crisis had been averted, but the decisions Kennedy had been forced to make were fraught with peril, and his actions revealed the necessary balance of initiative and caution required by a contemporary President. Unlike the Bay of Pigs disaster, he insisted on obtaining clear evidence of Russian missiles before he took any action and having taken his stand he remained impervious to legislative criticism. Yet he always allowed Khrushchev an option or alternative plan of response. The decision to set up a blockade allowed Khrushchev the choice of ordering Russian ships to be diverted. Kennedy, in turn, kept certain options. He did not wholly rely on the blockade, but speeded mobilisation and readiness of American forces and so put additional pressure on Khrushchev. The President also was careful to escalate the crisis slowly in order to allow Khrushchev to consider developments, and also to keep the final decisions about the blockade and its implementation in his own hands. Khrushchev in turn perhaps underestimated Kennedy, bearing in mind the Bay of Pigs disaster.

Crisis produces distinctive patterns of decision-making and administrative activity from a President. Crisis makes a President more dependent on his staff and on his ability to utilise their expertise, yet makes it more necessary for him to take final decisions himself. Kennedy recognised that in this particular instance three important factors worked in his favour. The crisis took place in an area where the United States enjoyed local conventional superiority, and where Soviet national security was not directly affected. Moreover, it was not a situation where the Russians could plausibly sustain their position before the world. Presidents since have not always found themselves in such a favourable position, nor found their actions supported by the public or indeed Congress.

2. *The Demonstration Cities and Metropolitan Development Act of 1966*

In November 1966 President Johnson signed into law a new programme whose main feature was a three-year $1·2 thousand million 'demonstration cities' plan. Housing officials later renamed the programme 'model cities' so as to avoid association with street demonstrations and riots which had taken place in many American cities in 1966. The plan was designed to rebuild entire urban areas by tying together existing federal and local programmes and also involving local community organisations in participating cities.

In 1965 Congress had passed two other major pieces of housing legislation, one establishing a Department of Housing and Urban Development, the other an omnibus bill expanding existing urban renewal programmes and authorising new programmes such as rent supplementals to low-income families. Earlier housing legislation in 1932 and 1933 was intended to help people, through improved credit facilities, to maintain home ownership and provide national funds for low-cost housing and slum-clearance projects as part of a general effort to alleviate unemployment.

There have been three distinct types of national government activity relating to housing. Since the 1930s the national government encouraged the flow of private capital into housing construction and sought to help in the insurance of home mortgages. This, combined with cheap credit facilities, makes house purchase in America for the ordinary white working man generally easier than acquiring a council house in Britain, and the quality is often higher. Yet many poor Americans cannot take advantage of this and are forced to remain in slum housing in decaying city centres.

A second government activity involved assistance to state and local governments in slum clearance and urban redevelopment as established by the Housing Act of 1949 and expanded in the Housing Act of 1954. Under these acts, national grants can be obtained to provide two-thirds of the funds for urban renewal projects. A third programme is public housing. In 1937 Congress provided for loans and grants to state and local governments for construction of public housing maintained by cities as low-rent housing, with the national government providing a capital grant or annual subsidy. However, such public housing was usually available only to families with incomes below a certain level. All of these programmes were opposed in Congress and by private groups, and development of many of the programmes was slow.[6] The lack of a co-ordinated policy caused administrative problems in Washington which also undermined their implementation. In the 1950s and early 1960s, however, a growing body of professional opinion, including administrators, social workers, members of the building industry, and finance corporations, began to press for more efficient co-ordinated action.

In 1964, President Johnson, in his famous 'Great Society' speech, made extensive reference to the need to act to improve the quality of urban life. Late in 1965 the President appointed a special Task Force on Urban Problems headed by Robert Wood, an academic urbanologist, and the basic concept of the demonstration cities plan came from their recommendations. The success of President Johnson in 1964 and 1965 with housing legislation prompted him to take swift action. In his State of the Union message on January 12th, 1966, he called for public and private efforts to eliminate urban blight. On January 26th the President submitted to Congress a special message outlining his proposals for city development.

In his message President Johnson emphasised the need to concentrate available resources and skills in a co-ordinated effort to improve the conditions of life in urban areas and to mobilise local leadership and citizen participation through governmental financial and administrative aid. Johnson emphasised the

[6] See *Congress and the Nation 1945–1964*, Washington, D.C.: Congressional Quarterly Inc., 1965, pp. 468–9.

importance of establishing a programme of demonstration grants to selected cities for co-ordinated local programmes designed to show how urban renovations and other activities could revitalise the centre of large cities.

The legislative recommendations presented to Congress involved several major proposals. Communities could apply for planning grants to take part in the project and would be financed by grants of up to 80% by the Department of Housing and Urban Development. After approval of initial plans, further funds and technical assistance would be available. On completion of planning, cities might then apply for grants to carry out their projects, and the programme was designed to encourage the integration of various welfare and renewal projects at all levels. The President estimated the total cost of the six-year programme at $2·3 thousand million.

The demonstration cities proposal was referred to the Housing Sub-committee of the House Banking and Currency Committee. Other bills relating to housing and urban development were also pending at the same time. The sub-committee held hearings on all these, plus a substitute bill sponsored by a Republican which sought to lessen the degree of co-ordination and control exercised by national agencies. Hearings were held between February 28th and March 26th, 1966, and Robert Weaver as Secretary of the Department of Housing and Urban Development was the major witness (along with the mayors of several large cities) in support of the Administration proposals, while spokesmen for the National Association of Real Estate Boards, the U.S. Chamber of Commerce, the National Association of Manufacturers, and several smaller groups, testified against the demonstration cities bill.

The House Banking and Currency Committee reported an omnibus version of the Administration bills following Sub-committee approval by a 7–3 vote and full Committee approval by an 18–8 vote, after rejecting two amendments, one by a Democrat and the other by a Republican. Approval came only after intense lobbying by Administration officials following reports that a bipartisan group on the Sub-committee sought to reduce the demonstration cities programme from $2·3 thousand million to a mere $12 million in project planning funds, because they did not think the original measure could pass the House.

The final Committee recommendation on July 15th included minor changes to the original request. No rule was granted for full House consideration of these recommendations, and there was no further action until after the Senate passed a resolution in August, dealing with the demonstration cities proposals.

The Housing Sub-committee of the Senate Banking and Currency Committee held hearings on the proposals from April 19th to 29th, and heard testimony from Weaver and a representative of the U.S. Conference of Mayors in support of the bill, along with Senators from both parties. Criticism of the bill came from the mayor of Louisville, Kentucky, and a representative of the General Improvement Contractors Association. On August 9th the full Committee reported to the Senate, and reduced demonstration city planning and action funds from $2·3 thousand million to $924 million, and the duration of the programme from six to three years. The Committee also reduced an Administration request for additional funds which was submitted after hearings had been completed. The total cost of the revised legislation was to be $1·2 thousand million. Certain other modifications were made to the legislation.

The bill, by August 1966, was clearly under heavy attack in Congress. What was the explanation for this? Several factors appeared to be responsible. Firstly, the Department of Housing and Urban Development, sponsor of the bill, was a new department relatively unskilled in the art of dealing with Congress. The timing of the introduction of the legislation was not ideal. Despite the existence of a strong 'liberal' Democratic majority in the House, many House members had reservations about the bill, and the new Chairman of the House Sub-committee on Housing was something of an unknown quantity to the Administration. In the Senate, the Chairman of the Sub-committee on Housing of the Banking and Currency Committee, Senator Sparkman of Alabama, felt that Johnson should not be demanding new legislation so soon after the omnibus bill of 1965 and its controversial provisions. The interest of the Senator was further dampened by the approach of a stiff party primary election fight in May 1966 to retain his Senate seat.

Further, the legislation itself was selective. No Congressman could vote for the bill and be certain it would bring assistance or national funds to an urban area in his constituency. The original fund request, $2·3 thousand million spread over six years, seemed too little for those Congressmen directly concerned with city problems, and far too much for those who were not. Many city officials who testified before both sub-committees, while keen to receive national funds, had some reservations about the degree of control over their activities envisaged by the Department of Housing and Urban Development, and were especially critical of the possible existence of so-called 'federal co-ordinators'.

The Administration was therefore forced to develop several distinct strategies to counter opposition. Initially, Presidential advisers and department administrators alike were pessimistic about the chances of the bill, but were encouraged by a strong speech from Lawrence O'Brien, Johnson's appointee as Postmaster-General, but better known as chief 'troubleshooter' in Congress for both Presidents Kennedy and Johnson. Two broad strategies of Congressional pressure were adopted. A deliberate attempt was made to compromise on some aspects of the bill and so persuade 'waverers' in Congress to support the bill, and at the same time persuade the unwilling, inside and outside Congress, to accept the President's programme. Before this strategy could get under way the House Sub-committee had prepared its recommendations, but on June 1st the Chairman was persuaded to delay action on the bill for three weeks by senior members of the Administration. This delay enabled Administration lobbyists to concentrate on the consideration of the bill in the Senate.

The original measure had little support within the Senate Banking and Currency Committee, members being concerned about the costs of the bill and its objectives. In an effort to work out a compromise, President Johnson took the unusal step of sending members of the White House staff to participate in the actual committee 'mark up' of the bill, and the deletion of certain items and a cut-back in the duration of the programme finally satisfied several critics, and the modified bill was approved by an 8–6 margin. The Administration had some difficulty in securing a suitable manager of the bill to steer it through committee and get support on the Senate floor. Two members of the Committee who in the past had supported liberal housing legislation, Senators Sparkman, of Alabama, and Douglas, of

Illinois, were senior full Committee members and Housing Sub-committee chairman and second ranking member respectively. However, both faced strong election opposition in 1966 and feared the political consequences of close association with such controversial legislation. Senator Muskie, of Maine, was finally persuaded to undertake the task, but only in return for certain compromises by the Administration. One of these included provision in the bill for participation by small metropolitan areas, which might help small towns in Maine. Muskie also found that further compromises were necessary to obtain majority support in the Sub-committee and get the approval of the full Committee.

The majority report of the Senate Banking and Currency Committee strongly supported the compromise proposals, but the four Republicans on the Committee issued a minority report criticising both the original proposals and the compromise recommendations. On August 19th the Senate, by a 53–22 roll-call vote, passed the demonstration cities bill. Before passing the bill, the Senate defeated a move by Senator Tower, Republican from Texas, to delete all funds to implement the demonstration programme, leaving only planning funds. Tower, backed by Senate Minority Leader Dirksen, argued that such large domestic spending should be deferred until the country could afford it. Seven minor amendments were accepted by voice votes.

With the bill through the Senate, it was up to the House to consider the matter. House Speaker McCormack advised delay, but fears of inflation and the victories of 'conservative' Democrats in primary elections in Maryland and Georgia increased pessimism among supporters of the bill in the House. Outside the immediate Congressional battle, members of the Administration were seeking to unite private and semi-public organisations in support of the legislation. A new 'Urban Alliance' was formed which began to hold regular meetings in Washington and put pressure on Congress.

The Housing Sub-committee in the House was persuaded to reconvene and consider the Senate proposals. The Sub-committee met in late August and approved these proposals, and added some general amendments. The full Banking and Currency Committee reported the bill to the House on September 1st. A minority report by eight of the eleven Republican members of the Committee stated that they felt that actual costs would be far higher than indicated, and separate supplemental views were submitted by individual Republicans on the Committee criticising specific aspects of the bill. Before the House considered the bill, the House Republican Policy Committee issued a statement criticising the control over the new programme to be exercised by the Secretary of Housing and Urban Development. Later, however, a group of senior business executives, including several prominent Republicans, issued a statement urging the House to pass the bill promptly.

The House took up the bill in mid-October, and, after a bitter floor debate, passed the measure, with amendments, on a roll-call vote. Before passage the House rejected by roll-call vote a motion by a Republican to recommit the bill to the Banking and Currency Committee with instructions to delete the $900 million authorisation for demonstration city projects. An amendment by another Republican, who had opposed the bill in committee, sought to require the Justice Department to investigate local group participation in the programme to ensure they were not connected with any 'black power' or racist organisations. After strong debate this amendment was rejected, but several amendments were accepted which would limit Departmental responsibility for co-ordinating the programme.

The majority in favour of passage was small, and few members changed their votes from the roll-call vote to recommit to Committee. Once a recommittal vote is defeated, some Congressmen normally take the opportunity of changing their vote to one of support or do not vote on the roll-call vote for passage of the bill, but in this instance there was little or no change.

On October 17th, conference committee members from the House and Senate resolved differences between House and Senate versions and agreed on a tentative compromise version. The conference report was presented on October 18th, but two House Republican conferees did not sign the document. Conferees agreed to a Senate provision not in the House bill requiring that demonstration city assistance first be used to finance new programmes not federally assisted before being used to defray costs of the local share of programmes receiving federal aid. A minor House provision, not included in the Senate bill, was also accepted.

On October 18th, the Senate adopted the conference report by a 38–22 roll-call vote and the House two days later by a 142–126 roll-call vote, and on November 3rd President Johnson signed it into law. The Administration requested $12 million for planning demonstration city projects in a special supplemental appropriations request which went before the Senate Appropriations Committee on October 19th, and which it approved. As a result of conference committee consideration by members of the House and Senate Appropriations Committees, the conference report recommended $11 million and this was accepted by voice votes in the House and Senate on October 21st and 22nd respectively.

Voting on the final stages of authorisation of the legislation saw Congressmen consciously lining up as 'liberals' or 'conservatives'. Party cohesion and strength of turnout, however, was especially marked among Republicans in the House, and there was a good deal of evidence of Southern Democrats joining with Republicans in opposition. On the three House roll-call votes a very high percentage of the Democratic votes against the measure in the House came from the South.

The case-study illustrates some of the difficulties a President must overcome if he lacks strong support in Congress. In a situation of maximum political strength in the 89th Congress, with massive Democratic majorities (295–140 in the House, 68–32 in the Senate) and after a highly successful first session of Congress for legislation instigated by the President, this attempt to extend and build on legislation accepted in 1965 to solve problems in the cities, a platform on which the President campaigned in the 1964 election, obtained only modest results after eight months of intensive pressure by the Administration. An initial request for a six-year programme costing $2·3 thousand million ended in a compromise bill providing only $1·2 thousand million over three years. Despite compromises, the bill came under strong floor assault from Republicans in both the House and Senate, and its outcome was never a foregone conclusion in either House. In formal roll-call votes there were substantial Democratic defections, especially by Southern Democrats.

Having obtained legislative authorisation, however, proved to be only half of the battle. The executive now had to ensure that sufficient funds would be appropriated annually to make the legislation effective. Yet, of the $12 million requested for immediate use as planning funds for fiscal 1967, only $11 million were obtained. In 1967, faced with a larger Republican membership and a depleted 'liberal' Democratic membership in the House, the programme was almost eliminated. Despite intensive lobbying, original requests for $662 million for fiscal 1968 ($12 million in planning funds, $400 million for grants to implement the programme, and $250 million in urban renewal funds to be used as part of the programme) were cut to $312 million by Congressional action. Close to 80% of House Republicans voted to recommit and delete all funds for the demonstration cities programme, and they were supported in their general opposition by a majority of Southern Democrats. The result was that the share of the money available to participants in the programme (191 cities and counties) was cut drastically. Fears of inflation, possible tax increases, the rising costs of the Vietnam war and a decreased Democratic majority, cut support in the House for the programme to a bare minimum except on the final roll-call vote adopting a second conference report (the first conference could not agree on funds for the programme) recommending $312 million. Without Senate resistance to House demands, the programme would have been cut more heavily. As Congress has so often demonstrated, it is one thing to pass legislation and another to be able to implement it. Many supporters of the demonstration cities programme in 1967 must have wondered if indeed half a loaf is better than none, especially in a situation where there was real doubt as to whether programmes financed and administered largely by the national government (but subject to the vagaries of Congress) are more likely to provide a solution to the major problems of the cities than comprehensive co-ordinated action by private groups at the local level.

The legislation seemed badly timed, final voting coming too close to election time for many Congressmen. Moreover it was a bill many Democrats dare not oppose, while others would have preferred not to have to make a decision, and where the Republicans gained electoral propaganda through organised opposition. In the end the efforts of the Democratic Administration were hardly worthwhile. Controversy continued over implementation, critics arguing that it suffered from insufficient federal funds and too much federal control, while at the local level there was conflict between citizen groups and city government over control of the programme. Early in the Nixon Administration a Presidential task force advocated continuation, but with greater control by city government and financial organisation more in line with Nixon's revenue-sharing plans. Despite this attempt to remodel a Great Society programme to conform to new patterns of intergovernmental relations, there is little evidence that the Republicans sought in any way to extend or develop legislation which itself almost 'died' in 1966 in Congress.

Problems of Federalism

1. Civil Rights 1964–1968

The American federal system has been criticised because it has sheltered opponents of civil rights. William Riker has argued that the main beneficiary of American federalism has been the white Southerner, who has been free to oppress Negroes as slaves and later as a depressed caste. It also aided special business interests by protecting them from regulation in the period 1890–1936. His conclusion – that if one approves of Southern white racists and the values of a privileged minority one should approve of American federalism – is harsh, but it demonstrates that federalism has not always served to guarantee full political and social equality for all.[7] Problems relating to racial discrimination are affected by the nature of the federal system. No consideration of political action in this area can escape questions of federal jurisdiction, states' rights, the position of the U.S. Supreme Court as arbiter of federal–state relations, or the internal autonomy of the states.

The problem of Negro rights demonstrates that the role of the states in the federal system is not just a question of structure, for very often this structural question becomes a political question. The guarantee of Negro rights depends on the willingness of states to carry out or comply with national policy, and the differing responses of different states indicate that states may reflect very different political cultures and attitudes towards matters they consider to be local rather than national. Only in

[7] See W. H. Riker, *Federalism. Origin, Operation, Significance, op. cit.*

cases where it can be demonstrated clearly that the states cannot or will not implement the Constitution as interpreted by the judiciary is it possible for national authorities to intervene, and this too may only be possible with the aid of special statutory authority.

This conflict illustrates the simple fact that the American federal system provides little or no coercive power for the national government to enforce national legislation or U.S. Supreme Court decisions upon state governments who refuse to co-operate. This tradition of American federalism has an important symbolic effect. Even when the national government has the authority, it is reluctant to use coercion upon states because the effectiveness of the federal system is believed to depend upon compliance not coercion. In many instances, of which civil rights for Negroes is a prime example, the national government has not sought to dominate, or deprive states of powers which they believe belong constitutionally to them, but has tried to avoid open conflict by seeking to persuade states to comply voluntarily with decisions of the national government rather than coerce states into compliance by the use of limited or temporary authority. The extent to which such self-restraint can continue when individual rights are being violated has led to cruel dilemmas. Civil rights groups demand national governmental action to uphold the Constitution; the national government seeks to avoid direct conflict between state and national authority because of the disintegrative effect it may have on the federal system as a whole, yet failure to act also causes tension and hostility on the part of Negroes which in turn creates internal unrest.[8]

This situation can be related to both historical and practical experience. In part it is a consequence of the traditional recollection of the difficulties of trying to impose and maintain national authority in the Southern states during the Reconstruction period after the Civil War, along with a practical recognition of the major administrative obstacles involved in such activity at the present time. It may also be related to a cultural unwillingness, which must be overcome, to coerce white men in American society on behalf of Negroes.

[8] See H. F. Way, Jr., *Liberty in the Balance*, New York: McGraw-Hill, 1964, Chapter 1.

The existence of state legislation relating to civil rights prior to national governmental legislation in the 1960s indicates the different political cultures existing in many states. In 1966 no state in the Deep South had any anti-discrimination statutes, whereas elsewhere thirty-eight states had legislated in some form against discrimination, and there was no correlation between the scope of such legislation and the size of the Negro population in these states.[9] In certain states like Oregon and Minnesota, the total black population is very small yet they have quite extensive legislation, while four states (Illinois, Kentucky, Missouri and Oklahoma) have been tardy about enacting anti-discrimination laws yet have an average or higher percentage of Negro residents. In geographic terms the area with the greatest number of states in 1966 with extensive laws relating to fair employment practices, fair housing, and open public accommodations was the North-East, and the area where the least had been done outside the South was in those states bordering the South. Where state party politics is highly competitive there is a greater likelihood of stronger state anti-discrimination laws.[10]

In the 1950s and 1960s, however, states have been under severe pressure to end racial segregation, and resistance in many Southern states forced the national government to assume a more coercive role to enforce constitutional guarantees. Attempts to pass civil rights legislation since 1945 found formidable obstacles in Congress, especially among Southern Democrats, who were able to combine influence based on seniority and procedural rights, notably the filibuster in the Senate, to prevent any extensive legislation. Civil rights groups therefore sought to persuade the Supreme Court to take action in the absence of legislation to end segregation in schools and other public places.

In 1954 the Supreme Court responded to such pressure through litigation, and, in the case of *Brown* v. *Board of Education of Topeka, Kansas*, required the desegregation of public schools 'with all deliberate speed', and asked lower courts to require a

[9] See W. B. Graves, *op. cit.*, Chapter 9; also M. R. Konvitz, *A Century of Civil Rights*, New York: Columbia University Press, 1961.
[10] See D. Lockard, *Toward Equal Opportunity*, London: Collier–Macmillan, 1968, Chapters 2 and 6.

'prompt and reasonable start towards full compliance'. This decision led to some school desegregation in all segregated states except Mississippi, yet by 1964 less than 10% of the school children in states bordering the Deep South, and less than 1% in Deep South States, were in integrated schools. Legal and other resistance to the Supreme Court decision took a variety of forms in different states, and posed problems for federal judges in many Southern states required to implement the 1954 decision.[11] The national government had no direct way, except by the lengthy process of litigation, of enforcing compliance with the decision or preventing state governments from encouraging resistance by school boards backed by interest groups, and allowing private schools to be created and public schools closed.[12] In 1958, in a further decision, *Cooper* v. *Aaron*, the Supreme Court called on local school board officials to make a prompt start with school desegregation, and in 1963, in a decision on another desegregation case, the Supreme Court expressed impatience with the pace of school desegregation. In 1964 the Supreme Court, noting that there was 'too much deliberation and not enough speed', declared unconstitutional (as violating the equal protection clause of the 14th Amendment) the closing of all public schools in Prince Edward County, Virginia, to avoid integration. In 1965, the Court on several occasions showed its impatience with the rate of desegregation, and in 1967 denied a stay sought by six Louisiana school districts from a court order for desegregation of all classes in six states by September 1967.

However, judicial remedies for violations of civil rights in these areas are costly, slow, and lacking in sanctions. In 1964, President Johnson succeeded in obtaining comprehensive legislation from Congress, and the 1964 Civil Rights Act gave the national government certain sanctions to eliminate segregation and racial discrimination. For example, Title 6 of the 1964 Act allowed for the withholding of federal funds from school districts which continued to provide segregated public education. By late 1965 many school districts in the Deep South indi-

[11] See J. W. Peltason, *Fifty Eight Lonely Men, op. cit.*

[12] For an analysis of the variety of tactics used in the state of Virginia, see R. L. Gates, *The Making of Massive Resistance*, Chapel Hill: University of North Carolina Press, 1964.

cated they would seek to comply with the new legislation. The use of powers granted under Title 6 by the Office of Education, however, led to complaints by Southern states and to Congressional action to limit the scope of the guidelines given to administrators and to a revision of these guidelines in 1966 and the centralisation of enforcement within the Department of Health, Education and Welfare.[13] While legislative action did not guarantee the full elimination of segregation in public schools, it made such activities difficult to maintain, and it served to provide federal officials with some sanctions to aid enforcement of constitutional guarantees against state and local actions. The national government, however, can exercise only a minimal influence on the pattern of education at the state and local level, though the effects of legislation such as the Elementary and Secondary Education Act of 1965 will be to increase national influence over an area formerly regarded as primarily a state and local responsibility.

The major problem in guaranteeing the civil rights of all American citizens is that while there is a legal and constitutional commitment to one set of norms and attitudes about the problem there is also a strong *de facto* cultural commitment to a conflicting set of norms, and therefore there is resistance to formal action designed to translate constitutional guarantees into practical reality. In 1965, however, a major breakthrough was achieved with the passage of a Voting Rights Act. This followed extensive pressure by civil rights groups and Negro demonstrations in the South, and it was designed to prevent certain states from using their powers to control election procedures to deprive Negroes of their voting rights as guaranteed by the Fifteenth Amendment of the Constitution.[14] The result has been increased participation by Negroes in national and other elections in the South, and the election of more Negroes to state and local offices, and ultimately to Congress.

In other areas of civil rights the availability of legislative or judicial authority has not been as evident. The United States does not have a national police force such as exists in Britain,

[13] See *Revolution in Civil Rights*, Washington, D.C.: Congressional Quarterly Service, 3rd edition, 1967, pp. 111–15.
[14] See B. Marshall, *Federalism and Civil Rights*, New York: Columbia University Press, 1964, pp. 10–41.

and the national government is given no general police power unless a state can no longer maintain law and order. Federal government officials cannot protect the constitutional rights of a citizen from infringement by a state or local official because this is the responsibility of the state or local police. Federal officials can only intervene in a matter once a constitutional right has been violated or made the subject of a federal court action.

The general question of the administration of justice in the United States is a good illustration of the dilemmas which federalism can create. The following brief commentary provides a specific example. In December 1960, the U.S. Supreme Court ruled that passengers using bus lines which crossed state boundaries had a federal right to be free from racial discrimination in bus terminals. The decision provided the impetus for the so-called 'Freedom Rides' by whites and Negroes to test whether this federal right would be recognised in bus terminals in the Deep South. At Anniston and Birmingham, Alabama, the riders met with violence, and President Kennedy sought to persuade Governor Patterson, of Alabama, and local authorities to accept police responsibility for the safety of bus passengers, and obtained such assurance. The arrival of the Freedom Riders in Montgomery, Alabama, led to riots and violence, and a federal court later declared that the Montgomery police had engaged in wilful and deliberate failure to provide protection on the arrival of the bus. The U.S. Department of Justice had meanwhile made plans, in the event of continued failure to protect American citizens travelling across state boundaries seeking to exercise their federal rights in the face of local aggression, and obtained a court order preventing the Montgomery police from continuing to fail to provide protection for interstate travellers.

The groundwork was also laid for the use of direct federal police action to enforce the court order. Federal officers were instructed to proceed to Montgomery and be sworn in as deputy federal marshals. They later performed police duty and protected a Negro church where the late Martin Luther King was holding a mass meeting, and broke up the attempts of a mob to invade the church. Local police arrived, but the Governor put Montgomery under martial law and used his authority to call out the National Guard.

The Freedom Riders demanded to proceed to Jackson, Mississippi, and the U.S. Attorney General sought assurances from state and local officials in Mississippi that order would be preserved. In Jackson there was no disorder, but federal law was challenged with the arrest of the Freedom Riders when they sought to use the bus terminal facilities on an integrated basis, and attempts by others also led to arrests which could not be prevented by obtaining federal court orders.

The acceptance of a temporary federal responsibility to protect persons exercising federal rights in Alabama when the state failed to provide protection caused some confusion, but it forced state and local authorities to renew acceptance of responsibilities. In Mississippi, however, on the pretext of maintaining order, the federal rights of individuals were violated and this raised the question whether a federal court could be empowered in advance to prevent such action. The national government chose not to take such action but used the federal courts to prevent police and city authorities from maintaining segregation in terminals, and so avoided the delicate question of interference with local police functions. Reliance on voluntary compliance to legal decisions, federal court injunctions, and the implementation of civil rights legislation do not alone guarantee full civil rights. The murder of civil rights workers in Mississippi in 1964,[15] and the refusal of local authorities to try those suspected of the crime, followed by the fact that the federal courts could only try the suspects for conspiracy to violate the civil rights of the individuals, highlights the fact that federalism is heavily dependent on the voluntary compliance of all citizens of the United States with the laws of the land, and that laws at all levels should be applied equally by those officials given the authority to enforce the law, though clearly on many occasions they are not.

In 1966, Congress reversed its previous support and rejected a major piece of civil rights legislation. The measure was accepted, despite attack, in the House but 'died' in the Senate. An attempt in the legislation to bar racial discrimination in the sale and rental of all housing proved too controversial for Congress to accept until 1968, when a compromise bill was accepted. While, in the South, thousands of Negroes registered to vote for

[15] See W. B. Huie, *Three Lives for Mississippi*, London: Heinemann, 1965.

the first time in their lives, in the North the black ghettoes of the major Northern cities erupted in violence, school boards in the cities grappled with the problem of *de facto* segregation caused by the existence of ghetto communities, and relations between minority groups and city police forces deteriorated. A pre-1966 Gallup poll indicated that 52% of whites believed that the Johnson Administration was pushing racial integration too rapidly.

The nature of the problem was reflected in a few simple statistics. In 1910, over 90% of American Negroes lived in the South; by 1966, while the Negro population had doubled to 21·5 million, over 14 million now lived in metropolitan areas, and the number living outside the South increased elevenfold to 9·7 millions. In conjunction with an equally rapid white exodus from the centres of the cities, by 1968 one-third of all American Negroes and over two-thirds of those Negroes living outside the South resided in the twelve largest cities of the United States, seven of these cities being over 30% Negro, and one (Washington, D.C.) being two-thirds Negro.[16]

In the summer of 1967, the tempo of violence and rioting in Negro ghetto areas in cities large and small across the nation increased to crisis proportions, but Congress again rejected attempts to pass further civil rights legislation. There were grave doubts that even a compromise bill would be accepted in 1968, but the assassination of the black civil rights leader, Martin Luther King, in Memphis, Tennessee, in April 1968, followed by violent racial unrest, led Congress to approve a new piece of civil rights legislation. This legislation provided severe penalties to prevent the use of force or threats to interfere with an individual's right to vote, obtain any benefits from federal or federally aided programmes, obtain schooling, private or state employment, and use public accommodations. It also outlawed discrimination in the sale, rental, or advertisement of housing, both public and private, with only limited exceptions. This legislation seemed for many to be a far-reaching extension of the powers of the national government to guarantee the civil rights of all American citizens. After the Civil War, a series of compromises and adjustments to the federal system were

[16] See *Report of the National Advisory Commission on Civil Disorders*, New York: E. P. Dutton Co., 1968, Chapter 6.

made in order to save the union. By 1968 the new adjustments in the federal system marked by extensive federal guarantees of civil rights for black Americans were significant, but despite a diminution in the scope of urban rioting, problems remained which could perhaps be alleviated best by changes in personal attitudes and values rather than by governmental action alone.

2. *The Politics of Education*

While the education of Negroes has been one of the major sources of political conflict over civil rights in the United States since at least 1954, the formulation of governmental policies towards education as a whole has been affected by the nature of the federal system. As was indicated earlier, schools in the United States not only transmit learning and vocational skills, but also impart to the student broad cultural values. Because the state school system affects the political socialisation of every generation of Americans, education becomes inextricably linked with politics and the political system.

It has been a traditional article of faith in American society to protect the local control of public schools. The local school district has been the historical unit for administration of the primary and secondary school system. Schools are objects of local control, and control is exercised by the people in a school district through an elected school board who appoint a superintendent to act as the chief administrator in the district. While there are minor variations from this pattern, this was the most common arrangement in the 27,000 or so school districts in the United States in 1967.

Yet local control of the public schools no longer really exists. The boundaries of school districts, even their very existence, depend on state action. A major proportion of their revenue is provided from state funds (which in turn involves an increasing percentage of national funds). School districts are governmental units and school boards are engaged in political activity. They are forced to make important decisions on curriculum, facilities, personnel, and general organisation, and affecting all this is the basic issue of finance.

In the 1960s the support of public education became a major expenditure for many states. In the 1960–61 school year, it is estimated that public school revenue accounted for 33·9% of the revenue of state and local governments.[17] In some states there are state school boards, and such boards are often involved in considerable political controversy. While there are no formal groups opposed to state spending on public education, the fact that a public school system is a costly operation means that educators are in competition for the allocation of scarce financial resources. Major educational innovations are likely to involve increased expenditure and may require delicate negotiation and bargaining with political officials pressured by other interests seeking conflicting goals such as tax reductions. Interest group activity is therefore an essential part of the political activities of those responsible for public education in the United States.

Yet the activities of such organisations depend upon the political and social environment. Many of the basic conflicts in the American federal system affect education. The conflict between rural and urban interests affects the pattern of education and the extent of state financing of its public school system. Conflict over states' rights and national financial intervention into areas traditionally reserved to the states affects the public school system in many states, especially in the South. The controversial question of the separation of church and state in the United States and the role of church-aided private schools has affected governmental policies for the public school system, and it is very clear how racial conflict in American society has also been linked with matters relating to the nature of the public schools, and the type and quality of the education provided.[18]

As a result of these facts of life, organisations have developed in different states as spokesmen for the interests of the public school system. In Missouri, the State Teachers Association defines the school needs of Missouri, adjusts them to the political traditions of the state, and works to get their demands accepted by the state politicians. In Illinois an entirely different influence is exerted. The politics of education at the state level is dominated by the Illinois School Problems Commission, an agency

[17] See N. A. Masters, R. H. Salisbury, and T. H. Eliot, *State Politics and the Public Schools*, New York: Alfred A. Knopf, 1964, p. 4.

[18] See R. L. Crain, *The Politics of School Desegregation*, Chicago: Aldine Publishing Co., 1968; and L. Kushnick, 'Race, Class and Power: The New York Decentralization Controversy', *Journal of American Studies*, December 1969, pp. 201–20.

created by the state legislature in 1957. This agency seeks to combine the goals of educators with the realities of the political system. It has been successful in allowing considerable autonomy for the Chicago public school system in return for their support on school measures affecting the rest of the state, or the state as a whole.[19] Despite the fact that there are no organised groups opposing public schools, political conflict occurs over questions such as the amount of money a state can afford to spend on schools and on higher education, the effect of the reorganisation of school districts, or the extent of state as compared with local fiscal responsibilities. Some state legislators act as direct representatives of educational interests and can help to obtain favourable legislative action, and state superintendents of education may seek to exercise direct political influence.

The overriding political influence on public schools in the early 1960s came primarily from the increased involvement in elementary and secondary education by the national government, culminating in the Elementary and Secondary Education Act of 1965. Though the national government has exercised some influence over public schools in the past, the U.S. Office of Education being formed in 1867, the passage of this legislation came at the end of a long political struggle against those who argued that education was traditionally a state and local concern, and believed that national control and national regulations would inevitably follow federal aid. Supporters of the legislation had long argued that the level of education provided was a national concern and its determination could no longer be left to the states. Local tax resources in many of the poorer states were inadequate to provide the necessary standard of education which was the right of every child.

Opponents of federal aid were, however, aided by other factors. The existence of many private or church-sponsored schools raised the question as to whether such schools should or would be supported by federal aid. Catholics generally opposed attempts to omit such schools, while others refused to

[19] See N. A. Masters, *et al.*, *op. cit.*, Chapters 2 and 3. See also S. K. Bailey, R. T. Frost, P. E. Marsh and R. C. Wood, *Schoolmen and Politics: A Study Aid to Education in the Northeast*, Syracuse, New York: Syracuse University Press, 1962.

support any legislation which included provisions for aid to such schools. The question of federal aid to school districts with segregated schools also caused conflict, especially after the Supreme Court decision of 1954. Liberals insisted on preventing federal funds from being given to segregated schools, while many Southern politicians feared that federal funds would be used as a bait to force school districts to desegregate. Some politicians also supported federal aid for school construction but not for paying teachers' salaries, since the latter might lead to federal direction over what they taught, and others raised questions about the equity of the distribution of federal funds among the states.

President Kennedy began a major effort in 1961 to obtain a federal aid to education bill, and asked for a three-year authorisation of over $2·4 thousand million to help states build elementary and secondary schools and improve the salaries of teachers. In 1961, and again in 1963, such bills were defeated in Congress.[20]

In April 1965, however, a federal aid to education bill was passed. In the 1964 Presidential campaign, Johnson decided to make this question and the elimination of poverty central domestic issues. He believed the latter would be helped by the former. The co-ordinated efforts of the Office of Education and a special Task Force on Education created by Johnson sought to present a bill which would be acceptable to many of the interest groups concerned with this question, and would be politically realistic. Political factors in the 89th Congress, such as a 'liberalised' House Rules Committee and a large Democratic majority, were exploited, along with changes in public opinion about the importance of education prompted by Soviet space exploits, the plight of the urban poor, and the Negro in the South. Fears of federal control and matters such as support for religious schools had, however, to be considered in drawing up legislation.

Title I of the bill provided for federal grants to local school districts where at least 100, or alternatively 3%, of school-age children came from low-income families. Incentive grants were also provided, and the money was to be spent on programmes

<hr />

[20] See F. Munger and R. F. Fenno, Jr., *National Politics and Federal Aid to Education, op. cit.*; and R. Bendiner, *Obstacle Course on Capitol Hill, op. cit.*

designed to help the educationally deprived children. Poverty was established as the criteria for aid, and the formula was likely to affect approximately 95% of all counties in the United States, and would benefit, in particular, central urban areas in the North and rural areas in the South (the major bases of Democratic party support). Assistance would be given to educationally deprived children in private schools without giving money or facilities to such schools directly. State departments of education were given a major role in administering such grants.

Further concessions were made to religious educational institutions to allow them to participate in other aid programmes without receiving funds directly. Certain other provisions involved direct local–national co-ordination, though modest funds were also provided to strengthen state departments of education and so allay suspicions of excessive federal control. Considerable efforts were made by the Administration to ensure that the bill had a strong chance of passage before it was presented to Congress. Submitted to the House in January 1965, it received only minor changes by the House Committee on Education and Labour, was accepted by the Rules Committee, and was passed in March by a 263–153 roll-call vote (supported by almost all Northern Democrats, almost half the Southern Democrats, and by 25% of voting Republicans).

The Education Sub-committee of the Senate Labour and Welfare Committee considered the legislation, and the full Committee reported the bill without amendments, though several Republicans were unhappy about the increase in federal control involved. Eleven amendments were rejected during Senate debate, four by roll-call vote. The bill was accepted by a 73–18 roll-call vote and was exactly as the House had approved it. This avoided a conference committee which in the past had caused trouble for similar legislation. On April 11th, 1965, President Johnson signed the bill into law.[21] It marked the end of a lengthy battle and was the result of careful planning to produce legislation which would provide the necessary finances and assuage the opponents of federal aid to education.

Elementary and secondary education in Britain is not divorced

[21] See P. Meranto, *The Politics of Federal Aid to Education in 1965: A Study in Political Innovation*, Syracuse, New York: Syracuse University Press, 1967.

from political conflict or interest group activity, as has been shown by the attempts to obtain local authority support for comprehensive schools. The organisational framework within which public education is administered and conducted is, however, rather different. The extent to which such responsibilities have remained under the control of state and local authority in the United States produced a diversity of structure and organisation which is affected by the culture and traditions of the state, and by particular local influences. Organisational structure, and increasing financial dependence on state and national government, has brought education in the United States more and more into the political arena, and the federal system itself, plus the traditional adherence to state and local autonomy, has increased this involvement and stimulated political controversy. In 1967 close to two thousand million dollars were appropriated to implement the Elementary and Secondary Education Act of 1965, and over three thousand million dollars authorised for fiscal 1968. While state and local funds still provide the major portion of revenue available for public schools, national outlays for education have taken on a permanent, institutional, character which may have a significant effect on American education in the future.

The Making of Policy by Judicial Decision: the Case of Legislative Apportionment and Redistricting in the 1960s

In 1946, Kenneth Colegrove filed a complaint in the Federal District Court in Chicago, arguing that, as a resident of the Seventh Congressional District of Illinois, he was deprived of his constitutional right to equal protection of the laws as guaranteed by the 14th Amendment of the U.S. Constitution. The Seventh District contained some 900,000 people, and the Fifth District little more than 100,000. Such a disparity meant that his vote was worth about one-eighth of that of a resident of the Fifth District. The suit was dismissed by the district court, but he appealed to the Supreme Court, who also dismissed the suit, but disagreed as to whether they had jurisdiction to try the case. Justice Frankfurter wrote the opinion dismissing the complaint, and asserted that the whole matter of the apportionment of legislative representation was a 'political question' over which the federal courts had no jurisdiction. The remedy lay in securing state legislators prepared to apportion properly, or in obtaining Congressional legislation. Two other Justices agreed with Frankfurter, one Justice wrote a separate concurring opinion but did not accept that the federal courts lacked jurisdiction, and three Justices strongly dissented. Justice Black wrote the dissent, and argued that the Court had jurisdiction and should have decided the case in favour of Colegrove.

The rejection of this claim illustrates the hazards of seeking political remedies by legal action. It was easy for members of the Supreme Court to shelter behind the well-established doctrine of avoiding 'political questions'. As this case concerned Congressional districts, it was indeed possible for Congress to act. Yet the actual legal implications of the decision were not clear because of the conflicting opinions. However, in 1947, the Supreme Court refused to consider another suit by Colegrove, and in the next twelve years rejected eleven attempts to bring a case before them concerning legislative apportionment. The *Colegrove* decision also reinforced the disinclination of state legislatures to reapportion, or adjust Congressional district boundaries to reflect population changes revealed by the 1950 census.

However, the general question of malapportionment remained a controversial one. It affected political discussion in many states where it was most obvious, and was a source of a good deal of academic writing. In some states, citizens formed Committees for Fair Representation. Law journals also published articles critical of Frankfurter's opinion in the *Colegrove* case. In 1958, a Minnesota federal court ruled that it possessed jurisdiction to decide an apportionment case, but withheld judgment in order to allow the state legislature to act. The legislature did act.

External factors affecting the Supreme Court itself also began to change the general picture. In the 1950s the Supreme Court used the equal protection clause of the 14th Amendment to demand desegregation of public schools, and other public places. Between 1953 and 1960, four new appointments were made to the Court. Earl Warren became Chief Justice, and three Associate Justices remained who were on the Court when the *Colegrove* decision was given, and two of these had dissented from it. It was also apparent that, despite Frankfurter's plea to look to Congress or the state legislatures for action, few legislatures seemed prepared to take any action to remedy the inequities.

In 1959 and 1960, however, five separate lawsuits were initiated at the state level, designed to force the Supreme Court to consider the question again. In Tennessee, Michigan, New Jersey, Maryland, and New York, the suits were considered by the state courts or the Federal District court. Meanwhile another case had come before the Supreme Court in 1960 indirectly concerned with legislative reapportionment. In Tuskegee, Alabama, the Negro voting population had grown considerably, and to preserve white domination of the city, the Alabama state legislature redrew the city boundaries of Tuskegee, including only a small proportion of Negroes within the city limits. Negroes challenged this action, and brought a suit in the federal courts. Obtaining no protection from the Federal District court, the case was appealed to the Supreme Court.

The Supreme Court, in a unanimous decision, held that the action of the Alabama state legislature was proscribed by the 15th Amendment. Justice Frankfurter wrote the Court opinion and carefully distinguished between this case, *Gomillion* v. *Lightfoot*, and the question of equal representation. One of the Justices, however, could not accept the distinction, and in a concurring opinion argued that the case should have been decided in terms of the equal protection clause of the 14th Amendment since it was a clear case of changing electoral boundaries without regard to the effectiveness and equality of the vote. Despite Frankfurter's distinction, the decision did appear to weaken the effect of the *Colegrove* decision, and strengthened the claims of those seeking Supreme Court action against the failure of state legislatures to reapportion.

The case in Tennessee, *Baker* v. *Carr*, came before the Supreme Court in 1962. On the surface the citizens of Nashville, Tennessee, bringing the suit, had a strong case. The Tennessee state legislature had not reapportioned since 1901. State remedies were exhausted, and the key issue was whether the matter came under the jurisdiction of the Supreme Court and whether they could provide a remedy. One important strategy was to seek to get the Solicitor General, the chief attorney for the U.S. government, to present a supporting brief arguing that the national government had a vital interest in the case. The support given to those seeking a Supreme Court ruling on school segregation in 1954 by the Solicitor General helped to get the Supreme Court to consider the case. The Solicitor General agreed to enter the case, and filed an *amicus curiae* (friend of the court) brief in support of Baker.

In April 1961 the Supreme Court heard oral argument on the case, and ordered reargument at the beginning of the new term in October 1961. On March 25th, 1962, Justice Brennan, supported by five other members of the Court, decided only on the specific and narrow issues of the case. A citizen could sue in a federal court, and federal courts had jurisdiction of the subject matter of cases dealing with legislative apportionment and could make a decision on them. An individual had a federal right to be represented fairly. Two of the Justices who supported Brennan on this point believed he should have gone further and set a standard for testing the constitutionality of reapportionment plans. Justice Frankfurter wrote a dissenting opinion attacking the majority for accepting jurisdiction, and for involving the Court in political matters requiring choice between competing theories of representation.

Yet Frankfurter's view itself was not free from political implications. The decision not to interfere with 'political questions' can itself be based on political rather than constitutional views about the role of the Supreme Court in American politics. Also, not taking action when it was clear that few legislatures would take action on their own initiative, and were prepared to ignore provisions in their own state constitutions requiring regular reapportionment, in itself implicitly supported a flexible theory of representation as applied to apportionment of legislative districts rather than requiring equality of population in each legislative district.

However, while an alternative was now available to individuals, many problems remained. The decision of the Court provided a paradox. Those who viewed the Supreme Court as the protector of minorities now saw the Court acting in a 'political' way to curb the power of minorities to prevent majority rule in the state legislatures. It was also paradoxical for those who, with Justice Frankfurter, advocated judicial self-restraint, to criticise the Court for helping to make majority rule effective. The case for self-restraint is based on the argument that the Court, as an appointed body, should not presume to challenge legislative acts of elected representatives depending for their position on the support of a majority of those who elect them. As malapportionment destroys this argument, judicial action to remove obstacles to majority rule may thus be more acceptable than helping to perpetuate minority rule.

Having paved the way for judicial action, the Supreme Court had to face the consequences. As Justice Frankfurter warned, the decision empowered 'the courts of the country to devise what should constitute the proper composition of the legislatures of the fifty states'.[22] The Supreme Court was forced to use 'substantial equality' as a constitutional requirement in assessing state legislative apportionment action, thus elevating the principle of 'one person, one vote – one vote, one value' to the stature of a federal constitutional requirement.[23]

Two cases decided after *Baker* v. *Carr* indicate the development of the principle of 'one vote, one value' by the Supreme Court. In 1963, in *Gray* v. *Sanders*, the Court upheld claims that the county-unit system of voting in state-wide and congressional primary elections in Georgia violated the 14th Amendment. The unit vote system gave each county a certain number of votes, usually the number of its seats in the state legislature. The candidate gaining the most votes in a county won all its unit votes. However, a candidate might have the largest total vote but lose the nomination by failing to win counties in rural areas which often had more unit votes than counties in more populous areas. In 1964, in *Wesberry* v. *Sanders*, the Supreme Court reversed a lower court decision and invalidated a Georgia statute creating congressional election districts, the largest of which contained a population three times that of the smallest. The Court argued that the requirement in Article 1 of the Constitution that Representatives to Congress be chosen 'by the People of the several States' meant that as near as possible the vote of an individual in a congressional election is to be worth as much as any other individual.

[22] See *Baker* v. *Carr*, 369 U.S. 186 (1962), p. 269.
[23] See C. A. Auerbach, 'The Reapportionment Cases: One Person, One Vote – One Vote, One Value', in P. B. Kurland (ed.), *The Supreme Court Review, 1964*, Chicago: University of Chicago Press, 1964, pp. 1–87.

On June 15th, 1964, the Supreme Court decided that the apportionment of seats in the legislatures of six states failed to meet the requirements of the equal protection clause of the 14th Amendment, and a week later invalidated the apportionment of seats in nine more state legislatures. In doing so, the Court laid down certain basic constitutional standards. Seats in both houses of a bicameral state legislature must be apportioned on a population basis and states should make an honest effort to construct districts, in both houses of its legislature, as near to equal in population as practicable. Departures from this standard may possibly be justified in the apportionment of state legislative districts only to enable the state to use political subdivisions as bases for electoral districts and to construct compact and contiguous districts. Federal constitutional requirements would be satisfied if a state reapportioned its legislative seats once in every ten years. The Court did not determine precisely the permissible bounds of deviation from strict apportionment, indicating that state legislative districts might be more flexible than Congressional districts, which in 1969 it declared had to be as equal in population as practicable.

Despite the attempts of state legislature to avoid the implications of the *Baker* decision by legal and other devices, the 1964 decisions indicated that the Supreme Court was prepared to delve into the 'political thicket'. Inevitably there were immediate political reactions. Certain Congressmen demanded a constitutional amendment to allow one house of a state legislature to depart from the population basis, and before the end of June 1964 the senior Republican member of the House Committee on the Judiciary introduced a constitutional amendment allowing one house to be based on a pattern other than population if such a plan were approved by a referendum. The Republican National Convention adopted in their platform a statement urging a constitutional amendment and proposing a legislative moratorium on federal court action until such an amendment was ratified.

Several alternative schemes were tried in Congress. The most subtle was a bill introduced by the Senate Minority Leader, Everett Dirksen, which would have the effect of placing at least a two-year moratorium on reapportionment in all states. On August 4th, 1964, the Republican leader obtained approval of his bill by the Senate Judiciary Committee. Dirksen then announced he would offer the bill as an amendment or rider to the Administration's foreign aid authorisation bill. House rules forbid such amendments or riders which are not germane or relevant to a bill, but such action is permitted in the Senate. The foreign aid bill was vital to the Administration, and Dirksen hoped that in conference committee the rider would be accepted as the price for Senate concurrence in the authorisation. With Congress close to adjournment, and a Presidential election campaign already begun, it would be difficult for the President to veto his own foreign aid bill or for liberal Democrats to vote against the programme in order to defeat the rider.

Congressional opponents of the Dirksen rider claimed it was unconstitutional, and the Democratic Study Group in the House obtained over sixty supporters to a statement claiming they would vote against the foreign aid bill if the Dirksen rider remained. A small group of Senate liberals threatened a filibuster against adoption of the rider. Meanwhile, in the House, the Rules Committee chairman invoked a House rule which was rarely used, and in spite of objections by the House Judiciary Committee, sent a bill sponsored by Representative Tuck, Democrat, of Virginia, for consideration on the floor of the House. This bill sought to strip the federal courts of jurisdiction over apportionment cases. Opponents of this bill believed it was unconstitutional, but supporters claimed it was necessary to prevent the usurpation of legislative functions by the judiciary. After debate the bill was passed in the House by a 218–175 vote, on August 19th, 1964.

Meanwhile, in the Senate, attempts were made to prevent the foreign aid bill from coming up for a vote, and pressure was also brought on the Administration by urban groups to oppose the rider. When Dirkson filed a cloture petition to end debate on the rider, President Johnson indicated that he would prefer the Senate to adopt a 'sense of Congress' resolution on the matter as a compromise. This would have no legal effect, but three Senators co-sponsored such a resolution as a substitute for the Dirksen rider. On September 10th, 1964, the Senate refused to invoke cloture on the Dirksen rider by a 63–30 vote, and later rejected by 42–40 the substitute amendment and also an attempt to substitute the Tuck bill which had passed the House.

However, both the Majority and Minority Leaders in the Senate sought to obtain a further substitute rider directing the courts to allow state legislatures a reasonable time to comply with the Supreme Court decisions, and if no action was taken then the courts would be required to reapportion. Such a resolution, which did not have the force of law, was passed on September 24th, 1964, by a 44–38 vote, but House–Senate conferees eliminated it after Senator Dirksen refused finally to support it.

In 1964 there was considerable opposition in Congress to the actions of the Supreme Court, and support for some attempt to allow a state to apportion one branch of the legislature on a non-population basis. In 1965 a serious but unsuccessful attempt was made to get Congress to accept a constitutional amendment. Opposition outside Congress was also generated. The American Farm Bureau Federation and the U.S. Chamber of Commerce endorsed a constitutional amendment, as did the Council of State Governments. Plans were laid to try to obtain a constitutional amendment by an alternative procedure outlined in the Constitution requiring two-thirds of the states to apply to Congress to call a national constitutional convention which would consider an anti-reapportionment amendment and submit it to the states for ratification. Meanwhile, supporters of reapportionment organised and created a National Committee for Fair Representation.[24] The challenge by Congress continued in 1966. Outside Congress, groups continued to work to seek to obtain some limitation on the jurisdiction of the Supreme Court. As in the 1930s, but for different reasons, the Supreme Court in the 1960s became a source of political controversy. In the 1930s the Court came under attack for declaring acts of Congress unconstitutional. In the 1950s and 1960s it became a source of political controversy by taking action to uphold the constitutional rights of individuals in the absence of action by elected representatives. By 1966, legislatures in forty-six states were in substantial compliance with the equal-population principle upheld by the Court.

The Supreme Court has become the protector of the Constitution and constitutionalism in the United States by a combina-

[24] See R. Hansen, *The Political Thicket: Reapportionment and Constitutional Democracy*, Englewood Cliffs, N.J.: Prentice-Hall Inc., 1966, pp. 92–101.

tion of custom, judicial practice, and the abdication of responsibilities by other branches of government. However, just as there is disagreement over the values the American Constitution should support, there is disagreement about the role the Supreme Court should play in the political system. Moreover, the political role played by the Court is determined by the composition of the Court, the circumstances of the case, and the political environment. In 1961 there could be little doubt about the political implications of the question of legislative apportionment. The failure of state legislatures to reapportion meant that considerable political power could remain in the hands of rural-based interests at a time when population movement was into the metropolitan areas.[25] Advocates of change had to convince the Court that the constitutional guarantee of 'equal protection of the laws' required individual equality of access to the political process through equal representation in legislatures. The Court had several choices open to it. Initially the Court chose to allow the matter to be settled by the elected representatives of the people, but later accepted that they should take some action, and that there was widespread sentiment in favour of the reapportionment of legislatures on a population basis. A majority of the Court chose to support majoritarian and egalitarian values, and to give the demands of reformers a firm constitutional backing. In so doing the Court made a deliberate decision of policy which was challenged by other participants in the political process and provoked additional political conflict and debate about the nature of representative government in the United States in the mid-twentieth century.

Conclusion

These case-studies demonstrate the significance of the interaction of major political institutions with social forces, and the influence of personal disposition, political skill, and accident on decision-making in these institutions. The success or failure of a policy may depend on historical or other circumstances which individuals can only influence in part. If the Democrats had not made sweeping gains in the 1964 Congressional elections,

[25] See C. H. Pritchett, 'Equal Protection and the Urban Majority', *American Political Science Review*, December 1964, pp. 869–75.

the Model Cities programme would never have been initiated, while modest changes in public attitudes, caused by a series of events and circumstances, also affected the will of the national government to legislate to guarantee civil rights. No individual, whether President or Chief Justice, can guarantee success in making policy, yet policy changes depend on the actions of individuals: of President Kennedy and his ability to learn from mistakes in making foreign policy decisions, or of a Supreme Court prepared to take action to support legitimate citizen demands ignored by their elected representatives.

No single institution can make radical changes alone, or on its own authority. The political process at the national level in the United States normally requires a high degree of conciliation, negotiation, and bargaining between different institutions composed of heterogeneous groups of individuals responsible for making decisions. It also involves conflict and co-operation between different levels of government whose relationships may change over time. Those making governmental decisions possess a high degree of independence to determine the role they intend to play, the interests they seek to represent, and the influence they seek to exert on policy. Too often perhaps such independence is best exploited by cohesive minorities intent on limiting rather than supporting policy initiatives. Too often also it is confidently assumed that every problem in American society is capable of a political solution.

While political power in Britain is more dispersed than is often believed, in the United States it is often less divided if no less diffuse than was originally intended. Conflict within American society may be intensified and exacerbated by the difficulty of obtaining drastic changes in policy in certain areas, while in others the ability to make decisions may serve to lower the political temperature to manageable proportions. The balance is rarely ever maintained in the United States, but the attempt to strike such a balance has provided a modicum of stability for a complex, largely apolitical, acquisitive, and often violent society.

Chapter Eleven

THE POLITICAL SYSTEM AND
SOCIAL CHANGE

Despite massive economic and social changes, the political system in the United States has retained a basic structural and cultural similarity to the kind of government planned at Philadelphia in 1787. As Bernard Bailyn has indicated, the political culture of the United States in the mid-eighteenth century did not develop merely as an amalgam of ideas and beliefs current in eighteenth-century England, nor was it a distillation of the minds of a few political philosophers.[1] It possessed a strong anti-authoritarian, anti-faction, libertarian strain which strongly influenced those responsible for creating the American Constitution and implementing a framework of government whose major political institutions (President, Congress, Supreme Court, state governments) remain today, but whose functions and powers have often changed in response to social and political pressure. The basic structural pattern of federalism also remains, though the functions performed by the different units and the relationships between these units are now different. The major constitutional vehicle for change has been the Supreme Court, and the practical vehicles have been political parties and interest groups.

The Governmental Community in Perspective

Some indication of the influence of social and political change may be revealed by a brief comparison of the Washington of the Jeffersonian period at the beginning of the nineteenth century with contemporary Washington.

James Young demonstrates that, despite the intentions of the

[1] See B. Bailyn, *The Origins of American Politics*, New York: A. A. Knopf, 1968.

Founding Fathers, the national government in Jeffersonian times was not an important institution either by virtue of its social presence or its impact on the everyday life of the five million or more citizens and slaves in the United States. Nor were those who came to Washington as elected persons happy to stay there and build a strong national government. Between 1797 and 1829, in a Congress much less than half its present size, there were, on average, many more resignations than in the modern Congress, and of those who resigned, over two-thirds continued their office-holding elsewhere than in Washington.[2] The size of the government establishment was also small. The total civil establishment was less than three thousand (less indeed than the staff of a minor bureau today), and the official members of the governmental community numbered less than three hundred. Congress and the Supreme Court met for very brief periods in the year, whereas today Congress is in session almost the whole year round even in election years. The President and the Cabinet were also absent for as much as three months in the year.

Young also shows how isolated were the early politicians in Washington. As a provider of services and benefits to citizens, the national government was insignificant, as was its knowledge of the population and its attitudes while in session. There were no encounters with 'those critically important surrogates of the popular will that bother but also aid and inform men in office today – the citizen delegates trooping to the capital full of opinions to air and demands to press, the quasi-official cadres of reporters, lobbyists, pollsters, professional party politicians, bringing the office-holders' constituencies within talking distance and providing clues to the popular mood'.[3]

Both the Capitol building and the White House were uncomfortable and shabby, and facilities provided for Congressmen were scanty. Social life in Washington in 1800, however, as today, was simply another arena of politics. Congressmen regarded themselves as 'outsiders' in Washington and were happy to beat an early retreat, a state of mind which may afflict some Congressmen today though they find it difficult to carry out in

[2] See J. S. Young, *The Washington Community, 1800–1828, op. cit.*, pp. 258 and 263.

[3] J. S. Young, *op. cit.*, p. 33.

practice. Members of the political community in the Jeffersonian period were also inclined to view political power and politics as essentially evil, a view which reflected that of he citizenry as a whole. They lacked the feeling of performing vital functions as managers of a large organisational empire which is conveyed to many Congressmen today by the hordes of reporters and citizen petitioners who demand their attention. The absence of party cohesion in Congress at this time was the result of a lack of cultural support for such organisation and the institutionalisation of sub-communities based on boarding-house cliques, which suggests that similar cultural demands and the sub-communities produced by committee specialisation or membership of state party delegations may be responsible for the similar lack of consistent party cohesion in the contemporary Congress.

The Supreme Court in 1800 provides a marked contrast to that of today. It was of little significance, met briefly, with members knowing each other well and having similar backgrounds, and knowing few of their fellow members of the governmental community. Today the Supreme Court is very busy, its composition reflects the religious, ethnic and racial diversity of the country, its decisions are often of considerable political importance, and its members have often had considerable practical political experience.

In the Jeffersonian period, however, evidence indicates that each branch of government took literally the doctrine of 'separation of powers' and a constitutional structure where separated institutions shared power even when there were few citizen pressures demanding such separation. Thus Congress fashioned an internal structure which, though different in its nature, like the modern Congress proved excellent in terms of representing the cultural attitudes of the people but was grossly deficient in the means for governing the people.

The Constitution clearly provided a wholly inadequate vehicle for presidential leadership of Congress, and the nature of the governmental community in 1800 supplemented this. Presidential power in Congress, then as today, largely depended on the exercise of political skill and statecraft by the President. Attempts by Jefferson to create personal communication and liaison channels with legislators, deputise cabinet members for political liaison with Congress, and even lobby legislators socially (all tactics dear to the heart of President Lyndon Johnson, who unlike Jefferson held a major leadership position in the Senate before moving to the executive), emphasised that success in mobilising Congress depended more upon personal abilities than ties of party.[4] Today, while the President can use the media and other techniques to mobilise public support against Congress, both President Johnson and President Nixon found that in particular situations Congress can become an effective countervailing force.

In 1800, as today, evidence suggests that the executive community in Washington was very different from the congressional community. It was certainly more stable in terms of personnel, but there existed similar inequalities of status between departments. Patterns of rivalry between departments have continued to exist and to hamper executive co-ordination. Jefferson, though faced with a small bureaucracy, had fewer weapons of control than the modern President and his difficulties were compounded as they are today by congressional attempts to influence particular elements of administrative activity.

Though the scope and extent of governmental activity in Washington has grown extensively since the Jeffersonian period, the basic procedural and institutional patterns of governmental decision-making remain substantially the same. The growth of organised political parties, more democratic election procedures, the changing balance of governmental responsibility and activity, and the rise of mass communications, have provided greater opportunities for Presidential leadership. In general terms, foreign and defence matters have become increasingly important, and the regulatory responsibilities of the national government have increased, while all levels of government have come to assume responsibilities for social, economic and civil concerns once conducted by individuals or private groups. As the economic wealth of many states and the country as a whole has grown to massive proportions, so the fiscal responsibilities of the national government have grown.

The expansion of national governmental authority and the growing complexity of many social and economic issues has also

[4] See J. S. Young, *op cit.*, Chapter 8.

increased political tensions. This has been reflected in the increase in political violence, as expressed by demonstrations and disturbances such as those that surrounded the 1968 Democratic national convention, and in the assassination of a President and two major political figures between 1963 and 1968, and the attempted assassination of a likely Presidential candidate during the 1972 Democratic Presidential primaries.

Parties and Social Change

The growth in the authority and responsibilities of the national government did not develop without consistent social and cultural opposition. Power required justification, and only after massive economic hardship and the collapse of the economic system did this become inevitable in the 1930s. With this came a vast increase in the numbers of federal government officials. In 1802 there was one federal official for every 1,914 citizens, on the eve of the Civil War only 1·5 federal bureaucrats per 1,000 citizens. By 1900 this ratio had reached only 2·7, but by 1940 it became 7 per 1,000 and had more than doubled by the mid-1900s.[5] This growth of governmental bureaucracy has raised formidable problems of accountability, as the American people have come to expect more of government yet retain an inherent scepticism as to the virtues and efficiency of public rather than private activities.

As the United States expanded in population and territory, so it became more diverse. The federal system helped in part to contain this diversity, providing a means whereby those states which sought unsuccessfully to secede in the Civil War were ultimately brought back into the political system. The most significant organisation maintaining unity as well as diversity in the United States has been the political party. Hence the prime function of the major political parties in the United States, in contrast to parties in many European countries, has been to provide vehicles of integration, channelling conflict between regional, ethnic or class interests for control of political offices, and thus performing a 'constituent' or constitutional function in a political system where power was deliberately decentralised or dispersed. They have rarely presented clear alternatives of

[5] See T. J. Lowi, 'The Public Philosophy: Interest Group Liberalism', *American Political Science Review*, March 1967, pp. 5–24, especially p. 5.

policy and have engaged in accommodationist politics. One consequence of this integrative role is that it is difficult for the parties to move from performing primarily constituent functions towards a stronger policy-making and initiating role. At times – 1856–60, 1910–14 or 1932–36 – there have been clear differences between the parties on specific issues, but not until the latter period did something approaching a dialogue develop over the question of the expansion of governmental authority.[6]

The ultimate triumph of attitudes more susceptible to an expansion of national governmental responsibilities led to the establishment of a new liberal consensus, and the differences between the two major parties were again obscured. The need to reconcile this change with traditional attitudes separating private life and public authority promoted in domestic affairs (especially over policies affecting established economic interests) a form of interest group liberalism which dominated policy-making in the 1950s and 1960s.[7] Over foreign policy questions the political parties between 1948 and 1964 sought to encourage and promote bipartisanship, often failing to provide a meaningful dialogue in election campaigns or through the formal institutions such as Congress. One consequence was an increase in the 'independent' authority of the President in the conduct of foreign affairs, but severe limitations on his ability to obtain and implement comprehensive domestic legislation. The ultimate results of these developments were intra and extra-party pressures as demonstrated by student and black protest over specific questions like the war in Vietnam, race or poverty which heightened social and political tensions. These increased during the Johnson Administration after the 1964 Presidential elections, despite the fact that the election seemed on the surface to offer the electorate a real choice between Presidential candidates.

The 'mixed' results of the Great Society programme launched by President Johnson,[8] together with increased dissatisfaction

[6] See the contributions by T. J. Lowi and W. D. Burnham in W. N. Chambers and W. D. Burnham (eds.), *The American Party Systems*, New York: Oxford University Press, 1967.

[7] See T. J. Lowi, *The End of Liberalism*, New York: Norton, 1969.

[8] For an evaluation of the effects of the Great Society legislation, see the symposium entitled 'Nixon, the Great Society, and the Future of Social Policy', *Commentary*, May 1973, pp. 31–61.

with the policies of the Johnson Administration as American involvement in the Vietnam war escalated,[9] produced, or coincided with, a growing concern for issues among distinctive groups of voters. This was reflected in both the preliminaries to, and the results of, the 1968 Presidential election. The growing volatility of the electorate as a whole was reflected in increases in the number of 'independent' voters and in ticket-splitting, also the large popular vote support for a third party candidate. The emergence of a more 'ideologically' committed set of activists, backed by opposition to the war in Vietnam, severely strained the unity of the Democratic party. They prompted the decision of President Johnson not to seek renomination, and produced a Democratic convention marked by violence and unrest outside and division within. The narrow victory of the Republican, Richard Nixon, emphasised the unnatural nature of the 1964 Democratic landslide, but the impact of the combination of electoral volatility and intra-party manœuvre was shown even more forcefully in the 1972 election, when a Nixon Republican Presidential landslide together with the Democratic party continuing to retain their control of Congress, confirmed that while the old dynamic of party coalitions[10] and accommodationist politics was ended, new patterns of electoral support and internal party stability were unlikely to be discernible or to be consolidated in the immediate future. The decade since 1964 has proved to be one of a secular decline in the strength of party organisation, the emergence of more issue-oriented participants in both major parties, committed to a more programmatic or ideological politics, and an electorate which has become more issue and candidate-oriented. It produced in 1972 (as in 1964) a situation in which a major party nominated a candidate who was the minority choice of the rank and file, was considered to be 'too extreme' and who was massively defeated despite the fact that his opponent was not highly popular in either personality or policy terms. Whether

[9] For extensive discussion of the impact on public opinion of the Korean and Vietnam wars, and on Presidential popularity, see J. E. Mueller, *War, Presidents and Public Opinion*, New York: Wiley, 1973.

[10] On this matter, see R. Axelrod, 'Where the Votes Come From: An Analysis of Electoral Coalitions, 1952–1968', *American Political Science Review*, March 1972, pp. 11–20.

the unpredictable nature of party performance is indicative of a critical realignment, i.e. the establishment of a new partisan identification for significant segments of the electorate,[11] or of a series of elections in which an 'unnatural' landslide will be as likely a result as any,[12] the major political parties will continue to seek to adjust to changing social attitudes. The American parties are finding it more and more difficult to be all things to all citizens, and they may never again be dominant all-purpose agents of political and social change. It is indeed difficult to meet the expectations of more ideological politics as well as pragmatic electoral politics, and in effecting internal change parties may court short-term electoral setbacks in their attempts to remain both channels of influence for the political activist and powerful reference symbols for the wider electorate.

Social Change and Political Power

Some of the political conflict in the United States since the early 1960s has emanated in part from dissatisfaction and disquiet among many concerned citizens about the location of political power. While argument on this subject has primarily been of an academic nature it has important practical implications which manifested themselves clearly in debate over American involvement in the war in Vietnam, and are also implicit in the series of events triggered off by the Watergate affair. They are brought into sharper relief by evidence over a series of national elections of a continued relative decline in voting, and public opinion poll evidence of a growing public suspicion and distrust of political leaders and the political process. For many observers government deception, supported by a pervasive system of official secrecy, has caused this distrust, altering traditional political relationships, shattering the necessary bond of confidence between government and the people and under-

[11] For sophisticated analysis of this phenomenon, see W. D. Burnham, *Critical Elections and the Mainsprings of American Politics*, New York: Norton, 1970. See also E. C. Ladd Jr., *et al.*, 'A New Political Realignment?' *The Public Interest*, Spring 1971, pp. 46–63.

[12] See E. C. Ladd Jr. and S. M. Lipset, *Academics, Politics, and the 1972 Election*, Washington, D.C.: American Enterprise Institute for Public Policy Research, 1973, Chapter 2.

mining the leaven of trust and legitimacy vital to any democratic government.[13]

The question 'who governs' (and how) has therefore an important empirical as well as theoretical relevance in the United
States in the 1970s, though initial debate predates both Vietnam and Watergate. At least three different interpretations can
be baldly identified. A body of opinion has, since the mid-
1950s, held that power in the United States is highly concentrated in the hands of a 'power élite' which is little concerned
with the values of a liberal society. Moreover, the major locus of
this power does not rest within the political process, nor is it
directly accountable to the people. C. Wright Mills saw it as
composed of the higher leadership of major corporations and
the military who essentially control political authority even if
they do not make political decisions.[14] Others have defined it as
an 'upper class' or establishment who hold power and influence
irrespective of what administration or individual occupies the
White House.[15]

Such analysis produced an alternative interpretation, originating in the work of Robert Dahl,[16] sometimes known as the
'pluralist' analysis. This does not reject the existence of élites but
basically holds that power is scattered, balanced and checked by
competing but responsible élite groups. In the sphere of national
government it postulates the existence of multiple centres of
power, none of which is wholly sovereign. While this view has
had its critics both on practical and methodological grounds,
the multiplicity of organised interest group activity in the
United States claiming to speak on behalf of large 'publics' in
American society supports this view of competing, and often
temporary, élite groups. However, in the mid-1960s, as a consequence of political and social unrest, a third view emerged.
This was essentially critical not so much of the 'pluralist' interpretation as the tacit acceptance of this pattern of government

13 See, for example, D. Wise, *The Politics of Lying: Government Deception,
Secrecy and Power*, New York: Random House, 1973.

14 See C. W. Mills, *The Power Elite*, New York: Oxford University Press,
1959.

15 See among others G. W. Domhoff, *Who Rules America?*, Englewood
Cliffs, N.J.: Prentice-Hall Inc., 1967.

16 See R. A. Dahl, *Who Governs?*, op. cit., and *Pluralist Democracy in the
United States: Conflict and Consent*, op. cit.

in the United States. It took the form of criticism of the nature of élite group competition as being both unrepresentative and undemocratic, and of attacks as indicated earlier on the so-called pattern of interest group liberalism which dominated the thinking and actions of governmental decision-makers. At its worse this made the possibility of government by a power élite or establishment more likely. At its best it produced a pre-occupation with consensus and incremental policy-making, the uneven sharing of power among groups with narrow interests and the virtual exclusion from the purview of political decision-makers of the claims of those in society who found organisation and the articulation of their demands difficult. Such criticism of the so-called 'theory' of democratic élitism inevitably took different forms.[17] The major normative thrust was for a return to a more citizen-based pattern of influence on government, and a recognition that government by consensus, far from main-taining stability, was increasing political conflict, along with the view that such conflict within the political system need not be dysfunctional[18] and might indeed be necessary if government and administration[19] were to respond to public as well as group interests, if political apathy and alienation were to be alleviated and if government by a power élite was to be avoided.

This sketch of the debate about the nature of political power in the United States, while grossly oversimplified, is an im-portant prologue to the final section of this chapter which seeks to identify the major political and social developments in the United States since the 1968 election through to 1974, and assess their implications for the future pattern of American politics. Before doing this, however, it might be useful to identify a further strand of analysis which has emerged since the Democratic Presidential defeat in 1968. It reflects, in part, traditional sentiments about the use of national governmental power to achieve major domestic social change, and the cross-pressures this may arouse. It infers that contradictory and often

[17] See, for example, P. Bachrach, *The Theory of Democratic Elitism, op. cit.*; J. Walker, 'A Critique of the Elitist Theory of Democracy', *American Political Science Review*, June 1966, pp. 285–95; and G. Beam, *Usual Politics*, New York: Holt, Rinehart and Winston, 1970.

[18] See T. J. Lowi, *The Politics of Disorder*, New York: Basic Books, 1971.

[19] On the matter of bureaucratic power, see L. C. Gawthrop, *Administrative Politics and Social Change*, New York: St. Martin's Press, 1971.

incompatible demands have been made of the national government, with the public having come to expect it to do so much, yet ultimately trusting it less. Hence studies have sought to demonstrate the limits of national governmental performance in trying to deal, for example, with urban problems[20] (along with the view that some of these problems are not as bad as they seem or are unlikely to be further alleviated by national governmental action). Some have also argued that the actual well-being of most Americans, including blacks, has improved considerably in the past decade.[21] Yet there is little evidence that the public feels this is so or that it is the result of governmental policies. Rather government may be seen to have tried to do too much and attempted things it was unlikely to do well. The fact that since 1968 a Republican President has faced a Congress controlled by the Democrats may be the clearest indicator of such ambivalence.[22]

The 1972 Election, Watergate and the Future

The election of Richard Nixon as the 37th President of the United States in 1968 was a significant event, not merely for Republicans, and was the subject of extensive discussion and debate.[23] In itself the election campaign was unspectacular, though there were some intriguing aspects to the election results as a whole. Nixon obtained less than 45% of the total popular vote, the lowest percentage for a winning Presidential candidate since 1912, and for the first time since 1848 the new President faced a Congress in which his party was in the minority. The performance of George Wallace as the Presi-

---

[20] See E. Banfield, *The Unheavenly City*, Boston: Little, Brown, 1970.

[21] See, for example, A. Wildavsky, 'Government and the People', *Commentary*, August 1973, pp. 25–32; and B. J. Wattenberg and R. M. Scammon, 'Black Progress and Liberal Rhetoric', *Commentary*, April 1973, pp. 35–44.

[22] For a detailed study of the ultimate irony – President Nixon's failure to get Congress to accept a guaranteed income policy – see D. P. Moynihan, *The Politics of a Guaranteed Income*, New York: Random House, 1973.

[23] For general analysis from a British perspective see J. D. Lees, 'Deviation and Dissent – The American National Election of 1968', *Parliamentary Affairs*, Spring 1969, pp. 134–43; and H. G. Nicholas, 'The 1968 Presidential Elections', *Journal of American Studies*, July 1969, pp. 1–15.

dential candidate of the American Independent Party in polling over 13% of the vote, winning five Deep South states and coming second in several 'border' states, reflected the growing decline in support for Democratic Presidential candidates in a former stronghold and more general ambivalence towards their party by other voters who traditionally identified themselves as Democrats.[24] If the latter was a consequence of the policies of the Democratic party nationally since 1964, and activities within the party in the pre-election period, rather than the inadequacies of their candidate, Hubert Humphrey, the lessons for the party were not learnt. Consolidation of Democratic control of Congress in the 1970 congressional elections,[25] and the political difficulties of President Nixon, masked the extent to which reforms within the Democratic party designed to open up their procedures for choosing national party convention delegates and conducting the national party convention were to reap a bitter Presidential election harvest in 1972.

Few Democrats, however, had any illusions about the fact that the election of Nixon would mean significant changes in Washington. Having only narrowly won an election he at one time seemed to have comfortably in his grasp, Nixon returned to a Washington still dominated by Democrats, not only in Congress but in the upper echelons of the bureaucracy and in the press corps. Moreover, outside government, the anti-war movement still seemed a significant and vocal threat, a force that had debilitated Johnson and might conceivably undermine the authority of the new President.

The seeds of Watergate undoubtedly precede the accession of Nixon to the White House. This is so, not merely in terms of the 'checkered' political career of Nixon himself or the tradition of conspiracy theory in the United States, but also given the political events since 1945, from McCarthyism through the John Birch Society to the Goldwater campaign in 1964 and the rise of the New Left, and changes in the nature of the institu-

---

[24] For close analysis of these and other matters, see P. E. Converse et al., 'Continuity and Change in American Politics: Parties and Issues in the 1968 Election', American Political Science Review, December 1969, pp. 1083–1105.

[25] See J. D. Lees, 'Campaigns and Parties: The 1970 American Mid-Term Elections and Beyond', Parliamentary Affairs, Autumn 1971, pp. 312–20.

tional structure of government (in particular the Presidency). For Johnson, no less than Nixon ultimately, the White House, and in particular the Executive Office of the President, became the refuge or castle of a political leader buffeted by political pressures and complex affairs of state. Nixon inherited from his former chief, Eisenhower, a belief in the virtue of efficiency in government and the importance of organisation within the White House. His first major action on becoming chief executive, significant in the light of future events, was to make all the major appointments to his personal staff before selecting his Cabinet. Controversy over his appointment of Henry Kissinger, as national security adviser, diverted attention from the relative anonymity and political inexperience of many of his other personal appointees. From this base began the gradual but consistent consolidation of power within the Executive Office, and in particular the White House staff, with a corollary weakening of the influence of members of the Cabinet, especially the Secretary of State. This led eventually to the creation of a new Domestic Council, a revamped Bureau of the Budget, and an extensive Executive Reorganisation bill. The political implications of these initiatives were reflected in traditional congressional opposition to such developments, but the wider consequences were barely apparent during Nixon's first administration. They were not inconsistent with a legitimate executive desire (especially for a Republican) to exercise tighter control over the bureaucracy and promote greater governmental efficiency, even if they did not entirely square with the goal of cutting back bureaucracy. Furthermore, Nixon was not so much initiating a new development as building on existing trends. If ultimately this led to attempts to conduct foreign and defence policy without the Senate, budget policy without the House and a domestic national security policy without the judiciary, it is by no means clear that Nixon intended such developments when he took up office.[26]

However, this does not mean that Nixon had no clear view of his intentions, beyond a long-term desire to concentrate on major matters of foreign policy and the short-term necessity of an honourable military withdrawal from Vietnam. From the outset in the domestic sphere he faced the ambiguous and

[26] See on this point A. Wildavsky, 'Government and the People', pp. 30–1.

ultimately contradictory problem of the broader demands for unity, a theme he emphasised in his victory statement, and the specific and less conciliatory demands of the constituency that elected him (in particular, pledges to the South of judicial appointments), in a situation where congressional hostility seemed inevitable.

The most noteworthy features of the first Nixon administration were the persistent tensions between the executive and the legislature, and the pragmatism of Nixon, which combined an adherence to Republican traditions and an almost apolitical response to particular situations. In the first two years he faced growing congressional and public opposition to his Vietnamisation policy, and suffered severe reverses when he attempted to appoint two Southerners to the Supreme Court. He also got little response from Congress to his revenue-sharing legislation and a veto strategy on his part eclipsed efforts to get his own legislation passed. A tax reform bill and postal reform were the sole accomplishments. His initial efforts to deal with inflation through 'Nixonomics' were unsuccessful, but his later policies after the 1970 elections, though offending traditional Republicans, were more successful. Though he did not seek to change dramatically the Great Society programmes of his predecessor, he did little to encourage their extension, yet his own initiative to deal with poverty, family assistance legislation, was ultimately defeated in Congress. His main concerns lay, however, in foreign policy, not simply in dealing with Vietnam but in initiating a new so-called Nixon Doctrine. In essence the doctrine was in part a cover for getting American troops out of Vietnam and in part a challenge to American allies to do more in the age of nuclear parity to maintain their own defence, with the United States providing a shield against nuclear threats and also furnishing military and economic assistance.

In the face of the disappointing election results in 1970 and growing evidence of opposition and loss of credibility in the eyes of the public, Nixon, aware of the precedents in the latter part of Johnson's Administration, began to take a more independent line in dealing with economic and law and order problems at home, and sought to divert attention from the albatross of Vietnam through daring new initiatives towards China and the U.S.S.R. In January 1971 he proposed six 'great domestic goals' which included new revenue-sharing legislation, an executive reorganisation bill, an expansionary full-employment budget, welfare reform and health and environment legislation. Though few of these initiatives reached full legislative fruition, his efforts to deal with the basic issues troubling the electorate succeeded in reversing strong public opposition, despite continued congressional hostility to his unilateral foreign policy actions, evidence of a growing consolidation of authority within the White House itself, and the embarrassment of revelations of atrocities in Vietnam and the unauthorised publication of the Pentagon Papers. As the 1972 election neared, though Nixon still lacked the personal popularity he craved for, his position was stronger and re-election seemed possible. Yet at the beginning of 1972 few if any observers would have predicted the demise of his likely Democratic opponent, Senator Muskie, and the ultimate landslide victory he achieved in November 1972 over the Democratic candidate, Senator McGovern.

In time the 1972 Presidential election seems likely to be viewed either as an electoral anachronism (but not an aberration) or as part of the new 'normal' pattern of national elections.[27] It produced the greatest electoral victory for a Republican Presidential candidate since 1920, yet it was a victory for neither man, party or ideology, but rather the solid rejection of the Democratic candidate McGovern, his assumed supporters and policies and his inept campaign. It was, in part, also the result of the traditional advantages held by an incumbent President in a situation where pragmatic action had appeared to alleviate domestic economic difficulties and bold initiatives seemed to have secured 'peace with honour' in Vietnam and the basis of a new policy towards China and the U.S.S.R.

The roots of the Democratic Presidential defeat (once again not reflected in the congressional elections where they continued to maintain a majority in both the House and Senate) lay as indicated earlier within the party itself, and illustrate the paradoxes of electoral politics for political parties. The major

[27] For more detailed evaluation, again from a British perspective, see H. G. Nicholas, 'The 1972 Elections', *Journal of American Studies*, April 1973, pp. 1–15; and G. K. Wilson and P. M. Williams, 'Mr. Nixon's Triumph', *Parliamentary Affairs*, Spring 1973, pp. 186–200.

irony was the fact that extensive attempts by the Democratic party after 1968 to reform their convention procedures to create a more representative and open convention so that their nominee might more accurately reflect the ideas and sentiments of Democratic voters led to the nomination of a candidate who succeeded in tripping off an unprecedented defection of rank-and-file Democrats to the Republican candidate. The reasons for this may be a combination of idealism and self-deception, but the consequences raise important questions about the role of national party conventions for national political parties in the United States and the definition of 're-presentative' in party terms.[28] The intentions of the reform committees set up in 1968 have been considered by most independent observers to be legitimate and desirable, and indeed the Republicans also sought similar modest changes in their convention procedures. The results, however, gained more qualified approval. The committees cannot be criticised for lack of thoroughness or action; indeed the McGovern-Fraser commission on party structure and delegate selection may be said to have gone beyond its terms of reference in defining guidelines for the selection of convention delegates and developing a quota rule intended to ensure the most inclusive process of delegate selection on pain of formal challenge at the convention itself. While the final consequences seemed to some to benefit McGovern himself and his followers as part-authors of the rules and players in the game, there is little doubt that the final result was a very different 'mix' of convention delegates. Yet the convention was not in fact more representative of the diverse range of Democratic party supporters, as was perceived by many 'traditional' Democrats participating in the convention courtesy of the media. The increase in presidential primaries and other methods by which convention delegates were elected rather than appointed did not guarantee a more 'representative'

[28] For a detailed appraisal of the contemporary situation, see J. H. Parris, *The Convention Problem: Issues in the Reform of Presidential Nominating Procedures*, Washington, D.C.: Brookings Institution, 1972. For a critical view of the 1972 Democratic convention, see P. Kemble and J. Muravchik, 'The New Politics and the Democrats', *Commentary*, December 1972, pp. 78–84, and for evidence of the electoral dangers implicit in such developments for the Democratic party, see R. M. Scammon and B. J. Wattenberg, *The Real Majority*, New York: Coward, McCann Inc., 1970.

convention and gave an advantage to the dedicated and well-organised supporters of McGovern. This process also identified McGovern as a firm upholder of their attitudes and life-styles. The openness of the convention allowed full expression to the divisions of policy and attitude between different elements in the party, but normal incentives to unite behind the candidate did not materialise.

McGovern's crusader image, an asset at the pre-convention stage, was tarnished by the impression of ruthlessness in gaining the nomination. Immediate defections by elements of the old Democratic coalition were accelerated by the debacle over the selection and later rejection of Senator Eagleton as Vice-Presidential candidate. Again it was the impression created, of carelessness and vacillation, rather than the actual event, that further damaged his standing among traditional Democratic voters. As the election campaign began, parallels with the Goldwater 'caper' in 1964 seemed apparent to all but the most devoted and myopic McGovernites. The shift from factional to coalitional leader was difficult, and many Democratic voters saw him not as a crusader but as an 'extremist' in his advocacy of a more radical and élite form of interest group liberalism. In a period of disturbing social and economic change, such fears were based less on opposition to new social or economic policies as such, but reflected cultural resistance to change which might occur in a non-traditional manner. Paradoxically, McGovern's moralism became 'immoral' because in many respects it conflicted with the conventional political morality of personal achievement, individualism and nationalism which still dominates the thinking of many Americans.[29] The election therefore provided several ironies. At a time of high voter discontent, the incumbent succeeded in diverting attention away from the inadequacies of his own Administration and presented himself as the champion of traditional American virtues. The response was a reluctant one in personal terms, producing a landslide victory which was almost wholly negatively based, though it was a real one in terms of votes.

The most significant indicator of McGovern's deficiencies, however, was the fact that one 'moral' issue, Watergate, had

[29] For evidence of the specific issue-context of this, see S. Lubell, *The Future While It Happened*, New York: W. W. Norton, 1973.

little impact on voting in November 1972. It officially began on June 17th, 1972, when five men were caught on the premises of the Democratic National Committee headquarters in Washington. One of the men, James McCord, was a security expert on the staff of the Campaign to Re-Elect the President. The ensuing investigations and press and television disclosures revealed potentially grave evidence of possible electoral malpractices by Republican campaigners, involvement on the part of White House officials close to the President, and possible help from government departments such as the Department of Justice. On June 19th, 1972, John Mitchell, the former Attorney General, resigned as the President's campaign manager. In April 1973 he admitted to knowledge of the plan to 'bug' the Democratic National Committee headquarters. Despite strong circumstantial evidence, few voters seemed influenced by the Watergate affair, and the White House was able to issue blanket denials and delay any serious investigation of any allegations until after the election. Nixon, picking up the 1968 Wallace vote in the South and becoming the first Republican candidate to win a majority of the Catholic vote and a high percentage of 'blue collar' Democratic support, won every state except Massachusetts.

With re-election assured, Nixon resumed his battle with Congress, stirring up resentment by his use of the veto power and the rarely-used authority to impound appropriated funds. He completed negotiations for American withdrawal from Vietnam and set out the goals of his new administration. However, further revelations linking key members of his staff with events and incidents related to the Watergate break-in ultimately developed into a major political and constitutional crisis.[30] Beginning with the trial and conviction of the Watergate burglars, and the appointment in February 1973 of a Senate Select Committee on Presidential Campaign Activities chaired by Senator Ervin, the year was dominated politically by a series of exposés, investigations, firings, court trials and political resignations.

It is impossible to chronicle here the complex development of

[30] For detailed information see C. Bernstein and B. Woodward, *All the President's Men*, London: Secker and Warburg, 1974; also L. A. Chester *et al.*, *Watergate*, London: André Deutsch, 1973.

the Watergate crisis, but it is necessary to try to assess the nature of the constitutional crisis, and the wider crisis of legitimacy and respect for government it spawned. What began in Washington as a Congressional investigation into the Watergate break-in and other campaign irregularities escalated into criminal investigations into activities of former Cabinet members and key officials of the White House staff. It led to the resignation of an Attorney General, the firing by Nixon of a special prosecutor appointed to investigate allegations of illegal activities by members of his Administration, and the consequent resignation of the current Attorney General and his Deputy. In October 1973, Vice-President Agnew resigned in the face of criminal charges relating to his activities as Governor of Maryland. Under the terms of the 25th Amendment he was succeeded by Gerald Ford, formerly Republican Minority Leader in the House of Representatives. In February 1974, the House Judiciary Committee began enquiries, backed by strong subpoena powers, to determine if grounds existed for recommending the impeachment of President Nixon. By May, when they began formal impeachment hearings, possible grounds included much more than initial charges of the authorisation of secret bombing raids in Cambodia or failure to spend funds voted by Congress.[31]

The activities of the Senate investigating committee and of the courts gradually revealed the astonishing pervasiveness of corruption among Nixon's political and official associates. Their misguided conspiracy theories and loyalty to the cause led to many of them being convicted of crimes or indicted on charges which included perjury, burglary, illegal wiretapping, obstruction of justice, destruction of evidence, fraud, extortion, solicitation of illegal campaign contributions, violation of campaign funding laws and various forms of conspiracy to commit illegal acts. Despite strenuous efforts by the President to deny that he was in any way involved in initiating the Watergate break-in and other illegal activities, his reluctance about dismissing key former aides and his initial refusal to give either to the courts, the investigating committee or the special prosecutor recorded tapes of White House meetings and telephone calls, cast

---

[31] For a study of the intent of the impeachment clause of the Constitution see R. Berger, *Impeachment: The Constitutional Problem*, Cambridge, Mass.: Harvard University Press, 1973.

genuine doubts on his total innocence. His dismissal of the special prosecutor and evidence that certain tapes, which he released following court action, had been tampered with, increased suspicion.

Gradually the President was drawn into the centre of the controversy. On April 30th, 1974, the White House released over one thousand pages of edited transcripts which revealed brutally frank discussion about Watergate and certain political personalities. Public reaction was hostile. A week later the President's chief defence lawyer stated that no more White House conversations about Watergate would be released to the House Judiciary Committee or the new special prosecutor. On May 24th the latter appealed directly to the Supreme Court to decide whether the President could withhold evidence requested by subpoena prior to the pending criminal trial of certain former aides. A month later the Supreme Court ruled unanimously that the President had no right to withhold such evidence, and ordered him to release certain material to the District Court. The House Judiciary Committee also began debate on articles of impeachment. Three articles were ultimately drawn up, recommending impeachment because the President had engaged in a 'course of conduct or plan' to obstruct investigation of the Watergate break-in and to cover up other unlawful activities, had repeatedly engaged in conduct 'violating the constitutional rights of citizens', and had wilfully disobeyed subpoenas issued by the committee. On August 5th the White House released three new transcripts of conversations between the President and his staff on June 23rd, 1972, which revealed that the President had personally ordered a cover-up of Watergate. Three days later, President Nixon announced to the nation that he would resign at noon on August 9th, and Gerald Ford was sworn in as the new President at that time.

The consequences of these dramatic series of events for the political process are incalculable. The manner and circumstances of the resignation of a President so recently elected by a massive majority increased the already considerable public disenchantment, cynicism and distrust of the national governmental process. It brought into question not merely Presidential government in Washington but the efficacy and legitimacy of the electoral and governmental processes. While many Americans have always been ambivalent about the national government and conscious of its potential for corruption, the magnitude of the misdeeds of a President who had gained the office by appeals to latent morality and puritanism provoked a sustained public reaction against politics and politicians. Some observers saw in these events confirmation of their views about the importance of presidential character, the crisis being the predictable consequence of the accretion of executive authority. Others found succour in the fact that the constitutional process seemed ultimately to have been vindicated, though acutely conscious of the fact that the crisis demonstrated the relative ease in which weak parties and a fragmented political process could be manipulated by groups indifferent to the established norms and rules of the political game. Watergate provided a dramatic demonstration of the paradoxes and ironies of American politics. One example was the betrayal by Nixon of those who supported him electorally in his efforts to lessen the influence of the national government on domestic decision-making by his use of a new and frightening structure of national executive authority.

The immediate political legacy of Watergate was revealed by the November 1974 mid-term elections. After the initial euphoria of a new President and a return to more conventional political practices, public hostility was again aroused when Ford officially pardoned Nixon, despite the fact that several of his close advisors and assistants were still on trial. Opinion polls showed depressing evidence of public concern and pessimism about the relative state of the nation and their own individual well-being, as well as a low regard for 'traditional' politicians. This was amply demonstrated by the derisory turnout of voters in November and strong evidence of the negative attitudes motivating many of the 40% who did vote. Though the Democrats made substantial gains in Congress, it was the election of the anti-politician, reflecting concern over the scandals and the collapsing economy. The task of restoring faith in the integrity and legitimacy of government and the ability of politicians to deal with critical immediate economic problems was left in the hands of the first non-elected President in American history and a restless but uncertain Congress.

THE CONSTITUTION OF THE
UNITED STATES OF AMERICA

PREAMBLE

We, the people of the United States, in order to form a more perfect Union, establish justice, insure domestic tranquility, provide for the common defense, promote the general welfare, and secure the blessings of liberty to ourselves and our posterity, do ordain and establish this Constitution for the United States of America.

ARTICLE I

Section 1. All legislative powers herein granted shall be vested in a Congress of the United States, which shall consist of a Senate and House of Representatives.

Section 2. The House of Representatives shall be composed of members chosen every second year by the people of the several States, and the electors in each State shall have the qualifications requisite for electors of the most numerous branch of the State Legislature.

No person shall be a representative who shall not have attained to the age of twenty-five years, and been seven years a citizen of the United States, and who shall not, when elected, be an inhabitant of that State in which he shall be chosen.

Representatives and direct taxes shall be apportioned among the several States which may be included within this Union, according to their respective numbers, which shall be determined by adding to the whole number of free persons, including those bound to service for a term of years, and excluding Indians not taxed, three-fifths of all other persons. The actual enumeration shall be made within three years after the first meeting of the Congress of the United States, and within every subsequent term of ten years, in such manner as they shall by law direct. The number of representatives shall not exceed one for every thirty thousand, but each State shall have at least one representative; and until such enumeration shall be made, the State of New Hampshire shall be entitled to choose three, Massachusetts eight, Rhode Island and Providence Plantations one, Connecticut five, New York six, New Jersey four, Pennsylvania eight, Delaware one, Maryland six, Virginia ten, North Carolina five, South Carolina five, and Georgia three.

When vacancies happen in the representation from any State, the executive authority thereof shall issue writs of election to fill such vacancies.

The House of Representatives shall choose their Speaker and other officers; and shall have the sole power of impeachment.

Section 3. The Senate of the United States shall be composed of two senators from each State, chosen by the legislature thereof, for six years; and each senator shall have one vote.

Immediately after they shall be assembled in consequence of the first election, they shall be divided as equally as may be into three classes. The seats of the senators of the first class shall be vacated at the expiration of the second year, of the second class at the expiration of the fourth year, and of the third class at the expiration of the sixth year, so that one-third may be chosen every second year; and if vacancies happen by resignation, or otherwise, during the recess of the legislature of any State, the executive thereof may make temporary appointments until the next meeting of the legislature, which shall then fill such vacancies.

No person shall be a senator who shall not have attained to the age of thirty-years, and been nine years a citizen of the United States, and who shall not, when elected, be an inhabitant of that State for which he shall be chosen.

The Vice President of the United States shall be President of the Senate, but shall have no vote, unless they be equally divided.

The Senate shall choose their other officers, and also a President pro tempore, in the absence of the Vice President, or when he shall exercise the office of President of the United States.

The Senate shall have the sole power to try all impeachments. When sitting for that purpose, they shall be on oath or affirmation. When the President of the United States is tried, the Chief Justice shall preside: And no person shall be convicted without the concurrence of two-thirds of the members present.

Judgment in cases of impeachment shall not extend further than to removal from office, and disqualification to hold and enjoy any office of honor, trust or profit under the United States: but the party convicted shall nevertheless be liable and subject to indictment, trial, judgment and punishment, according to law.

Section 4. The times, places and manner of holding elections for senators and representatives, shall be prescribed in each State by the legislature thereof; but the Congress may at any time by law make or alter such regulations, except as to the places of choosing senators.

The Congress shall assemble at least once in every year, and such meeting shall be on the first Monday in December, unless they shall by law appoint a different day.

Section 5. Each House shall be the judge of the elections, returns and qualifications of its own members, and a majority of each shall constitute a quorum to do business; but a smaller number may adjourn from day to day, and may be authorised to compel the attendance of absent members, in such manner, and under such penalties as each House may provide.

Each House may determine the rules of its proceedings, punish its members for disorderly behavior, and, with the concurrence of two-thirds, expel a member.

Each House shall keep a journal of its proceedings, and from time to time publish the same, excepting such parts as may in their judgment require secrecy; and the yeas and nays of the members of either House on any question shall, at the desire of one-fifth of those present, be entered on the journal.

Neither House, during the session of Congress, shall, without the consent of the other, adjourn for more than three days, nor to any other place than that in which the two Houses shall be sitting.

Section 6. The senators and representatives shall receive a compensation for their services, to be ascertained by law, and paid out of the Treasury of the United States. They shall in all cases, except treason, felony and breach of the peace, be privileged from arrest during their attendance at the session of their respective Houses, and in going to and returning from the same; and for any speech or debate in either House, they shall not be questioned in any other place.

No senator or representative shall, during the time for which he was elected, be appointed to any civil office under the authority of the United States, which shall have been created, or the emoluments whereof shall have been increased during such time; and no person holding any office under the United States, shall be a member of either House during his continuance in office.

Section 7. All bills for raising revenue shall originate in the House of Representatives; but the Senate may propose or concur with amendments as on other bills.

Every bill which shall have passed the House of Representatives and the Senate, shall, before it becomes a law, be presented to the President of the United States; if he approve he shall sign it, but if not he shall return it, with his objections to that House in which it shall have originated, who shall enter the objections at large on their journal, and proceed to reconsider it. If after such reconsideration two-thirds of that House shall agree to pass the bill, it shall be sent, together with the objections, to the other House, by which it shall likewise be reconsidered, and if approved by two-thirds of that House, it shall become a law. But in all such cases the votes of both Houses shall be determined by yeas and nays, and the names of the persons voting for and against the bill shall be entered on the journal of each House respectively. If any bill shall not be returned by the President within ten days (Sundays excepted) after it shall have been presented to him, the same shall be a law, in like manner as if he had signed it, unless the Congress by their adjournment prevent its return, in which case it shall not be a law.

Every order, resolution, or vote to which the concurrence of the Senate and House of Representatives may be necessary (except on a question of adjournment) shall be presented to the President of the United States; and before the same shall take effect, shall be approved by him, or being disapproved by him, shall be repassed by two-thirds of the Senate and House of Representatives, according to the rules and limitations prescribed in the case of a bill.

Section 8. The Congress shall have the power to lay and collect taxes, duties, imposts and excises, to pay the debts and provide for the common defense and general welfare of the United States; but all duties, imposts and excises shall be uniform throughout the United States;

To borrow money on the credit of the United States;

To regulate commerce with foreign nations, and among the several States, and with the Indian tribes;

To establish a uniform rule of naturalization, and uniform laws on the subject of bankruptcies throughout the United States;

To coin money, regulate the value thereof, and of foreign coin, and fix the standard of weights and measures;

To provide for the punishment of counterfeiting the securities and current coin of the United States;

To establish post offices and post roads;

To promote the progress of science and useful arts, by securing for limited times to authors and inventors the exclusive rights to their respective writings and discoveries;

To constitute tribunals inferior to the Supreme Court;

To define and punish piracies and felonies committed on the high seas, and offenses against the law of nations;

To declare war, grant letters of marque and reprisal, and make rules concerning captures on land and water;

To raise and support armies, but no appropriation of money to that use shall be for a longer term than two years;

To provide and maintain a Navy;

To make rules for the government and regulation of the land and naval forces;

To provide for calling forth the militia to execute the laws of the Union, suppress insurrections and repel invasions;

To provide for organizing, arming, and disciplining, the militia, and for governing such part of them as may be employed in the service of the United States, reserving to the States respectively, the appointment of the officers, and the authority of training the militia according to the discipline prescribed by Congress;

To exercise exclusive legislation in all cases whatsoever, over such district (not exceeding ten miles square) as may, by cession of particular States, and the acceptance of Congress, become the seat of the Government of the United States, and to exercise like authority over all places purchased by the consent of the legislature of the State in which the same shall be, for the erection of forts, magazines, arsenals, dock-yards, and other needful buildings; – And

To make all laws which shall be necessary and proper for carrying into execution the foregoing powers, and all other powers vested by this Constitution in the Government of the United States, or in any department or officer thereof.

Section 9. The migration or importation of such persons as any of the States now existing shall think proper to admit, shall not be prohibited by the Congress prior to the year one thousand eight hundred and eight, but a tax or duty may be imposed on such importation, not exceeding ten dollars for each person.

The privilege of the writ of habeas corpus shall not be suspended, unless when in cases of rebellion or invasion the public safety may require it.

No bill of attainder or ex post facto law shall be passed.

No capitation, or other direct tax shall be laid, unless in proportion to the census or enumeration herein before directed to be taken.

No tax or duty shall be laid on articles exported from any State.

No preference shall be given by any regulation of commerce or revenue to the ports of one State over those of another; nor shall vessels bound to, or from, one State, be obliged to enter, clear or pay duties in another.

No money shall be drawn from the Treasury, but in consequence of appropriations made by law; and a regular statement and account of the receipts and expenditures of all public money shall be published from time to time.

No title of nobility shall be granted by the United States: And no person holding any office of profit or trust under them, shall, without the consent of the Congress, accept of any present, emolument, office, or title, of any kind whatever, from any King, Prince, or foreign State.

Section 10. No State shall enter into any treaty, alliance, or confederation; grant letters of marque and reprisal; coin money; emit bills of credit; make anything but gold and silver coin a tender in payment of debts; pass any bill of attainder, ex post facto law, or law impairing the obligation of contracts, or grant any title of nobility.

No State shall, without the consent of Congress, lay any duty of tonnage, keep troops, or ships of war in time of peace, enter into agreement or compact with another State, or with a foreign power, or engage in war, unless actually invaded or in such imminent danger as will not admit of delay.

ARTICLE II

Section 1. The executive power shall be vested in a President of the United States of America. He shall hold his office during the term of four years, and, together with the Vice President, chosen for the same term, be elected as follows:

Each State shall appoint, in such manner as the legislature thereof may direct, a number of electors, equal to the whole number of senators and representatives to which the State may be entitled in the Congress: but no senator or representative, or person holding an office of trust or profit under the United States, shall be appointed an elector.

The electors shall meet in their respective States, and vote by ballot for two persons, of whom one at least shall not be an inhabitant of the same State with themselves. And they shall make a list of all the persons voted for, and of the number of votes for each; which list they shall sign and certify, and transmit sealed to the seat of the Government of the United States, directed to the President of the Senate. The President of the Senate shall, in the presence of the Senate and the House of Representatives, open all the certificates, and the votes shall then be counted. The person having the greatest number of votes shall be the President, if such number be a majority of the whole number of electors appointed; and if there be more than one who have such majority, and have an equal number of votes, then the House of Representatives shall immediately choose by ballot one of them for President; and if no person have a majority, then from the five highest on the list the said

House shall in like manner choose the President. But in choosing the President, the votes shall be taken by States, the representation from each State having one vote; a quorum for this purpose shall consist of a member or members from two-thirds of the States, and a majority of all the States shall be necessary to a choice. In every case, after the choice of the President, the person having the greatest number of votes of the electors shall be the Vice President. But if there there should remain two or more who have equal votes, the Senate shall choose from them by ballot the Vice President.

The Congress may determine the time of choosing the electors, and the day on which they shall give their votes; which day shall be the same throughout the United States.

No person except a natural born citizen, or a citizen of the United States, at the time of the adoption of this Constitution, shall be eligible to the office of President; neither shall any person be eligible to that office who shall not have attained to the age of thirty-five years and been fourteen years a resident within the United States.

In case of the removal of the President from office, or of his death, resignation, or inability to discharge the powers and duties of the said office, the same shall devolve on the Vice President, and the Congress may by law provide for the case of removal, death, resignation, or inability, both of the President and Vice President, declaring what officer shall then act as President, and such officer shall act accordingly, until the disability be removed, or a President shall be elected.

The President shall, at stated times, receive for his services a compensation, which shall neither be increased nor diminished during the period for which he shall have been elected, and he shall not receive within that period any other emolument from the United States, or any of them.

Before he enter on the execution of his office, he shall take the following oath or affirmation:—'I do solemnly swear (or affirm) that I will faithfully execute the office of President of the United States, and will to the best of my ability, preserve, protect and defend the Constitution of the United States.'

Section 2. The President shall be Commander in Chief of the Army and Navy of the United States, and of the militia of the several States, when called into the actual service of the United States; he may require the opinion, in writing of the principal officer in each of the Executive Departments, upon any subject relating to the duties of their respective offices, and he shall have power to grant reprieves and pardons for offences against the United States, except in cases of impeachment.

He shall have power, by and with the advice and consent of the Senate, to make treaties, provided two-thirds of the senators present concur; and he shall nominate, and by and with the advice and consent of the Senate, shall appoint ambassadors, other public ministers and consuls, judges of the Supreme Court, and all other officers of the United States, whose appointments are not herein otherwise provided for, and which shall be established by law: but the Congress may by law vest the appointment of such inferior officers, as they think proper, in the President alone, in the courts of law, or in the heads of departments.

The President shall have power to fill up all vacancies that may happen during the recess of the Senate, by granting commissions which shall expire at the end of their next session.

Section 3. He shall from time to time give to the Congress information of the state of the Union, and recommend to their consideration such measures as he shall judge necessary and expedient; he may, on extraordinary occasions, convene both Houses, or either of them, and in case of disagreement between them, with respect to the time of adjournment, he may adjourn them to such time as he shall think proper; he shall receive ambassadors and other public ministers; he shall take care that the laws be faithfully executed, and shall commission all the officers of the United States.

Section 4. The President, Vice President and all civil officers of the United States, shall be removed from office on impeachment for, and conviction of, treason, bribery, or other high crimes and misdemeanors.

ARTICLE III

Section 1. The judicial power of the United States shall be vested in one Supreme Court, and in such inferior courts as the Congress may from time to time ordain and establish. The judges, both of the supreme and inferior courts, shall hold their offices during good behaviour, and shall, at stated times, receive for their services, a compensation, which shall not be diminished during their continuance in office.

Section 2. The judicial power shall extend to all cases, in law and equity, arising under this Constitution, the laws of the United States, and treaties made, or which shall be made, under their authority; to all cases affecting ambassadors, other public ministers and consuls; to all cases of admiralty and maritime jurisdiction; to controversies to which the United States shall be a party; to controversies between two or more States; between a State and citizens of another State; between citizens of different States; between citizens of the same State claiming lands under grants of different States, and between a State, or the citizens thereof, and foreign States, citizens, or subjects.

In all cases affecting ambassadors, other public ministers and consuls, and those in which a State shall be party, the Supreme Court shall have original jurisdiction. In all the other cases before mentioned, the Supreme Court shall have appellate jurisdiction, both as to law and fact, with such exceptions, and under such regulations as the Congress shall make.

The trial of all crimes, except in cases of impeachment, shall be by jury; and such trial shall be held in the State where the said crimes shall have been committed; but when not committed within any State, the trial shall be at such place or places as the Congress may by law have directed.

Section 3. Treason against the United States, shall consist only in levying war against them, or in adhering to their enemies, giving them aid and comfort. No person shall be convicted of treason unless on the testimony of two witnesses to the same overt act, or on confession in open court.

The Congress shall have power to declare the punishment of treason, but no attainder of treason shall work corruption of blood, or forfeiture except during the life of the person attainted.

ARTICLE IV

Section 1. Full faith and credit shall be given in each State to the public acts, records, and judicial proceedings of every other State. And the Congress may by general laws prescribe the manner in which such acts, records and proceedings shall be proved, and the effect thereof.

Section 2. The citizens of each State shall be entitled to all privileges and immunities of citizens in the several States.

A person charged in any State with treason, felony, or other crime, who shall flee from justice, and be found in another State, shall on demand of the executive authority of the State from which he fled, be delivered up, to be removed to the State having jurisdiction of the crime.

No person held to service or labor in one State, under the laws thereof, escaping into another, shall, in consequence of any law or regulation therein, be discharged from such service or labor, but shall be delivered up on claim of the party to whom such service or labor may be due.

Section 3. New States may be admitted by the Congress into this Union; but no new State shall be formed or erected within the jurisdiction of any other State; nor any State be formed by the junction of two or more States, or parts of States, without the consent of the legislature of the States concerned as well as of the Congress.

The Congress shall have power to dispose of and make all needful rules and regulations respecting the Territory or other property belonging to the United States; and nothing in this Constitution shall be so construed as to prejudice any claims of the United States, or of any particular State.

Section 4. The United States shall guarantee to every State in this Union a republican form of Government, and shall protect each of them against invasion; and on application of the legislature, or of the executive (when the legislature cannot be convened) against domestic violence.

ARTICLE V

The Congress, whenever two-thirds of both Houses shall deem it necessary, shall propose amendments to this Constitution, or, on the application of the legislatures of two-thirds of the several

States, shall call a convention for proposing amendments, which, in either case, shall be valid to all intents and purposes, as part of this Constitution, when ratified by the legislatures of three-fourths of the several States, or by convention in three-fourths thereof, as the one or the other mode of ratification may be proposed by the Congress; provided that no amendment which may be made prior to the year one thousand eight hundred and eight shall in any manner affect the first and fourth clauses in the Ninth Section of the First Article; and that no State, without its consent, shall be deprived of its equal suffrage in the Senate.

ARTICLE VI

All debts contracted and engagements entered into, before the adoption of this Constitution, shall be as valid against the United States under this Constitution, as under the Confederation.

This Constitution, and the laws of the United States which shall be made in pursuance thereof; and all treaties made, or which shall be made, under the authority of the United States, shall be the supreme law of the land; and the judges in every State shall be bound thereby, anything in the Constitution or laws of any State to the contrary notwithstanding.

The senators and representatives before mentioned, and the members of the several State legislatures, and all executive and judicial officers, both of the United States and of the several States, shall be bound by oath or affirmation, to support this Constitution; but no religious test shall ever be required as a qualification to any office or public trust under the United States.

ARTICLE VII

The ratification of the conventions of nine States shall be sufficient for the establishment of this Constitution between the States so ratifying the same.

Done in convention by the unanimous consent of the States present the seventeenth day of September in the year of Our Lord one thousand seven hundred and eighty-seven and of the Independence of the United States of America the twelfth. In witness whereof we have hereunto subscribed our names.

AMENDMENTS TO THE CONSTITUTION

(The first 10 Amendments are known as 'The Bill of Rights')

Amendment I (December 15, 1791)

Congress shall make no law respecting an establishment of religion or prohibiting the free exercise thereof; or abridging the freedom of speech, or of the press; or the right of the people peaceably to assemble, and to petition the government for a redress of grievances.

Amendment II (December 15, 1791)

A well regulated militia, being necessary to the security of a free State, the right of the people to keep and bear arms shall not be infringed.

Amendment III (December 15, 1791)

No soldier shall, in time of peace, be quartered in any house, without the consent of the owner, nor in time of war, but in a manner to be prescribed by law.

Amendment IV (December 15, 1791)

The right of the people to be secure in their persons, houses, papers, and effects, against unreasonable searches and seizures, shall not be violated, and no warrants shall issue, but upon probable cause, supported by oath or affirmation, and particularly describing the place to be searched, and the persons or things to be seized.

Amendment V (December 15, 1791)

No person shall be held to answer for a capital, or otherwise infamous crime, unless on a presentment or indictment of a grand jury, except in cases arising in the land or naval forces, or in the militia, when in actual service in time of war or public danger; nor shall any person be subject for the same offence to be twice put in jeopardy of life or limb; nor shall be compelled in any criminal case to be a witness against himself, nor be deprived of life, liberty, or property without due process of law; nor shall private property be taken for public use, without just compensation.

Amendment VI (December 15, 1791)

In all criminal prosecutions the accused shall enjoy the right to a speedy and public trial, by an impartial jury of the State and district wherein the crime shall have been committed, which district shall have been previously ascertained by law, and to be informed of the nature and cause of the accusation: to be confronted with the witnesses against him; to have compulsory process for obtaining witnesses in his favor, and to have the assistance of counsel for his defense.

Amendment VII (December 15, 1791)

In suits at common law, where the value in controversy shall exceed twenty dollars, the right of trial by jury shall be preserved, and no fact tried by a jury shall be otherwise re-examined in any court of the United States, than according to the rules of the common law.

Amendment VIII (December 15, 1791)

Excessive bail shall not be required, nor excessive fines imposed, nor cruel and unusual punishments inflicted.

Amendment IX (December 15, 1791)

The enumeration in the Constitution of certain rights shall not be construed to deny or disparage others retained by the people.

Amendment X (December 15, 1791)

The powers not delegated to the United States by the Constitution, nor prohibited by it to the States, are reserved to the States respectively, or to the people.

Amendment XI (January 8, 1798)

The judicial power of the United States shall not be construed to extend to any suit in law or equity, commenced or prosecuted against one of the United States by citizens of another State, or by citizens or subjects of any foreign State.

Amendment XII (September 25, 1804)

The electors shall meet in their respective States, and vote by ballot for President and Vice President, one of whom, at least, shall not be an inhabitant of the same State with themselves; they shall name in their ballots the person voted for as President, and in distinct ballots the person voted for as Vice President, and they shall make distinct lists of all persons voted for as President, and of all persons voted for as Vice President, and of the number of votes for each, which lists they shall sign and certify, and transmit sealed to the seat of the government of the United States, directed to the President of the Senate; – the President of the Senate shall, in the presence of the Senate and House of Representatives, open all the certificates, and the votes shall then be counted; – the person having the greatest number of votes for President, shall be the President, if such number be a majority of the whole number of electors appointed; and if no person have such majority, then from the persons having the highest numbers not exceeding three on the list of those voted for as President, the House of Representatives shall choose immediately, by ballot, the President. But in choosing the President, the votes shall be taken by States, the representation from each State having one vote; a quorum for this purpose shall consist of a member or members from two-thirds of the States, and a majority of all the States shall be necessary to a choice. And if the House of Representatives shall not choose a President whenever the right of choice shall devolve upon them, before the fourth day of March next following, then the Vice President shall act as President, as in the case of the death or other constitutional disability of the President. — The person having the greatest number of votes as Vice President, shall be the Vice President, if such number be a majority of the whole of electors appointed, and if no person have a majority, then from the two highest numbers on the list, the Senate shall choose the Vice President; a quorum for the purpose shall consist of two-thirds of the whole number of Senators, and a majority of the whole number shall be necessary to a choice. But no person constitutionally ineligible to the office of President shall be eligible to that of Vice President of the United States.

Amendment XIII (December 18, 1865)
Section 1. Neither slavery nor involuntary servitude, except as a punishment for crime whereof the party shall have been duly convicted, shall exist within the United States, or any place subject to their jurisdiction.
Section 2. Congress shall have power to enforce this article by appropriate legislation.

Amendment XIV (July 28, 1868)
Section 1. All persons born or naturalized in the United States,

and subject to the jurisdiction thereof, are citizens of the United States and of the State wherein they reside. No State shall make or enforce any law which shall abridge the privileges or immunities of citizens of the United States; nor shall any State deprive any person of life, liberty, or property, without due process of law; nor deny to any person within its jurisdiction the equal protection of the laws.

Section 2. Representatives shall be apportioned among the several States according to their respective numbers, counting the whole number of persons in each State, excluding Indians not taxed. But when the right to vote at any election for the choice of electors for President and Vice President of the United States, representatives in Congress, the executive and judicial officers of a State, or the members of the legislature thereof, is denied to any of the male inhabitants of such State, being twenty-one years of age, and citizens of the United States, or in any way abridged, except for participation in rebellion, or other crime, the basis of representation therein shall be reduced in the proportion which the number of such male citizens shall bear to the whole number of male citizens twenty-one years of age in such State.

Section 3. No person shall be a Senator or Representative in Congress, or elector of President and Vice President, or hold any office, civil or military, under the United States, or under any State, who, having previously taken an oath, as a member of Congress, or as an officer of the United States, or as a member of any State legislature, or as an executive or judicial officer of any State, to support the Constitution of the United States, shall have engaged in insurrection or rebellion against the same, or given aid or comfort to the enemies thereof. But Congress may by a vote of two-thirds of each House, remove such disability.

Section 4. The validity of the public debt of the United States, authorized by law, including debts incurred for payment of pensions and bounties for services in suppressing insurrection or rebellion, shall not be questioned. But neither the United States nor any State shall assume or pay any debt or obligation incurred in aid of insurrection or rebellion against the United States, or any claim for the loss or emancipation of any slave; but all such debts, obligations, and claims shall be held illegal and void.

Section 5. The Congress shall have power to enforce, by appropriate legislation, the provisions of this article.

Amendment XV (March 30, 1870)
Section 1. The right of citizens of the United States to vote shall not be denied or abridged by the United States or by any State on account of race, color, or previous condition of servitude.
Section 2. The Congress shall have power to enforce this article by appropriate legislation.

Amendment XVI (February 25, 1913)
The Congress shall have power to lay and collect taxes on incomes, from whatever source derived, without apportionment among the several States, and without regard to any census or enumeration.

Amendment XVII (May 31, 1913)
Section 1. The Senate of the United States shall be composed of two senators from each State, elected by the people thereof, for six years; and each senator shall have one vote. The electors in each State shall have the qualifications requisite for electors of the most numerous branch of the State legislature.
Section 2. When vacancies happen in the representation of any State in the Senate, the executive authority of such State shall issue writs of election to fill such vacancies: Provided, that the legislature of any State may empower the executive thereof to make temporary appointments until the people fill the vacancies by election as the legislature may direct.
Section 3. This amendment shall not be so construed as to affect the election or term of any senator chosen before it becomes valid as part of the Constitution.

Amendment XVIII (January 29, 1919)
Section 1. After one year from the ratification of this article the manufacture, sale, or transportation of intoxicating liquors within, the importation thereof into, or the exportation thereof from the United States and all territory subject to the jurisdiction thereof for beverage purposes is hereby prohibited.
Section 2. The Congress and the several States shall have concurrent power to enforce this article by appropriate legislation.
Section 3. This article shall be inoperative unless it shall have been ratified as an amendment to the Constitution by the

legislatures of the several States, as provided in the Constitution, within seven years from the date of the submission hereof to the States by the Congress.

Amendment XIX (August 26, 1920)
Section 1. The right of citizens of the United States to vote shall not be denied or abridged by the United States or by any State on account of sex.
Section 2. Congress shall have power to enforce this article by appropriate legislation.

Amendment XX (February 6, 1933)
Section 1. The terms of the President and Vice President shall end at noon on the 20th day of January, and the terms of senators and representatives at noon on the 3rd day of January, of the years in which such terms would have ended if this article had not been ratified; and the terms of their successors shall then begin.
Section 2. The Congress shall assemble at least once in every year, and such meeting shall begin at noon on the 3rd day of January, unless they shall by law appoint a different day.
Section 3. If, at the time fixed for the beginning of the term of the President, the President elect shall have died, the Vice President elect shall become President. If a President shall not have been chosen before the time fixed for the beginning of his term, or if the President elect shall have failed to qualify, then the Vice President elect shall act as President until a President shall have qualified; and the Congress may by law provide for the case wherein neither a President elect nor a Vice President elect shall have qualified, declaring who shall then act as President, or the manner in which one who is to act shall be selected, and such person shall act accordingly until a President or Vice President shall have qualified.
Section 4. The Congress may by law provide for the case of the death of any of the persons from whom the House of Representatives may choose a President whenever the right of choice shall have devolved upon them, and for the case of the death of any of the persons from whom the Senate may choose a Vice President whenever the right of choice shall have devolved upon them.
Section 5. Sections 1 and 2 shall take effect on the 15th day of October following the ratification of this article.

Section 6. This article shall be inoperative unless it shall have been ratified as an amendment to the Constitution by the legislatures of three-fourths of the several States within seven years from the date of its submission.

Amendment XXI (December 5, 1933)
Section 1. The eighteenth article of amendment to the Constitution of the United States is hereby repealed.
Section 2. The transportation or importation into any State, Territory, or possession of the United States for delivery or use therein of intoxicating liquors, in violation of the laws thereof, is hereby prohibited.
Section 3. This article shall be inoperative unless it shall have been ratified as an amendment to the Constitution by conventions in the several States, as provided in the Constitution, within seven years from the date of the submission hereof to the States by the Congress.

Amendment XXII (February 27, 1951)
No person shall be elected to the office of the President more than twice, and no person who has held the office of President, or acted as President, for more than two years of a term to which some other person was elected President shall be elected to the office of President more than once. But this Article shall not apply to any person holding the office of President, when this Amendment was proposed by the Congress, and shall not prevent any person who may be holding the office of President, or acting as President, during the term within which this Amendment becomes operative from holding the office of President or acting as President during the remainder of such term.

Amendment XXIII (March 29, 1961)
Section 1. The District constituting the seat of Government o the United States shall appoint in such manner as the Congress may direct:
A number of electors of President and Vice President equal to the whole number of senators and representatives in Congress to which the District would be entitled if it were a State, but in no event more than the least populous State; they shall be in addition to those appointed by the States, but they shall be considered, for the purposes of the election of President and

Vice President, to be electors appointed by a State; and they shall meet in the District and perform such duties as provided by the twelfth Article of amendment.

Section 2. The Congress shall have power to enforce this Amendment by appropriate legislation.

Amendment XXIV (January 23, 1964)

The right of citizens of the United States to vote in any primary or other election for President or Vice President, for electors for President or Vice President, or for senator or representative in Congress, shall not be denied or abridged by the United States or any State by reason of failure to pay any Poll Tax or other tax.

Amendment XXV (February 23, 1967)

Section 1. In case of the removal of the President from office or of his death or resignation the Vice President shall become President.

Section 2. Whenever there is a vacancy in the office of the Vice President, the President shall nominate a Vice President who shall take office upon confirmation by a majority vote of both houses of Congress.

Section 3. Whenever the President transmits to the President pro tempore of the Senate and the Speaker of the House of Representatives his written declaration that he is unable to discharge the powers and duties of his office, and until he transmits to them a written declaration to the contrary, such powers and duties shall be discharged by the Vice President as Acting President.

Section 4. Whenever the Vice President and a majority of either the principal officers of the Executive departments or of such other body as Congress may by law provide, transmit to the President pro tempore of the Senate and the Speaker of the House of Representatives their written declaration that the President is unable to discharge the powers and duties of his office, the Vice President shall immediately assume the powers and duties of the office as Acting President

Thereafter, when the President transmits to the President pro tempore of the Senate and the Speaker of the House of Representatives his written declaration that no inability exists, he shall resume the powers and duties of his office unless the

Vice President and a majority of either the principal officers of the Executive departments or of such other body as Congress may by law provide, transmit within four days to the President pro tempore of the Senate and the Speaker of the House of Representatives their written declaration that the President is unable to discharge the powers and duties of his office. Thereupon Congress shall decide the issue, assembling within forty-eight hours for that purpose if not in session. If the Congress, within twenty-one days after receipt of the latter written declaration, or, if Congress is not in session, within twenty-one days after Congress is required to assemble, determines by two-thirds vote of both houses that the President is unable to discharge the powers and duties of his office, the Vice President shall continue to discharge the same as Acting President; otherwise, the President shall resume the powers and duties of his office.

Amendment XXVI (June 30, 1971)
Section 1. The right of citizens of the United States, who are eighteen years of age or older, to vote shall not be denied or abridged by the United States or by any State on account of age.
Section 2. The Congress shall have power to enforce this article by appropriate legislation.

Appendix B

PRESIDENTS OF
THE UNITED STATES

	Term of Office	Politics	State of Residence	Age at Inauguration
George Washington	1789–1797	Fed.	Va.	57
John Adams	1797–1801	Fed.	Mass.	61
Thomas Jefferson	1801–1809	Dem.-Rep.	Va.	57
James Madison	1809–1817	Dem.-Rep.	Va.	57
James Monroe	1817–1825	Dem.-Rep.	Va.	58
John Quincy Adams	1825–1829	Dem.-Rep.	Mass.	57
Andrew Jackson	1829–1837	Dem.	Tenn.	61
Martin Van Buren	1837–1841	Dem.	N.Y.	54
William H. Harrison	1841 (1 mo.)	Whig	Ind.	68
John Tyler	1841–1845	Whig	Va.	51
James K. Polk	1845–1849	Dem.	Tenn.	49
Zachary Taylor	1849–1850 (1 yr., 4 mos.)	Whig	La.	64
Millard Fillmore	1850–1853	Whig	N.Y.	50
Franklin Pierce	1853–1857	Dem.	N.H.	48
James Buchanan	1857–1861	Dem.	Pa.	65
Abraham Lincoln	1861–1865 (4 yrs., 1 mo.)	Rep.	Ill.	52
Andrew Johnson	1865–1869	Dem. (Union)	Tenn.	56
Ulysses S. Grant	1869–1877	Rep.	Ohio	46
Rutherford B. Hayes	1877–1881	Rep.	Ohio	54
James A. Garfield	1881 (6½ mos.)	Rep.	Ohio	49
Chester A. Arthur	1881–1885	Rep.	N.Y.	50
Grover Cleveland	1885–1889	Dem.	N.Y.	47
Benjamin Harrison	1889–1893	Rep.	Ind.	55
Grover Cleveland	1893–1897			
William McKinley	1897–1901 (4 yrs., 6 mos.)	Rep.	Ohio	54
Theodore Roosevelt	1901–1909	Rep.	N.Y.	42
William Howard Taft	1909–1913	Rep.	Ohio	51
Woodrow Wilson	1913–1921	Dem.	N.J.	56

Warren G. Harding	1921–1923 (2 yrs., 6 mos.)	Rep.	Ohio	55
Calvin Coolidge	1923–1929	Rep.	Mass.	51
Herbert Hoover	1929–1933	Rep.	Calif.	54
Franklin D. Roosevelt	1933–1945 (12 yrs., 1 mo.)	Dem.	N.Y.	51
Harry S. Truman	1945–1953	Dem.	Mo.	60
Dwight D. Eisenhower	1953–1961	Rep.	N.Y.	62
John F. Kennedy	1961–1963 (2 yrs., 10 mos.)	Dem.	Mass.	43
Lyndon B. Johnson	1963–1969	Dem.	Texas	55
Richard M. Nixon	1969–1974 (resigned Aug. 9, 1974)	Rep.	N.Y.	56
Gerald R. Ford	1974–	Rep.	Mich.	61

Appendix C

ELECTION RESULTS 1944 – 1974

Congress and the Presidency

Election Year	Congress	Dem.	House Rep.	Others	Senate Dem.	Rep.	Others	Presidency
1944	79th	243	190	2	57	38	1	Roosevelt (D)
1946	80th	188	246	1	45	51		Truman (D)
1948	81st	263	171	1	54	42		Truman
1950	82nd	234	199	2	48	47	1	
1952	83rd	213	221	1	47	48	1	Eisenhower (R)
1954	84th	232	203		48	47	1	
1956	85th	234	201		49	47		Eisenhower (R)
1958	86th	283	154		66	34		
1960	87th	263	174		64	36		Kennedy (D)
1962	88th	259	176		68	32		
1964	89th	295	140		68	32		Johnson (D)
1966	90th	248	187		64	36		
1968	91st	243	192		57	43		Nixon (R)
1970	92nd	255	180		54	44	2	
1972	93rd	243	192		56	42	2	Nixon (R)
1974	94th	291	144		61	37	2	

Presidential Elections 1944–1972

	Candidates	Electoral Vote	Popular Vote
1944	Franklin D. Roosevelt (D)	432–81%	25,602,504–53·5%
	Thomas E. Dewey (R)	99–19%	22,006,285–46·0%
1948	Harry S. Truman (D)	303–57%	24,104,030–49·5%
	Thomas E. Dewey (R)	189–36%	21,971,004–45·1%
	J. S. Thurmond (States Rights)	39– 7%	1,169,063– 2·4%
1952	D. D. Eisenhower (R)	442–83%	33,778,963–55·1%
	Adlai E. Stevenson (D)	89–17%	27,314,992–44·4%
1956	D. D. Eisenhower (R)	457–86%	35,579,190–57·4%
	Adlai E. Stevenson (D)	74–14%	26,027,983–42·0%
1960	J. F. Kennedy (D)	303–57%	34,221,349–49·71%
	R. M. Nixon (R)	219–41%	34,108,546–49·55%
	H. F. Byrd	15– 2%	
1964	L. B. Johnson (D)	486–90%	43,128,956–61·1%
	B. Goldwater (R)	52–10%	27,177,873–38·5%
1968	R. M. Nixon (R)	301–56%	31,785,480–43·4%
	H. H. Humphrey (D)	191–36%	31,275,165–42·7%
	G. C. Wallace (AIP)	46–8%	9,906,473–13·5%
1972	R. M. Nixon (R)	521–97%	47,169,911–60·7%
	G. McGovern (D)	17–3%	29,170,383–37·5%

Source: Congress and the Nation 1945–1964, Congressional Quarterly Service, Washington, D.C., 1965, pp. 62–3 (amended).

Appendix D
NOTES ON FURTHER READING

The Annual *Statistical Abstract of the United States* provides an extensive range of political, economic, and social information about the United States. *The Congressional Record* contains verbatim records of debates in Congress and a good deal of additional material inserted by Congressmen. *The Congressional Quarterly Almanac* and *Congressional Quarterly Weekly Reports* provide a comprehensive view of major political activities in Washington, especially Congress, and in particular give detailed breakdowns of roll-call votes along with factual articles on specific and important legislation. *The Congressional Directory* and a companion volume with more limited circulation, *The Congressional Staff Directory*, provide annual information about Congressmen, committees, and their staffs. *The U.S. Government Organisation Manual* provides basic factual information about governmental departments, agencies, and commissions, while the *United States Reports* contain the decisions and opinions of the U.S. Supreme Court.

The footnotes in the book provide a detailed bibliography to allow particular questions to be followed up, but the following books and articles are also of especial value for further general study.

Chapter 1

Monsma, S. V., *American Politics – A Systems Approach*, 2nd edit., Hinsdale, Ill.: The Dryden Press, 1973.

Parenti, M., 'Ethnic Politics and the Persistence of Ethnic Identification', *American Political Science Review*, September 1967, pp. 717–26.

Russett, B. M., *Community and Contention: Britain and America in the Twentieth Century*, Cambridge, Mass.: M.I.T. Press, 1963.

Taylor, C. L., and Hudson, M. C., *World Handbook of Political and Social Indicators*, 2nd edit., New Haven: Yale University Press, 1972.

Vile, M. J. C., *Politics in the U.S.A.*, London: Allen Lane, The Penguin Press, 1970.

Chapter 2

Black, C. L., Jr., *Perspectives in Constitutional Law*, Englewood Cliffs, N.J.: Prentice-Hall, Inc., 1963.

Fischer, D. H., *The Revolution of American Conservatism*, New York: Harper and Row, 1965.

McCloskey, R. G., *The American Supreme Court*, Chicago: University of Chicago Press, 1960.

Pritchett, C. H., *The American Constitutional System*, New York: McGraw-Hill, 1963.

Schubert, G. A., *The Judicial Mind*, Evanston, Ill.: North Western University Press, 1965.

Solberg, W. U. (ed.), *The Federal Convention and the Formation of the Union of American States*, New York: Liberal Arts Press, 1958.

Westin, A. F., *The Anatomy of a Constitutional Law Case*, New York: Macmillan Co., 1958.

Chapter 3

Banfield, E. C., *Big City Politics*, New York: Random House Inc., 1965.

Cohen, J., and Grodzins, M., 'How Much Economic Sharing in American Federalism?', *American Political Science Review*, March 1963, pp. 5–23.

Dye, T. R., and Hawkins, B. W. (eds.), *Politics in the Metropolis*, Columbus, Ohio: C. E. Merrill Publishing Co., 1967.

Leach, R., *American Federalism*, New York: W. W. Norton and Company, 1970.

Metropolitan America: Challenge to Federalism, Study by Advisory Commission on Intergovernmental Relations, Washington, D.C.: U.S. Government Printing Office, 1966.

Rockefeller, N. A., *The Future of Federalism*, Cambridge, Mass.: Harvard University Press, 1962.

Senate Sub-Committee on Intergovernmental Relations, *Hearings on Creative Federalism*, 89th Congress, 2nd Session, Washington, D.C.: U.S. Government Printing Office, 1967; also *The Federal System as Seen by State and Local Officials*, Washington, D.C.: U.S. Government Printing Office, 1963.

Sundquist, J., *Making Federalism Work*, Washington, D.C.: Brookings Institution, 1969.

Wilson, J. Q., *City Politics and Public Policy*, New York: John Wiley Sons, 1968.

Chapter 4

Devine, D., *The Political Culture of the United States*, Boston: Little, Brown, 1972.

Goldman, E., *Rendezvous with Destiny: A History of Modern American Reform*, New York: A. A. Knopf, 1952.

Hofstadter, R., *The Age of Reform: From Bryan to F.D.R.*, New York: A. A. Knopf, 1955.

Hyneman, C. S., and Carey, G. W. (eds.), *A Second Federalist. Congress Creates a Government*, New York: Appleton-Century-Crofts, 1967.

Kennan, G., *American Diplomacy 1900–1950*, Chicago: University of Chicago Press, 1951.

Lipset, S. M., *The First New Nation*, London: Heinemann, 1963.

Potter, D., *People of Plenty: Economic Abundance and the American Character*, Chicago: University of Chicago Press, 1954.

Rosenau, J. N. (ed.), *Domestic Sources of Foreign Policy*, New York: The Free Press, 1967.

Silbey, J. H., *The Transformation of American Politics 1840–1860*, Englewood Cliffs, N.J.: Prentice-Hall Inc., 1967.

Woodward, C. Vann, *Reunion and Reaction: The Compromise of 1877 and the End of Reconstruction*, Boston: Little, Brown, 1957.

Chapter 5

Adler, N., and Harrington, C. (eds.), *The Learning of Political Behavior*, Glenview, Ill.: Scott, Foresman and Company, 1970.

Easton, D., and Dennis, J., *Children in the Political System*, New York: McGraw-Hill, 1969.

Hess, R. D., and Torney, J. V., *The Development of Political Attitudes in Children*, Chicago: Aldine Publishing Co., 1967.

Jennings, M. K., and Niemi, R. G., 'The Transmission of Political Values from Parent to Child', *American Political Science Review*, March 1968, pp. 169–84.

Langton, K. P., *Political Socialisation*, New York: Oxford University Press, 1969.

Langton, K. P., and Jennings, M. K., 'Political Socialisation and the High School Civics Curriculum in the United States', *American Political Science Review*, September 1968, pp. 852–67.

Litt, E. (ed.), *The Political Imagination*, Glenview, Ill.: Scott, Foresman and Co., 1966.

Merelman, R. M., 'The Development of Policy Thinking in Adolescence', *American Political Science Review*, December 1971, pp. 1033–47.

Chapter 6

Brock, C., *Americans for Democratic Action*, Washington, D.C.: Public Affairs Press, 1962.

Broyles, J. A., *The John Birch Society*, Boston: Beacon Press, 1964.

Burrow, J. G., *A.M.A., Voice of American Medicine*, Baltimore: The Johns Hopkins Press, 1963.

Kariel, H. S., *The Decline of American Pluralism*, Stanford, Calif.: Stanford University Press, 1961.

Mahood, H. R. (ed.), *Pressure Groups in American Politics*, New York: Scribners, 1967.

Marmor, T. R., *The Politics of Medicare*, London: Routledge and Kegan Paul, 1970.

Salisbury, R. H. (ed.), *Interest Group Politics in America*, New York: Harper and Row, 1970.

Chapter 7

Davis, J. W., *Presidential Primaries: The Road to the White House*, New York: Thomas Y. Crowell, 1967.

Eaton, H. A., *Presidential Timber. A History of Nominating Conventions 1868–1960*, Glencoe, Ill.: The Free Press, 1964.

Goldman, R., *The Democratic Party in American Politics*, London: Collier-Macmillan, 1966.

Ladd, E. C., Jr., *American Political Parties: Social Change and Political Response*, New York: W. W. Norton Company, 1970.

Mayer, G. H., *The Republican Party 1854–1966*, 2nd edition, New York: Oxford University Press, 1968.

Phillips, K. P., *The Emerging Republican Majority*, New Rochelle, N.Y.: Arlington House, 1969.

Pomper, G., *Elections in America*, New York: Dodd, Mead, 1968.

Sayre, W. S., and Parris, J. H., *Voting for President*, Washington, D.C.: Brookings Institution, 1970.

Sindler, A. P., *Political Parties in the United States*, New York: St. Martin's Press, 1966.

Sorauf, F. J., *Party Politics in America*, 2nd edit., Boston: Little, Brown, 1972.

Chapter 8

Bailey, S. K., *Congress in the Seventies*, New York: St. Martin's Press, 1970.

Congress. The First Branch of Government, Washington, D.C.: American Enterprise Institute for Public Policy Research, 1966.

Cummings, M. C., Jr., *Congressmen and the Electorate*, New York: The Free Press, 1966.

Froman, L. A., Jr., *The Congressional Process. Strategies, Rules, Procedures*, Boston: Little, Brown, 1967.

Harris, J. P., *Congressional Control of Administration*, Washington, D.C.: Brookings Institution, 1964.

Jewell, M. E., and Patterson, S. C., *The Legislative Process in the United States*, 2nd edit., New York: Random House Inc., 1972.

Keefe, W. J., and Ogul, M. S., *American Legislative Process: The Congress and the States*, Englewood Cliffs, N.J.: Prentice-Hall Inc., 1968.

Polsby, N. W., *Congress and the Presidency*, 2nd edit., Englewood Cliffs, N.J.: Prentice-Hall Inc., 1971.

Reiselbach, L. N., *Congressional Politics*, New York: McGraw-Hill, 1973.

Tacheron, D. G., and Udall, M. K., *The Job of the Congressman*, Indianapolis: Bobbs-Merrill Co., 1966.

Chapter 9

Cronin, T. E., and Greenberg, S. D., (eds.), *The Presidential Advisory System*, New York: Harper and Row, 1969.

Dean, H. E., *Judicial Review and Democracy*, New York: Random House Inc., 1966.

Evans, R., and Novak, R., *Lyndon B. Johnson: The Exercise of Power*, London: Allen and Unwin, 1967.

Jacob, C. E., *Policy and Bureaucracy*, Princeton, N.J.: Van Nostrand Co., 1966.

Krislov, S., *The Supreme Court in the Political Process*, London: Collier-Macmillan, 1965.

Polsby, N. W., (ed.), *The Modern Presidency*, New York: Random House Inc., 1973.

Rourke, F. E. (ed.), *Bureaucratic Power in National Politics*, 2nd edit., Boston: Little, Brown, 1972.

Seidman, H., *Politics, Position and Power: The Dynamics of Federal Organization*, New York: Oxford University Press, 1970.

Thomas, N. C., and Baade, H. W., *The Institutionalized Presidency*, Dobbs Ferry, N.Y.: Oceana Publications Inc., 1972.

Wann, A. J., *The President as Chief Administrator*, Washington, D.C.: Public Affairs Press, 1968.

Chapter 10

Allison, G. T., *Essence of Decision: Explaining the Cuban Missile Crisis*, Boston: Little, Brown, 1971.

Carmichael, S., and Hamilton, C. V., *Black Power: The Politics of Liberation in America*, London: Cape, 1968.

Carroll, H. N., *The House of Representatives and Foreign Affairs*, Boston: Little, Brown, 1966.

Destler, I. M., *Presidents, Bureaucrats and Foreign Policy*, Princeton, N.J.: Princeton University Press, 1972.

Eidenberg, E., and Morey, R. D., *An Act of Congress*, New York: W. W. Norton and Company, 1969.

Fisher, L., *President and Congress: Power and Policy*, New York: Free Press, Macmillan, 1972.

Lewis, A. (ed.), *Portrait of a Decade*, New York: Random House Inc., 1964.

Moynihan, D. P., *The Politics of a Guaranteed Income: The Nixon Administration and the Family Assistance Plan*, New York: Random House Inc., 1973.

O'Leary, M. K., *The Politics of Foreign Aid*, New York: Atherton Press, 1967.

Peabody, R. L., *et al.*, *To Enact a Law: Congress and Campaign Financing*, New York: Praeger, 1972.

Robinson, J. A., *Congress and Foreign Policy-Making*, Homewood, Illinois: The Dorsey Press, rev. ed., 1967.

Chapter 11

Barber, J. D., *The Presidential Character: Predicting Performance in the White House*, Englewood Cliffs, N. J.: Prentice-Hall, 1973.

Evans, R., and Novak, R., *Nixon in the White House*, New York: Random House Inc., 1971.

Halberstam, D., *The Best and the Brightest*, London: Barrie and Jenkins, 1972.

Lockard, D., *The Perverted Priorities of American Politics*, New York: Macmillan, 1971.

Schlesinger, A. M., Jr., *The Imperial Presidency*, Boston: Houghton Mifflin, 1973.

Verba, S., and Nie, N. H., *Participation in America: Political Democracy and Social Equality*, New York: Harper and Row, 1972.

Wills, G., *Nixon Agonistes*, New York: Houghton Mifflin Co., 1969.

Yarmolinski, A., *The Military Establishment*, New York: Harper and Row, 1971.

INDEX

Ackley, Gardner, 231
Adams, D. K., 90n.
Adams, Sherman, 237, 237n.
Adelstein, A. S., 113n.
Adrian, C. R., 54n., 244n.
Advisory Commission on Inter-
governmental Relations, 63
Agency for International Develop-
ment, 233, 266
Agnew, Spiro T., 329
Albany, poverty programme in, 65
Alexander, H. E., 186n.
Alford, R., 126n.
Alien and Sedition Acts of 1798, 94
Allen, H. W., 217n.
Alliance for Progress, 269, 270
Almendinger, V., 62n.
Almond, G. A., 92n., 98, 99n. 131,
131n.
American Automobile Association,,
143
American Bar Association, 142, 147;
Committee on the Federal Judi-
ciary of, 147
American Cancer Association, 143
American Civil Liberties Union,
100, 142, 148
American Coalition of Patriotic
Societies, 142
American Farm Bureau Federation,
136, 138–40, 142, 143, 147, 155,
166, 308
American Federation of Labour –
Congress of Industrial Organi-
sation, 131, 135, 138–45, 153, 158;
Committee of Public Education
of, 153

American Federation of Teachers,
142
American Humane Society, 137
American Independent Party, 322
American Institute of Public Opin-
ion, 128n., 129n., 295
American Jewish Committee, 143
American Legion, 142, 145, 148
American Medical Association, 136,
142, 152; Political Action Com-
mittee of, 152–5
American Nurses Association, 154
American Public Health Associa-
tion, 154
American Public Welfare Associa-
tion, 154
American Revolution, 68–9, 71, 111
Americans for Democratic Action,
142, 154, 166
amicus curiae brief, 304
Annapolis meeting of 1786, 72
anthracite coal strike of 1902, 256
Anti-Masonic Party, 160
Arieli, Y., 83n.
Arizona, immigrants into, 26
Arnold, T., 87n.
Aronson, S. H., 243n.
Articles of Confederation, 19, 32, 38,
71–2, 195
Ashwander v. *Tennessee Valley Authority*,
297 U.S. 288 (1936), 250
Assistant Secretaries, recruitment
of, 245–7
Atomic Energy Commission, 238,
242
Attlee, Clement, 235
Attorney General, 294, 328–9